Keywords for Comics Studies

Keywords

Collaborative in design and execution, the books in the Keywords series bring together scholars across a wide range of disciplines in the humanities and social sciences, with each essay on a single term to help trace the contours and debates of a particular field. Keywords are the nodal points in many of today's most dynamic and vexed discussions of political and social life, both inside and outside of the academy. Providing accessible A-to-Z surveys of prevailing scholarly concepts, the books serve as flexible tools for carving out new areas of inquiry.

For more information, visit http://keywords.nyupress.org.

Titles in the series include the following:

Keywords for American Cultural Studies, Third Edition
Edited by Bruce Burgett and Glenn Hendler

Keywords for Children's Literature, Second Edition
Edited by Philip Nel, Lissa Paul, and Nina Christensen

Keywords for Asian American Studies
Edited by Cathy J. Schlund-Vials, Linda Trinh Võ, and K. Scott Wong

Keywords for Disability Studies
Edited by Rachel Adams, Benjamin Reiss, and David Serlin

Keywords for Environmental Studies
Edited by Joni Adamson, William A. Gleason, and David N. Pellow

Keywords for Media Studies
Edited by Laurie Ouellette and Jonathan Gray

Keywords for Latina/o Studies
Edited by Deborah R. Vargas, Nancy Raquel Mirabal, and Lawrence La Fountain-Stokes

Keywords for African American Studies
Edited by Erica R. Edwards, Roderick A. Ferguson, and Jeffrey O. G. Ogbar

Keywords for Comics Studies
Edited by Ramzi Fawaz, Shelley Streeby, and Deborah Elizabeth Whaley

For a complete list of books in the series, see www.nyupress.org.

Keywords for Comics Studies

Edited by

Ramzi Fawaz, Shelley Streeby, and Deborah Elizabeth Whaley

NEW YORK UNIVERSITY PRESS New York

NEW YORK UNIVERSITY PRESS
New York
www.nyupress.org

References to internet websites (URLs) were accurate at the time of writing. Neither the author nor New York University Press is responsible for URLs that may have expired or changed since the manuscript was prepared.

Library of Congress Cataloging-in-Publication Data
Names: Fawaz, Ramzi, editor. | Streeby, Shelley, 1963– editor. | Whaley, Deborah Elizabeth, editor.
Title: Keywords for comics studies / edited by Ramzi Fawaz, Shelley Streeby, Deborah Elizabeth Whaley.
Description: New York : New York University Press, [2021] | Series: Keywords | Includes bibliographical references.
Identifiers: LCCN 2020055474 | ISBN 9781479816682 (hardback) | ISBN 9781479831968 (paperback) | ISBN 9781479825431 (ebook) | ISBN 9781479862702 (ebook)
Subjects: LCSH: Comic books, strips, etc.—Terminology. | Comic books, strips, etc.—Encyclopedias. | Comic books, strips, etc.—History and criticism.
Classification: LCC PN6707 .K49 2021 | DDC 741.5/03—dc23
LC record available at https://lccn.loc.gov/2020055474

Hardback ISBN: 9781479816682
Paperback ISBN: 9781479831968
Consumer Ebook ISBN: 9781479825431
Library Ebook ISBN: 9781479862702

New York University Press books are printed on acid-free paper, and their binding materials are chosen for strength and durability. We strive to use environmentally responsible suppliers and materials to the greatest extent possible in publishing our books.

Manufactured in the United States of America

10 9 8 7 6 5 4 3 2 1

Also available as an ebook

The chapter "Queer" was originally published in Scott, Darieck, and Ramzi Fawaz. 2018. "Introduction: Queer about Comics." *American Literature* 90, no. 2, 197–219. Reprinted by permission of Duke University Press.

Contents

Introduction

Ramzi Fawaz, Shelley Streeby, and
Deborah Elizabeth Whaley

Writers, artists, inkers, editors, and readers of comic books and comic book adaptions leave an indelible imprint on cultures across the globe. Popular film adaptions of classical comics characters and narratives, including *Black Panther, Wonder Woman, Avengers,* and the *X-Men* series, yield immense profit because of an ongoing yearning to witness strength, perseverance, and heroism in the face of social struggle, political uncertainty, and the many forms of global cruelty and wickedness. Small-screen televisual and digital adaptions of wildly popular comic book series, from the earliest iterations of *Superman* and *Batman* to the twenty-first-century installments of *The Flash, Black Lightning, Luke Cage, Jessica Jones, Batwoman,* and *Supergirl,* underscore that widespread interest in heroic narratives and increasingly diverse representations of heroic power in comics media remains an enduring impulse over decades of cultural production and across multiple visual platforms.

In the academy, we often refer to the various forms of comics as sequential art, which is somewhat of a catchall for all kinds of images in sequence, whether in the form of anime, manga, comic books, graphic novels, zines, television, animation, and film creations and adaptions. Our authors discuss these many forms in this volume. Deborah Elizabeth Whaley has coined the sophisticated process of reading comics as "optic cognitive"—that is, the ways in which image and text are simultaneously encoded and decoded and deeply understood by readers and viewers. This eschews the enduring but misguided understanding of comics as a remedial form, thereby understanding comics as a highly elaborate process of meaning making to take in, deconstruct, and reconstruct multiple forms of visual information, from drawn figures and shapes, to text, to color, to the size and shape of a sequential panel, a page, or an entire printed, bound book.

The thrill, excitement, and the materiality of comic books—the feel of turning pages between your fingers; looking to the right, left, top, and bottom; pausing on images and rereading the narratives again and again—spark interest among the editors, authors, and artists in *Keywords for Comics Studies.* This volume gathers a series of rich and timely meditations on comics' extraordinary multiplicity—that is, the medium's capacity to multiply meaning through a vast number of variables in the reading and viewing experience. By taking time to unpack an equally wide range of such variables—from the cultural meanings attached to ink on paper, to the conceptual possibilities of narratives told in visual sequences, to the deep affective and cultural attachments built around enduring comics characters such as Archie and the X-Men—*Keywords for Comics Studies* recognizes and honors the heterogeneity of the medium, its myriad stories, and its aesthetic forms. Moreover, all contributors to this project know that we are in good company and joining a growing list of *Keywords* volumes on the ideas, theories, words, movements, and forms in American culture, media, disability, Latinx, Asian American, and African American studies. Taken as a whole, this volume forcefully contends that comics are an aesthetic medium that also doubles as a conceptual terrain upon which the most central concerns of humanistic inquiry have and continue to be spectacularly rendered.

Beyond Heroic Narratives and on to the (Inter)Disciplines: The Scholarly Impact of Comics Studies

The last half decade has signaled a renaissance in comics studies unprecedented in the history of humanities scholarship in the US. Between 2015 and 2016 alone, more than twelve highly anticipated monographs on comics and sequential art appeared from leading academic presses, among them Bart Beaty's *Twelve-Cent Archie* (Rutgers University Press), Scott Bukatman's *Hellboy's World* (University of California Press), andré carrington's *Speculative Blackness* (University of Minnesota Press), Hillary Chute's *Disaster Drawn* (Harvard University Press), Ramzi Fawaz's *The New Mutants* (New York University Press), Nick Sousanis's *Unflattening* (Harvard University Press), Frederick Louis Aldama's *Latinx Superheroes in Mainstream Comics* (University of Arizona Press), and Deborah Elizabeth Whaley's *Black Women in Sequence* (University of Washington Press). Moreover, during this same period, comics scholars organized the Comics Studies Society, the first international association dedicated to supporting the study of graphic narrative and sequential art; the Modern Language Association (MLA) approved an official Comics and Graphic Narratives Forum and accepted more comics-themed panels for its annual conference than at any time previously in MLA history; the *Journal of Graphic Novels and Comics* celebrated more than a decade of publication; *The Blacker the Ink*, a groundbreaking 2015 anthology of scholarly essays on "constructions of black identity in comics and sequential art," co-edited by John Jennings and Frances Gateward, won the Eisner Award, the most prestigious honor granted in the field of comics publishing; the academic journal *American Literature* approved what would become an award-winning special issue on queer theory and comics studies, edited by Darieck Scott and Ramzi Fawaz, the first of its kind in any academic publishing venue; and the inaugural Queers and Comics Conference, the largest gathering of LGBTQ+ comics artists, writers, and scholars in the world, debuted at the CUNY Graduate Center in New York City. This potent moment of scholarly and institutional efflorescence has been accompanied by a wave of similar milestones in comics cultural production, including a Broadway musical adaptation of Alison Bechdel's extraordinarily successful graphic memoir *Fun Home*, Roxane Gay and Ta-Nehisi Coates's celebrated runs on the *Black Panther* comics series, historian Jill Lepore's best-selling book *The Secret History of Wonder Woman*, and Nick Drnaso's nomination for the Man Booker Prize for his graphic novel *Sabrina*. In 2019, the *Publications of the Modern Language Association of America* (*PMLA*) published a Theories and Methodologies Forum on Hillary Chute's *Why Comics?*; this was the first time that the flagship journal of the MLA had ever dedicated an entire section to a discussion of the comics medium. It is not an understatement to say that comics studies is booming and here to stay.

Our *Keywords* volume creates a new toolbox for comics studies by providing short, user-friendly, analytical essays on the most significant concepts, questions, and debates in this vibrant field. Inspired in part by Raymond Williams's *Keywords: A Vocabulary of Culture and Society* (1976), our authors analyze "the issues and problems" that are "there inside the vocabulary," as Williams put it in his introduction to the first edition of his classic cultural studies text. As it was for Williams, our inquiry is interdisciplinary, straddling "an area where several disciplines converge but in general do not meet." It is also "necessarily unfinished and incomplete," since it involves live struggles and debates over historically changing meanings. But while Williams sought to analyze "a vocabulary of meanings in a deliberately selected area of argument and concern" that centered on the terms *culture*, *class*, *art*, *industry*, and *democracy*, which he could "feel" as "a kind of structure," our focus, like those of the other NYU *Keywords* volumes, is a field imaginary in motion—in this case, the burgeoning field of comics studies.

While comics studies today is indebted to British cultural studies, and although each of Williams's structuring terms shows up frequently within individual essays, only one—*Industry*—is a keyword in the present volume. Still, there are many convergences, including our shared purpose of thinking about these vocabularies in not only historical but also aesthetic terms; it is too rarely recalled that the first entry in Williams's *Keywords* is "Aesthetics." Although we have no other common terms, a few are close: Williams's "Creative" becomes "Creator," his "Formalist" is "Form," and "Racial" shifts to "Race" in our *Keywords* volume. We also share terms, parts of words, and methodologies with other books in the NYU *Keywords* series, especially with Burgett and Hendler's foundational *Keywords for American Cultural Studies*, partly because of the impact of American studies scholarship on comics studies.

In the US context, though perhaps no less globally, comics are not only popular entertainment but cultural objects that magnetized nationwide debates over censorship, youth rebellion, multiculturalism, and literacy while producing some of the most enduring fictional characters in US literary production. They are the cultural studies objects par excellence, demanding to be accounted for from a rich interdisciplinary perspective that considers the conditions of their production, aesthetic and formal codes, circulation, and audience reception. Building on earlier cultural studies frameworks as well as new approaches to comics studies, we believe that our *Keywords for Comics Studies* volume, shaped by an interdisciplinary cultural studies vision, provides scholars and nonacademic readers alike with a wide range of terms that speak to the formal and historical specificities of the medium while also showing how the key aesthetic, political, and cultural questions comics raise have wide-reaching relevance to the humanities.

Certainly, comics studies is not a new field, emerging as far back as Gilbert Seldes's classic 1957 study of American popular culture, *The Seven Lively Arts*, and most explicitly with the publication of Scott McCloud's *Understanding Comics: The Invisible Art* in 1993. Yet the recent exponential growth of comics scholarship and intellectual communities points to the field's newfound relevance to a range of humanities disciplines and interdisciplinary formations, including media and cultural studies; art history; women's, gender, and sexuality studies; ethnic studies; American studies; history; anthropology; the medical humanities; and beyond. Quite simply, the recent renaissance in comics studies is in large part due to the field's increasing interdisciplinarity and the daring scholarship of a new generation of researchers who have explored the medium's unique formal properties in direct relation to its distinct historical, political, and cultural contexts of production and circulation. Some of the field's most classical debates regarding the value of lowbrow cultural forms, the distinct formal and aesthetic affordances of hand-drawn and sequential art, the effects of print circulation, and the development of nontraditional and youth audiences have been either placed into new contexts or else revalued for their generative insights into the reading experience.

The relative obscurity and marginality of comics studies have often resulted from two factors. First, there is the traditional dismissal of so-called lowbrow or popular culture forms as undeserving of legitimate study in the humanities, a critique that has generated enough intellectual heat over a half century of scholarship and is now considered a cliché (though for that reason, it is no less relevant today). Second, traditionally formalist approaches to comics, which attempted to clarify the aesthetic stakes of the medium and its unique artistic contributions to visual culture, have sometimes unwittingly confounded those who are either unfamiliar with comics or not predisposed to take them seriously. The production of specialized formal vocabularies for studying distinct mediums of artistic production is certainly not unique to comics studies; in fact, the development of such a vocabulary for comics remains a necessary part of the field's constitution and provides the groundwork for any cross-disciplinary discussion of the medium's specificity as a distinct and valuable cultural product. Yet an already existing bias against comics as a "trash" medium in the US and European intellectual imagination, combined with a perception of specialization in the field as an extension of "fannish" overenthusiasm for comics among a niche cadre of scholars, often creates a conceptual gap between the generative formal work of comics scholars and this work's potential broader appeal to the humanities. In other words, comics studies is quietly generating some of the most important frameworks for exploring the aesthetic work of visual print culture for decades while often being dismissed for its very precision and focus.

One problematic effect of developing such vocabularies has also been a tendency to approach comics from one or two vantage points—including historical context, politics and ideology, business history, or aesthetic theory—while neglecting their simultaneous or interconnected weave. Alternatively, many scholars have focused intently on the biographical lives of particular comics artists and writers in an effort to recuperate the denigrated creative labor of important comics practitioners. This work has been essential to underscoring the imaginative power of comics as a medium driven by numerous artistic minds working in every subfield of comics production from independent to mainstream. Yet a persistent focus on the individual biographies of creators can also limit interpretative possibilities of actual comics texts by reducing readings of comics content to authorial intention or else canonizing a small number of vaunted creators, reifying the cult of the genius rather than expanding our understanding of the medium and its possibilities. On this latter point, one need only consider the fact that the vast range of comics scholarship up until 2014 focused extensively on a short list of celebrated creators such as Art Spiegelman, R. Crumb, Alison Bechdel, Alan Moore, and Marjane Satrapi, with a few additional outliers. Without question, these authors and their rich imaginative oeuvres deserve continued scholarly attention, but we contend that their aesthetic accomplishments should not obscure the compelling creative output of thousands of other comics creators working in numerous genres and styles to expand and reinvent what sequential art constitutes. For all the vibrant scholarship emerging around comics today, the medium remains a largely unplumbed and uncanonized field of lesser known texts. Go to a local comic book store and dip your hand at random into any long box containing back issues of comics from any period or in any genre, and you'll likely have in your hand a comic book that no scholar has ever published about in a peer-reviewed journal. To point out these conceptual limitations is not to denigrate the development of the field or to suggest that comics studies is in any way uniquely problematic compared to other media-specific areas of study. Rather it is to illuminate some of comics studies' perceived stumbling blocks as well as some of the ways in which the field's most generative contributions to the study of visual culture have been unfairly elided, glossed over, or misunderstood.

The dramatic growth of recent comics scholarship at the highest levels of academic research and publishing is, in part, a direct outcome of contemporary comics scholars' work to vastly expand the coordinates or variables by which the medium is understood without losing its attention to media specificity, which defined its most daring early interventions. Contemporary comics scholarship (covering nearly two decades of recent academic production) has increasingly considered the medium's unique aesthetic qualities alongside the relationship of comics to distinct audiences and their practices of reading; political, social, and intellectual history; the evolution of print technologies and methods of distribution; the shifting demographics of creators; the corporatization of comics production; the development of underground comics communities; fan writing and association; transmedia uses of comics; and much more. It is at this moment when comics studies are being reinvented for an interdisciplinary audience willing to rethink earlier dismissals of the field that a *Keywords for Comics Studies* volume is most necessary and relevant. Despite the widespread interest in comics—whether among digital humanists seeking to expand the range of their multimedia teaching sources, art historians attempting to recover obscured histories of illustration and printmaking, or queer studies scholars tracing the evolution of alternative sexual cultures in visual art and fandom—there exists no single anthology, encyclopedia, or reference guide that enumerates the key concepts, debates, and histories that animate the field for an interdisciplinary audience. This means that countless scholars are teaching and studying comics without a shared vocabulary to instruct students on how to read and engage this dynamic and multifaceted medium across multiple genres and styles. This volume bridges that gap.

What Goes into the Toolbox: Building a Comics Studies Vocabulary

Comics is a widely accessible mode of popular culture and a distinct art form; thus, *Keywords for Comics Studies* necessarily includes a range of terms that link the political and historical dimensions of cultural production with aesthetics and creative production, one of the signal strengths of comics studies since its inception. We believe this will make *Keywords for Comics Studies* relevant to any scholar interested in popular culture, media, art, and other forms of cultural production. With this in mind, we have crafted a list of keywords that carefully toggles back and forth between aesthetic terms that are distinct to the medium of comics but also relevant to a vast range of cultural forms and terms that capture the kind of cultural, political, and historical debates that comics have fomented due to their changing content and public perceptions of their uses and misuses. Consequently, unlike other *Keywords* volumes, we include certain technical terms such as *editor*, *ink*, *gutter*, and *creator* alongside more classically conceptual terms such as *disability*, *lowbrow*, *genre*, and *fantasy*.

These former keywords not only describe elements of craft or creative labor in comics but are deeply contentious, ambivalent ideas in the field that have rich conceptual meaning beyond the limits of comics. For instance, *ink* refers not only to the long history of technical transformations in four-color printing technology but also to (1) the ways skin tone (and hence racial representation) has shifted in comics and other print media across time, (2) how the often-unrecognized creative labor of inkers has shaped the medium, and (3) how recent innovations in digital coloring technologies affect contemporary representational politics of comics and the creative labor required to produce sequential narratives. Similarly, a term such as *creator* opens up long-running questions about authorship and proper ownership of intellectual property, the collaborative nature of comics art, and the very meaning of creative labor in the culture industry. In our list, we never include a technical term that is not also a conceptual "problem" for the field or comics studies and more broadly, for cultural studies, too. We see this as being especially helpful for people teaching about comics because the essays will both provide students basic definitional understanding of terms specific to comics and stress the cultural politics and broader conceptual stakes of these terms.

Second, our *Keywords* oscillate between concepts that consistently reappear across time in the history of comics—including *collecting*, *funnies*, *seriality*, and *caricature*—and those that are of a more recent vintage such as *zine*, *webcomics*, *diversity*, *trans-/**, or *cosplay*. We believe it is important to cover classical elements of comics and remain up to date with where the cultural field is today. These latter terms also speak to the increasing interdisciplinarity of comics by showing how the current study of graphic narrative and sequential art requires a basic understanding of digital media cultures, performance, audience reception, race, gender, sexuality, and ability, among others. For example, *cosplay*, a term that refers to fans who dress up as versions of their favorite comic book and fantasy characters, has become an incredibly popular phenomenon at comic book conventions and other fan venues. Cosplay is especially celebrated and taken up by queer, feminist, and minority fan communities who use the practice to perform

or inhabit a vast range of fantasy identities, including characters traditionally presented as white, straight, and normatively gendered. Cosplay then has extremely important links to key conceptual questions in cultural studies, including practices of appropriation, "camp performance," disidentification, reparative reading, and the production of counterpublics. By offering essays that theorize these expanded locations for the field and offer grounded assessments of previous approaches to studying different aspects of comics production and circulation, *Keywords for Comics Studies* can function as a resource guide for young scholars needing an orientation or starting point for their research.

Since so much of comics research and teaching relies on historically constituted genre categories within the larger field of comics production, we provide space for terms that speak to distinct genres—such as superhero comics, alternative comics, and memoirs—but that also have rich uses beyond the limits of generic constraints. For example, we include terms like *universe*, *nostalgia*, and *pornography*, which refer to specific elements of genre comics (such as superhero, memoir, and erotic comics) but have wide-ranging relevance to literary and cultural production. We also carefully selected a small handful of terms that are simultaneously specific to comics culture—*Archie*, *X-Men*, *EC Comics*, *Watchmen*, *Love and Rockets*—and thus garner enough attention to exist and work as theoretical terms. For instance, the X-Men, traditionally the name given to a popular team of mutant superheroes invented by creators at Marvel Comics in the early 1960s, has since become an iconic reference point for the idea of diversity and multiculturalism in mainstream superhero comics. Similarly, Archie, once the red-haired title character of a comic strip about middle American high schoolers, has come to embody the notion of ideal "Americanness" as well as its potential subversion. These terms are not intended as comprehensive but rather as touchstones in a larger lexicon.

Ultimately, our list is distinguished by its synthetic approach to the study of comics form and content (seeing the two as interwoven rather than isolated), its inclusion of terms that have relevance to multiple fields and disciplines simultaneously, its use of terms that are both specific to the comics medium and encompass broader debates in the humanities, and its attention to historical and methodological change in comics studies. Our list of contributors represents a variety of interdisciplinary thinkers, including scholars from literary studies; art history; visual cultural studies; American studies; performance studies; women's, gender, and sexuality studies; comparative literature; African American studies; sociology; disability studies; and more. Since these scholars also use many approaches outside of comics studies to explore the medium from their distinct locations, their essays provide potential readers a wealth of different intellectual vantage points from which they might approach comics without denigrating or eliding the field's most foundational interventions in the study of this important print media. In this sense, we see the volume as a foundation for and an incitement to producing more innovative and intellectually capacious scholarship on comics. We see the true value of this book lying not only in its ability to produce powerful interdisciplinary vocabulary for comics studies but also in its commitment to linking the questions, concepts, and debates in comics studies to cultural studies writ large.

In the Gutter: Teaching *Keywords for Comics Studies*

The popular comic strip and Afroanime television show *The Boondocks* is best understood when one contemplates its chief creator, Aaron McGruder, as one trained in the field of African American studies at the University of Maryland. His images and narratives are not created in isolation. Rather, his work is informed by the history of people of African descent living in America, and Japanese comics and anime is an influence for him, as it is for a large majority of comic creators today, especially regarding how characters are drawn and how they move in and through space and time. Afroanime can be understood as an articulation of Black cultural idioms, signifiers, and historical and contemporary narratives of agency and action with the visual cues and complex, postmodern narratives of Japanese comic production. In this sense, Afroanime itself is an example of the work that *Keywords* does in connecting the dots between the historical, social, political, and material. Comics studies, as readers will see in the following entries, constitutes the interpretive space between narrative and visuality in sequential works.

For an entry into the pedagogical work of *Keywords*, we see the concept and the space of the gutter—where readers and viewers engage in interpretation and fill in the narrative with their own references in history, culture, and social relations—as the "key" part. Since our volume has a commitment to this space—that is, the space of the reader's meaning making that is in concert with, and paradoxically also in opposition to, what lies before them on the page—we weight this project in terms of its place in various concepts of "the classroom." For us, the classroom is more than a physical space with students and instructors. The classroom is the conversations readers will have with others in a multitude of spaces—in hallways, on public transportation, and online—as well as the journey of writing and seeking to understand and work within the comics form anew. A high school teacher may choose select entries in this volume in a way that aids students with the space of the gutter, to craft lectures, and to help provide an intensified context for the forms of sequential art, artistic practice, and the impact of genres, characters, and the complex identities that one negotiates as learners of comics and learners of the world. How might the form of manga help one understand the Japanese comics and animation shorts and features that have an immense impact on artists and writers of comics today, McGruder included? In what ways might we consider how the concept of borders strengthens our understanding of the geographical markers that are as much analytical as they are material and tied to emerging categories such as Latinx? As a pedagogical tool, the entries here do not consist of a monolith of understanding or the last definitive word on any given term, practice, or genre; each entry is an opening for everyday readers; students; researchers; art practitioners; film, television, and animation producers; and certainly instructors to travel with and beyond us into the sequential art and interpretive space of the gutter.

In tandem with this volume, many exercises will assist a variety of educational levels and learning spaces. Instructors who have no training in the drawing of comics can begin units on the form or a discussion of a particular work with a simple and powerful exercise to emphasize the impact of comics and the use of icons and iconography to convey larger ideas. Readers might find an exercise of artist and cultural critic Joel Gill instructive in this regard. He conducts talks with an adjacent workshop where he asks participants to draw a few simple forms: a house, a car, a flower, and the sun. The artistry of the mixed audience is irrelevant. A learning aspect from this is that as participants share their images, differences abound among them in terms of identity, but all have drawn basically the same image for each form. This is not because we are all the same or because we all think the same; it is because our experiences and reference points of understanding are

as much individualist as they are shared within common contexts of culture. This is an entry space into the gutter in order to begin to contemplate what is shared, specific, and contested as we think about iconography and signs that are used to move from the simple to the complex and from the individual to universal, even when no words or narrative are present. Perhaps this is what draws instructors to the form as a way of engaging learners in interdisciplinary and multicognitive ways. Indeed, many instructors teach graphic novels, comic books, animation, and film adaptions of sequential art in courses as an entry point into understanding constructions of identity and difference, illuminating the affective experience of distinct historical moments, and exploring aesthetic exchanges, both appropriative and genuine, between cultures and geographical locations. For example, blockbuster film and television productions, prominently addressed in Matt Yockey's opening entry, "Adaptation," might be used by media and communications scholars to teach about global media markets, fandom, media production, the business of comics, and multiple narrative forms. Educators in business may instruct students to reimagine human resource business cases that rely on problem making and problem solving in the form of a graphic novel. Many business cases *as* graphic novels have become best sellers, such as Richard Horwath's *StrategyMan vs. the Antistrategy Squad* (2018); these graphic case studies help readers see, through simultaneous reading and viewing, integral steps in management and human resource decision-making. Health practitioners and community workers can use comics to better communicate to and with community members about health practices, including developing and distributing accessible visual information about conditions, treatment, patient care, and community health philosophies; social studies instructors can use comics to convey how social relations, group identities, and shared histories are visually imagined and narrated in a range of aesthetic styles and comic book genres; and film scholars and practitioners can meditate on the aesthetic, production, reception, and narrative work of the moving image. The terms, genres, characters, and innovations in comics discussed here can play a part in and provide an opportunity to dive deep into the gutter—the open space of possibility between panels but also between conversations, comics texts, and readers—and to strengthen course content and engagement through the entries that inform the visual and written wonderment of the comics form. Instructors, artists, and students can take the terms that are sharply theoretical in this volume and create visual diagrams that draw from the explanations of our authors to bridge the written with the visual. Practitioners of sequential artworks will find our *Keywords* volume useful in making their art and narratives sharper and attuned to the various ideas and schools from which their work may draw and depart. Much of what occurs when we watch and read a sequential form is instinctive, happening in electric flashes of creative "optic-cognitive" work in the mind's eye; *Keywords for Comics Studies* helps in connecting these instinctive and canny interpretations enacted by comics fans and readers to the analytical and practical ideas that constitute an expansive field of inquiry.

Take, for example, just a small handful of contemporary flashpoints in comics cultural production that dovetail with learning opportunities in comics studies: The wildly successful film *Black Panther* (2018) ignited universities, high schools, and community centers to institute "Black Superhero Week" across the globe—this included screenings of documentaries and popular moving image depictions, tutorials on drawing characters that were ethnically specific instead of debased, forums on Black political leaders and activists that do

the practical work of change every day, and collective readings of comics in libraries. The extraordinary and surprising global popularity of "boy love manga"—the genre of shojo and narrative of *shoen-ai*, which lovingly depict the blossoming of same-sex romance among adolescent boys—among women readers has caught the attention of gender and women's studies scholars; these researchers have developed sophisticated analyses of the unexpected forms of cross-gender and sexual identification boy love manga elicits from diverse readers internationally. The critical public response of readers and viewers on the aggressive and abusive relationship between the Batman franchise's Joker and Harley Quinn, their celebration of the queerness of Batwoman in her titles and Iceman in the X-Men franchise, and their embrace of Muslim characters like the new Ms. Marvel reflect audiences' sophisticated, even intersectional interpretations of their most cherished series and characters. Scholars in critical race and visual studies have rigorously traced the intertextual links between blaxploitation films, blaxplocomics, and the recent appearances of iconic Black superheroes like Luke Cage and Black Lightning in small-screen televisual adaptations; their analyses show how these depictions are both wedded to *and* seek to move beyond limited understandings of Blackness and its relationship to economic and social blight, class, power, gender, sexualities, and policing. The groundbreaking comics collection Jeff Yang's *Secret Identities: The Asian American Superhero Anthology* (2009) displays how comic artists and writers have historically depicted Asian immigration, transnational labor, US Japanese internment, the bombings of Hiroshima and Nagasaki, American and Islamic conflict, and anti-Asian violence while grappling with broader issues of multiracial and ethnic Asian representation. And the list could go on. All of these scholarly and fan interventions are significant in helping us make sense of cultural conflicts over the role that comic book representations play in the major debates of our time. For instance, when there is a public debate among readers and viewers over the whitewashed casting of Asian and Asian-inspired superheroic characters like Iron Fist and Major Motoko Kusanagi on the small and big screen, where should interested parties turn to engage with critical ideas on the debate? In moments like these, collections of comics like Yang's *Secret Identity*, which contains the original comics in which these characters appeared, and the essays in this *Keywords* volume can all offer a toolbox of images and concepts to encourage critical conversations on the history of racial representation, including the historical and contemporary social and political relations that continue to fetishize Asian bodies even as those bodies are repeatedly subjected to color-blind casting. We see the kaleidoscopic nature of the essays in this volume as making it exceptionally adaptable for entering countless conversations about the cultural power, utility, and futures of the comics medium. We thus encourage readers to approach the words, concepts, and movements within these pages as both a start and an invitation to edit and perform *a deep and fantastical dive into and beyond the sequential magic of the gutter*.

1

Adaptation

Matt Yockey

At the conclusion of *Spider-Man*, director Sam Raimi's 2002 film adaptation featuring the popular Marvel Comics superhero, Peter Parker denies his love for Mary Jane Watson and accepts the responsibilities of being Spider-Man. Upon Peter's voice-over declaration "Who am I? I'm Spider-Man," Raimi cuts to a brief sequence of Spider-Man swooping across the Manhattan skyline that ends with him pausing on a flagpole before swinging toward the camera. This narratively superfluous and affectively excessive coda mirrors the often emotionally rich and visually spectacular moments captured by a superhero comic book splash page or cover, acting as an emphatic visual declaration that Peter Parker has, at least for the time being, resolved the identity crisis that has plagued him throughout the film. Following the iterative narrative structure of the comic books, this crisis reappears in Raimi's 2004 sequel *Spider-Man 2*. At one point in the film, Peter Parker abandons his Spider-Man identity and tosses his costume into a garbage bin in an alley. Raimi cuts to a long shot of Peter, shoulders slumped, walking away from the bin with part of his Spider-Man costume hanging limply off its side. Raimi's composition of this shot directly recalls a splash page in the story "Spider-Man No More!" that appeared in *The Amazing Spider-Man* no. 50 (July 1967). Raimi, a reader of Spider-Man comics in the 1960s, offers a cinematic quotation of an iconic image that many fellow Spider-Man comic book readers will immediately recognize. Thus the affect-saturated narrative moment

of Peter Parker's disavowal of his "great responsibility" is amplified by the feelings produced for those viewers who recognize Raimi's quotation. The visual citation is reinforced by Peter's assertion prior to the moment in the alley that he will be "Spider-Man no more." Consequently, the subjectivities of the protagonist, director, and viewers synthesize in this highly charged affective moment produced by the intersection of the comic book and filmic texts.

These spectacular moments in adaptations of superhero comic books reflect the adaptor's understanding of the affective appeal of the source material and actualize the relationship between texts, producers, and audience. Such a relationship confirms that what Sara Ahmed terms "affective economies" are at the heart of comic book adaptations (2004, 8). Ahmed regards emotions as a kind of capital "produced as an effect of its circulation . . . the more signs circulate, the more affective they become" (45). Consequently, any consideration of comic book adaptation must consider the degree to which a cluster of texts (the source text, the adaptation, and other texts that circulate around and within a larger textual matrix) become more affective, or saturated with feeling, according to the ways in which adaptations interact with other texts and how readers and viewers consume them. Central to this are the methods by which film adaptations of comic books signal their relationship to their source material. In this way, adaptations of comic books should be regarded not as sequential links in a textual chain but according to affective histories attached to the texts, which are always particular to individual reading and viewing experiences.

Since at least Winsor McCay's animated cartoon *Little Nemo* (1911), an adaptation of his own comic strip, filmmakers, particularly those in Hollywood, have turned to comic books and newspaper strips for material. Unsurprisingly, given the long-standing and widespread conflation of the superhero genre with the comic book medium, the most well-known adaptations of comic book material have been superhero films, which exploded in popularity in the twenty-first century, beginning with *X-Men* (Bryan Singer, 2000). Raimi's exploitation of the affective appeal of comic book superhero spectacle has become de rigueur in the numerous film adaptations of comic book superheroes that have followed. For example, the colorful visualization of the mythical realm of Asgard in *Thor: Ragnarok* (Taika Waititi, 2017) evokes Jack Kirby's cosmic architectural designs in the comic books, while a scene in which a group of young women asks for a selfie with Thor on the streets of Manhattan echoes the Stan Lee–Jack Kirby comic books of the 1960s, in which Thor is often treated like a celebrity when he is out and about in New York City. Such instances confirm and expand upon Hans-Christian Christiansen's observation that through an emphasis on visuals, comic books "foreground the presence of enunciator" (2000, 115). Cinematic quotations of comic book elements such as those in *Thor: Ragnarok* foreground the comic book creators and filmmakers equally, with the viewer at the fulcrum of these points of enunciation.

As films that draw directly from comic books for their affective appeal, it is useful to consider these texts as components of transmedia franchises that are in a dialogic relationship with one another and their source material (Burke 2015, 21). It is the goal of many comic book adaptations, then, to translate signature stylistic codes of comic books to film and television, and consequently, they engage with and contribute to the source material's already abundant meanings. Consider, for example, the prominent use in the television series *Batman* (1966–68) of onomatopoeia inserts or the use in early twenty-first-century superhero comic book adaptations such as *Watchmen* (Zack Snyder, 2009) of digital effects such as ramping (or bullet time), in which the subject in motion is slowed down, an effect often accompanied by the camera rotating around the subject in order to affect a three-dimensional study of the subject. These live-action appropriations of comic book style foreground the presence of the source material, indicating the value of audience recognition of these texts as adaptations of comic books. Such signaling reveals the shifting cultural value of comic books. In *Batman*, the onomatopoeia effects—the visual representation of "Bam!" and "Pow!" when characters fight on-screen—satirize the bloodless violence of contemporaneous comic books, while the ramping in *Watchmen* reflects the general shift in superhero comic books from the mid-1980s onward toward ostensibly more realistic depictions of violence. In both cases, the circulation of affect attached to the comic book–style visual effects is central to the value and meaning of the adaptation.

Such an approach can be understood in terms of remediation, the multiplication of media, and their relationship to one another within texts (Bolter and Grusin 1999, 5). A consideration of adaptations as remediating texts allows for a deeper understanding of the role of affect in the production and consumption of these texts. The role of state-of-the-art special effects in translating superhero comic books to film is often a primary aspect of the affective appeal of such adaptations. For example, "You'll believe a man can fly" was a central marketing tagline for *Superman: The Movie* (1978), promising audiences that the film would achieve a degree of realism not possible in comic books while still relying on those comic books as a source of an affectively defined relationship to Superman. As such, the comic books are regarded as texts strongly associated with childhood, while the film is positioned to appeal to adults as well as children. Audience members of all ages will, the ad campaign promises, collectively believe in the fantastic. This strategy is foregrounded in the film's prologue, in which the viewer is placed in the point of view of a child reading a Superman comic book aloud and recalling Superman's Depression-era origin. The camera zooms in on a panel showing the *Daily Planet* building and then dissolves to a matching live-action shot of the building. The camera then dramatically dollies above the *Daily Planet*, past the moon, and into space. At this point, the black-and-white photography shifts to color, and the curtains that had confined the image to the Academy ratio used in classical Hollywood cinema open up, allowing for a widescreen presentation for the remainder of the film. The credits then dramatically rush into the foreground of the shot, accompanied by a "wooshing" sound effect and John Williams's rousing score. This prologue compels the viewer, regardless of age, to assume a childlike perspective as they enter the story world. This world is simultaneously linked to the past, which is constructed as both personal and public (the child reading a 1938 *Superman* comic book), and the future (the promised realization of the childhood fantasy of believing a man can fly). Superman's textual history, of which the film immediately becomes a part, is held together by the circulation of affect, including magnetizing powerful feelings of wonder, enchantment, thrill, power, and even fear and terror in witnessing the fantastic.

As with the examples cited in the Spider-Man films, the first Superman film self-reflexively foregrounds the theme of identity. Origin stories are an expected trope of the genre, and superhero stories in general are concerned with the inherent fluidity of identity. Yet the dominance of film adaptations of superhero comic books should not blind us to the fact that a significant number of nonsuperhero comic books have been adapted to film and that many of these adaptations have been equally, if not more so, invested in exploring the theme of identity. Such explorations are enhanced by the self-reflexive nature of adaptation and by the more autobiographical nature of many of these works. Consider, for example, writer-artist Marjane Satrapi's autobiographical *Persepolis*, which was initially published as a graphic novel in 2000 and adapted into a film codirected by Satrapi and Vincent Parannoud in 2007. If live-action adaptations of superhero comic books can affectively engage viewers with moments of action and emotion-based spectacle that cite their source material, the animated feature adaption of *Persepolis* fully immerses the viewer into the story world of Satrapi's graphic novel. The film's visual approach exactly duplicates Satrapi's artistic style in the graphic novel. Further, given that she also wrote the screenplay for the film, the narrative closely hews to that of the graphic novel. The story details her childhood and young adulthood growing up in Iran before and after the Islamic Revolution of 1979 and her later life in Europe. Her coming-of-age story is expressly linked to her political identity as a dissident in her native country and as an émigré in Europe. In starting her story in childhood, Satrapi's work places her readers and viewers in the subjectivity of childhood, similar to the strategy used at the beginning of *Superman: The Movie*. Like that film, *Persepolis*—both as a graphic novel and a movie—is invested in the text as an enunciation of memory that conflates the past and present in an exercise of affective signaling.

The film adaptation of *Persepolis* itself becomes a self-reflexive component of the graphic novel's textual history and Satrapi's personal history. In this way, it is productive to consider the degree to which film adaptations of comic books thematically extend the formal properties of the medium upon which they are based. Thierry Groensteen characterizes static panels that sequentially present forward movement (spatially, temporally, narratively) as a "double maneuver of progression/retention" ([1999] 2007, 45). If every panel both advances and arrests the story, per Groensteen, the same dynamic is evident in the act of adaptation. This is not to suggest that stasis is the end result of the relationship between panels or between texts but rather that a dialogic space is created in the intersection of panels and texts. Likewise, when such texts explicitly engage with the theme of identity, they reflect the ways in which we engage with these texts affectively in a dialogue with our own histories, memories, and identity.

While conventional adaptation studies often regard adaptations as diminished or compromised versions of their source material, a metatextual perspective dispenses with overly restrictive textual hierarchies and enhances an understanding of authorship within a broader cultural context that allows for reader agency and textual fluidity (Horton and McDougal 1998, 2–3). Further, a metatextual approach encourages a consideration of the role played by comic book adaptations of other texts, as affect and memory, the key components of adaptations of comic books, play comparably vital roles in the other direction. Consider, for example, the 2017 graphic novel adaptation by writer Damian Duffy and artist John Jennings of Octavia E. Butler's 1979 science fiction novel *Kindred*. The story is about Dana, an African American woman in 1976 who is transported back in time to 1815, where she discovers she has a deeply affective connection with the son of a plantation owner. When he is in a moment of life-threatening crisis, she is transported from her time to his. Similarly, when she herself experiences tremendous emotional duress while in the past, she returns to 1976. The original novel's disruption of time and place and its thematic concerns with identity render its graphic novel adaptation as a highly self-reflexive work. Like Dana, affect is the vehicle by which we travel in time and space when we engage with texts and their histories. Through them one can better understand oneself as a sign that becomes more affective the more it circulates within that metatextual flow.

2

Alternative
Charles Hatfield

The term *alternative comics* implies opposition: an alternative *to* something. Its meaning depends on the ever-shifting context in which the opposition is staged. While comparisons to other oppositional forms (say, indie music or film) are helpful, the term is rooted in comics' distinctive culture, where it performs work not quite analogous to that accomplished by, for example, "alternative rock." In truth, defining alternative comics has always been a matter of position-taking within comics culture rather than any single aesthetic formation or genre. Broadly, alternative comics overturn familiar commercial formulas—beyond that, defining them is tough.

Historically, the label *alternative comics* has served to claim cultural capital for comics marginalized in Anglophone commercial production. Though alternative comics cannot be corralled into one type of story, still they constitute a distinct outsider genre: the "mainstream" comic's shadow self, using the same form yet insisting on thematic and ideological differences. In the sociology of culture established by Pierre Bourdieu, alternative comics would be a field in which capital, or prestige, is inversely proportional to commercial clout; indeed, fans often affirm the artistic seriousness of alternative comics by highlighting the genre's economic precarity and combative anticommercialism.

However, after Spiegelman's *Maus* (1986, 1992), the commercial and critical success of certain alternative comics, as graphic novels, memoirs, and so on, has challenged this marginality, positioning some comics within mainstream literary criticism and legitimizing the "literary" graphic novel. Usual suspects here would include Satrapi's *Persepolis* ([2000] 2004), Bechdel's *Fun Home* (2006), and more recent titles like Drnaso's *Sabrina* (2018)—books that have won or been nominated for literary prizes and made their way onto syllabi as contemporary literature. Such works, though arguably inspired by underground publishing practices, are now consecrated by literary critics. Alternative comics and the recent literary comic movement overlap, as the former prepared for and fed into the latter. However, many alternative comic fans reject literariness as emphatically as they reject comics' commercial mainstream.

Alternative comics have both a historically specific and a broader, more inclusive definition. The broader one operates today: an independent, artistically aspiring approach to comics that rejects commercial formula. The narrower definition, though, is the more easily defined: it recognizes *alternative comics* as a term specific to the US-based direct market in comic books—that is, the culture of comic shops as developed in the 1970s and after. In that context, "alternative comics" gained currency as a shorthand for comics distributed and sold within the direct market yet resistant to the market's focus on superhero comic collecting (the hobby that still fuels North American comic shops). Direct-market retailing merged the once-mainstream periodical comic book, a Depression-era innovation that peaked commercially in the early 1950s, with an underground mode of distribution—thus creating a specialized market favoring the superhero and nostalgic pulp genres in which stakeholders nonetheless insisted that their interests were "mainstream." This model provided not only a new means of distributing what remained of a once-mainstream medium but also a marketplace for collectible back issues and sometimes a new venue for underground comix. In fact, the direct market quickly birthed a new species of specialized, fan-oriented comic books and graphic novels (Gearino 2017; Hatfield 2005). By the late 1970s, these postunderground "independent" comics were a distinct trend, whether alternatives to superhero fare or opportunistic riders on the superhero wave; thus, alternative comics publishing took root as an idea.

This independent publishing boom exploited the direct market's unusual terms of business, including nonreturnable sales to shops and the placing of orders in advance of publication: essentially, a subscription system advantaging publishers while exposing shops to higher risks (offset somewhat by a loyal clientele). The result of all this activity, on the levels of creation, retail, and distribution, was an era of spirited entrepreneurship—and a cultural hothouse in which appeals to nostalgia collided with quixotic independent comics determined to use the new system to their advantage. In this market, *independent comics* came to refer to conditions of ownership and scale, specifically to small, independently owned companies distinct from the large-scale superhero brands Marvel and DC (owned by conglomerates). A grassroots ethos of independence bloomed, testimony to the undergrounds and the longer history of comic books as participatory culture yet ironically supported by a collecting hobby centered on Marvel and DC.

The comic shop is easy to mock as a geek preserve: a hideout nurturing the esoteric interests of a narrow, self-marginalizing fandom insulated from the social and political "real world." The typical "local comic shop" and its clientele can be typecast as a willed holdout against "growing up." Yet ironically, many of the publications that enabled US comics to adopt a rhetoric of greater maturity—what Christopher Pizzino (2016) has labeled the *bildungsroman discourse*—arose from the

direct market. From revisionist superhero comics such as Frank Miller et al.'s *Batman: The Dark Knight Returns* (DC Comics, 1986) and Alan Moore and Dave Gibbons's *Watchmen* (DC, 1986–87) to creator-owned projects such as the Hernandez brothers' *Love and Rockets* (Fantagraphics, 1982–present), direct-market comics took advantage of the market's devoted clientele to experiment with new formats and new content. By the 1980s, the market inspired a sort of barracks revolution in comic books.

The new "independent" comics, owned and operated by fan entrepreneurs, followed direct-market practices that would have been untenable in conventional magazine publishing: small print runs, fannish content relying on insider knowledge, and an emergent "star system" touting favorite creators. While "independent" in publishing structure, many offered superhero and fantasy tales that appealed to traditional fans and competed with Marvel and DC (*Nexus*, *Mage*, *Elementals*, etc.). Pioneering independent publishers included Star*Reach (1974–79), Eclipse (1979–94), First Comics (1983–91), Comico (1983–90), and self-publishers Dave Sim (Aardvark-Vanaheim, 1977–present) and Wendy and Richard Pini (WaRP Graphics, 1978–present). At times, independent titles indulged nostalgia while still twisting superhero formulas; at times, they pushed into new territory graphically and thematically. For example, Howard Chaykin's satirical science fiction series *American Flagg!* (First, 1983–89) is now recognized as a thematic and aesthetic breakthrough (Costello 2017).

While independent comics touted auteurist self-expression, their roots in superheroes and pulp revivalism made them ideal for direct-market shops. Groundbreaking efforts such as the *Star*Reach* anthology (1974–79), Jack Katz's *The First Kingdom* (Comics and Comix / Bud Plant, 1974–86), Sim's *Cerebus*, and the Pinis' *Elfquest* offered fantasy, SF, and swashbuckling adventure. By the early 1980s, independent comics reliably provided monthly doses of such work. Neither wholly underground nor mainstream in spirit, these were the so-called ground-level comics, successors to the fantastical undergrounds of, say, Wally Wood, Vaughn Bodē, Trina Robbins, or Richard Corben. The celebrated *Love and Rockets*, by Gilbert, Jaime, and Mario Hernandez, began that way, with *Heavy Metal*–style forays into absurdist fantasy and retro sci-fi. Launched as a self-published zine in 1981, *Love and Rockets* relaunched with publisher Fantagraphics in 1982 and soon became a roughly bimonthly serial offering sprawling story arcs by Jaime and Gilbert. However, it quickly ditched its pulp and fantasy trappings and thus modeled a new type of direct-market alternative comic.

Love and Rockets was a bellwether, offering a radical new conception of what periodical comics could be. Scrappy, punk inspired, and DIY, it spotlighted characters of color, strong women and queer characters, and new explorations of identity. It claimed the freedom of the underground but entirely avoided the malaise of the wilted counterculture. Though begun as a ground-level mix of fantasy and realism, *Love and Rockets* jettisoned (or ironized) familiar genre tropes and instead emphasized a gritty, everyday viewpoint, shot through with romance, magic realism, absurdist humor, and ambitious, nonlinear storytelling. Its casual mastery inspired a new fandom and ushered in periodical alternative comics as a distinct market niche in comic shops (Sobel and Valenti 2013; García 2017; Hatfield 2005). The publisher of *Love and Rockets*, Fantagraphics, known for the hard-hitting *Comics Journal* and a defiantly art-first attitude, became the leading alternative publisher of the 1980s direct market (Spurgeon 2016). Fantagraphics went on to publish Daniel Clowes's *Eightball* (1989–2004), Peter Bagge's *Hate* (1990–98), Roberta Gregory's *Naughty Bits* (1991–2004), the early issues of Chris Ware's *ACME Novelty Library* (ca. 1993–2001), and other key alternative titles. These comics vary drastically in style and temper; alternative comics opened up, among other things, a wider stylistic range than had been the case for the market's mainstream. Like the underground before them, they valorized individual graphic expression.

Within the direct market, *alternative comics* became the byword for personal cartooning and edgy, provoking content—developments embraced by some and ignored or disavowed by others. Certain pioneers predating *Love and Rockets* originated outside the market's fan culture but nonetheless became available in some comic shops, where they helped solidify alternative comics as a movement. Notably, Francoise Mouly and Art Spiegelman's avant-garde anthology *Raw* (Raw Books & Graphics, 1980–86; Penguin, 1989–91) was at once cosmopolitan, championing artistic innovators from abroad, and postpunk, introducing (alongside veteran undergrounders) a generation of new artists who connected as much with New York's downtown art scene as they did with past comics (Heer 2013; Spiegelman 2013). *Raw*, of course, serialized Spiegelman's *Maus*, a landmark alternative comic and catalyst of the literary comics movement. In addition, it promoted artists as diverse and influential as Charles Burns, Sue Coe, Richard McGuire, and Chris Ware. Around the same time, underground innovator Robert Crumb launched his own anthology, *Weirdo* (1981–93), later edited by Peter Bagge and Aline Kominsky-Crumb. *Weirdo* channeled the old underground spirit and became tagged as a "lowlife" alternative to the highbrow *Raw* (though some artists appeared in both anthologies). If *Raw*'s avant-gardism drew more academic attention, *Weirdo* was also groundbreaking, not least in championing women cartoonists (Cooke 2019). Both carried on the underground project of confessional autographics, a tradition also extended by writer-publisher Harvey

Pekar's *American Splendor* (1976–2008), a series consisting of collaborative autobiographical stories by Pekar and various artists (Crumb at first). Pekar sidestepped the fantastical flourishes of earlier autographics, favoring a drab yet revelatory naturalism; his work inspired many autobiographical comics in the direct market of the 1980s to the 1990s. Indeed, for a time, autobiography became the expected default for alternative comic books, so much so that in 1993, the *Comics Journal* devoted an issue to examining (and spoofing) the genre. Autographics has proved a durable—and critically consecrated—genre. Canadian publisher Drawn & Quarterly has excelled in this area, with its flagship anthology *Drawn & Quarterly*, volumes 1 and 2 (1990–97), leading the way, as well as other key autobiographical works such as Julie Doucet's *Dirty Plotte* (1990–98) and the later issues of Chester Brown's *Yummy Fur* (1991–94; see Rogers and Heer 2015).

Thus the direct market, though beholden to pulp and superhero fandom, helped enable alternative genres and styles, including both serials a la *Love and Rockets* and episodic autobiographical work. Yet this definition of alternative comics, centered on direct-market comic books, favors a scene that was largely white, male, straight, cis, often politically disengaged, and (as the market urged on the commodification of alternative genres) at risk of succumbing to formula. Alternative comic books, despite their performative marginality, were subsidized by the direct market's conditions and bred their own clichés and limitations—they were not alternatives in *every* sense. Publications that did not cater to the direct market, such as *World War 3 Illustrated* (1979–present), founded by artists Seth Tobocman and Peter Kuper and rooted in radical political cartooning, tended to be even further marginalized. While the best alternative comics rejected cliché and inspired creators whose perspectives were genuinely alternative (carrying forward the promise of *Love and Rockets*), in a narrow, direct-market sense, alternative comics were simply a sideshow to the market's business as usual.

In any case, this particular definition of alternative comics is outdated due to changes within the direct market and comics culture. Disastrous upheavals within—and the consolidation of—the direct market threatened the whole field in the 1990s, and a less competitive, more straitened market emerged from the chaos, post-1996. In this new phase, a single distributor, Maryland-based Diamond Comics Distributors, achieved a near monopoly on the distribution of periodical comic books. Diamond has a history of rejecting or criticizing controversial content in comics and catering to nostalgia-oriented fandom. Further, market fluctuations have urged publishers and retailers toward proven sellers. Thus the distinctive conditions that supported the direct-market alternative comic book have passed (Hatfield 2014).

Yet the local comic shop has never been the whole show; alternative comics have also been sustained by other currents. For one thing, publishers like Fantagraphics, while relying on the direct market, have sold comics through channels other than comic shops; in particular, record stores that favored "indie" music in the late 1980s sometimes carried comics like *Love and Rockets*. (Tower Records, in particular, stocked alternative comics and zines.) The underground ethos of the alternatives resonated with the postpunk DIY culture of indie rock, an overlap that provided another outlet for quirky, anticommercial comics. In addition, a thriving if commercially invisible culture of minicomics creation has flourished since at least the 1960s and became more prominent with the spread of self-service photocopy shops by the early 1980s, a trend that, as Lloyd Dunn (2007) puts it, led to "the rise of the casual publisher." Minicomix, a lively movement sometimes called "newave" (in the US) or "small press" (in the UK), encouraged the spread of handmade comic books (Dowers 2010). Some alternative publishers have had roots in minicomics, such as Seattle-based Starhead Comix (1984–99) and Portland, Oregon-based Sparkplug (2002–16), and that tradition continues.

Today, alternative comics persist—indeed, are flourishing: again, an independent approach that upends familiar market genres, transforming comics traditions into a personal graphic language that defies commercialization. *Alternative comics*, then, means more than a window in the history of comic book shops. Alternative comics now, decoupled from direct-market serialization, represent a radically accessible and decentralized artistic culture that does not rely on any one distribution company or channel to reach readers. Instead, alternative comics now circulate within dynamic networks constituted by festivals, independent bookstores, webcomics, crowdfunding, social media, and a minority of comic book and zine stores in big cities.

This independent activity coincides with, as noted, the tentative mainstreaming of graphic books. Today conglomerates or their subsidiaries, such as Pantheon, First Second, or Abrams, publish for the general book trade what once would have been labeled alternative comics, while veteran alternative publishers like Fantagraphics and Drawn & Quarterly enjoy distribution arrangements with long-standing literary ones. These trends dissolve the once-assumed link between alternative content and "independent" ownership; as Fantagraphics publisher Gary Groth has remarked, "Alternative used to be coterminous with independent, but not now" (pers. comm.). Yet even as these trends bring alternatives into the literary mainstream, a grassroots comics culture continues to resist or refuse commercial business as usual—and it is more robust now than ever.

To see this culture in action, one may attend small-press festivals such as Bethesda, Maryland's Small Press Expo (SPX, 1994–present), the Toronto Comic Arts Festival (TCAF, 2003–present), Seattle's Short Run (2011–present), or Comic Arts Los Angeles (CALA, 2014–present). At such shows, publishers like Fantagraphics tend to be among the largest exhibitors or may even be so large as to be excluded (whereas they are underdogs at larger-scale conventions such as San Diego Comic-Con International). Self-publishing artists, who may combine printed work with webcomics, are the norm and often band together to afford and cooperatively manage an exhibitor's table for the weekend. Besides self-publishing individuals, small presses are a fixture, including well-regarded boutique publishers like Czap Books, Koyama Press, and Youth in Decline (and many more). These publishers sometimes sell to direct-market comic book shops and/or the general book trade, but all are rooted in the small-press scene; doing well at these festivals is vital to their business. Tables may be small and modest, but the range of items on offer can be dizzying: from hand-sized minicomics, to buttons, to hand-crafted art objects (tchotchkes, apparel), to prints or original art—a startling variety of handmade works that, to paraphrase Czap Books' mission statement, "celebrate and explore the poetic, the personal, and the weird."

Today's alternative scene celebrates diversity; small-press festivals tend to welcome—if not proactively invite—creators of color and queer creators. LGBTQ+ representation has bloomed, surpassing pioneering underground and direct-market efforts such as *Gay Comix* (1980–91, later *Gay Comics*, 1992–98; Hall 2012). New creators, influenced by anime and shojo manga, autographics, and queer and trans webcomics, are reinterpreting existing genres to destabilize gender and sexual norms. Racism and ableism are also contested in today's alternative comics, which constitute a new frontier for identity work, including tales of disability and neuro-divergence and ethnoracially complex identities. The festivals' mission statements publicly encourage such work: CALA "foster[s] interactions among creators and readers alike by providing the community a diverse, inclusive space"; Short Run is "committed to creating safe spaces" celebrating "indie comix and self-published, small press, and handmade books of all kinds." In reality, LGBTQ+; Black, Indigenous, and people of color (BIPOC); and disabled representation remains an ongoing challenge rather than an achieved goal; not every festival has succeeded in diversifying its guests, volunteer communities, and leadership, and the politics of representation in such spaces can be fraught. Yet the culture has decisively shifted to recognize the importance of this struggle. In any case, these festivals deemphasize cosplay and other fandom-oriented activities in favor of an art-first ethos and the sharing of new reading experiences, often across borders of culture or genre. TCAF (partly sponsored by the Toronto Public Library) sums up the reigning spirit by offering "a literary festival and not a con." Small-press comics festivals, then, focus on the "coalescence of art and literature," as Short Run puts it, and "the intimate experience" of reading. A community spirit, often informed by feminist collective practice, unites these festivals, counterbalancing the strikingly individual work of the comics themselves. Hence contemporary alternative comics appear more progressive and deliberate about inclusion than their forebears.

Such generalizations are of course made to be broken, and alternative comics remain a borderland in which work of all kinds, progressive and reactionary, can happen. In any case, contemporary comics festivals, and the burgeoning internet commerce around self-made comics, confirm that alternative comics are a more flexible and robust form than an emphasis on the direct-market comic shop would indicate. The current scene reminds us that reaching outside of comics fandom was vital to what made alternative comics different in the first place—and this spirit lives on in the decentered yet fertile alternative comics culture of today.

3

Archie

Bart Beaty

The 2017 launch of the *Riverdale* series on the CW channel cast one of the longest-running franchises in the American comic book industry in an entirely new light. The popular teen drama, with its emphasis on sex and violence, served as a radical reimagining of a comics franchise that had, for more than seventy-five years until its more adult transformation in print by Mark Waid in 2016, traded on its wholesome and family-friendly reputation. For generations, Archie Comics represented an image of American comics that many actors in the field hoped to eliminate. Archie Comics have been commonly dismissed as the unserious, commercial work against which more important works are arrayed, just as the readership of Archie Comics (predominantly young, overwhelmingly female) is regarded as a problematic demographic that graphic novels struggled to overthrow. For example, writing in a new introduction to his 1979 interview with science fiction writer Harlan Ellison, Fantagraphics publisher Gary Groth describes the cultural desolation of "a monolithic Comics Industry composed primarily of Marvel and DC, which comprised what was then called the 'mainstream' and which published probably 98% of the comics being consumed by the American public (excepting *Archie*, which was under everyone's radar, especially mine)" (2018). Groth's blindness in this instance is tellingly distorting: the aggressively masculine disposition valorized by him and Ellison could find no room for comic books published for children and, particularly, girls.

The early history of the American comic book is one in which a publishing industry catered to two groups: young children (aged approximately three to eight years old) and children or preadolescents (eight to twelve). Any reasonable history of the comic book form must center, in its first quarter century, on the enormous success of Dell Comics, the sales leader who held the licenses for characters belonging to Walt Disney Productions, Warner Brothers, and the Walter Lantz Studio, among many others. Dell's market dominance stemmed from their leadership among the most prized demographic in comic book publishing, young children, and they were challenged by publishers like St. John, Toby Press, Fawcett, and Harvey Comics until their separation from Western Publishing in 1962 and their gradual decline due to the expansive reach of television animation.

Archie Comics, on the other hand, catered primarily to children who were slightly too old for comics featuring funny animals and found themselves competing with publishers of superhero comic books for a slightly older demographic. Archie Comics began as MLJ Magazines, founded in 1939 by Maurice Coyne, Louis Silberkleit, and John Goldwater, each of whom lent their first initial to the name of the company. In 1940, the company launched *Pep Comics*, an anthology title whose lead feature was the Shield, a red, white, and blue patriotic superhero who predated the first appearance of Captain America by more than a year. *Pep* was a moderate success. Archie Andrews was introduced with no fanfare in the twenty-second issue (cover-dated December 1941) as one of many backup features. Over the next several years, however, the exploits of Archie and his friends at Riverdale High began to inch into the spotlight. First, the Archie stories slowly marched toward the front of the title; then Archie began to appear on the cover alongside the Shield; and in 1944, Archie displaced the Shield from the covers entirely as *Pep Comics* became predominantly a vehicle for humorous stories about America's most lovable teenager.

The earliest Archie stories were drawn by Bob Montana and written by Vic Bloom. The duo slowly established the core characters and setting over the first several years before Montana departed the comic book to become the cartoonist behind the *Archie* daily newspaper strip in 1947 (a job that he held until his death in 1975). The flagship *Archie* title was launched in 1942, giving the character two venues, and that expanded to three with the creation of *Laugh Comics* in 1946. In 1949, the company launched its first spin-off title, *Archie's Pal Jughead*, and followed that with *Archie's Girls Betty and Veronica* in 1950. Over the coming years, Archie Comics would continue to add monthly, bimonthly, and quarterly titles featuring the Riverdale crew, including *Little Archie*, *Life with Archie*, *Archie's Joke Book*, *Archie's Pals 'n Gals*, *Betty and Me*, *Archie and Me*, and *Archie's Rival Reggie*, among dozens of others. By the 1960s, Archie Comics was among the most successful of all comic book companies and had virtually cornered the market on comics for young girls (with romance comic books targeted a slightly older female readership with varying degrees of success). In 1969, when *Archie* was the best-selling comic book in the United States and Archie Comics published seven of the top twenty best-selling titles, the industry might be understood to be composed of comic books for very young children (Gold Key and Harvey Comics), comic books for young readers (Archie Comics), and comic books for young readers and teens (DC Comics, Marvel Comics, Charlton Comics, *MAD Magazine*), with an extremely marginal market segment for adult readers in the undergrounds that existed on the periphery of the industry. In the 1970s, new publishers like Warren and Skywald and magazines like *Heavy Metal* would help usher in a young adult category dominated by the kinds of male-centered concerns relevant to figures like Groth and Ellison, paving the way for the graphic novel revolution of the 1980s and 1990s that would strive to separate comic books from their historically juvenile audience.

The invisibility of Archie Comics within the comics world stems, at least in part, from the fact that their core elements rely on repetition and simplicity. Because Archie Comics historically targeted a readership that turned over approximately every five years, more than any other comic book publisher, they were able to rely on the recirculation of old material (as in the digest-sized comic books that they popularized as a format). In support of this, the publisher insisted on an extremely narrowly defined house style so that new and reprinted material would be minimally differentiated. During the height of their popularity, Archie stories tended to be as short as a single-panel gag and only as long as six pages (*Life with Archie* was the exception to this rule, as early issues tended to feature a single story). Archie stories were always lightheartedly comic in tone, brightly colored, and wholesome in nature. The comics featured Archie Andrews, an all-American redheaded young man, as the lead. He courts the wealthy Veronica Lodge and the girl-next-door Betty Cooper. His best friend, Jughead Jones, is a laconic overeater and girl hater, and his rival, Reggie Mantle, is a well-to-do narcissist. The cast is filled out with dozens of supporting characters, many of whom are little more than clichés (the brainy Dilton Doiley, the dumb jock Moose). While the core group existed for decades virtually unaltered, the publisher added Chuck Clayton, an African American friend, in 1971, and Cheryl Blossom, a rival of Betty and Veronica, in 1982. In 2010, the company added Kevin Keller, a gay student, providing him with his own short-lived title in 2011. For most of its history, Archie Comics focused on creating work that is the antithesis of the types of graphic novels that are most celebrated in comics scholarship and within contemporary fandom. Archie Comics published short, funny stories about these characters that had no continuity—each story was set in an eternal present that allowed them to be endlessly repackaged in reprint collections for decades. The formula was a tremendous success, and as late as 1969, the flagship *Archie* title sold more than 515,000 copies per issue.

Despite the heights attained in the 1960s, Archie Comics has been in a state of decline that almost precisely mirrors the state of the American comic book industry since that time. Changes to magazine distribution in the 1970s reduced the reach of Archie Comics. As distribution dried up, the company made a number of missteps, including going public, launching a restaurant chain, and creating a fantasy and horror imprint (Red Circle Comics). In 1983, Richard Goldwater, the son of John, and Michael Silberkleit, the son of Louis, took the company private again. As comic book sales shifted toward the more restrictive and adult-focused direct market, Archie Comics remained a force within traditional magazine distribution channels at a time when that system was in decay. When Harvey Comics, the other publisher focused on comic books for younger children, ceased operation in 1982, Archie Comics was the primary—and at times exclusive—publisher focusing on comic books for young readers.

While Archie Comics remains a private, family-owned business, its direction changed with the deaths of the sons of the cofounders (Goldwater in 2007 and Silberkleit in 2008). The company is currently owned by Michael Silberkleit's widow, Nancy, and Richard Goldwater's half brother, Jonathan. In the 2010s, Archie Comics has pursued a variety of projects targeted toward the comic book direct market in efforts to revitalize their properties as newsstand distribution all but disappeared. These projects have included a much-publicized story in 2010 where Archie marries Veronica in one story line

and Betty in another and the death of Archie Andrews in 2014. In December 2014, Archie Comics relaunched its flagship title under the creative direction of writer Mark Waid and artist Fiona Staples and began featuring ongoing serial story lines that were a radical break from the company's traditions; new titles featuring Jughead and Betty and Veronica soon followed as the company sought to shift toward a more mature readership. While the initial relaunch of Archie, with its many variant covers, sold well in comic shops, sales have declined significantly over time (Miller 2017). Archie Comics continues to produce digest-sized reprint comics for channels outside the direct market.

Presently, Archie and his friends are much more prominent as the characters on the CW's *Riverdale* than they are as comic book characters. While *Riverdale* is not the first Archie television series (the company produced animated television series in 1968, 1987, and 1999 and has also produced both live-action and animated versions of their characters Sabrina and Josie with varying degrees of success), *Riverdale* dominates contemporary thinking about Archie. *Riverdale* courts an older viewership with its frank depictions of sexuality and story lines involving queerness, drug use, rape, and murder. The ironic inversion of nostalgia for *Riverdale*'s utopian image of Middle America has become a hallmark not only for the television show but for other imaginings of Archie and his friends. Ed Brubaker and Sean Phillips put a noirish spin on the Archie gang in their 2011 series *Criminal: Last of the Innocent*, and even Archie Comics itself embraced a dark vision with the satiric zombie-horror comic book series *Afterlife with Archie* (2013). The uses of irony in Archie Comics are closely tied processes of masculinization and adultification that were earlier used by Frank Miller to reshape the cultural understanding of Batman in *The Dark Knight Returns*. To this end, in the face of the transformation of the economics of the comic book industry that has resulted from the abandonment of young readers, *Archie Comics* has sought with varying degrees of success to emerge from the position of cultural valuelessness identified by Groth, abandoning its status of the graphic novel's other by embracing the norms of the industry as they have developed over the past two decades as the graphic novel has displaced the ephemeral comic book, a category that Archie once ideally embodied.

4

Archive
Margaret Galvan

Comics are not designed to be remembered. Accordingly, it may seem strange to think of comics in relation to archives given that throughout their history, floppy comics in the form of short, bound, and stapled booklets have been created to be more or less disposable, often printed on poor-quality paper. Even in the era of the graphic novel, titles from major comics publishers go out of print with regularity, and the rise of crowd-funded titles, where fans donate money directly to comics creators to underwrite the making and printing of their work, means that such productions have no guarantee of futurity past the initial print run. Beyond that, the marginal status of comics has often kept them out of archives: the very institutions dedicated to memory. Many archives have independent collectors to thank for their rich collections, like Bill Blackbeard, whose amassing of early newspaper comics across three decades now forms the heart of the Billy Ireland Cartoon Library & Museum at the Ohio State University (Robb 2009). Despite all of these challenges, comics are inextricably bound up with archives, and the recent archival turn has fueled debate over what archives mean for materials like comics. The ability of archives to bring visibility to largely forgotten or ignored works of comics production not only expands our sense of the field and its history but also offers new methods of understanding comics that complement comics scholarship's focus on questions of form that explore the stylistic or aesthetic qualities of comics art.

Jacques Derrida's *Archive Fever* (1996) ignited the archival turn wherein scholars examined the functioning of archives to preserve cultural memory. Derrida built his argument around the origins of archives as a space that safeguarded legal documents in private domiciles, but scholars in the years since have traced the development and proliferation of the concept as archives have prospered in museums, university libraries, private collections, grassroots spaces, and so on (Derrida 1996; Steedman 2001; Blouin and Rosenberg 2011). In her book *An Archive of Feelings* (2003), Ann Cvetkovich explored how the artifacts and affiliated feelings of queer lives have been preserved in a variety of formats and spaces that in periods prior to grassroots institutions like the Lesbian Herstory Archives would be lost and forgotten. Given comics' status as an ephemeral, marginalized art form, this approach to archives is relevant to comics in general, but it also points us to comics created by queer and other marginal folks that were not produced within traditional comics venues. In the introduction to *No Straight Lines*, a collection recuperating four decades of queer comics, cartoonist Justin Hall documents how these comics have been created "in a parallel universe alongside the rest of comics, appearing almost exclusively in gay newspapers and gay bookstores, and published by gay publishers" (2012). Engaging comics in an expansive set of archives reveals forgotten works, formats, artists, histories, and so on. Extending from Cvetkovich, the examination of politically radical archives has animated several special journal issues and monographs over the past five years, relevant for how scholars analyze both the practices of grassroots archives and the archiving of radical materials used for political actions and those documenting the lives of marginalized individuals (Eichhorn 2013; Kumbier 2014; Marshall, Murphy, and Tortorici 2014; Darms and Eichhorn 2015; Rawson and Devor 2015; Stone and Cantrell 2015;

Dittmar and Entin 2016; Adkins and Dever 2017; Bessette 2017).

Comics studies participates in the archival turn in two ways: some scholars examine how comics operate *as* archives, and others theorize how comics circulate and reside *in* archives. Those who study comics *as* archives consider questions of form that further formalist approaches foundational to the field, including asking how the visual and narrative structures of a given comics text organize and memorialize different kinds of bodies, lives, affects, and experiences; scholars who look to comics *in* archives reassess the cultural history of comics and often deploy new methodological approaches. While archives preserve all sorts of comics, a queer approach to recovery allows us to see a wider expanse of comics and encourages us to be aware of the assumptions scholars often make when constructing histories.

Some scholars who study comics as archives formally examine how comics represent marginalized culture. This approach involves conceptualizing comics as an "archival genre," meaning that comics structurally echo practices that we attribute to archives like "collecting, preservation, and ordering" (Eichhorn 2008; Galvan 2015). In his work, Jared Gardner describes how comics act as archives by encoding "excess data—the remains of the everyday" in their very form (2006, 802). The prevalence of graphic memoir as a contemporary genre and central site of comics scholarship furthers this discussion as scholars analyze how the alliance of comics with archives often involves comics representing and arguably preserving archival material within their narratives. A glance at the scholarship on Alison Bechdel's *Fun Home* neatly demonstrates the archival impulse of the comic, where Bechdel catalogs her family story amid a larger queer history present in the books she reads throughout the narratives and in references to historical events like Stonewall and the AIDS crisis (Cvetkovich

2008; Watson 2008; Chute 2010; Rohy 2010; Warhol 2011). While formalist-driven analyses of comics train us to consider the archival aspect inherent in *Fun Home* in how she redraws family photographs and other personal ephemera, we can also look to how the comic documents Bechdel's own participation in the archival turn. This kind of reading understands Bechdel as a visual theorist across her oeuvre who contends with the ephemerality of queer history by preserving it in comics, inscribing what she has gleaned from participating and publishing in grassroots newspapers into the content of her work while she also collects and preserves records of these publications amid her papers archived at Smith College (Galvan 2018). Her practices point toward those scholars who locate comics in archives as her approach gestures toward undertheorized locations for comics—both in grassroots newspapers and in archival collections not explicitly dedicated to comics.

Theorizing comics in archives means analyzing comics and affiliated materials preserved in these spaces and asking what new histories we can trace with this recuperative approach. The lack of accessibility of many comics—the fact that many have been destroyed, badly preserved, or only exist in a handful of well-maintained collections and archives—skews scholarship toward contemporary creators and in-print titles and thereby distorts the histories we tell about various kinds of comics production. Archives and the comics therein encourage comics scholarship both to reconsider its history making and to examine the biases of collectors who have donated archival collections. For example, we can consider how we can differently understand the legacy of the comic series *Wimmen's Comix* (1972–92), unique for being a feminist comic produced by women in the overwhelmingly misogynist underground scene dominated by male cartoonists, based on how it is collected in numerous archives (Galvan 2017, 23; Sammond

2018). In most collections of underground comics, *Wimmen's Comix* exists as a lone counterpoint to the usual understanding of the underground, while its existence in feminist and lesbian collections embeds the series in a wholly different history and challenges us to reconceive the underground and its impact (Galvan 2017, 23; Sammond 2018). Further, feminist comics artist Trina Robbins recuperated the stories of hundreds of forgotten female creators and their comics in the pages of her *Women and the Comics*, which relate the history of women in the field alongside visual samples of the work of many of these artists (Robbins and Yronwode 1985; Robbins 1993, 1996, 1999, 2001, 2013). Nancy Goldstein recovered the memory and strips of pioneering African American artist Jackie Ormes, who published her work in Black newspapers during the early years of civil rights activism (Goldstein 2008). Carol Tilley is rewriting our understanding of Fredric Wertham's midcentury morality crusade against comics by working with his archived documents at the Library of Congress (Tilley 2012). These examples jointly demonstrate how archives can support revisionist scholarship that reworks comics histories in ways that excavate marginalized creators and readers who were earlier dismissed.

This emerging strand of comics scholarship is supported by university archivists actively seeking out collections to preserve; the archival acquisitions shepherded by Karen Green at Columbia University in recent years—of the papers and records of Chris Claremont, Howard Cruse, Al Jaffee, Kitchen Sink Press, Wendy and Richard Pini, and so on—suggest a rich tapestry of histories yet to be written (Gustines 2011; Reid 2011; Vo 2012; Reid 2013a, 2013b; Grimes 2013a, 2013b; Galvan 2015; McCabe 2016; Sousanis 2017; Tilley 2017a; Green, n.d.). Other American institutions that preserve large archival collections of comics and material affiliated with the making of comics include Bowling Green State

University, Duke University, University of Florida, Library of Congress, Michigan State University, Portland State University, the Ohio State University, Syracuse University, and Virginia Commonwealth University and online at the Alexander Street Press Underground and Independent Comics database. Granted, comics as an art form that has circulated within magazines, newspapers, pamphlets, posters, zines, and so on also exist in unremarked plentitude within archives not focused on the medium. All of these collections forecast a future history of comics that appreciates the multifaceted nature of the form and that considers how archives intertwine with its ephemeral material.

5

Border
Cathy Schlund-Vials

In *Comics and Sequential Art* (1985), US cartoonist/ writer Will Eisner (1917–2005) establishes—by way of particularized form and via specialized function—the art medium's disciplinary, rhetorical, and speculative stakes. Stressing that a serious study of comics (a.k.a. "sequential art") lays bare "the unique aesthetics" that are part and parcel of the widely popular yet undertheorized genre, Eisner's illustrated treatise subsequently settles its critical attention on the blended literary/art mode's compositional, spatial, and affective dimensions ("Foreword"). While much of *Comics and Sequential Art* concerns the roles imagery, anatomy, scale, and framing play in the making of drawn narrative, and whereas extensive attention is paid to multivalent significations rendered evident in strategic uses of line, shading, shadow, and perspective, Eisner likewise interrogates the art form's uncanny ability to simultaneously traverse space and time. These traversals, which pivot on a concomitant attention to panel area and pictorial frame, very much depend on a multivalent, multidisciplinary understanding of the role borders play in the making of graphic narrative. As important, such multifaceted attention to form, function, movement, and narrative takes centrally Ramzi Fawaz's convincing insistence that comics is "a medium that demands an exceptionally rigorous account of multiplicity" (Fawaz 2019, 591).

Given this essay's overt focus on "border" as an intelligible comics "keyword," consonant with Fawaz's characterization of comics-focused "multiplicity," and consistent with Eisner's "successive" argument, it is perhaps apropos that Eisner—as a foundational graphic narrative theorist—alludes to a fellow groundbreaking logician in *Comics and Sequential Art*'s assessment of narrative temporality in a chapter appositely titled "Timing." Expressly, in that chapter's second subsection (designated "Framing Time"), Eisner turns to Nobel Prize–winning theoretical physicist Albert Einstein and his special theory of relativity. As Eisner synopsizes, the special theory of relativity states that time is not absolute but relative to the position of the observer. In essence the panel (or box) makes that postulate a reality for the comic book reader. The act of paneling or boxing the action not only defines its perimeters but establishes the position of the reader in relation to the scene and indicates the duration of the event. Indeed, it "tells" time (Eisner 1985, 28). Situated adjacent to Einstein's hypothetical deliberations on the structure of "space-time," Eisner's use of relativity—as a principal means of relaying both narrative proximity and spectator propinquity—places the reader in a discernible space (e.g., of "the scene") and situates that same subject within a distinctive time (explicitly vis-à-vis "the duration of the event"). Equally noteworthy is Eisner's successive suggestion that the lines that demarcate a panel or box—constitutive of visible edges and projected perimeters—concurrently delineate the drawn form's spatial proportions (via two-dimensional drawings on the page) and instantiate a flexible temporality (a la Einstein's aforementioned theorization of "space-time").

On the one hand, Eisner's pointed reference to Einstein's theory inadvertently though constructively accentuates the critic's preponderant portrayal of sequential art as an exceptionally interactive mode; this mid-1980s categorization, which presages what Hillary Chute and Marianne DeKoven note in 2006 is a "cross-discursive" aspect of comics, pivots on an improvisational interplay between artist and audience. Notwithstanding such fluid inventiveness, and despite Eisner's emphasis on audience refraction, integral to these comics interactions is an implicit acknowledgment of narrative limits and visual "borders." Often obscured in comics criticism by terms such as *panel*, *box*, or *gutter*, border as an analytical descriptor in sequential art is paradoxically commonplace (as an illustrated means of containing action box, staging panel, speech bubble, and caption) and all-encompassing (via its reiterative utilization as panel/box separator and page frame). The relativistic position of "border" as hypervisible/invisible schema in comics theory is replicated in the word's better-known usages and the meanings connected therein.

Politically connotative of "a line separating two countries, administrative divisions, or other areas," a border can nevertheless be governmentally porous (as evidenced by the present-day movement of people, goods, and ideas across state-established boundaries, current conceptualizations of transnationalism, and contemporary debates concerning immigration policy), historically contingent (e.g., wartime "demilitarized zones" or strictly policed checkpoints), or contiguous (e.g., a district or area wherein two borders converge, such as a refugee camp; "Border"). Shifting from geopolitical imaginary to artistic composition, a border also refers to a "decorative strip around the edge of something." Such focalized framing on one level corresponds to an overall reading of comics as *art* and individual panels as stand-alone artworks. On another level, the use of borders in graphic narrative—particularly via the signification of time and articulation of space—resonates with the cinematic tenets of mise-en-scène via panel design, visual theming, and storyboarding ("Border").

On the other hand, when considered a proximal signifier, a "border"—as Eisner's "relativity" reference underscores—figures keenly in contemporaneous evaluations of comics as a complex hermeneutic mode. Analogous to the ways in which Einstein's theory of special relativity upended the primacy of Newtonian physics and transformed other disciplines (particularly astronomy), Eisner's treatise on sequential art—along with Scott McCloud's *Understanding Comics: The Invisible Art* (1993)—dramatically altered the relationship between academics and comics by elevating the latter to the interpretation-worthy status of the former. In so doing, *Comics and Sequential Art* redraws the disciplinary borders of established fields such as English, comparative literature, linguistics, and art history so that they are—to varying degrees and divergent ends—in dialogue with one another. Such redrawing is, as Fawaz notes, indicative of the medium's "greatest conceptual power" vis-à-vis its "ability to perform a queer disruption of the field's existing logics" (2019, 592).

Such recalibrations with regard to analytic site and evaluative methodology, which attend to a complex mode that is both "written and drawn," meaningfully correspond to what Chute and DeKoven argue is a primary aspect of comics, a "form that . . . always refuses a problematic transparency, through an explicit awareness of its own surfaces" (2012, 767). Accordingly, these comics-generated refusals—wherein the superficial overtness of line, the seeming clarity of color, and the ostensible simplicity of cartoon drawing converge to form the "diegetical horizon of each page"—are, according to Chute and DeKoven, made discernible through bordered "boxes of time" (769). While Chute and DeKoven's characterization immediately speaks to the division of panels on a page and their ability to convey an experiential duration, such "boxes of time" are also resonant with Einstein's "space-time" hypothesis, which posits that the collision of the three dimensions of space and the singular dimension of time produces a single four-dimensional continuum.

Though coincidental, Einstein's argument concerning special relativity (featured in a paper titled "On the Electrodynamics of Moving Bodies") was published the same year (1905) that Winsor McCay's *Little Nemo in Slumberland* debuted in the *New York Herald*. Known for its experimental use of form, manipulation of panel size, deployment of multiple perspectives, and utilization of detailed architectural drawings, *Little Nemo in Slumberland* as a full-page endeavor consistently pushed against the boundaries of newspaper comics. As suggested by the series title, *Little Nemo in Slumberland* drew inspiration and plot from the protagonist's fantastical dreams. Despite the initial appearance of "real-time" narration and chronological sequence, *Little Nemo in Slumberland* was more often than not "otherwise," echoing the imaginary registers of a dreamlike state. Set within a shifting dreamscape, McCay's graphic narrative assumed by way of moving vantage point the multilayered dimensions of Einstein's notion of space-time. Notwithstanding such expansiveness, the oversized comic strip would come to an abrupt end when the protagonist awoke, signaling a move from borderless imagination to bordered reality.

Such endings—in which the limits of the page function as an impassible boundary—highlight what was, until recently, the ultimate comics border and presage what is possibly a new "frontier" in sequential art production. As Scott McCloud notes in his turn-of-the-twenty-first-century meditation on the future of comics, "Print cartoonists . . . make a constant series of compromises in pacing and design to stuff our stories into pages. We add and subtract panels, restrict size variation, break reading flow, and rarely if ever vary the distance between panels for fear of wasting paper" (n.d.). Faced with these limits, McCloud has consistently pushed artists and critics to consider the unexplored possibilities of a so-termed infinite canvas, which utilizes an online format that "measures time using space." In so doing, McCloud articulates a new way of seeing sequential art, making visible through the underused platform the paramount *borderlessness* of comics.

6

Caricature

Rebecca Wanzo

The term *caricature* emerged in Italy in the sixteenth century and was a form of exaggerated portrait drawing. The distortion or exaggerated representation of people's features had a long history before that and can be seen in visual work produced by ancient Egyptians, Greeks, and Romans (Robinson 1917). It has often been used for comic effect. Part of what can make caricature comic is the way in which phenotypic excess can suggest the grotesque—a liminality between humanness and something else. Many caricatures of people are anthropomorphic, sometimes producing a feeling of the uncanny.

The fusion of excess, comedy, and the grotesque has made caricatures an aesthetic practice valuable for political commentary and indicting the characters of public figures. It has thus been foundational to the art of editorial cartooning and satirical humor in cartoon art. Political cartooning came of age in the nineteenth century, with artists such as Honoré Daumier producing work for *La Caricature* (1830–1943), George de Maurier for *Punch* (1841–2002), and Thomas Nast for *Harper's Weekly* (1857–1916). It was considered such a powerful tool in attacking political figures that in 1903, a Pennsylvania state legislator introduced a bill to make editorial cartoons illegal if someone is portrayed, described, or represented in a publication "either by distortion, innuendo or otherwise, in the form of a likeness of beast, bird, fish, insect, or other inhuman animal, thereby tending to expose such person to public hatred, contempt, or ridicule" (Lamb 2004). He was unsuccessful. Satirizing the powerful, however, is not the only common use of caricature. It has also been a frequent tool in circulating discriminatory discourses.

Nast, well known for playing a role in bringing down the corrupt political administration of "Boss" William M. Tweed in nineteenth-century New York, also made use of racist caricature to disparage the Irish and African Americans. While the treatment of Black visages was more realistic when he produced abolitionist cartoons in the war, he descended into racist stereotypes to suggest neither Black people nor Irish Americans were capable of full participation in democracy. Racist caricature was present in some of the most celebrated comic strips in United States history. Richard F. Outcault made use of racist caricature in his influential comic strips *The Yellow Kid* (1895). An African imp accompanied the dreaming title character in Winsor McCay's *Little Nemo in Slumberland* (1905–26), a beautiful comic celebrated for its use of color and inventive comic layouts. Will Eisner's masked vigilante, the Spirit (1940), was assisted by an amphibian-looking sidekick named Ebony White. These are but a few examples, as cartoon and comic art have been a prominent place for circulating racist representations.

The idea that the face is a way of representing the essential characters of a group of people, of course, is not confined to cartoon art. It is perhaps no accident that caricature and scientific racism came of age somewhat concurrently in the same historical moment that improvements in printing technology allowed drawings to be produced more cheaply and circulate more widely in the nineteenth century. While eighteenth-century scientific texts such as Carl Linnaeus's *Systema Naturae* (1759) established some of the Enlightenment foundations for attaching character to physiognomy, nineteenth-century scientific literature such as Arthur Gobineau's *An Essay on the Inequality of the Human Races* ([1853] 1967), Samuel George Morton's *Crania Americana* (1839), and James. W. Redfield's *Comparative Physiognomy* (1852) contributed to an influential anthropological and medical discourse that posited racial differences in intelligence and character. Their arguments were often accompanied by drawings that tried to present the relationship between character difference and visual features as self-evident.

This nexus between character and physiognomy also illustrates the ways in which caricatures are not always negative representations. Caricatures can also represent ideal types. Just as the European man was held up as the height of human superiority in scientific racism, cartoonists also used caricature to represent citizenship ideals. The best example in comic art is the superhero. Superman's musculature and perfect character modeled a fantasy of not only the model citizen-soldier but the ideal immigrant for the nation. But perfection is not the predominant work done by cartooning—characters often represented "types" through their excessive depiction, and the excess can produce not only comic effect but grounds for reader identification. Cathy Guisewite's long-running comic strip *Cathy* (1976–2010), for example, was a stereotype of a single, professional white woman in the United States. She is slightly overweight, often wearing expressions that might be characterized as "ditzy" or hysterical, and many readers found these highly gendered constructions of her foibles endearing.

The words *caricature* and *stereotype* are sometimes used interchangeably; thus, it is also useful to highlight their relationship with each other and their dissimilarities. A caricature can be about an individual, while stereotypes are always about groups. Caricatures are defined by exaggeration or excess, while stereotypes are defined by simplification and reductiveness. A caricature can present a stereotype and vice versa. And both have been a means of circulating celebratory and discriminatory discourses about identity groups.

The use of caricature to contribute to nationalist scripts or intervene in them, indict oppression or participate in it, thus make the art form one of the most politically charged aspects of cartoon and comic art. Art Spiegelman's *Maus*, for example, recast the victims and perpetrators in the Holocaust as animals. Given the history of the association of Jews with animals, this could have been a disastrous representational move. But critical history has judged his choice to use animals as a brilliant way of understanding the structural and psychological issues of the Holocaust. Editorial cartoonists around the globe have been persecuted for their indictments of powerful people and ideologies they contest. The most famous example of persecuted cartoonists was undoubtedly the murder of the *Charlie Hebdo* cartoonists. But the debates that emerged in the wake of their deaths also exemplify how caricature is a complex art form that can highlight differences in reading practices and ethical commitments in the world.

On January 7, 2015, two terrorists associated with a branch of the Islamic fundamentalist group Al-Qaeda went to the Paris office of the satirical magazine *Charlie Hebdo* and shot and killed Stephane Charbonnier (Charb), Jean Cabut, George Wolinski, Bernard Verlhac, Bernard Maris, Phillipe Honore, Michel Renaud, Elsa Cayat, Frederic Boisseau, Mustapha Ourrad, Ahmed Merabet, and Franck Brinsolaro. The ostensible motive for the horrifying murders of cartoonists, staff, and officers was the cartoonists' choice to represent the Prophet Muhammad satirically, with images seen by some as deploying racial, ethnic, and religious stereotypes (and representing Muhammad at all is a sacrilege to many followers of Islam). While some people assert that the representation of Muhammad in itself is offensive, nothing in the Koran actually prohibits the representation of the prophet, and in fact representations of Muhammad have been produced by worshippers for centuries (Gruber 2019). Cartoons that satirized Muhammad also were in the news when the Danish newspaper *Jyllands-Posten* produced twelve cartoons of Muhammad in 2005 and then again in 2011, when the *Charlie Hebdo* offices were bombed. The comics did not produce the violence. The agents in those acts are the terrorists. But the conversations that followed the violence were produced by the content of the comics—debates about speech, satire, tradition, citizenship, and identity. Hermeneutical conflict reigned, with leftist allies all condemning the murders but divided on the interpretation of the cartoons. Some people argued that *Hebdo* was employing the tradition of *bête et méchant* humor for leftist, secular critique, while others argued that they still trafficked in discriminatory stereotypical representations. In both scholarly and popular circles, people argued over how to read caricature in comic art.

While it may seem a special case, we should not lose sight of the fact that caricature has been a kind of Western nationalist grammar that quickly describes citizenship excesses and failures since the eighteenth and nineteenth centuries. As Martha Banta argues, caricatures structure much of our relationality as citizens in the West, as many people "are doomed to be defined by representations of what they say they are not" (Banta 2003). The word *caricature* is a common part of our Western vocabulary as a way to describe an exaggerated visual or linguistic depiction that flattens out the complexity of its referent, but its reach is much bigger than mimesis. Our political discourse would be unrecognizable without reductive and excessive depictions of real and imagined flaws.

7

Cartoon

Michael Mark Cohen

In a Gary Larson cartoon from *The Far Side* (1980–95), a pair of archeologists wearing pith helmets and short pants discover "the mummified remains of a prehistoric cave-painter—still clutching his brush!" The artist's skeleton lies on the cave floor with a stone-tipped spear lodged in his ribcage. On the wall is the artist's final work, a black-line drawing of a bison in the style of Lascaux but with the face of a slack-jawed caveman protruding from the bison's ass. Our scientists offer their expert assessment: "Seems he made an enemy, though."

Maybe it is my own nostalgia for the twentieth century's printed "funny pages" in which I read *The Far Side* as a kid, but Larson's violent origin story of the political cartoon provides clear insights into the history of cartoons. First, it shows that the cartoon is rooted in the oldest forms of human visual representation, such as cave paintings, pictographs, and hieroglyphics. Some scholars date the origin of the political cartoon to 1360 BCE with a caricature of the pharaoh Akhenaten protesting his effort to impose monotheism over Egypt. (The archive leaves no word on the fortunes of the satirist.) Second, Larson makes light of a very serious issue—namely, that the work of representation is a comingling of the aesthetic and the political. It may seem a "cartoonish" exaggeration to insist that the stakes of political cartooning are that of life and death. Yet that is precisely the point on which I will conclude this essay. Therefore, in what follows, I consider several highlights in the political history of cartooning and its

relationship to problems of political representation. In short, this is a story of how silly pictures can often produce very serious consequences.

In its modern form, the cartoon is a mass-reproduced black-line drawing or engraving, often with dialogue text or captions, that employs a caricatured, nonrealistic, or humorous style of visual storytelling. The geography of daily newspapers that once thrived on this popular art published two types of cartoons: the gag cartoons that appear at the back in the "funny pages" and the political cartoons that appear on the editorial page. Gag cartoons are supposed to be inoffensive *and* funny; political cartoons are supposed to be partisan *but* funny. As an artistic medium, the *political* cartoon sits at the meeting point between art and propaganda, specific political context and broad ideological abstractions, crude humor and state power. Far more than the fine arts or comic book superheroes, political cartoons have a long history of challenging and enacting political power, both for good and for ill.

Cultural theorist Stuart Hall (2002) has argued that the concept of representation takes two forms: representation enables us *to depict* our ideas, and it allows something *to stand in for* something else, to be where others cannot go. If the cartoon image can depict the fossilized remains of a murdered prehistoric artist, it can also represent more abstract concepts like political agendas, national identity, racial difference, class struggle, and ideals of gender and sexual freedom. In this light, Hall reminds us that the concept of representation is equally critical to communication and art as it is to democracy and hegemony (S. Hall 2002). This elected official or that political idea can be said to "represent" my beliefs; it stands in for me or us; or, conversely, it stands against us and represents the enemy. When I read a cartoon and agree with its editorial message, it has the power of representing my beliefs, of standing in for them and giving them a conceptual shape. In this way, cartoons are adjuncts of political power, and through this conceptual power, they have long provided American politics with its necessary and omnipresent symbolism, stereotypes, and allegories.

As the "father of American political cartooning," nineteenth-century artist Thomas Nast invented both the Democratic donkey and the Republican elephant as well as the image of the gift-giving, capitalist Santa Claus. In 1812, a cartoon by Elkanah Tilsdale attacking the reorganization of voting districts in Massachusetts by Governor Elbridge Gerry introduced "the Gerry-mander—new species of Monster." In 1954, *Washington Post* cartoonist Herblock coined the phrase "McCarthyism" in a drawing of the eponymous Wisconsin senator wielding a tar bucket and brush.

By such means, American political cartoons have become both institutionalized and professionalized. Starting in 1922, Pulitzer Prizes have been handed out for editorial cartooning. White men held on to this source of political power so tightly that it took until 1992 for Signe Wilkinson to become the first woman to win. Cartoons have historically had deep ties to specific publications, linking artist to editorial politics and style, like Nast at *Harper's*, Peter Arno at the *New Yorker*, or E. Simms Campbell at *Esquire*. And when publications are tied to social movements, like the Socialist cartoonists for the *Masses* or Emory Douglas's Black Power drawings for *Black Panther*, cartoons reveal how visual styles can shape social movements.

It is when politics, publication, and artist combine to confront the powerful that these simple drawings reveal their fullest potential for causing trouble. This is, after all, how the art form earned its name.

The term *cartoon* first enters the arts from the Italian *cartone*, meaning a heavy paper used for a full-sized study for a tapestry, fresco, or stained-glass window. Europe's grandest museums house cartoons painted by Raphael and Goya that have been woven into tapestries to hang on royal or holy walls. In the preparation of a fresco, cartoons were perforated with small holes along the lines, and when "pounced" with a bag of chalk or soot on a freshly plastered wall, they leave an outline for the artist to follow.

In an engraving by John Leech from 1843 for the British satirical magazine *Punch*, we see the preparatory cartoons of the frescoes in Westminster Hall, images of puffed-up aristocrats on display before an audience of the ragged and starving poor. Bearing the caption "Cartoon No. 1—Substance and Shadow," this image changed the term forever by satirizing the meaninglessness of high art forms in the face of the suffering masses. In siding with the poor and disabled, represented as both a collection of haggard individuals and a class standing in subaltern relation to a buffoonish elite, the popularity of *Punch*'s version of the cartoon gave the new illustrated press a form for representing mass politics.

In the United States, the most heroic version of the political cartoonist is Thomas Nast. Born in Germany in 1840, Nast helped establish the detailed, cross-hatched illustration style and political allegories that elevated him from a political commentator into a feared political actor. For his contribution to the Union cause in the Civil War, Abraham Lincoln referred to Nast as "our best recruiting sergeant" whose "emblematic cartoons have never failed to arouse enthusiasm and patriotism." But Nast's greatest fame came after the war, when his cartoons brought down the corrupt "Boss" William M. Tweed of New York's Tammany Hall. After refusing a bribe to abandon cartooning and study art in Paris, Nast's attacks grew sharper until Tweed was voted out and convicted of fraud. Legend has it that when Tweed attempted to flee the country in 1875, Spanish customs officials identified the fugitive using one of Nast's cartoons.

During Reconstruction, Nast's cartoons taught Americans how to see race in politics. A committed Republican, Nast championed the rights of African American freedmen against the terrorism of Southern Democrats. In one of his most stirring cartoons, "This Is a White Man's Government" published in September 1868, Nast depicts three white men standing on the back of a prostrate Black man. Each standing figure represents a faction in the reconstruction of whiteness in the wake of emancipation: the bestial Irish immigrant who led the mob during the New York City draft riots of 1863, the former Confederates represented by Nathan Bedford Forrest who readies a dagger labeled "the lost cause," and the Northern Democratic elite in the form of August Belmont who wields the power of "Capital." These three different types of white men find a common cause in racial supremacy, symbolized by pressing one boot firmly down onto the back of a Black Union soldier, his body along with the American flag ground into the dirt, the ballot box wrested from his hand. Nast's image reveals how the historical fiction of whiteness grows out of a political alliance forged in violent antiblackness.

Despite Nast's support for Reconstruction, he also drew images of shocking racism and nativism. One of his most famous images illustrates Catholic immigration in the 1870s as an invasion of papist crocodiles emerging from the "American River Ganges." And in 1876, Nast placed the same simian Northern Irishman opposite a barefoot and smiling Southern Negro on an enormous hanging scale, weighing each as subhuman and together representing the "Ignorant Vote" (see figure A.4). Such cartoons translated visual stereotypes of racial difference and hierarchy into the very substance of partisan politics.

While Nast's drawings focused primarily on national politics, *The Forbidden Book: The Philippine-American War in Political Cartoons* collects images from a new generation of cartoonists who turned the style and stereotypes of Nast into the melodrama of American imperialism (Ignacio, Emmanuel, and Toribio 2004). Between 1890 and 1910, hundreds of cartoons in *Puck*, *Judge*, and *Life* magazines illustrated "The White Man's Burden" in which a stern but patient Uncle Sam attempts to bathe the infantilized people of Hawaii, the Philippines, Puerto Rico, and Cuba—depicted as Kipling's "half devil and half child"—into the cleansing waters of "Civilization." These cartoons translated racial science and a growing American militarism into cartoon visions of Darwinian progress, global white supremacy, and American empire. Yet they also produced a powerful and talented opposition.

America's greatest generation of political cartoonists arose to prominence in the early twentieth century, coalescing around the Greenwich Village bohemian and Socialist magazine the *Masses*. The magazine's cartoon editor, Art Young, once worked under Nast, where he discovered cartooning's power. "I have always felt," Young wrote in 1928, "that there is more power in my talent than in the mind of the statesman" (236). Working alongside artists like Maurice Becker, William Gropper, Stuart Davis, and George Bellows, Young's cartoons took on the global class struggle rather than the petty squabbling of party politics. Radical cartoons of this era made stock characters out of bloated plutocrats, puppet politicians, bull-necked police, the harlot "capitalist press," the dignified yet dispossessed poor, and the heroic union organizer.

We can see Young's gift for radical abstraction in a cartoon simply labeled "Capitalism," published in his own magazine *Good Morning* in 1920 (figure A.1). Young's drawing embodies the global capitalist system as a singular, enormously fat, bald, well-dressed white man. Tipping back on his chair over an unseen chasm, the capitalist grotesquely pours more food from gilded bowls down his insatiable gullet. The image draws upon the legal fiction of corporate personhood to transform the abstract logic of capital accumulation into a socially ruinous act of private gluttony. By personifying capitalism in this single image, Young offers a critical vision of a global economic system mired in greed and waste, using a figure that cannot imagine a shared future for all and thus unknowingly tilting toward crisis, collapse, and doom.

For his efforts, Young was censored by the US Postal Service and sued by the Associated Press, and in 1918, he and his fellow editors at the *Masses*, Max Eastman and John Reed, faced two criminal trials for conspiring against America's entry into the Great War. Saved by two hung juries, Young faced decades of incarceration for drawing in a style that Socialist Party presidential candidate Eugene V. Debs once called "cartooning capitalism."

If Young specialized in anticapitalist cartoons, Lou Rogers became the nation's first professional female cartoonist by drawing for the cause of woman's suffrage, birth control access, and radical feminism. To break into the all-male world of newspaper cartooning, Annie Lucastia Rogers began mailing out cartoons as "Lou," and in 1908, she published her first cartoon in *Judge* magazine. By 1913, *Cartoons Magazine* proclaimed, "Her pen is destined to win battles for the Woman's Movement and her name will be recorded when the history of the early days of the fight for equal rights is written." Committed equally to the causes of feminism and socialism, Rogers became art director for Margaret Sanger's *Birth Control Review* in 1917. And in the pages of *Judge*, she illustrated a weekly column entitled "The Modern Woman" in which she famously depicted Columbia as a young woman chained and bound by the bonds of sexism and law.

Not content to merely illustrate politics, as activist artists, Rogers and Young sought to participate in it directly. Young ran for office as a Socialist Party candidate in New York City. Ralph Chaplin drew hundreds of class war cartoons for the Industrial Workers of the World, wrote the labor anthem "Solidarity Forever," and eventually faced twenty years in federal prison for his revolutionary activism. Robert Minor was a successful mainstream cartoonist before his political convictions turned to the left, leading him to quit the capitalist press and draw cartoons for the *Masses* and the *Blast* before giving up art altogether to become a leader in the newly formed US Communist Party.

These were not the first nor the last cartoonists to face censorship and repression. In 1832, the French artist Honoré Daumier was sentenced to six months in prison for a caricature of King Louis Philippe. When the offended king lifted press censorship two years later, he preserved restriction on cartoons, arguing, "Whereas a pamphlet is no more than a violation of opinion, a caricature amounts to an act of violence."

While many celebrate artists who push the boundaries of free speech, we dismiss the notion of cartoons as an "act of violence" at our own peril. The cartoons published in Julius Streicher's newspaper *Der Stürmer* helped educate interwar Germans in the crudest forms of Nazi anti-Semitism, a crime for which Streicher was executed after the Nuremberg trials. More recently, an Islamophobic stunt by a Danish satirical journal published cartoons of the Prophet Muhammad, not only violating Islam's prohibitions against graven images but provocatively depicting the prophet as a terrorist and a pedophile. These cartoons led to weeks of riots in 2006 and several hundred deaths across the Muslim world. Incensed by similar images in 2015, Islamic fundamentalists massacred twelve employees of the French satirical magazine *Charlie Hebdo* in Paris. Writing on these controversies, Art Spiegelman defended cartoonists' right to free speech while insisting upon their political and aesthetic responsibilities. "It's just that cartoons are most aesthetically pleasing," wrote Spiegelman, "when they manage to speak truth to power, not when they afflict the afflicted" (2006, 45).

Perhaps the most stirring example of the political stakes of cartooning is the Palestinian artist Naji al-Ali. Born in 1936 in the Palestinian village of al-Shajara, al-Ali and his family were uprooted in 1948 by the Israeli ethnic cleansing known as the *Nakba* (Arabic for "catastrophe"). Like hundreds of thousands of displaced Palestinians, al-Ali's family became refugees in southern Lebanon. In 1961, al-Ali's drawings began appearing in Arab-language newspapers around the world, and in 1969, he first drew his most celebrated creation, the character Hanthala (figure A.2). A refugee child of ten years old, Hanthala is shoeless, dressed in patched rags, and stands with his back permanently turned to the reader. As a symbol of the Palestinian people, Hanthala refused to grow up in exile, impatiently awaiting the right of his people to return to their homeland. "His hands are clasped behind his back," explained al-Ali, "as a sign of rejection at a time when solutions are presented to us the American way" (2009, viii). While living in Kuwait in 1980, Naji al-Ali criticized the US policy of selling weapons to both Iran and Iraq in their war against each other, leaving two Islamic societies destroyed while the US alone grew stronger. After being expelled from Kuwait, al-Ali returned to Lebanon where he illustrated Israel's invasion in 1982 and the start of the first Palestinian intifada in 1987.

Giving voice to the "Arab street," al-Ali's cartoons protested the crime of occupation, condemned the corruption of Arab regimes, and ridiculed the hypocrisy of American imperialism. Fiercely independent and repeatedly censored and jailed by his many powerful enemies, Naji moved to London in 1985, where he continued to publish cartoons until July 22, 1987, when he was shot outside the Chelsea offices of the *al-Qabas* newspaper. His murder remains the source of much controversy, leading to a major international row in which Margaret Thatcher expelled three Israeli diplomats and closed Mossad's office in England. Today, in the West Bank, Hanthala remains an icon of Palestinian self-determination and identity; his image is found on T-shirts, tattooed on bodies, minted into souvenirs, and graffitied on the apartheid wall. Naji al-Ali's forty thousand cartoons represent a record of popular art that shaped the consciousness of a people and created an icon for a nation in exile and under occupation, and for his talents and commitments, he paid with his life.

All of which is to say, Gary Larson's cartoon isn't as funny as we wish it were.

8

Censorship

Amy Kiste Nyberg

Since their debut in the late 1930s, comic books have come under fire from a variety of sources. Criticism originated from three distinct groups, each with its own agenda. First, teachers and librarians objected to comic books, arguing that the simplistic storytelling, colloquial language, and reliance on illustrations hampered children's ability to appreciate fine literature. The second group was composed of religious and civic organizations, whose objections to comics were an outgrowth of the nineteenth-century decency crusades. Their concerns centered on the moral corruption of young readers. They objected to depictions of sex and violence, the use of blasphemous or obscene language, and any content that demonstrated disrespect for authority. Finally, child study experts and psychiatrists shifted the focus from education and morality to media effects on children's behavior. This criticism resonated with a public alarmed by a perceived rise in juvenile delinquency in postwar America. The attacks on comics from these three groups resulted in efforts to regulate reading, sales, and content of comic books.

The first group, comic books' earliest critics, targeted comic book reading and essentially struggled to control children's culture. While librarians and teachers traditionally selected children's books, comics targeted the child reader directly. The inexpensive format allowed children to purchase their own comics, and an informal network of pass-along readership gave children access to a wide variety of material. Readership studies from the 1940s suggest that nearly all children read comics.

Librarians, educators, and parents responded to this shift by attacking comics and seeking to curtail—or even eliminate—comic book reading. Education journals featured articles decrying the effects of comic book reading on their pupils. The integration of text and image was dismissed as "looking at pictures" rather than true reading. Comics discouraged progression in reading skills. In addition, comic books were badly designed, with garish colors and crude drawings. Opponents offered a number of strategies for weaning youngsters off comics and providing them with more suitable literature. This criticism of the impact of comics on children's reading persisted even after research showed the fears of educators were largely unfounded. As noted, fears over the loss of authority over children's reading help explain why teachers and librarians clung to their beliefs. Another explanation is that classroom teachers were likely not familiar with the scholarly research on comic book reading or, if they were, may have dismissed it as contrary to common sense.

Parents, too, were warned about the act of reading comics. Articles in popular magazines urged parents to combat the waste of time and money on comics. Early attacks on comics used the language of disease, warning of "contamination" by comics and urging parents to provide a suitable alternative to this undesirable reading material. The most widely published example of this vitriol was literary critic Sterling North's editorial in the *Chicago Daily News* in 1941. He wrote that "the antidote to the 'comic' magazine poison can be found in any library or good bookstore. The parent who does not acquire that antidote for his child is guilty of criminal negligence" (16–17).

Criticism also targeted the types of stories included in comics. The sensational stories about superheroes did little to develop readers' appreciation for good litera-ture. The "challenge" was to determine what youngsters found attractive about comics and steer them toward more suitable material that offered the same type of content.

Despite these efforts, children continued to read comics, and the number of titles available grew. Efforts shifted from discouraging reading to evaluating content in order to determine which comics children should read and which were inappropriate. To that end, various organizations began monitoring comic book content in order to provide lists of acceptable and unacceptable comic book titles. One well-publicized resource for par-ents was the work of the Committee on the Evaluation of Comic Books in Cincinnati, founded in 1948, whose ratings of comics were published in *Parents* magazine. Another nationally available ranking was the Catholic Church's Office of Decent Literature reviews of comic books, starting in 1947.

However, the efforts of the National Organization for Decent Literature (NODL) went beyond simply provid-ing a list of comics. For the first time, organized efforts focused on retailers rather than readers. Catholics and other concerned members of the public were encour-aged to conduct local "decency campaigns" that tar-geted retailers carrying comics. Teams visited various stores to encourage managers to remove undesirable titles from their racks. The local campaigns presented their efforts as concern over child welfare rather than censorship.

While decency campaigns were localized and compli-ance voluntary, legislators sought to formalize and ex-pand restrictions on sales. Legislative attempts to limit or eliminate the sales of comics, however, ran afoul of the First Amendment. For example, in 1948, the Los Angeles Board of Supervisors passed an ordinance that prohibited the sale of crime comics to minors. Groups supporting the legislation hoped that a state-level ban would be enacted, but the California Superior Court struck down the ordinance as unconstitutional in 1949.

At the state level, about a third of the states inves-tigated legislation regarding the sale and distribution of comics, but such efforts also failed to pass consti-tutional muster. One of the more aggressive attempts at comic book legislation was undertaken in New York. A bill that would have banned the sale of crime com-ics to minors passed both houses but was vetoed by Governor Thomas Dewey in April 1949 on the grounds that it was unconstitutional. Legislators also sought to create a division in the State Department of Education charged with reviewing all comic books and issuing permits for publication. That bill was approved by the state senate in February 1949 but died in committee in the assembly.

Historically, it was the popularity of crime and horror comics in the 1940s and early 1950s that triggered cen-sorship attempts aimed at limiting the sales of comics. Later efforts targeting retailers stemmed from two very different developments. The first was the rise of under-ground comics in the 1960s, and the second was the ad-dition of more adult-oriented fare in both mainstream and alternative comics in the 1980s.

Underground comics were a product of the 1960s counterculture, and artists appropriated the form of comics to produce works that were decidedly not ap-propriate for children. The graphic sexual content of the underground comics attracted the attention of law enforcement, and police and prosecutors used obscenity laws to arrest and try retailers. Store owners and employ-ees, not the artists, were put in the position of having to defend graphic sexual content as having social and ar-tistic value. After the 1970 conviction of two Manhattan store managers and a landmark case in 1973 in which the Supreme Court set new tests for obscenity, many retailers judged the risk of carrying such titles too great, and underground comics disappeared from shelves.

The next censorship effort targeting retailers came about as a result of the rise of a new system that shifted the distribution of comics away from companies that handled magazines. New distributors, who purchased comics directly from the publishers, serviced a growing number of comics specialty retailers. This change, called direct-market distribution, led to the emergence of alternative, independent comics publishing and encouraged mainstream publishers to develop comics aimed at a mature audience. Comics historians identify the mid-1980s as a fertile period in which comic books and graphic novels escaped, to some extent, the perception of the art form as strictly juvenile literature. The iconic titles from this period include *Maus*, *Watchmen*, and *Batman: The Dark Knight Returns*. Art Spiegelman's *Maus*, a Holocaust narrative that garnered wide public attention and acclaim, demonstrated that the form of comics could be used for serious subject matter. The other two titles reimagined the superhero genre for an adult audience. Both *Batman: The Dark Knight Returns* and *Watchmen* evoke and upend the genre conventions to produce a sophisticated inquiry into what it really means to be a superhero.

Just as was the case with underground comics, law enforcement was at the forefront of efforts to curb the sales of adult-oriented comics. Police conducted raids on individual stores, and prosecution was based on obscenity laws. One such incident that spurred what would become an ongoing effort to defend comics occurred in 1986, with the arrest of a comic book store manager in Illinois. Comic book publisher Denis Kitchen and a number of prominent artists raised money to assist in the defense. Recognizing the battle over comic book content was not resolved, they used their remaining funds to establish the nonprofit Comic Book Legal Defense Fund (CBLDF) in 1990. The CBLDF assists in legal challenges to comics, responds to legislation against comics, and aids libraries whose collections of comics are targeted.

Censoring comics by trying to restrict access and by prosecuting retailers worked at the local level and, to a limited extent, at the state level. However, the regulations that had the most lasting and far-reaching impact on comic books were those imposed on content by the publishers themselves. The origins of industry self-censorship are rooted in changes in the criticism of comic books in postwar America. Increased fears about juvenile delinquency, combined with a rise in popularity of crime comics, led to the belief by many that there was a cause-and-effect relationship between the two. Experts in the area of child behavior began to weigh in on the effects of comic book reading.

The best known of these was Dr. Fredric Wertham, a psychiatrist whose objections to comics received national attention through two influential articles published in 1948 in *Collier's* magazine and in the *Saturday Review of Literature*. Both of these articles included anecdotes about children who imitated what they read in the comics and committed violent acts.

The negative publicity spurred the Association of Comics Magazine Publishers (ACMP), a trade association that had been largely dormant since its formation in 1947, to reorganize in June 1948 and adopt an industry code to regulate the content of comic books. The six-point code forbade the depiction of sex or sadistic torture, the use of vulgar and obscene language, the ridicule of religious and racial groups, and the humorous treatment of divorce. A staff of reviewers read comics before publication, and those passing muster were allowed to carry the association's seal on their covers. However, only about a third of the publishers actually supported the code, and within a few short years, the prepublication review process was abandoned.

Dr. Wertham had little faith in the industry to regulate itself and continued to push for laws banning the sale of comics to children. Discouraged by the failure of the states, particularly New York, to ban sales of comics to minors, Dr. Wertham collected his articles and lectures about his research on the negative effects of comics on children into a book manuscript. The book, published in spring 1954, was titled *Seduction of the Innocent*. Excerpts of the book were published in the November 1953 issue of *Ladies' Home Journal*.

The timing was significant because earlier that year, the US Senate formed its Subcommittee on Juvenile Delinquency, with hearings set to begin in November. It scheduled a series of hearings on the possible relationship between mass media and juvenile delinquency. The subcommittee opened its investigation of comic books in New York City in April 1954. Witnesses included experts on the effects of comics on children, industry representatives, people involved with distribution and sales, and individuals with experience in industry self-regulation or legislation involving comics. Without a doubt, the two witnesses who received the most attention from both the senators and the media were Dr. Wertham and William Gaines, publisher of EC Comics.

In his testimony, Wertham recited his credentials and regaled the committee with anecdotes drawn from his articles and his book about how comics influenced children to imitate the crime and violence in the titles they read. He told senators he had no doubt that comic book reading was an important contributing factor to juvenile delinquency.

Gaines's testimony, which was fodder for a front-page *New York Times* story the next day, was intended to present comic book reading as harmless entertainment. When asked whether there was anything he would not include in a comic, Gaines answered that he would rely on what he determined was "good taste" for a horror comic. That set him up for the infamous "severed head" exchange, in which one of the committee staffers held up the cover of an issue of *Crime SuspenStories* featuring a man holding a bloody ax and a woman's severed head. "Do you think that is in good taste?" the staffer demanded. Gaines had little choice but to answer, "Yes, sir, I do, for the cover of a horror comic."

Although the hearing yielded some sensational testimony, the subcommittee was well aware of the legal difficulties involved in legislating against comics. The real goal of the senators was to force the publishers to take on the task of policing comic book content. They succeeded. Publishers, concerned about the comic book hearing and public perception, hurried to do damage control. They formed a trade association to replace the defunct Association of Comics Magazine Publishers, establishing the Comics Magazine Association of America (CMAA). They implemented a new code to govern content, designed a "seal of approval" to be carried on the cover of all comics passing muster, and appointed a comics czar with unimpeachable credentials to oversee the prepublication review of members' comics: Charles F. Murphy. He began his job on October 1, 1954.

The code itself was a hastily written adaptation of the 1934 Film Production Code. It contained forty-one specific regulations regarding content, focusing on the two genres that had drawn the ire of the public and the senators—crime and horror. Not only would the provisions ensure that comics would curtail violence and sex; they also mandated moral values, such as respect for authority, the triumph of good over evil, and the proper treatment of women. Censorship of content fell to a panel of five women who reviewed the pages submitted by publishers and demanded changes where deemed necessary.

The most notable casualty of industry self-regulation was William Gaines. He discontinued his line of controversial comics, but he fought with the CMAA regarding the content of his new line. Frustrated by his treatment at the hands of the regulators, he resigned from the CMAA in December 1955 and left comics publishing altogether.

The CMAA code succeeded where the ACMP failed in large part due to the enforcement mechanism put in place. Distributors signed on to the effort to clean up comics, refusing to carry titles unless they bore the seal of approval or the company's reputation was such that the distributors felt its titles were no risk, such as Dell Comics.

The Comics Code remained in effect until 2011, undergoing revisions in 1971 and 1989. Despite changes to the code, the underlying principle that comic books should contain only material appropriate for children was retained. Restrictions on violence, sex, and language remained central to the policies governing content. While publishers may have chafed under the restrictions, they largely adhered to the CMAA's standards.

One notable challenge to industry self-censorship came from Marvel Comics. The company sought approval for a *Spider-Man* story arc that dealt with drug addiction but was denied. Marvel published the story without the seal of approval. This episode led to the 1971 revision of the code along with a renewed pledge by member publishers—including Marvel—that they would comply with the code in the future.

The power of the CMAA waned with the rise of direct-market distribution. Since magazine distributors served as the enforcers of the code by refusing to distribute noncode comics, publishers who took advantage of the new distribution and retail system could bypass industry censorship altogether. Mainstream comic book publishers developed comic book titles intended for mature audiences. The CMAA took no action regarding this

development other than to specify that such titles not be distributed through traditional newsstand outlets.

The second revision of the code, in 1989, gave publishers the opportunity to acknowledge changes in the market and audience for comics. The revised code initially proposed a two-tiered system of evaluating content based on whether the comic book was intended for a general audience or for adults. Publishers ultimately rejected the distinction, however, deciding the code's seal of approval would continue to designate content appropriate for all ages.

Although the code's influence was greatly reduced by the time of its demise in 2011, the censorship standards imposed on decades of mainstream comic book artists, writers, and publishers severely limited the creative growth of the medium. Going forward, creators and publishers are freer to expand the types of stories they tell and how they tell those stories.

9

Circulation

Benjamin Woo

To be in circulation is to be in motion, to flow along or through some course or circuit. *Circulation* may refer to any movement between people or places, but the term has special meanings for print media such as comic books. In the strictest sense, a periodical's circulation refers to how many copies are sold on average; circulation thus has a relationship—albeit an inexact one—with audience. In its broadest sense, it opens onto a rich vein of theorizing about how culture shapes our experiences of space, time, and social connection.

Since the rise of the penny press in the early to mid-nineteenth century, most periodical publishers have adopted a hybrid business model, selling both the newspaper or the magazine itself and advertising space inside. Ads subsidize lower cover prices, encouraging larger circulations, and everybody wins. In this arrangement, then, publishers serve two masters: the reader, who must be persuaded to buy a copy, and the advertiser, who must believe these readers are worth addressing. Both audience size and quality must be considered. Some publishers—the great general-interest magazines of the twentieth century such as *Look* and *Life*, for example—seek to maximize their readership, pitching content to their conception of the broadest audience possible while trying to alienate as few readers as possible. More recently, however, niche marketing has become the norm, as smaller but demographically "purer" audiences can be more valuable if they match an advertiser's target consumer. But both strategies require that everyone involved knows who is buying and reading a publication.

As Eileen Meehan (2005) has argued of radio and television broadcasting, measuring audiences always involves a clash of interests. Media companies want to be able to point to the largest possible number so they can charge higher rates, while advertisers don't want to pay for hypothetical or less desirable readers. Unlike broadcasters, publishers can measure their readerships by keeping track of how many copies are printed, sold, and returned, and since 1960, periodicals published in the United States have been required to print statements detailing their average circulation in order to qualify for cheaper postage rates. These annual statements of circulation are the clearest and most direct evidence we have of historical trends in comic book sales. As industry analyst John Jackson Miller (2017) explains, however, few of today's comic book publishers use periodical-class mail, and therefore most are not required to print the statements. We are relatively in the dark about the circulations of more recent comic books, relying on estimations and extrapolations from partial data released by Diamond Comics Distributors, Nielsen BookScan, and more recently Amazon's ComiXology (Woo 2018b). Moreover, the already tenuous equation of a sale and a reader is even more questionable because comic books are often viewed as collectibles or investments as well as entertainment products. Some copies find their way into several readers' hands, perhaps being resold multiple times, while others are preserved in Mylar bags or encased ("slabbed") in tamper-proof plastic boxes to prevent anyone from opening them and touching their pages. Some never even leave the comic book store. As a result, even the best-informed observers of the field must at times rely on hunches and guesswork as much as cold, hard data.

Despite—or perhaps because of—the lack of valid and reliable circulation figures, claims about what comics sell and who is buying them have been central to the politics of comic book culture in recent years, as progressive and reactionary readers argue over which comics count and who they are *really* for. One response to these debates would be to intensify the quest for more and better sales data in order to finally get to the truth of whether the middle-aged, straight, white, male fan collectors, who have been the presumed target demographic for mainstream comic book publishers for several decades now, are really the core audience of comic books (Kashtan 2017; Woo 2018a). Even if shifts toward digital distribution and reading of comics fulfilled their (arguably, creepily dystopian) promise of total and complete comic book analytics, there is much we would still never know about the relationships between readers and text, interactions between readers, and how what they do or think might change as a result of these experiences. While there remains much to learn about the quantitative aspects of comic book reading, we should not stop at enumerating who reads comic books and graphic novels. The publishing industries use *circulation* narrowly as little more than a synonym for *sales* or *distribution*, but scholars have also developed a broader sense of circulation that asks us to think very differently about cultural goods.

Rather than simply asking how many copies of something are in circulation, we might instead look at what difference it makes that an object moves as it does: What audiences does it reach? Under what economic or market conditions is it accessed? How do social or cultural conventions teach people to treat it? Benjamin Lee and Edward LiPuma (2002, 191) argue circulation should be seen as a "cultural process with its own forms of abstraction, evaluation, and constraint, which are created by the interactions between specific types of circulating forms and the interpretive communities built around them." In Gaonkar and Povinelli's programmatic formulation, the level of analysis moves from the text itself to the "circulatory fields" in which it moves. These fields are "populated by myriad forms" and demand "an almost neurotic attentiveness to the edges of forms as they circulate so that we can see what is motivating their movement across global social space" (2003, 391–92). This is, as Will Straw (2010, 23) notes, an anti-interpretive gesture. Most forms of analysis in the humanities traditionally start by paying close attention to what's on the page (or screen or canvas), but what happens on the page is among the least interesting things about a comic book. A comic's meaning comes from the outside, as it moves through one or more circulatory fields. Try as they might, no author, publisher, or individual reader can fully control these processes. In sum, then, this broader view of circulation posits a space in which *forms* move along *edges* that connect people as members of *interpretive communities*. Particular configurations of objects, people, and the paths that connect them produce a given "social texture"—understood as "the rhythms and geometries left as residues by successive communicational events" (Straw 2010, 21)—or what Lee and LiPuma (2002) call cultures of circulation. What would a comics studies animated by these insights look like?

An analysis of comics as a culture of circulation might begin with the spaces where people encounter comics and graphic novels, asking what these sites are like, who populates them, and how people are invited to interact within them. The tradition of (auto)ethnographies of comic shops (Pustz 1999; Swafford 2012; Woo 2011) and conventions (Bolling and Smith 2014) represents one attempt to answer some of these questions, but these studies often take a single shop or event as typical of their respective fields. A macroview is necessary to capture the dynamic interaction of people and forms, and broader frames are always possible. Casey Brienza (2016) and Leah Misemer (2018) both point to the limitations of adopting narrowly national perspectives; research on labor and production grounds comics culture in human brains and bodies (Norcliffe and Rendace 2003; Brienza and Johnston 2016); and recent attention to infrastructure in media studies serves to remind us that growing and cutting down trees, transporting raw materials and finished books, and storing digital files in data centers are fundamental conditions of possibility for comics culture.

Having given some thought to *where* comics meet their interpretive communities, we might ask about the speeds at which they move through these spaces. Writing of cultural scenes—some of which are oriented to innovation and fads, while others are rooted in nostalgia and conservation—Straw (2017, 197) asks how they speed up or slow down the movement of cultural objects. The periodicity of comics is relevant here, and the forms or formats themselves influence their velocity. The daily newspaper comic strip, monthly comic book series released to comic shops every Wednesday (and eventually collected into trade paperbacks), and single-authored, long-form comics that readers may have to wait several years to finally read each implies different speeds and rhythms of circulation and imposes different costs on readers. To a certain extent, forms also objectify understandings of comics' relationship to space and time—some inviting us to read them and pass them on, others, to hold onto them as collectibles—and what they are for—suggesting, variously, ephemeral entertainment, historical or cultural significance, and literary greatness through their physical design and accompanying paratexts (Woo 2012).

Finally, we could invert the figure and ground relationship. What if, rather than assuming the objectivity of objects carving paths as they move from place to place, we gave primacy to the circuits? How does the circulatory matrix enable things to "appear in a decisive form" in the first place (Gaonkar and Povinelli 2003, 395)? Institutions and institutionalized understandings have a gatekeeping function, one that is not merely restrictive but is also, like Foucault's conception of power, generative of what we conceptualize as comics. A visit to a zinefest or the artists' alley at a convention should remind us of how many comics are made that will never show up in the *Previews* catalog or the *Overstreet Guide*, and we can only guess how many interpretive communities are formed and thrive behind the backs of industry and traditional comics fandom (see, e.g., Sabeti 2011), yet these nonetheless represent vital encounters with the form.

Bart Beaty and I have argued that the preponderance of literary scholars in comics studies has consequences for the shape of our field (2016, 28–29)—not the least of which is an unshakeable faith that the truth of comics can be found in their pages, if only they're read correctly. A turn to circulation, in either sense, forces us to rethink that assumption. On the one hand, are we devoting attention to the right comics? The most "plausible" comics for scholarly analysis may be read by comparatively few people, while many with a significantly larger reach and arguably greater impact are not studied at all. On the other hand, what are we missing when we keep our noses in a comic book? In seeking "to foreground the social life *of* the form rather than reading social life *off* of it" (Gaonkar and Povinelli 2003, 387; emphasis in original), the circulatory turn presupposes that what texts do is more important than what they say. In "The Uses of Cultural Theory," Raymond Williams asserts that "the most significant cultural theory" doesn't simply occupy a middle space between culture and society but theorizes the relations between them by "specifying cultural formations" (1986, 20, 29). To do so, we must pay attention to how cultural objects such as comic books and graphic novels move through society and what they accomplish as they connect people and places together.

10

Cognition
Michael Chaney and Sara Biggs Chaney

To say that comics have to do with thinking is a bit like saying piano keys have to do with music. Popular culture already advances comics, graphic novels, and editorial cartoons as heralds of knowledge and thinking. That simple drawings, in whatever form, have a special capacity to construct, organize, and convey thought is of little surprise to those familiar with cultures around the globe. Sequential art, or some derivative form of it (drawn pictures often in sequence and with captions or balloons containing speech or thought), functions as a comic strip, an illustrated story intended to teach reading, a printed visual humor strip in a newspaper, a political voting ballot, or the instructions for safely executing a water landing from an airplane or assembling a newly purchased shelf from the package. These examples illustrate the connection between cognition and the sequential drawing that we call a comic. If cognition, in this context, describes the way comics are used to organize and express the products of our perception, then comics are both an instrument and an illustration of the cognitive process. The ubiquity of these simple pictures taken seriously attests to their effectiveness as a means of telling picture stories and learning through those stories. Part of this ubiquity stems from the fact that to many, comics signify remedial literacy—juvenile ways of seeing the world as well as being in the world.

Comics scholars assume close correspondences between comics and cognition. One may well think of the myriad schools or approaches in comics studies as cohering around a singular investigation of these correspondences. Beginning with a Cartesian analysis, one can see through Scott McCloud's exploration of closure the way comics mediate a mind-body split. For McCloud, comics are a type of Cartesian X-ray of how we see ourselves in our mind's eye. The generally exaggerated or unrealistic figure of the comics is a perceptual or cognitive analog to the supposed inner vision we may have of ourselves. From this perspective, comics are unique for their ability to convey the messily perceived world, the world not as it is but as an effect of an often-fragmentary, hyperbolic, fantastical, or ironic point-of-view. Folded within this tradition of those who resolutely find in the comics an apt expression of human ocular-centric being, we might include other practitioners such as Dylan Horrocks and Paul Karasik or, more recently, Nick Sousanis, Alison Bechdel, and Lynda Barry. These comic artists are also analysts of the form who provide grounded theories of the connections between comics, seeing, and thinking.

Less abstractly, comics artists routinely demonstrate the facility comics have for visualizing human thinking and reflection. From Snoopy's reveries in Charles Schultz's *Peanuts* and Calvin's philosophical discussion with his toy tiger, Hobbes, in Bill Watterson's *Calvin and Hobbes* to Ellen Forney's autobiographical dissections of psychoanalysis in her graphic novel *Marbles* and Keith Knight's *(Th)ink* comic strips, which center on a single reflective Black subject of consciousness, the comic strip or comic-based narrative has been a familiar medium for popular discussion of cognition, memory, and consciousness. All, moreover, rehearse an approach common to Cartesian thinking in the West: we think as we see; what we see is what we know, and what we know is who we are.

Many have followed the lead of Gunther Kress, employing a social semiotic analysis to further tease out the close correspondence between comics and cognition. Assuming that social cognition proceeds in part through the socially mediated apprehension and interpretation of signs, it is not difficult to posit a relationship between cognition and the reading of comics. From this point of view, every comic will necessarily draw on semiotic resources, both visual and verbal, that provide evidence of how meaning is constructed or contested within a culture. Refining and advancing these claims, Neil Cohn (2010) understands comics as vehicles for *visual language*, a term expressing the human capacity to conceptualize and communicate in the visual or graphic mode. Comics, then, are cultural forms or artifacts expressed in a visual language structured similarly to verbal language and thus amenable to linguistic methods of analysis.

To understand how comics structure narrative and impact perceptions in the process, we need only turn to narratological studies following in the footsteps of Genette. Within this conversation, there is a presumption that comics are adept at presenting plural points of view, which may be simultaneously contextual, explanatory, performative, or expressive. This multipresentation of structured views and viewings connects the study of comics to the study of thinking. By classifying comics according to their rhetorical effects, the narratologist presents them as a form of situated thinking. In other words, this view presents comics as a system of thought not necessarily embodied in any particular actor or agent but as a layered intricacy of communication, made up of overlapping cultural codes, systems, signs, and signifying structures.

Scholars prioritizing the subjects of comics and the subjectivities performed, testified to, or expressed therein may be less inclined to unpack the communicational systems surrounding a comic or represented in one for their own sake. Rather, those more interested in a comic's inscription of identity have looked to the way comics either efface or give a face to autobiographical subjects, identities at the margins, and socially legible or politically legible identities related to movements. Hillary Chute's research (2010) exemplifies this approach, as it analyzes Lynda Barry's autobiographical graphic narratives as instances of a feminist form of communication, involving the materiality of the collages that fringe Barry's autobiographical comics. What do Barry's collages have to do with thinking? Collage is collective and tactile; it makes use of artifacts and recombines them in a new temporality that triggers collective memory. The significant departure from a purely narratological approach, for Chute, would have to do with the psychoanalytic as Barry explores unknowable psychic terrain in her collage.

With cognition as a primary lens, we might consider as an origin for Chute's analysis those theorists whose concepts have been found most resonant with jokes and low comedy, the primary aim of so many comics and editorial cartoons. Indeed, just as Freud and Bakhtin inquire into humor and the world of jokes and dreams so as to decode its structures, so too do pioneering comics scholars as various as Coulton Waugh and E. E. Cummings discover an intelligence in comic strip's play with juxtaposition or reversal—the formula for humor. Thus the fascination with the comics' construction of the surreal, the imaginary, and the world of fantasy likewise depends on ongoing observations into the form's unique presentations of generic themes (as recurring thought formations). Images in comics seldom come wrapped with neutrality. Rather, they are saturated with style—whether funny, cutesy, childlike, photo-realistic, or high-contrast noir. Comics are themselves a doctored view, always already a perspective that is also partly an ego. On the one hand, comics conjure a perspective often in their very style that implies that a great deal of visual information in the world has been digested and abstracted prior to the drawing style presented on the page, and on the other, these abstractions of the world into object content afford a critical, conceptual distance. Reader-viewers of editorial political comics, for example, are given not just jokes about the political present in order to laugh about it in their favorite cartoons but also a position to inhabit and try on. If laughter is the customary response to an editorial cartoon, it covers as much as it affirms. Laughter may operate on a level of communication that precedes language. Laughter may signify a response that is neither affirming nor denying but emotionally engaging nevertheless. If laughter and humor are fundamentally associated with comics, then we might also think of comics as prelinguistic, operating at a remove from rational language.

Of course, comics and comics studies have undergone fruitful diversifications. Perspectives have been sought beyond those that secure subjects of power—other than the unspecified and thus anonymously masculinist point of view—in other words, which is also white, Western, Judeo-Christian, and many other assumed intersections of affiliation and power. Even when focused on the question of comics as a form of thought, objective treatments of comics as a form may thus conceal an interest in those perspectives most translatable into such abstractions. Within this line of thought, critics of comics and identity—Hillary Chute and Julia Watson, Jose Alaniz and Maaheen Ahmed, Frederick Aldama and Michael A. Sheyahshe, Quiana Whitted and Rebecca Wanzo—all force us to ask exactly who is doing the thinking and how that thinking has been shaped by cultural assumptions about race, gender, ability, and sexuality. According to the lenses provided by these and others, the cognitive constructions that comics both permit and require are built from preexisting cultural materials. From this view, Kyle Baker's *Nat Turner*

is not simply a collection of images and texts that make up or retell the story of the Nat Turner rebellion but a comic designed to invoke and disrupt certain models of thinking that some reader-viewers may wish to avail themselves of in order to see or to understand a nineteenth-century uprising of unjustly enslaved persons who end up killing dozens of whites. Ho Che Anderson uses his multivolume graphic biography of Martin Luther King Jr. to show how encrusted or enshrined ways of thinking about the past relate directly to the visual record used to create, adapt, and revise history. To the extent, then, that graphic novels, particularly autobiographical ones, for example, entertain questions of embedded knowledge, they too pursue ongoing experiments in comics creativity to tether a subjective mode of seeing the world to subjectivist models for cognizing the world. When thought of as highly coded messages about thinking, comics are only as relevant to the subject of cognition as cultural scripts will allow.

Although equated with instruction and thought and therefore assumed to have special, unique cognitive affordances, comics are just as susceptible to history as any other medium. Nevertheless, at its most basic organization, a comic is an editorialized (because obviously drawn and therefore imperfect or nonrealistic) unit of meaning that collapses registers of saying (didacticism, instruction, telling) and showing (depiction, illustration, positing, mimesis, demonstration). Thought to be preverbal, the comic has risen to the status of a communication tool in clinical settings where it functions as a means of diagnosing, remediating, and giving language to those without conventional written or vocal abilities. In this clinical functioning, as part of a PECS or a Picture Exchange Communication System, for example, the comic form is perhaps shown in the full light of its cognitive potential as a building block of thought.

11

Comic Book

Jared Gardner

When screenwriter and director Paul Schrader criticized *Star Wars* (1977) for "creat[ing] the big budget comic book mentality," there was little doubt as to the nature of his critique (quoted in Biskind 1999, 316). Since the 1940s, *comic book* has been used to encompass all that an observer might find puerile, simplistic, soulless, bombastic, and/or lazy in popular culture. This pejorative usage reveals a paradox: those who loathe comic books are more likely to agree upon its essential features than are those who actually read them. Indeed, even the field of comics studies cannot agree on a shared definition of one of its most vital forms. For some, *comic book* stands as the default for all graphic works—in periodical or book form—that are simply longer than the *comic strip*. Randy Duncan and Matthew J. Smith, for example, define a comic book as any "volume in which all aspects of the narrative are represented by pictorial and linguistic images encapsulated in a sequence of juxtaposed panels and pages"—essentially claiming for the comic book everything that collects multiple pages in a "volume" (Duncan and Smith 2009, 4).

On the other side are those whose definitions of the comic book are specific in terms of a range of qualities we associated with the modern form that emerges in the 1930s and 1940s. Santiago García defines the comic book as referencing "a stapled booklet, generally in color, between thirty-two and sixty-four pages, sold at newsstands at a price accessible to children's pockets, and collected in a series" (García 2015, 68). The 1994 Library of Congress definition is even more economical: "periodicals of pictorial fantasy" (Library of Congress Collections Policy Statements 1994, 19). While the Library of Congress has since complicated this definition, the assumption of comic books as periodicals remains ingrained, as seen in postal regulations that disqualify comic books from media mail on the ground that they are magazines.

Both definitional options present challenges. If, as Smith and Duncan suggest, any sequential comic of more than one page bound together is a comic book, then not only do they effectively dispense with the newer concept of the "graphic novel," but newspaper comics supplements would need to be read as "comic books" as well. If we exclude the comics supplement on the grounds that it contains different works on each page, then we would similarly need to dismiss anthology comic books made up of one-page stories. From this angle, *comic book* as a format becomes all but synonymous with *comics* as a medium. Similarly, definitions that inextricably link comics to the periodical format lose their power when describing one-shot titles, just as those that require advertising or seriality quickly run into numerous counterexamples. And of course, the 1994 Library of Congress definition of comics as "pictorial fantasy" fails to account for a broad range of nonfiction comic books dating back to the 1940s.

While pinning down a precise formal definition of the comic book is impossible, there are certain features generally agreed upon. Most users identify the comic book with the newsstand form that emerged in the US in the early 1930s: saddle-stitched magazines, 7¾" x 10½", with glossy color cover and four-color interior newsprint pages. Many features and conventions of this original format would change in the coming decades. For example, while newsstands had the monopoly on comic book distribution for several decades, in the early

1970s, a new distribution method emerged in the form of the direct market in which comic books were sold in comic shops. This distribution shift would have a significant impact not just on the economics of the industry but on the fandom cultures that gathered around the form, as the comic shop became a place where some fans found community and safe haven. Of course, what were safe havens for some could also be decidedly unwelcoming spaces for others, including women, people of color, and those new to the form. Thus in the late twentieth century, the comic book took on associations, positive and negative, that have as much to do with its distribution as with the format itself.

In the early decades of the twenty-first century, comic book culture is in many ways more inclusive, and the form's cultural visibility is arguably greater than it has been at any time since the 1940s. A growing roster of movies and television shows are based on serial comic books, from the megabudget spectacles of the Marvel Cinematic Universe to independent properties like *Preacher* and *Umbrella Academy* adapted for television. The comic book is also now rarely printed on newsprint. The rise of digital coloring in the 1990s brought with it a move to higher-quality paper, making comics slicker and more colorful than ever before—and increasingly expensive. Whereas the original comic books sold for a dime for almost thirty years, the median price of a comic book in 2019 is over four dollars. These growing costs are certainly one reason—even at this moment in which comics seem to be everywhere—that sales of comic books are down sharply. Motivated by the closing of comic book shops and overall declining sales, many comic publishers are moving to digital distribution platforms, such as ComiXology (owned by Amazon) or self-controlled "streaming" subscription models such as Marvel Unlimited. Here of course the comic book dimensions are dependent on the size of the device on which it

is read, and this digital comic book is no longer available for collecting, trading, and resale—the lifeblood of the organized fandom that emerged in the 1970s.

While the next chapter in the evolution of the comic book remains uncertain, examining the "prehistory" of the modern form provides insights into the fantasies and ambitions that the comic book has gathered to its pages since its origins and that transcend the various format and distribution changes the comic book has undergone.

Long before the modern "comic book" was devised in 1933, the idea of the comic book emerged in the 1860s, primarily through the marketing of one American publisher, C. W. Carleton. As technological advancements such as the steam-powered rotary press reduced costs, the mid-nineteenth century was awash with new print formats (penny papers, story papers, dime novels) and markets. Images, once scarce, became increasingly central to popular print culture, as new techniques (wood engraving, lithography) made mass printing images easier and cheaper. By the 1840s, US print culture was a visual popular culture, leading to the emergence of both the modern comic form and the birth of film at century's end.

It was during this period of experimentation that the Swiss artist and educator Rodolphe Töpffer developed a technique he termed "auto-lithography," in which the artist drew with a special pen on chemically treated paper, which was then transferred to a lithography stone. This allowed the printed image to capture the spontaneity and flow of the hand-drawn line. The illustrated mammoth weekly paper *Brother Jonathan* was at this time publishing heavily illustrated serialized fiction from Britain as fast as the typesetters could pirate it off the incoming ships. It was in the midst of this gold rush in 1842 that *Brother Jonathan* published the comic "The Adventures of Obadiah Oldbuck." The supplement proved so popular that it was soon reprinted in a bound format. Although not yet labeled a "comic book," the format for the bound *Oldbuck* would influence the comic book form in the US until 1919. The comic book had arrived in America via a very circuitous route: a British bootleg of a French unauthorized reworking of a book by Töpffer, originally published in Geneva in 1837. The popularity of *Oldbuck* in America led to subsequent slim volumes of sequential graphic narratives advertised as "new and cheap book[s] of funny pictures . . . similar to 'Obadiah Oldbuck.'" Thus it was that Töpffer's pirated work created the beginnings of an American market for the comic book that publishers in the late 1840s and 1850s worked to build upon.

When Carleton advertised items as "comic books," he was drawing on the world he found as a young cartoonist in the 1850s. Carleton had worked for some of the pioneering comic periodicals of the time, including the *Lantern* and the *New-York Picayune*, before starting a publishing house that specialized in books that, like these magazines, combined humorous prose with the work of some of the leading cartoonists of the day.

While these books would not be recognizable as comic books to most readers today, the label was not simply an anachronism. For example, among the comic books Carleton advertised was *Artemus Ward* (1865). The cartoonist for *Artemus Ward* was Henry Louis Stephens, who had begun his career at another new comics periodical, the short-lived *John-Donkey* in 1848. There Stephens had created two popular series—one setting familiar lines of poetry against cartoons of humble characters and another combining political caricatures with a bestiary drawn in the style of the popular *Birds of America*—that would spin off into two books significant in comics history. The writer was Charles Farrar Browne, a popular humorist of the period who had edited *Vanity Fair*, a comics magazine founded by Stephens that

emerged out of the bohemian circles at Pfaff's beer cellar, of which both men were members. Pfaff's served as a nexus for an emerging counterculture of the period, frequented by artists and poets—most famously Walt Whitman—as well as many cartoonists, including a young Thomas Nast, whose 1870s campaign against "Boss" William M. Tweed would make him the first celebrity cartoonist.

In grouping these works together under the new category of "comic book," Carleton hoped to capture and capitalize on the energies that had failed to find a permanent home in the short-lived comics magazines of his younger years. These comic books would be something to keep on the shelf and return to in the future, differentiated from the ephemeral weeklies in which this material predominantly circulated in these early years.

This origin story for the idea of the comic book brings to the fore certain things that might be lost if we focus solely on the format as it comes into being in the 1930s. First, the comic book has from the start existed in a complex, liminal relationship with other periodical forms, a fact that will play a central role in the development of the modern form. Second, the comic book has always entailed an ungainly combination of commercial ambition and bohemian idealism, a quality that continues to adhere to the form throughout the coming century and will contribute to the push-pull between standardization and experimentation that shapes its history. Finally, the comic book form was from the start about community—in this originary moment, an attempt to create a more lasting home for the transient periodical comics communities whose early magazines had gone under by the time Carleton started selling "comic books."

The communal ideal of the comic book would fall away for a time, as comics at the end of the nineteenth century begin to migrate from the illustrated magazine to the new medium of the newspaper comics supplement, leading to the birth of the first comics celebrities in the form of characters like the Yellow Kid, Happy Hooligan, and Foxy Grandpa. For the first time, periodical comics had recurring characters. And almost immediately, the comic book was reimagined as a place they could call home.

In 1902, William Randolph Hearst began to market comic books—softbound collections entirely made up of newspaper comics reprints. These comic books featured many of the most popular strips in Hearst's fast-growing stable, including Happy Hooligan, Buster Brown, and the Katzenjammer Kids. For the first time, *comic book* became a widely adopted marketing concept. Book stores advertise the latest "comic books that will please everyone" (*Evening World*, November 30, 1903); alongside its more familiar commodities, Bloomingdale's announces a "Sale of Comic Books at 36c. Printed in Brilliant and Attractive Colors" (*Evening World*, November 10, 1903); and following the holiday season, an Oregon paper announces a 50 percent sale on "all leftover Comic Books" (*Morning Oregonian*, January 7, 1905).

The early Hearst comic books were oblong and perfect bound and had thin, flexible cardboard covers with linen tape around the spine, a layout inherited from *Oldbuck*. When Hearst started licensing to other publishers, the basic format was retained for the next two decades, before Cupples & Leon, who emerged as the dominant publisher in this marketplace, shifted in 1919 to a square format that better accommodated reprints of the newer daily comic strip.

If the definition of the comic book is restricted solely to periodical formats, one might dismiss these early comic books as belonging to a different category entirely. But of course magazines in the early years of the twentieth century did not always look like our modern saddle-stitch magazines. Indeed, many popular

magazines—including the pulps to which modern comic books are closely related—were perfect bound and looked more like oversized paperbacks than what we conventionally think of as magazines. And while the earliest comic books were not periodicals, they were often published as numbered series.

Further, from the very start, these early comic books explored seriality and transmediality, attributes we associate with the modern comic book. For example, the 1903 edition of *Happy Hooligan* includes a strip from April 13, 1902, that was the source for the 1903 Edison film *Happy Hooligan Interferes*, the first movie adaptation of a comic text. And the volume opens with one of the first comics to have been initially serialized over two consecutive installments, with "to be continued" opening up serial possibilities previously unexplored in newspaper comics. Within a couple of years, seriality would explode in newspaper comics, beginning in 1905 with the adventures of *Little Nemo in Slumberland* and then with the first successful daily newspaper strip, *A. Mutt* (1907). The first *Happy Hooligan* to be continued over multiple installments was likely initially designed as a full Sunday page, then divided by Hearst's editors into two installments to provide more material for the new comic book, which could only print half pages. But in doing so, this first twentieth-century comic book opened up the serial possibilities of the comic strip and established the genealogy of serial storytelling in the comic book form that would be fully realized several decades later.

The first *periodical* comic arrives in January 1922. The *Comic Monthly* was roughly square, like the post-1919 Cupples & Leon titles, but it sought inroads into venues unavailable to earlier comic books: "newsstands, railroad trains, book stores, toy stores, department stores, hotels, drug stores, everywhere" (see the inside cover of issue 6 of *Comic Monthly*, 1922). As the inside cover of #2 suggests, "Tell your newsdealer *now* that you want one.

You will want the whole collection and it will be impossible to secure back numbers" (see the inside back cover in issue 2 of *Comic Monthly*, 1922). By issue #6, it was clear the venture was struggling, as the annual subscription price was lowered to $1. The series ended with issue #12. But this first newsstand comic forged the bridge between the first comic books of the century and the development of the modern comic book a decade later.

Even as we look forward in anticipation of that modern comic book, however, it is worth noting continuities between the comic book of the first two decades of the century and the more familiar format that emerges beginning with *Comic Monthly*. In addition to adopting the square format from the popular Cupples & Leon series, *Comic Monthly* printed a trompe l'oeil tape around its spine to imitate the binding of the earlier comic books. Periodical and saddle-stitched, the *Comic Monthly* looks at last like a modern comic book, but the magazine's editors sought to maintain connections to their nonperiodical predecessors. If the "comic books" of the nineteenth century sought to capture in a lasting format the periodical energies of the first comic magazines, the first periodical comic of the twentieth century sought to transfer *back* to periodical form the pleasures and rewards of the new comic books.

In 1933, one of the darkest years of the Great Depression, the printing business was struggling. While the popularity of newspaper comics—a cheap entertainment—continued to grow, the newspaper industry as a whole was in trouble. Advertising revenue was down 50 percent from its levels before the crash in 1929. And there were other signs of trouble on the horizon, as the new medium of serial radio was claiming more of business's advertising budget.

While contemplating the declines in its newspaper printing business, two employees of Eastern Color Printing realized that the standard printing plates used to print the Sunday newspaper comics supplements could be repurposed. As one of those employees, Max Gaines, would tell the story in 1943, "The discovery was pure accident. While inspecting a promotional folder published by the Ledger Syndicate in the early 1930s, in which four-color Sunday comic pages were shown in 7 by 9 inch size, it was suddenly realized that pages of these dimensions could be economically produced on a four-color rotary newspaper press" (Gaines 1943, 19).

While it would be the development of the superhero genre a few years later that would ignite the comic book boom, the success of the earliest modern comic books was a response to the growing popularity of the comic strip medium and the desire on the part of fans for a more permanent medium than the daily newspaper. As it had been some eight decades earlier, the impetus behind the newest version of the comic book was the desire to capture the ephemerality of a periodical format—in this case, the daily newspaper—in a form that could be owned, revisited, collected. Where the earliest Sunday comics made few serial demands on their readers, the open-ended seriality of the daily comic strip generated a desire for completism and the return to installments—a desire that grew more intense with the daily adventure strips of the 1920s and 1930s. The Cupples & Leon comic books were infrequent and sold in bookstores for twenty-five cents; what Gaines proposed was to create a regularly published periodical that sold on newsstands for only a dime.

Had it not been the Depression when the modern comic book was born, things might have gone in a different direction. However, with creative labor cheap and willing, it was inevitable that someone would see what could be made of nonreprint materials. In 1935, Malcolm Wheeler-Nicholson founded National Allied Publications with the goal of making comics without the expense of syndicate licenses, hiring artists to create work that the publisher would own outright. In 1935, *New Fun* became the first comic to publish entirely original (if highly derivate) material. Ultimately Nicholson's efforts were not rewarded by the marketplace, at least not in time to save his stake in the company that would become DC Comics. The last original title launched under his management was *Detective Comics*, which in 1939 would serve as the birthplace of Batman, the second character of the superhero boom. But by then Nicholson had been forced out by his business partners, Harry Donenfeld and Jack Liebowitz.

What stymied Nicholson in those early years was the fact that his original stories had no recognizable characters of the kinds his rivals were offering. In an increasingly crowded marketplace, the deliberations of the newsstand favored characters readers already trusted from relationships established through their daily newspaper encounters. If what initially drove the 1930s comic book was a desire to possess a permanent version of the transient comic strip, none of the early National Allied original material serviced that desire. Of course, with the arrival of the superhero in the comic book format, all of that would change. Now for the first time, the modern comic book had original material that generated demand independent of the newspaper comics.

But *how* independent was the first superhero of the newspaper comics? For one thing, Superman was originally conceived of as a newspaper strip, and only after it had been rejected by numerous syndicates were its creators willing to consider the new medium of the comic book. In addition by January 1939, soon after his first appearance in *Action Comics* in 1938, Superman was appearing daily in newspapers across the country. Before it was amplified by the newspaper strip, *Action Comics* was likely selling around two hundred thousand copies—remarkable numbers for an original comic book to be sure. The sparse sales data from the period indicate

that Eastern Color's *Famous Funnies* continued to sell over three hundred thousand copies monthly throughout 1939 and into early 1940, suggesting that the newspaper reprint comic book was not suddenly obsolete with the arrival of the superhero. But while we cannot recover the degree to which the *Superman* comic strip impacted the sales of the comic book (especially with the additional complication of the radio serial beginning in February 1940), it is certainly clear that on its own, *Superman* did not immediately transform the comic book industry. The comic book, then as now, was always bound up with other media.

What this history of some of the early "births" of the comic book teaches us is that few of the properties we likely most associate with the format today are essential to its definition, at least when we take the long view. That doesn't mean, however, that there are no claims to make on behalf of the comic book. From the long view, we can see that the comic book is a form that is always in conversation with a range of other forms and media economies—early on, books, pamphlets, periodicals, and newspapers; more recently, film, television, video games, and the internet. It is a format that has, from its nineteenth-century origins, been tied up with a nostalgic longing for the fleeting present—the desire to capture an ephemeral modern popular culture in a form that could allow for ownership, rereadings, collection, and recirculation. And it is a format that perhaps better than any other represents the often-contradictory fantasies and desires readers, artists, and publishers bring to comics more broadly. It is quite certain that, despite the historically poor sales of periodical comic books at this historical moment, the form will persist beyond the end of our current century. It is equally certain that were we to encounter the comic book of century's end, we would find it as unfamiliar as we do the comic books of the 1860s or the early 1900s.

12

Comic Strip

Jessica Quick Stark

Scholars typically will encounter two persistent points of contention when approaching the term *comic strip*: (1) when precisely comic strips began and, relatedly, (2) the comic strip's most accurate definition. As a medium that sustains multiple origins, the comic strip continually exceeds its own boundaries and concerted efforts to fix authorial ownership, reception practices, and definitions. Some accounts source comics' beginning as far back as the cave paintings of Altamira and Lascaux, the Egyptian bas-reliefs, the Pompeii murals, Trajan's column in Rome, or the Queen Mathilde tapestry in Bayeux. More frequently, comics historians trace the birth of the modern comic strip to US newspapers and the first appearance of R. F. Outcault's Yellow Kid in the *New York World* in 1895. In many respects, scholars are correct in identifying US origins. The advent of photoengraving in 1873 made possible relatively inexpensive newspaper illustrations, which allowed for the mass production of comic strips in US daily newspapers. Moreover, the circulation wars between William Randolph Hearst and Joseph Pulitzer and the competing versions of Outcault's original *The Yellow Kid* and Outcault's replacement at *The New York World* with George Luks's *The Yellow Kid* contributed to an origin story that aptly hinges on popular appeal, recognizable character iconography, and early practices of fan fiction. What's most interesting, moreover, about claiming an origin story in US newspapers and its history of petty, intellectual imitation relates to the ways that comics continually misbehave against ownership and attempts to keep them still. As such, efforts to affix orderly ancestries to the comic strip provide only reductions of a contentious yet potentially expansive history beyond its US roots. We might characterize comic strips and their lineage as characteristically fraught concepts; the wide range of origin points claimed for comic strips reflect the medium's definitional volatility, its provocative failures, and its most radical potential.

Indeed, claiming *any* origin point requires a working definition of the term *comic strip*. So what *makes* a comic strip? Picture writing (Spiegelman)? Sequential art (Eisner)? Graphic narratives (Chute)? Juxtaposed pictorial and other images in a deliberate sequence, intended to convey information and/or produce an aesthetic response in the viewer (McCloud)? Word balloons (Carrier)? Definitions of the comic strip almost always involve a form of failure: many definitions overlook the very important, holistic act of reading comic strips. Rather than identify key features within comic strips that account for this complex process in piecemeal, how might we provide a definition that addresses the affective, readerly movement that is unique to its form? Relatedly, how might we define *comic strip* as a mobile process? This proposal does not attempt to outdo or nullify comics scholars' previous field-defining theoretical approaches to the comic strip. On the contrary, approaching the "comic strip" as a *process* builds upon previous definitions, with the tenet that all definitions are possible yet significantly *imprecise* when approaching a medium that moves. Approaching a definition of the comic strip as movement—as process—resists tidy classifications of the medium that, despite convincing attention to its varying parts, fail to reconstruct an elusive wholeness of the medium.

A perhaps unexpected yet useful framework with which we might approach the comic strip and its movement derives from the philosopher and psychologist William James, who appropriately enough published his seminal text *The Principles of Psychology* around the birth of the US comic strip at the end of the nineteenth century in 1890. In it, he classifies five characters of thought to describe human consciousness essentially as movement, or as a "continuous stream." I consider his approach to human consciousness in relation to how we may approach the comic strip—its precarious definitions and slippery histories—in an effort to grasp the distinguishing quality of its unique, readerly movement. Comparing James's theories on human consciousness to an iconic strip from the US comic strip canon, Ernie Bushmiller's *Nancy*, I consider how comic strips begin and end with movement, seriality, and an expression of the complex processes of the human mind. As such, the comic strip as human consciousness provides scholars with a malleable foundation from which to work while resisting an impulse to privilege certain, formal features and exclude others. In this way, William James's definition of human consciousness provides for us the comic strip as bare movement, as (in his words) "a painter's first charcoal sketch upon his canvas, in which no niceties appear" (1890, 225).

In Mark Newgarden and Paul Karasik's famous 1988 essay, "How to Read Nancy" (now a full-length and luminous text), Newgarden and Karasik explore the myriad of formal elements at work in a seemingly "simple," gag-oriented *Nancy* newspaper strip by original creator Bushmiller. In their analysis, they meticulously break down a single comic strip that involves three panels: two panels that show Sluggo spraying a young boy and a girl with a water pistol as Nancy observes from a distance and a final panel that shows Sluggo approaching Nancy with the pistol. In preparation for his attack, Nancy conceals a turned-on garden hose in her hip holster—poised like a ready gunslinger to outdo an unprepared Sluggo. In all three panels, Sluggo says "Draw, you varmint" as a signal for his attack. Piece by piece, Newgarden and Karasik work through this sequence and analyze how each arrangement of visual features contributes to how we read a comic strip. They repeatedly display the three-panel strip but modify the panels to contain only the characteristics of focus (e.g., word balloons, panel size, certain characters) in order to enunciate the work of specific elements. The cumulative effect of these singular attentions underscores how many practices we take for granted in the intricate reading of comic strips. To build upon this understanding of the comic strip, however, one must account for a simultaneity of these singular features that, like human consciousness, resist a discrete breaking down of parts that Newgarden and Karasik have meticulously detailed.

Challenging scientific approaches to consciousness, James asks whether we can (or should) methodologically break down discernible "parts" in thinking about and describing human cognition. He states, "The aim of science is always to reduce complexity to simplicity; and in psychological science we have the celebrated 'theory of ideas' which, admitting the great difference among each other of what may be called concrete conditions of the mind, seeks to show how this is all the resultant effect of variations in the combination of certain simple elements of consciousness that always remain the same" (1890, 230). Analyzing the *Nancy* strip reveals how useful James's approach may be in defining the comic strip. In this three-panel sequence, we view a repetition of figures across the page: Nancy, Sluggo, the word balloon and its recurring text, and the water pistol. Bushmiller performs the rapid positionalities of consciousness that James argues are continuously negotiating within the human mind. Even objects or ideas that feel "identical" to previous thoughts and facts "only bear a resemblance of kind with our other thoughts of the same fact. When the identical fact recurs, we must think of it in a fresh manner, see it under a somewhat different angle, apprehend it in different relations from those in which it last appeared" (233). The comic strip barters heavily in this awareness—recurring figures and familiar icons, while never aging or significantly "changing" over time, are constantly evolving under new contexts, whether those contexts involve an unexpected inversion of power in a single strip (as seen in the Nancy strip and the water pistol) or the minute modifications of a familiar comic strip character over time under the influence of new generations of audiences and artists. The *Nancy* comic strip, for example, hosts several character shifts during its long history of publication. Over the past century, dozens of artists have continually redefined Nancy's character in response to Ernie Bushmiller's initial designs. Joe Brainard's *The Nancy Book*, a compilation of select, experimental works by the poet and visual artist, and the more recent update to Nancy's world by Olivia Jaimes are just a few examples of how artists have preserved Nancy's familiar, visual features while drastically repositioning the character's context, her personality, and her function within the comic strip art form. Meaningful repetition in the comics medium, while seemingly subtle, wields some of the most radical implications for agitating ethical and social thought. The comic strip has a unique purchase in recurrence that allows for critical engagement with personal, generational, and/or national habits of perception that we often take for granted. What makes the gag operative in the *Nancy* comic is a sudden shift in perspective and power structures—an abrupt disturbance within a petty history of violence outlined elegantly in a three-panel sequence.

Similar to how one might read a comic strip or a full comic book page, James argues that our human consciousness may be "read" as significantly continuous;

James defines "continuous" as "that which is without breach, crack, or division . . . that even where there is a time-gap the consciousness after it feels as if it belonged together with the consciousness before it" (1890, 237). Although scholars attend meticulously to the "time-gap" of comics—white space between frames, the gap, the gutter—we don't consciously read these features as content. We read comics as a continuous sequence in motion that relies on omission to signal the passage of time. In the *Nancy* comic, for example, we must interpret white space between panels in order to understand the sequence of events leading up to the punchline panel. In a process that McCloud defines as "closure," we approximate the duration of time and the proximity of characters by filling in the gutter. As well, Bushmiller withholds from readers the satisfaction of the final confrontation—we surmise an invisible climax between Nancy and Sluggo. This vanishing point in comics, the gutter between panels, ensures a space for consistent revision and imaginative potential outside of the frames of provided content. Although I imagine a confrontation between Nancy and Sluggo in which Nancy prevails, I cannot know for sure. James describes the stream of thought as contingent on how individuals conceptualize their flowing experience based on varying forms of necessary, cognitive simplifications. The productive tension in the comic strip involves a dance between an author's omissions and any given reader's assumptions, which provide for a reading experience as a continual and participatory process. We must approach comics and their definition as distinguished by an implied movement between (and inclusive of) its frames of content that reflect how human consciousness constructs "a world full of sharp contrasts, of sharp accents, of abrupt changes, of picturesque light and shade" (James 1890, 284–85). The potential for viewing the comic strip this way recognizes the characteristic plasticity of the medium, which allows for endless, revisionary play with what is typically considered "fixed." The agitating concept of human consciousness and of the unique art of the comic strip promises only more meddling and restless foundations for provoking new perspectives that lead potentially to both subtle and explicit revision in how we habitually view and interact socially, politically, and ethically with the world that we inhabit.

Drawing on James's concepts of consciousness moves us closer to a definition of the comic strip that preserves the perspectival multiplicities involved in its unique reading practices. As a mobile and participatory literature, the comic strip invites what James considers a "radical plurality" of personal consciousness that depicts human relations with each other and their shared world as contingent and multifarious. I began this account by offering two common issues scholars encounter when approaching the comic strip. A mobile definition, in reflection of the stream of consciousness described by James, resists attempts to fix comic strips and their origins as well as concrete definitions that unwittingly reduce or underestimate the radical potential of this medium. In this type of definition as movement, we may recognize "the process by means of which individuals conceptualize their flowing experience guarantees that the history of philosophy will never come to an end: each philosophical vision is a personal simplification" (J. Campbell 2017, 198). And let this interpretation end here, which is also a gross simplification of sorts, as a beginning. Perhaps this sketch will provide an invitation to imagine yet another interpretive panel in reflection of a form of literature and its scholarship that we can only hope will always (*essentially*) move.

13

Comix
Nicholas Sammond

Writing about underground comix in the comics and animation journal *Funnyworld* in 1971, underground comix creator and publisher Denis Kitchen proclaimed that "by ridiculing the outmoded social system we live in, we are quickening its demise. And in its place, hopefully, will be established a society in which no 'underground' is necessary" (quoted in Schelly 2015, 484). The optimism in that statement is admirable, if not—given today's social, political, and cultural struggles—enviable.

The key to understanding comix is, of course, the *x*. Robert Crumb is usually given credit for swapping the second *c* in comics to the *x* in comix when, in early 1968, so the story goes, he was peddling *Zap Comix* from a baby carriage (or shopping cart) in the Haight-Ashbury district of San Francisco. First and foremost, the new spelling was a rejection of the North American comics industry and its restrictive and prudish Comics Code, a self-imposed system of censorship by mainstream comics producers that severely limited what types of stories, words, and images could appear in mass-market comic books (see Nyberg in this volume). A potent signifier, the *x* invoked a rejection of the code in favor of unbridled, libidinous, and uncensored expression. It foreshadowed the X rating for movies, which was instituted in November 1968, only months after Crumb released *Zap Comix* #1. Like X-rated movies, comix repudiated the notion that a vernacular art form, comics, had to be "family friendly," embracing traditional standards of morality.

Instead, they celebrated nonmarital reproductive sexuality, unlimited freedom of speech, drug use (and the expansion of consciousness it was meant to promise), and a communalism that challenged the hegemony of the white, suburban, nuclear family. Graphically representing an emergent counterculture and mobilizing independent networks of production, distribution, and consumption, comix were an alternative to (not a replacement for) mainstream comics culture (see Hatfield in this volume).

The standard history of the rise of comix, then, begins with Crumb peddling *Zap Comix* on the streets of San Francisco and subsequently with that book's publishers—Apex Novelties, Print Mint, and Last Gasp Eco Funnies—distributing it to head shops (which sold drug-related paraphernalia), alternative bookstores, and record stores across North America, wherever a robust hippy scene was happening. That scene is important in situating the rise of underground comix because of the strong connections between the contents of those early comix and the communities from which they arose. Two *Zap Comix* artists, Victor Moscoso and Rick Griffin, were also prolific producers of concert posters for psychedelic bands such as the Grateful Dead and Jefferson Airplane. Griffin also created iconic posters for events like the 1967 Human Be-In, at which Beat poets and artists such as Allen Ginsberg, Ken Kesey, and Gary Snyder handed the countercultural torch to the hippies. All of which is merely to say that underground comix were part of the larger aesthetic, cultural, and (to a lesser extent) political currents of the day.

Yet the mere appearance of the letter *x* at the end of comix doesn't tell the definitive story of the rise of the underground. Another version would place its origin much earlier, in 1955, when EC Comics publisher William Gaines and cartoonist Harvey Kurtzman protested the strictures of the Comics Code by converting one of EC's comic books, *MAD*, into a magazine, thereby exempting it from the code. Though tame compared to its underground descendants, *MAD* offered satirical and parodic pieces that skewered the mores and hypocrisies of the day (yet only occasionally took *direct* aim at politics). More than a few countercultural figures, including Students for a Democratic Society (SDS) founder Tom Hayden and cartoonists such as Crumb, Art Spiegelman, and Denis Kitchen, have named *MAD* and Kurtzman as major influences on them. Even though Kurtzman left *MAD* after one year—replaced by Al Feldstein—he set the tone that the magazine has maintained for generations. He also went on to produce the short-lived but influential humor magazines *Trump* (1957), *Humbug* (1957–58), and *Help!* (1960–65), which showcased up-and-coming talents such as R. Crumb, Terry Gilliam, Jay Lynch, and Gilbert Shelton. Each of these titles—but especially *Help!*—was an important proving ground for the emerging form of underground comix.

Another important incubator for the comix that followed the publication of *Zap Comix* in 1968—with titles like *Bizarre Sex* (1972–82), *Bijou Funnies* (1968–73), *Cosmic Comix* (1969), *Felch Cumics* (1975), and *Young Lust* (1970–93)—was the alternative press. Before contributing to comix, many of the men and women who first fueled the underground scene published in radical and alternative publications such as *The East Village Other* (*EVO*) and its comix supplement *Gothic Blimp Works*, *Ramparts*, the *Sunday Paper*, the *Berkeley Barb*, the *Los Angeles Free Press*, and the *Bugle*. While comix in alternative newspapers were edgy and "countercultural" (transgressive by the standards of the day), most avoided the explicitly political statements found in their editorial content. They articulated the counterculture by breaking taboos around sex and sexuality, drugs, and middle-class manners but generally eschewed any specific ideological or political stance.

Access to alternative presses was also key to improving the visibility of women and queer cartoonists. In 1971, Lee Marrs cofounded Alternative Features Service (AFS), which distributed comics, articles, and artwork to college and alternative newspapers. Marrs has indicated that she was drawn to the underground scene when she moved to San Francisco but found it a "closed club. . . . There was no way a beginning artist could break in, no place for it. All the underground comics consisted of friends printing friends. They were all buddies; they didn't even let us in" (quoted in Robbins 2013, 125). AFS provided a more inclusive service, distributing early work by women and queer folks, such as Robbins's *Panthea* series (1969–76) and Howard Cruse's *Barefootz* (1971–79).

For many artists who weren't straight white men, these networks were essential for breaking into underground comix. Robbins has indicated that her first comix, *It Ain't Me, Babe* (1970), was supported and initially distributed by A Woman's Place Bookstore in Berkeley. Not only did Robbins's *It Ain't Me, Babe* have its genesis at a women's bookstore; it began in a short-lived women's newspaper of the same name, for which Robbins had worked as an illustrator and cartoonist before branching out into book format ("Interviews with Women Comic Artists: Trina Robbins" 1979). Other women's bookstores, such as Old Wives' Tales and Full Moon Café and Books in San Francisco, Mama Bears in Oakland, or Toronto Women's Bookstore, were often important outlets for women's comix. In Los Angeles, Joyce Farmer and Lyn Cheveley launched the sex-positive feminist comix *Tits & Clits* (Nanny Goat Productions, 1972–87) around the same time that *Wimmen's Comix* began and sold it in Cheveley's bookstore. Yet as Robbins has recently pointed out, most of those bookstores, unable to compete against chain stores and online sales, have long since closed. Thus the marginality and precarity of the women's community (or communities) initially provided outlets for women's comix and a network of distribution and sales, but those outlets were limited and that network somewhat unstable.

The rise of underground comix, then, was at one level very local and at that local level revealed tensions within and among countercultural and oppositional communities. Yet comix were also shaped by, and depicted, struggles between local communities and the state. Charles Hatfield (2005) identifies several causes for a gradual shift in format from alternative newspapers to comic books in the early 1970s and for a subsequent lack of a clearly defined politics in comix. The "community standards" test for obscenity put forward in the US Supreme Court decision *Miller v. California* (1973) gave local communities more freedom to censoring controversial materials such as comix. Likewise, laws that banned selling drug paraphernalia closed many of the head shops that had been important sales points for comix (Ornasaka 2006). Hatfield suggests that the change in format engendered creative independence but not critical engagement, pushing comix artists away from "larger political issues" and more toward biography (Hatfield 2005, 19). So the closing of many alternative newspapers, the increased enforcement of local obscenity laws, and the shuttering of head shops all played a role in changing the format and, to an extent, the focus of underground comix.

Yet how that repression was experienced and how it shaped the medium depended very much on who you were. The term *community standards*, as much as it became an anathema to free expression during the 1970s, speaks not just to the shuttering of venues for all underground comix but also to differences between underground comix and the communities from which they arose and whom they served. R. Crumb and other of the first-generation underground cartoonists—at least those who were straight white men—opted not so much for a specific political platform as for a more iconoclastic and generically "countercultural" assault on mainstream mores. For Crumb, particularly after San Francisco and the popular psychedelic drug LSD had expanded his consciousness, this entailed plumbing the depths of his darkest racial and psychosexual biases and desires. Speaking to *Comics Journal* in 1991, Crumb spelled out that dynamic in detail: "I know from my own work I have to let that stuff out, it can't stay inside of me; all the creepiness, the sexual stuff, the hostility toward women, the anger toward authority. . . . If it's acceptable or unacceptable to other people, if it's helpful to anyone else, I don't know" (Groth 1991). For these underground comix artists, rebelling against the status quo involved breaking the aesthetic norms for mainstream comics of the day, but they also imagined that they were addressing the inherent sexism, racism, and repressiveness of mainstream society by creating satire that paradoxically indulged in *those same excesses*. Discussing cartoonist Jay Kinney's lifting of blackface minstrel imagery from Crumb, Leonard Rifas notes that "Kinney had found in Crumb's strip 'Don't Gag on It, Goof on It' an artistic command: 'mock and satirize hypocrisy, cant, self-congratulation, injustice, and so on, wherever you find it.' The artist's satirical task became to lay bare and break the taboos of the mainstream and the counterculture, of the left and the right, of sexism, feminism, and racism" (2010, 36).

Yet if Crumb, Spiegelman, and others found expressing their unconscious rage and repression liberating, that feeling wasn't shared by all. Lyn Cheveley, discussing the inspiration for *Tits & Clits* (1972–87), claimed, "Neither of us was much of a comix fan, but at the time we started I owned a bookstore, sold [underground comix], and was impressed by their honesty but loathed their macho depiction of sex. Our work, originally, was

a reaction to the glut of testosterone in comics. . . . Our original commitment was to concentrate on female sexuality" (quoted in Rifas 2010, 34).

Similar sentiments were shared by a number of comix creators who were the objects of the unconscious impulses described by Crumb: women, people of color, and queer folk. For them, though, the shift to book format didn't necessarily lead to apolitical comix. Not for titles such as Chiveley and Sutton's pro-choice *Abortion Eve* (1973), published the same year as the *Roe v. Wade* decision, or for the work of Leonard Rifas, such as his *Corporate Crime Comics* (1977–80), *All Atomic Comics* (1976), or *Food Comics* (1980), each of which offered graphic critiques of corporate malfeasance, nuclear power/weapons, and agribusiness, respectively. Nor did many of the women who had also gotten their start through the alternative press in the 1960s, such as Lee Marrs, Nancy Kalish, and Willie Mendes, move away from explicit politics. For example, the founding collective of *Wimmen's Comix* (1972–92)—Michelle Brand, Marrs, Lora Fountain, Patti Moodian, Sharon Rudahl, Shelby Sampson, Aline Kominsky, Robbins, Marie Haskell, and Janet Wolf Stanley—was dedicated to featuring women's experience through sequential art, eventually devoting 50 percent of every issue to new artists. *Wimmen's Comix* never achieved the recognition that work by their male counterparts received, but the series ran successfully for twenty years (Robbins 2013, 129–38). Similarly, queer artists such as Burton Clarke, Mary Wings, Howard Cruse, and Tom of Finland (Touko Laaksonen) produced comix that played an important role in articulating and entertaining changing queer sensibilities and communities. Such vital work made by and for marginalized communities has not been central to most histories of the creation and development of the underground comix movement/industry, but it was essential not only as a necessary counter to the unconscious fantasies of artists such as Crumb but also as an articulation of truly alternative visions of life outside of the mainstream.

In the beginning, then, underground comix imagined an alternative aesthetic movement, countering and critiquing the narrow consensus in mainstream comics and newspapers. Yet many early comix simultaneously reproduced some of the worst gender, sexual, and racial exclusions of that mainstream, and their domination of what might be described as the "alternative mainstream" encouraged racial, gender, and sexual minorities to claim a voice for themselves and to develop their own networks of distribution and sales. This situation offers a visual correlate for failures of the New Left and its eventual fragmentation into the Black Power, women's and gay liberation movements, and the subsequent third-world movements such as the American Indian Movement (AIM) and La Raza.

At the same time, in titles like *Ebon* (1970), *White Whore Funnies* (1975–79), and *Super-Soul* (1972), African American cartoonists Richard "Grass" Green and Larry Fuller (who also published *Gay Hearthrobs* [1976–81]) tweaked comix' hypermasculine style to create more nuanced critiques of sexual normativity and racial stereotyping (see Wanzo 2020 for a detailed discussion of their work). And just down the hill from where Crumb, Wilson, Griffith, and the other founders of the mainstream alternative comix scene were at work, Emory Douglas and Tarika Lewis were publishing the weekly *Black Panther Black Community News Service*. Lewis and Douglas forged a truly international graphic style that was in conversation with a wide range of artistic movements and styles, from North Vietnamese propaganda posters, to the iconic African American artist Charles White, to woodcuts by Latin American resistance movements and Cuban revolutionary art. The work they produced was not simply vaguely "countercultural"; it was ideologically specific and revolutionary.

If 1967, when Crumb was assembling *Zap Comix* #1, is the putative birth year of underground comix, it is also a year that saw rebellions in numerous cities in the United States, poor African American and Latinx communities exploding in rage at oppressive, discriminatory, and exploitative labor and housing practices and at the policies that fueled and justified that immiseration. It's the year that the Black Panther Party opened its first office in Oakland, California, and the year that Jo Freeman and Shulamith Firestone broke with the National Conference of New Politics to argue for what they called *women's liberation*. And it is the year that the queer community in the Silver Lake neighborhood in Los Angeles protested raids by the notorious LA police on the Black Cat Tavern, in the process coining the term *pride*. The *x* in comix refers to all of those acts of rebellion.

14

Cosplay

Ellen Kirkpatrick

Cosplay—a neologism of "costume" and "(role) play"—is one of several modes of embodied participation in media fandom. As cosplayer Vivid Vivka tells us, "It's dress-up, yes, but it's so much more" (Linde 2014). American comics, notably superhero titles, are a perennially popular source of cosplayable characters. And yet female and other minority representation within the mainstream Western superhero genre—and pop culture more generally—is notoriously problematic, on- and off-page and screen. With a few valuable exceptions, mainstream superheroes are straight white men living in straight white worlds. Yet despite the absences, exclusions, and periodic hostility, the genre remains popular with minoritarian fans and cosplayers. Indeed, coverage of female cosplayers dominates the scene. Through a broader discussion of cosplay, minoritarian cosplayers resist and reform exclusionary, and often hostile, meaningscapes—text, lived, and fandom. Borrowing from José Esteban Muñoz, "I use the term minoritarian to index citizen-subjects who, due to antagonisms within the social such as race, class, and sex, are debased within the majoritarian public sphere" (Muñoz 2009, 56). It also theorizes connections between cosplay and the superhero genre alongside considering the mechanics behind transporting characters from boundless, fantastical textual realms to a bounded, mundane material realm.

As a diverse, global practice with a long-established history, cosplay is subject to definitional complexity and fluidity, but its descriptions typically include costume, dressing up, fan, identity, bodies, performance, transformation, boundaries, (fan) conventions, and community. The root of the descriptor *cosplay* (*kosupure*) is contested in scholarship. For some it first appeared in print, written as コスプレ in a photo-essay produced by anime exponent Takahashi Nobuyuki. The piece, published in June 1983 in the Japanese anime magazine *My Anime*, chronicles the costuming practices of manga and anime fans (see Jee 2008; Plunkett 2014). For others, pieces written by Takahashi in 1984 provide the origin point (see Bruno, n.d.; Hlozek 2004; Gilligan 2011). Whatever the date, however, Takahashi used *cosplay* to express the concept of fannish masquerade witnessed at pop culture conventions such as WorldCon (est. 1939) and Comiket (est. 1975). Media fans throughout the globe were certainly dressing and performing as their favorite characters and heroes long before the 1980s (Winge 2006). Indeed, there is nothing spectacularly new about dressing up as one's heroes. People have always used their bodies and clothing to play at being other beings—usually but not always more powerful beings. We might think of the costuming practices of classical antiquity where religious adherents would dress up as their favorite gods, Renaissance masquerades, or the totemic dressing practices of many Indigenous peoples. But gods—so the myths tell us—also like to dress up and become, or appear as, other beings. The world's mythologies are full of stories about the shapeshifting and costuming practices of gods visiting Earth to play at being human or animal, just as the godlike Kal-El does when he becomes, or plays at being, the earthly Clark Kent or as members of furry fandom do when they don a "fursuit" and play at being animals. What is spectacular today, however, is the sheer scale—range, texture, spaces, and variety—of costume play.

As an evolving branch of fandom research, early cosplay studies understandably foregrounded the idea of cosplay as fans dressing up within convention settings and role-playing as fictional characters; this frequently ethnographic work often documented practice and explored motivations (see Winge 2006; Gunnels 2009; Lamerichs 2010; Rahman, Wing-Sun, and Cheung 2012). Bakhtin's idea of "carnival," Goffman's "performance," and Butler's "performativity" (and work on drag) were popular conceptual lenses during this time and still are today. Discussions crisscrossed through concepts of performance (Lamerichs 2010; Gunnels 2009), identity, and embodiment (performance and politics), notably around gender and sexuality—at this time often discussing "crossplay" performances (e.g., when a self-identified female cosplayer cosplays as a male-identified character; Leng 2013; Bainbridge and Norris 2013)—and affective fan labor and/or gender (Norris and Bainbridge 2009; Scott 2015). Alternative modes of costuming practice, such as digital cosplay (Booth 2015) and "real-life superheroes" (Kirkpatrick 2013), also received some limited attention. Recent studies have, however, also started to explore these kinds of concepts against less costumey, "everyday" modes of fannish dress, often dubbed "stealth" or "closet" cosplay, including fan fashion and couture (Lamerichs 2018) and Disneybounding (dressing as contemporary versions of Disney characters in daily life [Brock 2017]). The idea of "bounding" is currently evolving to include other media texts, such as "Potter bounding" (referencing J. K. Rowling's *Harry Potter* series) and, more generally, "fandom bounding." Other overlooked modes of cosplay, such as intergenerational cosplay (Pett 2016), are also now being examined.

Fan responses and mainstream coverage of cosplay track these trends and themes and contemporaneously highlight and confront rampant sexism within cosplay culture and broader fan cultures (i.e., the "fake geek girls" slur). In 2010, for instance, we saw the first flashes of what became the "Cosplay Is Not Consent" movement and the anomalous and trailblazing "Geek Girls Exist" panel at San Diego Comic-Con that blossomed into the grassroots Geek Girl Con (est. 2011). (By 2013, the radical spirit of "Cosplay Is Not Consent" had morphed into a global awareness-raising intervention, one making substantial progress in speaking out against and stamping out sexual harassment within anime, comic book, and pop culture conventions [see Culp 2016].)

Yet as within other branches of fan studies, intersections of race, ethnicity, disability, class, and age were often noted in cosplay studies but received no substantive attention. This is slowly changing (see Pande 2018; Warner 2015; Kirkpatrick 2019). Fan-instigated movements and activism, such as the Twitter hashtag #28daysofblackcosplay founded by "blerd" (Black nerd) cosplayer Chaka Cumberbatch (Broadnax 2015), Indigenous Comic Con, Texas Latino Comic Con, and the budding CosAbility (cosplay for people with disabilities) movement, were critical to this awakening. Mainstream events, such as San Diego Comic-Con, are also spotlighting the often-overlooked diversity within comics and fan cultures by hosting awareness-raising sessions, such as the 2017 panel "We Are All Heroes: The Changing Landscape of Comics, Geekdom, and Fanboy Culture."

The increased amount of work engaging issues around marginalized identities and an exclusionary mediascape frequently points to racebending fanwork as disidentificatory work; in this way, racebending cosplay becomes theorizable as an embodied mode of disidentification and/or resistive or reparative enactment. Racebending refers to practices that rework the race and ethnicity of source characters. It has two expressions:

(1) the whitewashing practices—representing minority source characters as white—of the mainstream media (see Lopez 2011; Reid 2017; Bravo, n.d.) and the subsequent grassroots advocacy and activism against these injurious practices (see racebending.com) and (2) those fan practices that diversify exclusory and culturally appropriative texts by representing white source characters as people of color, such as "Racebent Disney" and the racebending practices of factions of *Harry Potter* fandom (Seymour 2018). Racebending cosplay is then an embodied costuming practice that reimagines the (usually white) source character's race and ethnicity. It illuminates, responds to, and confronts the white centrism of Western media, a mediascape grounded in traditions of racebending and whitewashing. Racebending cosplayers insert themselves into an exclusionary text's meaningscape (and an often equally clannish fan space). Arresting visualities and performances make the invisible visible, the unimaginable real, and the personal political. In creating alternative images and new ways of looking—at both the original image and the new image this kind of remediative play transforms not only the look of the present but how we view the past and (re)imagine the future. Racebending performances are often sites of empowerment, resistance, and activism. Racebending cosplayers can effect change on a range of intersecting levels: textual, civic, fandom, and personal. It must be stressed, however, that while conventions and "geek" culture can provide safe spaces for queer or minoritarian cosplayers, it is not always so (see Figa 2015a, 2015b; Micheline 2015; Gooden 2016). Women of color cosplayers are vulnerable to a particularly virulent and brazen strain of abuse that intersects through race and gender (Cumberbatch 2013). Flame Con, NYC's first queer comics convention, provides a much-needed guaranteed safe space. Social networking sites such as Twitter, Facebook, and Tumblr can similarly provide invaluable safe spaces, support networks, and community-building opportunities, and not just among cosplaying communities of color (see, for example, Jackson, Bailey, and Foucault Welles 2017).

Cosplay almost always concerns more than simply dressing up in the likeness of fictional (or self-created) characters, though that is definitely a large part of its pleasure. For many, cosplay is also about capturing the spirit, or "habitus" (Bainbridge and Norris 2013), of an often-beloved character. As cosplayer Katrina Meowsir comments, "I get to bring my favourite characters to 'life' so to speak" (McIsaac 2012). Cosplay does not, however, always signify such fannish devotion. Character choice is a rich and complex process. Some cosplayers perform one character repeatedly, while others perform many (Rahman, Wing-Sun, and Cheung 2012). While most feel a connection to the source character, some simply like the look of a character's costume (Winge 2006) or base their selection on a character's "trending" popularity or share a character's body type. Choosing a source character is just the first step of a cosplayer's journey. The next is to (re-)create the costume, another idiosyncratic process. Cosplay costumes and props may be lovingly handmade or crafted, commissioned, or "shop bought"—or a blend of these possibilities—and may involve body modification (e.g., contact lenses, dental prosthetics). For dedicated cosplayers, cosplay is not just about the material costuming of the body but also about the material performance of the body; devoted cosplayers learn signature poses, facial expressions, and even dialogue to fully render their cosplay (see Winge 2006; Rahman, Wing-Sun, and Cheung 2012). These mimetic modes of cosplay involve intricate movements as the cosplayer endeavors to transfer the (often fantastical) source character from the page or screen to the more mundane human bodyscape. I theorize this kind of cosplay as embodied translation and a mode of embodied reception (see Kirkpatrick 2013, 2015). (I describe translation as a continuous, fluid, and unassured meaning-making process and cosplayers, as translators, as empowered meaning makers.) These concepts are proposed as a way of theorizing connections and repetitions between diegetic superhero costuming practices and cosplay and the transference of the fantastic to the mundane.

Characters from anime, manga, and tokusatsu dominate the cosplay scene, but cosplayers also draw inspiration from other pop culture media. Fans today cosplay celebrities, musicians, and film directors. Witness, for example, Jessi Chartier's Patty Jenkins—director of *Wonder Woman* (2017)—cosplay at Chicago's Comic & Entertainment Expo (Hale-Stern 2018). Among these other sources, the mainstream American superhero genre proves incredibly popular—a genre rooted in American comic books. For while the superhero genre flourishes outside the comics medium, comics remains its homeland. The genre's popularity within cosplay culture is perhaps not that surprising given its ubiquity in today's mediascape and that American comic book fandom is "one of the most dedicated, active fandoms" (Perren and Felschow 2018, 309). Notions of cosplay also feature routinely in superhero stories, either directly or indirectly (Kirkpatrick 2015). Connections between the superhero genre and cosplay culture, I argue, run deep. Both are—through their preoccupations with concepts of "becoming" via experimental identity play, transforming bodies, and, of course, masking and costuming—in deep dialogue. The origin story created for the second rendering of the Flash, Barry Allen (1956), illustrates several moments of juncture between superhero comics and cosplay performance.

Just like comic book readers reading *Showcase* #4 (1956), Barry Allen, the Flash-to-be, was shown reading an old issue of *The Flash*. This image nods to the changing demographics of comics readers and opinions on comics readership; it also indicates Allen as both a reader of comics and a fan of the Flash—a rare representation. It functions too as an example of the real-life superhero costuming trope. The transformative accident endowing Allen with "superspeed" allows him to take his pleasure in his childhood hero a step further than most fans; it allows the fulfillment of his desire to *become* the (or a) Flash. It is not enough for Allen, however, to possess the Flash's powers; he wants to be seen as the Flash. Allen adopts his hero's code name, modifies his costume, and replicates his crime-fighting behavior. Allen does not have to: he chooses to. This origin story knowingly and deliberately plugs into the desires of many superhero genre fans and cosplayers. Similarly, sometimes it is not enough to know oneself as a fan; one must demonstrate their fandom. Cosplaying a favored character publicly displays the cosplayer as a fan and allows him or her to become and be seen for a moment as that beloved character. For superheroes and cosplayers, costuming creates another way of reading visually and thus another mode of being.

Cosplay, especially perhaps superhero cosplay, transfers the fantastical—and, regarding racebending cosplay, the often invisible—into the realm of the mundane, and much is lost, and gained, in translation. Cosplay in this sense is more about translation than transformation. Cosplayers of fantastical source characters, including superheroes, rewrite the ontology of these characters. Superhero cosplayers will never, unlike their heroes, become a "real" superhero by changing their mode of dress. The idea of delimited superhero performance speaks to the mode of costuming and identity play performed by a growing—and not unproblematic—subculture of social activists known as "real-life superheroes" (Kirkpatrick 2017). The superhero genre is a major source of inspiration for these civic-minded citizens, from its costuming practices to its moral code, with many "heroically" working for the benefit of, and to protect, their local communities. Curiously, although deeply invested in superhero ontology, aesthetics, and morality, the lack of fannishness in their performances and surrounding discourse is notable. The bounded performances of superhero cosplayers and real-life superheroes demonstrate that superheroes can only *really* exist in the genre's imaginary realms—cosplay eliminates the "super" from the superhero. Embodied translation speaks to the processes involved in performing the "extraordinary" within the limits of the "ordinary": it is "uniquely enacted within the frame and bounds of the material body of the cosplayer. Thus, in translating an established character, cosplayers are implicated in a process of (re)creation, [and] they produce simultaneously a new character and a revised version of the original" (Kirkpatrick 2013, 64). Remembering that there are few minoritarian source characters to draw from, transgressive cosplayers perform an additional layer of imaginary work. Through their performances, they deliver the "extraordinary" idea of minoritarian superheroes from their imaginations, via genre tropes, into the material realm. Superhero cosplay creates the idea of a Superman who cannot fly and a Spider-Man sans "spidey sense," but its transgressive modes also, critically, reveal the possibility of a Black disabled Superman or a Muslim female Captain America, each in their own way a radical reimagining—embodied translation—of the superhero as portrayed in the largely white heteropatriarchal genre. As with transgressive cosplay, real-life superheroes disrupt mainstream Western superhero ideology, ontology, and aesthetics and display the idea of the superhero as a rallying figure for change in personal, political, and even perhaps textual realms. This disruptive quality is not localized to the superhero cosplayer or the superhero genre but touches all types of cosplay involving fantastical source characters.

Like cosplayers, the meaning of cosplay is experiencing a transformation. It is expanding beyond one-off fan-centric events and out into everyday spaces. And although you perhaps wouldn't think it—given the hegemonic biases and privileges historically stifling fan studies—cosplay is performed by majoritarian *and* minoritarian fans. The challenge facing those mapping cosplay culture today is to decolonize cosplay studies by undertaking remedial work that documents and theorizes the motivations and practices of minoritarian cosplayers. It is also, more broadly, to reveal the transformative potential of cosplay on all (intersecting) levels: seen and unseen; desired and unsolicited; personal and political; ludic and activist; textual, material, and fannish. Doing so will allow the emergence of a more nuanced, expansive understanding of cosplay, one that accounts for cosplay not only in other spaces but performed by "other" kinds of fans.

15

Creator

Susan Kirtley

The *Oxford English Dictionary* defines *creator* as "the divine agent which creates all things from nothing," or the significantly less exalted "person who or thing which creates or brings something into existence." In the history of comics creation, however, far from receiving divine recognition for their handiworks, creators have, unfortunately, struggled for the rights to their own creations. Thus the term *creator* holds particular resonance within the history of comics, as creators have long fought to be acknowledged for their work producing comics and still endeavor to receive appropriate monetary and intellectual recognition.

Early innovators such as William Hogarth, Rudolph Töpffer, and Lynd Ward created highly influential works and did so as individuals, as did Richard Outcault. R. C. Harvey argues that "Outcault was probably the first to run up the flag for creator's rights" when he attempted to copyright his character the Yellow Kid in 1896, although Brian Walker suggests that "records at the Library of Congress indicate that his request was never officially granted due to an irregularity in the application process" (2004, 14). Outcault also engaged in one of the first legal controversies over creator rights when he sued the *New York Herald* over the rights to his popular strip *Buster Brown* in 1906. Unfortunately, according to Mark D. Winchester, "The court only recognized the composition and execution of a drawing, refusing to entertain the idea of a character . . . as a significant element of cartoon art. . . . Outcault's failed bid was an unfortunate precedent for other cartoonists who sought similar protection for their characters and artwork" (2017, 61). Thus as proven by Outcault's case, the individual rights of creators to their characters were tenuous at best, a situation that became even direr in the early days of superhero comics and the advent of the shop system of comics creation, in which separate individuals were in charge of writing, penciling, inking, coloring, and lettering comics, often with little interaction.

Ian Gordon notes that comic books were originally devised as a repackaging of comic strips for "advertising premiums" intended to "attract the interest of children" during the 1930s (1998, 130). Shortly thereafter, in 1938, Jerry Siegel and Joe Shuster created "both a character and a type, the comic book superhero" for DC Comics, in what is probably the most famous case of aggrieved creators (Gordon 1998, 132). As is well-known today, Siegel and Shuster sold the rights to their iconic creation, Superman, to DC Comics for $130. Given the success of the hero, they sued for rights and a "just share" of profits from the character, resulting in a legal battle that continued until well after the creators' deaths.

The popularity of comic books during the so-called Golden Age also gave rise to the "shop system" of comics production, which organized the process of producing comics into a team of people rather than individual creators. The shop or studio system employed a variety of artists and writers to create comics quickly and efficiently. Charles Hatfield explains that, in what was "an assembly-line affair, pages frequently changed hands and artists routinely finished each other's work" (2005, 9), a system that discouraged individual creators claiming ownership of characters or titles and put an emphasis on a fast turnaround. Although the shop system evolved over time, most of the mainstream publishers still employ a large team of professionals to collaborate throughout the production process, with separate writers, editors, pencilers, inkers, and colorists all working together on a final project.

Of course, as is well documented in various comics histories, with the rise of the Comics Code Authority (CCA) post-1954, creators began to push back against the stringent guidelines proposed by the CCA—and, for that matter, against mainstream taboos of polite behavior and social mores—through the underground and alternative comics movements. These actions were largely launched by independent auteurs such as R. Crumb, Justin Green, and Kim Deitch, later joined by alternative creators such as Art Spiegelman, Gilbert Shelton, and Jaime and Gilbert Hernandez, once again to name only a few key figures. While some underground and alternative creators collaborated, most retained independent auteur status and, significantly, maintained the rights to their own creations, whether they were self-published or published by one of the new independent publishing houses—a major contrast with creators working for mainstream publishers.

In 1988, several key figures in the independent comics movement met to discuss creators' rights, resulting in the "Bill of Rights for Comics Creators," a list of twelve rights drafted by Scott McCloud and signed by a number of luminaries in the field. Scott McCloud (2018) notes that "the Bill never generated much noise in the industry and I wouldn't want to exaggerate its influence, but it provides an interesting snapshot of our attitudes at the time, and of the climate that was fueling self-publishers, progressive business people, and artists trying to reinvent the comics industry." Although the "Bill of Rights" didn't necessarily produce an immediate or pronounced effect on the comics industry, the coming together of such important and influential figures in the field to render a statement clearly articulating the significance of creators in the creative process and arguing for their rights represents a key moment in comics history as the community united to make a case for intellectual ownership and appropriate compensation for creators.

Today, webcomics have, to a large extent, democratized comics production, offering a forum for self-publication that can translate into larger publishing deals. Self-publishing on the web also offers almost anyone the ability to publish their own work and assume the title of "comics creator." As avenues for comics publication have expanded, however, the scholarly study of comics remains a narrowly circumscribed domain, with academic studies of comics focusing, according to scholars such as Bart Beaty and Benjamin Woo, primarily on a few creators, notably "Art Spiegelman, Alan Moore, Neil Gaiman, and, to a lesser extent, Chris Ware" (2016, 6). In fact, the majority of what Hillary Chute has called "today's contemporary canon" (2010, 14) is composed of auteurs creating "literary" or "art house" comics rather than mainstream titles marketed to popular audiences. Thus although the web allows for more comics creators to share their work with a wide audience, in recent years, the study of comics has largely restricted its focus to comics in a certain style and from a certain type of creator—the singular auteur comics creator—rather than collaborative comics from mainstream publishers. While these few comics creators enjoy additional prestige in the academic and publishing worlds, the majority of creators of comics today still struggle for recognition and for the legal rights to their creations. Thus the creator lucky enough to channel that divine spark into comics art would be well served to remember the history of comics creators and their struggle to protect any and all accomplishments carefully.

16

Disability

José Alaniz

The comics representation of disability spans the modern history of the medium, reflecting popular preconceptions and prejudices of the disabled in a given era. *Disability* refers to a common aspect of living embodied existence centered on a physical and/or cognitive difference(s) as well as the social, cultural, architectural, and political responses to said difference(s). Often referred to as the largest minority both globally (with upwards of eight hundred million worldwide) and in the US (with 20 percent of the population, or some sixty million), the disabled remain among the most disadvantaged, stigmatized, and misunderstood groups. This despite their significant social progress in the late twentieth and early twenty-first centuries, most prominently in landmark legislation such as the Americans with Disabilities Act (1990) and the UN Convention on the Rights of Persons with Disabilities (2006; Goodley 2011).

Disability activism since the 1970s and the rise of disability studies as an academic field since the 1980s have given rise to numerous models of disability, all posing a challenge to the predominant twentieth-century model (which for many still obtains today): the medical model, whereby a health-care system rooted in eugenicist premises approaches disability as a defect or a lack of or deviation from a preferred norm or "average," subject to a cure (Davis 2013, 4–5). The medical model thus situates disability in the bodies of disabled people. In sharp opposition, the social model (by far the most successful

and influential alternative) arose in the UK and US to locate disability in the inaccessible spaces, paternalistic attitudes, and social stigma with which the disabled must routinely contend (Finkelstein 1980; Oliver 1990). As Dan Goodley described it, "Social model scholars turned attention away from a preoccupation with people's impairments to a focus on the causes of exclusion through social, economic, political, cultural, relational and psychological barriers" (2011, 11). They did this in part by making a distinction between *impairment* (defined as the physical difference itself, like blindness or a missing limb) and *disability* (the societal reaction to the impairment, which alone creates disabling environments). This move was emancipatory.

The social model has more recently been subjected to considerable critique from scholars for, among other things, its naturalizing of impairment (ignoring its status as itself a largely sociocultural construction) and elision of disability's nonsocial aspects such as pain and neurodivergences such as autism, learning disabilities, and so on (Shakespeare 2014, 22). Other models have proliferated as well, including the minority model (with ideological links to the various civil rights movements of the 1960s/1970s premised on identity politics) and—perhaps most relevant to graphic narrative—the cultural model, led by humanists (especially literary scholars). The latter has mounted strong critiques of the representation of disability as metaphor (Goodley 2011; Garland-Thomson 1997), whether as symbols for human evil or as "inspiration porn" for the able-bodied, and advanced deconstructive concepts such as "narrative prosthesis" to lay bare the storytelling function of disability since antiquity (Mitchell and Snyder 2000).

In the new millennium, disability studies scholars and disability historians have increasingly interrogated their own presentist and Western-centric biases, with more attention given to the premodern era (Scalenghe

2014), non-Western regions, and the Global South (where the vast majority of disabled people live, mostly in conditions very different from those in the richer developed nations). Other recent developments include the rise of crip theory (modeled in part on queer theory) as a challenge to the ideological biases of disability studies (McRuer 2006). Terms such as *ableism*, the reflexive discrimination against the disabled in favor of the able-bodied, have become common currency. The field has expanded dramatically, through associations such as the Society for Disability Studies (1982) and a slew of publications, including *Disability Studies Quarterly* (1980) and the *Journal of Literary and Cultural Disability Studies* (2007).

Comics scholars have highlighted how graphic narrative's unique image-text strategies present important opportunities for complex portraits of the disabled, a largely neglected population, especially in life writing (El Refaie 2012a; Squier 2008). Thomas Couser, for example, lauds the graphic memoir about illness/disability (or somatography) as an always-"embodied" text, calling it an "inherently sensuous, and thus somatic, medium" (2018, 353), in that it presents a visual-verbal double portrait of the memoirist, allowing them "greater control over self-image" (349). He persuasively faults much contemporary graphic narrative about illness and disability for the "fail[ure] to realize the potential of the medium" (361) through an overly staid "sanitation" of symptoms and compromised bodily states and, less convincingly, a "self-infantilization" of a visually abstracted narrating self, particularly in the case of animal avatars. "To put it simply," he concludes, "I find disabled characters more engaging and empathetic when drawn as fully human, their bodies rendered realistically" (372).

Couser's hyper-"realist" fixation (in discussing a medium that has long trafficked in talking animals, cosmic battles between demigod-like beings, and fantasy writ large) provides a useful representational limit to push against. Its overly narrow view helps by contrast in making a case for how comics does and does not work as a graphic language, for how a memoir like Art Spiegelman's *Maus* (1991) can earn critical accolades (including a special Pulitzer Prize) and become a perennial best seller even as it depicts the Holocaust through the highly stylized device of Jews as mice and Germans as cats. For Couser, the downplaying of that "realism" means much more than a simple surface resemblance to one's subject, as attested to by, among others, the graphic memoirist Allie Brosh, who in her devastating web series-turned-book about her depression, *Hyperbole and a Half* (2013), utilizes a ridiculous cartoony anthropomorphic fish as an avatar. As she told an interviewer, "It was simple and that's really what I'm like on the inside. That picture is *me*, more me than I am" (quoted in Chute 2017, 239; emphasis in original).

Mainstream representations of the disabled appear from nearly the beginning of the superhero genre. Most early depictions marked physical difference as villainy; Jerry Siegel and Joe Schuster made Superman's first archnemesis, the Ultrahumanite, a wheelchair user in 1939 (Alaniz 2014; Smith and Alaniz 2019). The Golden Age featured few disabled heroes, including the partially blind Dr. Mid-Nite (created by Charles Reizenstein and Stanley Josephs Aschmeier in 1941) and the Daredevil, who under creator Jack Binder debuted as mute in 1941 but was quickly rebooted as able-bodied by Jack Cole that same year. Such inconsistent portrayals of disability in superhero serials would continue into the Silver Age and beyond, most famously in the case of the sometimes-deaf Hawkeye/Clint Barton (Smith and Alaniz 2019).

Disability as a fully fledged constituent of superhero identity was first systematically worked into the genre only during the so-called Marvel Silver Age in the early 1960s, through figures such as Stan Lee and Jack Kirby's the Thing / Ben Grimm (1961, disfigured), Thor / Donald Blake (1962, lame), and the X-Men (1963, various disabilities) and Lee and Bill Everett's Daredevil / Matt Murdock (1964, blind; Alaniz 2014). The most complex and important disabled superhero remains a DC character, Oracle / Barbara Gordon, who became a paraplegic after a violent shooting and assault at the hands of the Joker in the Alan Moore / Brian Bolland graphic novel *A Killing Joke* (1988). DC's 2011 "retconning" of Gordon into the able-bodied Batgirl after two decades as a wheelchair user proved a profoundly divisive event for fandom (Alaniz 2016). The first Black female superheroine with a disability, Marvel's Misty Knight, appeared in 1975, though she remained a supporting character for decades, and only recently have there been talks of her appearing in her own self-titled publication.

Other genres, such as horror (see "Jenifer" by Rick Jones and Berni Wrightson in *Creepy* #63, July 1974), war (e.g., Robert Kanigher and Joe Kubert's the Unknown Soldier debuted in *Our Army at War* #168, June 1966), and romance (e.g., "Don't Pity Me—Love Me!" by an unknown writer and artist Ric Estrada in *Falling in Love* #108, July 1969) also represented the disabled in the twentieth century, though mostly in keeping with the medical model, or else depicted them as objects of pity, villainy, and monstrosity. As seen in the evolution of superheroes, times were changing.

The rise of comix brought new possibilities, and in fact through comix, disability played a central role in the development of graphic narrative for adults. Justin Green's landmark *Binky Brown Meets the Holy Virgin Mary* (1972), on his childhood experience with obsessive-compulsive disorder (OCD), launched the autobiography in the medium. Hillary Chute calls this tremendously influential forty-four-page epic of personal humiliation and religious angst the "ur-text of comics illness and disability narratives" (2017, 249), and its innovations forever altered perceptions of graphic narrative's potential for self-expression, even on the most recondite subject matter. In an afterword to the 2009 reprint of *Binky Brown*, Green himself acknowledged how the word/picture "double-trackedness" of comics uncannily correlated to the "double vision" workings of his disorder, whereby a judgmental inner commentary accompanied his uncontrolled compulsions. Green's work is an undeniably "embodied text," in Couser's terms, though its baroque, surreal, and for some excessive self-fashionings (replete with phallic imagery, grotesque figures, and parodies of Catholic iconography) shatter any orthodox notion of "realism" to convey the author's agonized mental state.

Key comics works foregrounding the social, "dysappearance" model of the disability/illness experience (El Refaie 2012a, 61) include Richard and Renee Jensen's underground comix *Amputee Love* (1975); Al Davison's *The Spiral Cage* ([1988] 2003), on spina bifida; Harvey Pekar and Joyce Brabner's *Our Cancer Year* (1994); Keiko Tobe's manga memoir *With the Light: Raising an Autistic Child* (2000, translation 2007); David B.'s *Epileptic* (2000, translation 2003); Alison Bechdel's *Fun Home* (2006), on OCD; Ellen Forney's *Marbles: Mania, Depression, Michelangelo, and Me: A Graphic Memoir* (2012), on bipolar disorder; E. T. Russian's *The Ring of Fire Anthology* (2014), on various disabilities; John Porcellino's *The Hospital Suite* (2014), on OCD; Peter Dunlap-Shohl's *My Degeneration: My Journey through Parkinsons* (2015); Emil Ferris's *My Favorite Thing Is Monsters* (2017), on deformity, depression, cancer, and "monstrosity"; the Russian graphic novel *I Am an Elephant* (2017), illustrated by Lena Uzhinova, on writer Vladimir Rudak's paraplegia; and Georgia Webber's *Dumb* (2018), on mutism.

Though not often discussed as a disability narrative, Chris Ware's multiformat graphic novel *Building Stories* (2012) breaks some intriguing new ground in its representation of an unnamed amputee protagonist. Margaret Fink Berman argues that Ware, through doggedly portraying the reveries, repetitive actions, "empty" moments, and humdrum routines of his heroine's everyday life, advances her "idiosyncratic belonging," whereby she "lives with her disability not as a member of a fixed category (never do we hear her self-identify as any type of person because of her leg), but as one whose movements across social and physical space are sometimes shaped by her body's variation and the technologies that she uses" (2010, 195). *Building Stories* thus presents the "realism" Couser demands of somatography while refusing to exoticize or other the disabled figure—on the contrary, Ware's approach if anything plays up what we might call the banality of disability. From highly charged narrative prosthesis of maleficence or compassion to nearly unmarked, at times invisible component of the everyday, disability in comics has traveled a considerable distance over the medium's development.

The second decade of the twenty-first century has seen the rise of graphic medicine, a movement of artists, scholars, and health-care workers to produce illness and disability narratives in what they consider an accessible comics form. They have held an annual conference since 2010 and published a number of books. Cripping the Con at the University of Syracuse (launched 2013) serves as a colorful annual nexus of disability studies scholars, activists, and comics fandom. Disabled artists produce diverse work online in webcomics series such as Matt and Kay Daigle's *That Deaf Guy* (2010) and Jessica and Lianna Oddi's *The Disabled Life* (2016). In the small press arena, Portland, Oregon, artists Sabine Rear (the "blind illustratrix") and Alecia Gatlin, who chronicles her experience with rheumatoid arthritis, as well as the Seattle comics collective the Hand (composed of disabled, queer, and persons of color [POC]) illustrate the vibrancy of the US scene. Just as disability rights movements changed the culture in the final decades of the twentieth century, then, so has the representation of disability shifted the landscape of comics, composing a significant portion of contemporary graphic narrative production.

17

Diversity

Frederick Luis Aldama

Everywhere we turn today, we see *diversity* in all iterations of comic book story worlds. People of color and women are behind and in front of the camera lens in many of today's wildly popular comic book films and TV shows. Netflix brought on African American music journalist and TV writer Cheo Hodari Coker to bring Luke Cage onto our smaller screens. Patty Jenkins gave a feminist touch to *Wonder Woman*. Ryan Coogler's *Black Panther* showed the world how hungry audiences are for a vibrant and vibrant and varied Black superhero cast. Maori director Taika Waititi centered *Thor: Ragnarok* on a nonbinary superhero and a postcolonial imaginary. With Australasian James Wan directing Indigenous (Polynesian and Pawnee) actor Jason Momoa as Aquaman, questions of surveillance of racial identities are put front and center. Diversity in mainstream and indie in-print comics is making tremendous headway too. From fully realized gay characters like Kevin Keller in the Archie Comics universe and Anishinabe-Métis Elizabeth LaPensée's Indigenous women in *Deer Woman*, to life for Arabic and West African French Parisians in the work of Caza (Philippe Cazaumayou) and Farid Boudjellal and Inoue Takehiko's exploration of differently abled Japanese athletes in *REAL* (2008–present), no stone is left unturned. Indeed, we can confidently say that when it comes to diversity in world comics production (mainstream, independent, and alternative), we are seeing a renaissance.

The drawn-word shaping devices used to build story worlds (fictional and nonfictional) have become a significant narrative tool for conveying complex experiences related to gender, race, sexuality, and differently abled subjectivities. While the degree of discrimination, exploitation, and oppression of intersectionally diverse groups differs in time (history) and place (geographic region), this has been and remains one of the central destructive forces ripping our social tissue apart across the globe. Diversity comic book creators and readers have been an important form of resistance to this history. A lay of the diversity comics landscape in terms of creation (authors/artists) and cocreation (readers and scholars) allows for an investigation of the diversity work of comics.

We might not think of animals as part of this diversity impulse, but they are and have been in the comics world since time immemorial. I think less here of Chuck Jones (*Looney Tunes*), Charles Schultz (*Peanuts*), Carl Barker (*Donald Duck*), or Walt Kelly (*Pogo*) and more so of the work of those like Brian K. Vaughan and Niko Henrichon with *Pride of Baghdad* (2006) or Vaughan (writer) and Fiona Staples (artist) with *Saga* (2012–present). In these latter story worlds, we see how careful line work and intricate story lines convey complex interactions, actions, and interior states of mind of animals that *make* new our perception of vulnerable populations—including animals—during times of war such as the US invasion of Iraq; in, for instance, *Saga*'s creation of talking cats and alligator women, they can also demand that readers reconceptualize hybrid subjectivities—and with this demand that we expand civil rights to mixed (and mixed-race) ontologies.

There is a rich and growing body of scholarship that attends to the ways that speciesism and diversity intersect. For instance, in "Animal Subjects of the Graphic Novels," Michael Chaney identifies how Gene Luen

Yang's comic *American Born Chinese* "performs the animal" (2017, 131) to destabilize a long history of mainstream iconography that stereotypes Asian Americans as only anthropomorphic buffoons. As Chaney states, "Yang's monkey functions, as does the African trickster, to destabilize boundaries between cosmic orders of being" (2017, 138). Several chapters included in David Herman's *Animal Comics* shed light on how ideologies of race, ethnicity, and sexuality reinscribe speciesism across cultures: the favoring of humans over animals. In Michael Chaney's essay "The Saga of the Animal as Visual Metaphor for Mixed-Race Identity in Comics," he identifies how *Saga* deploys visuals such as "sight gags" and "visual turnabouts" to create a resistant "animal aesthetic" that at once points to speciesism and its "established orders of expectations" *and* "violates" this order of things (2017, 115). Indeed, here and elsewhere, we see scholarship that attends to the unique ways that a visual geometrizing of story asks us to *read* race in and through a critically *performed* animality as well as open new ways of seeing, feeling, and thinking about race, sexuality, gender, differently abled, and species generally.

Of course, in the Indigenous comics tradition, anthropomorphized story worlds have been an important way of passing on ancestral histories and traditions to new generations—and this is especially important when oral and written records have been lost through centuries of genocide. Here I think of the twenty-one comic book vignettes that make up Matt Dembicki's edited *Trickster: Native American Tales* (2010), where we meet richly characterized tricksters such as coyotes, ravens, rabbits, raccoons, wolfs, and the like. These creators, who hail from Cherokee, Abenaki, Ioway/Otoe, Choctaw, and many other nations, share their particularized reconstructions of histories, cultures, and storytelling traditions. Of course, that Indigenous creators

have used anthropomorphic characters to populate story worlds cuts another way. There is a long history of "animalizing" people of color, women, and LGBTQ+ subjectivities. When such creators choose to "perform animality" in constructing their story worlds, it is a form of radical reinsertion that calls attention to the history of being denigrated.

The sky is the limit, of course, when it comes to storytelling envelopes for diversity comics creators, and with this also comes a revitalizing of conventional storytelling formats. We see, for instance, in Michael Nicoll Yahgulanaas's *Red: A Haida Manga* (2009) the insertion into the Japanese manga panel layout, but in ways that *indigenize* it through the use of the Haida painterly arts—and to call attention to the displacement of Haida peoples from their homeland, Haida Gwaii in British Columbia. We see this also with Latinx comic book creators who choose to revitalize pre-Columbian histories. I think, too, of Daniel Parada's *Zotz: Serpent and Shield* as well as the Taino-set story worlds produced and created by the Puerto Rican collective Editorial El Antillano.

The complex ways that creators of comics can use visuals (dominant) and verbal elements to create complex identities and enrich understanding of cultural and historical experiences are happening also in the area of disability. With Judy and Paul Karasik's alphabetic (large sections that are text only) and graphic memoir, *The Ride Together* (2003), we see the use of a conventional panel layout with deliberately messy line work to convey the impossibility of trying to contain life while growing up with their older sibling, David; along the way, not only do they deeply humanize those like David on the autism spectrum, but readers learn of his wondrous emotive and cognitive processes. Indeed, creators from around the globe are putting the experiences of the differently abled on the map in important ways. In Japan, for instance, we have the important interventions of

Inoue Takehiko with his ongoing manga series *REAL* (2008), which puts a spotlight on wheelchair basketball, and with this, his manga transforms and complicates a tradition of manga that naturalizes able-bodiedness.

Until relatively recently, comic books have been dominated by male creators building story worlds that have either erased completely the presence of women, gay, lesbian, and transgender peoples that make up the world or re-created such "diversity" subjectivities in ways that uphold a patriarchal, straight male status quo. This is changing—and radically so. We see this in the alternative comics world with creators like Roberta Gregory (*Bitchy Bitch*), Lynda Barry (*One Hundred! Demons!*), Alison Bechdel (*Fun Home*), and Katie Skelly (*My Lesbian Vampire*), among many others. In countries like Japan, the gender-bending tradition of shojo manga (Japanese girls' comics) and "Boys Love" stories have matured into Eisner Award–winning comics like Gengoroh Tagame's *My Brother's Husband* (2014–17) and Mikiyo Tsuda's *The Day of Revolution*; the latter, for instance, follows teenager Kei Yoshikawa, who has grown up as a "boy" who, after learning that they are chromosomally a "girl," returns to school in a girls' uniform and with the new name Megumi; as such, they learn what it means to be objectified and denigrated as a female (see also Mark McLelland and Romit Dasgupta's *Genders, Transgenders and Sexualities in Japan*; J. Hall 2012).

US superhero comics have also been putting queer and gender identities front and center. I think of not only A-listers like Thor being given a gender makeover when Jane Foster takes up the Mjolnir in *Thor: The Goddess of Thunder* #1 (2015) but also Latinx lesbian writer Gabby Rivera, who fleshed out a queer Latinx America Chavez (*America*, 2017–18). Marvel had been actively creating queer superheroes, especially in its parallel Earth universe story lines. And of course, as carefully excavated by queer comics scholar Ramzi Fawaz, the

introduction in 1963 of *The Uncanny X-Men* and especially as experienced in its more complex 1975 relaunch functioned as a metaphor for those otherwise swept to the gender, sexual, social, and ethnoracial margins (see also Darowski 2014). In the 1990s with the DC-bankrolled, all-African-American-run Milestone Comics, we saw the appearance of sophisticated Afrolatinx queer superheroes like Carlos Quinones Jr. as Fade, created by gay Latinx writers like Xeric Award–winning Ivan Velez Jr. DC has also introduced important queer intersectional superheroes, including Latinx Miguel "Bunker" Barragan, Batwoman, Green Lantern (Earth-2), and Catwoman, who has been created and re-created variously as white, Latina, and African American.

Notably, food has also functioned as a topic of radical insertion and revision. Again, when ethnoracial subjectivities have been traditionally objectified as *only bodies*, when creators such as John Layman and African American Rob Guillory (art) create the Asian American cibopath in their series *Chew* (2009–16), they self-reflexively use mainstream ethnoracial stereotypes (movies to cookbooks) to remind readers that food has functioned as a marker to delimit and delegitimize Asian American identities. When Tony Chu solves murders by tasting food (including bodies), the comic calls attention to how food has been used as part of the Asian threat narrative to police identity boundaries and uphold the purity of whiteness.

These are but a few of the massive numbers of comics created and being created that seek to put diversity in the limelight—and to complicate its representation of identities and experiences. We are also witnessing a huge explosion of comics scholarship that enriches our understanding of the great array of diversity comics and their story worlds. There is a growing body of scholarship on women creators in underground, alternative, and mainstream comics (superhero and manga).

With *Cartooning for Suffrage* (1994), Alice Sheppard digs deep into the cartoon strip archives (over two hundred) to re-create a history of early twentieth-century pro-suffrage women creators and activists. Trina Robbins's *From Girls to Grrrlz* (1999) reminds us that at one time in comics history, mainstream comics created for girl readers outsold all other comics but stumbled because of an increasingly male-dominated industry. Lillian S. Robinson's *Wonder Women: Feminisms and Superheroes* (2004) provides a thoroughgoing history of the way women in superhero comics and the various women's movements are intimately bound together. In *Straight from the Heart: Gender, Intimacy, and the Cultural Production of Shōjo Manga* (2011), Jennifer S. Prough's ethnographic research leads her to identify how communities of shojo manga (romance stories aimed at girls five to eighteen years old) are at once a capitalist consumptive practice *and* a clearing of a space for the articulation of new possibilities for gendered roles and relationships. And in *Graphic Women: Life Narrative and Contemporary Comics* (2010), Hillary Chute excavates a genealogy of feminist women cartoonists such as Aline Kominsky-Crumb and Trina Robbins to Gloeckner, Barry, and Bechdel. These and other women cartoonists use the shaping devices of comics to etch onto the page (the comics corpus) the "unspeakability, invisibility, and inaudibility" (Chute 2010, 3) of women's subjectivities and experiences.

Excavating sexuality in comics, in *The New Mutants* (2016), Ramzi Fawaz creates an analytical scaffold built from queer theory, woman of color feminism, media studies, psychoanalysis, and political economy to dig into mainstream comics like *Superman, Justice League of America, The Fantastic Four*, and especially *The X-Men*. Fawaz seeks to enrich understanding of how mainstream comics perpetuate stereotypes of nonnormative subjects as Other as well as how queer readers and

readers of color along with women's and gay liberation movements transformed comics story world building, or what he calls a "comic book cosmopolitics" (2016, 15). In Ramzi Fawaz and Darieck Scott's editing of a special issue of *American Literature* titled *Queer about Comics* (2018), we see the systematic gathering together of original scholarship that analyzes the important presence of queer sexuality and desire in comics; how queer comics have been an important shaper of the evolution of comics *and* how queer comics demand that we reframe and review the comics, literary, visual, and cultural studies disciplines.

There's also significant scholarship that excavates and explores race and intersectional identities in comics. With the publication in 2015 of *Black Women in Sequence: Re-inking Comics, Graphic Novels, and Anime*, Deborah Elizabeth Whaley presents the first scholarly study that center-stages African American women represented in and creators of comics (print, pixelated, televisual, and filmic). Whaley takes us on a journey that includes Eartha Kitt's Catwoman in the 1960s *Batman* TV series; the first African American comic book superhero, Butterfly; and the more contemporary Monica Rambeau to reveal how "women of African descent are semiotic referents for social relations and discourses about national and international politics, gender, race, and sexualities" (8). With *"How Come Boys Get to Keep Their Noses?": Women and Jewish American Identity in Contemporary Graphic Memoirs* (2016), Tahneer Oksman studies the complex ways that Jewish women creators such as Aline Kominsky-Crumb, Miriam Libicki, and Leanne Finck among many others use the graphic memoir form to express *and* self-referentially perform racial, ethnic, and gendered identity experiences. In *The Hernandez Brothers* (2017), Enrique García analyzes Jaime and Gilbert Hernandez's comics as ushering in a new era (post–Chicano movement) of self-representation that makes natural all variety of ways Latinxs exist: politicized and nonpoliticized, bilingual and monolingual, dark and light skinned, and across all geographies of the Americas. There are other scholarly excavations that seek to complicate erstwhile straight, white, and male superhero comics histories. In *Superwomen* (2016), Carolyn Cocca identifies how significant female superheroes have been in the shaping of mainstream superhero comics. In my book *Latinx Superheroes in Mainstream Comics* (2017) and like-titled film (2018), I build on and complicate work done in *Your Brain on Latino Comics* (2009). With a focus on excavating the presence of Latinx superheroes in mainstream comics (including print, filmic, and televisual means), I attend to how geometrizing devices—for instance, mise-en-page and layout in comics; editing, casting, and lensing in films; and voice acting in animation—can distill and reconstruct *Latinidad* in simplistic *or* complex ways. They can also erase entirely Latinx origin texts and characters, such as with Christopher Nolan's whitewashing of the Latinx Bane by casting Tom Hardy to play the role in *The Dark Knight Rises* (2012).

I think also of the scholarship published in anthologies such as *Multicultural Comics* (2010) and my coedited *Graphic Borders* (Aldama and González 2016) as well as Carolene Ayaka and Ian Hagues's *Representing Multiculturalism in Comics and Graphic Novels* (2018). For instance, in Sheena Howard and Ronald L. Jackson's *Black Comics: Politics of Race and Representation* (2013) and in Frances Gateward and John Jennings's *Blacker the Ink* (2016), we see all variety of scholarship that seeks to solidify a multilayered (creators, publishers, readers), interdisciplinary Black comics studies field. A. David Lewis and Martin Lund's edited *Muslim Superheroes: Comics, Islam, and Representation* (2017) identifies several of the ways that Muslims have been re-created in superhero comics: (1) as characters "to entertain with reference to the Orientalist exotic"; (2) as superheroes re-created in an "American template to provide role models for youth in the Muslim world"; (3) as superheroes to "critique inequalities in Muslim majority countries"; and (4) as superheroes that re-create Islam as a threat to the West (7).

Scholarship on disability in comics is also a rapidly growing field. We see the rich array of approaches and primary texts analyzed in José Alaniz's *Death, Disability, and the Superhero: The Silver Age and Beyond* (2014) as well as the scholarship collected in *Disability in Comic Books and Graphic Narratives* (Foss, Gray, and Whalen 2016). For instance, in their introduction to the latter, Chris Foss, Jonathan W. Gray, and Zach Whalen identify how the "interoperation of verbal and visual modalities . . . and emotive iconography" in comics can uniquely convey experiences of disability, trauma, and illness. Foss, Gray, and Whalen illustrate the form's potentialities through their close reading of how swirling frames in, for instance, *The Enchanted Prince* not only convey but also celebrate neurodiverse subjectivities. In Alaniz's work, we also see the analysis of how the visuals and verbal elements can and do push against and subvert stereotypical misrepresentations of disability in ways that vitally convey the complex lives of those with nonnormative physical, emotive, cognitive abilities.

This is but a brief sampling of the rich array of scholarship that seeks to dig into nonnormative archives to trace and analyze normative (able-bodied, white, male) comic book traditions. Moreover, the texts enrich our understanding of how using the visual (dominant) and verbal techniques give shape to protagonists of color and their experiences in vitally complex ways. One way or another, today's "diversity" comics scholarship seeks to clear a space for creating new possibilities of representing and embracing nonnormative subjectivities and experiences—and to set the record straight (and with it the mainstream imaginary) concerning problematic stereotypes and attitudes toward women, people of color, LGBTQ+ peoples, and those differently abled, among others.

In different ways, the previously mentioned scholarship touches on the importance of readers—diversity readers. It might come in the shape of a confessional such as what it meant to be a woman reading male-centric comixs or as a queer Brown or Black scholar reading superhero comics. It might be in the form of a systematic tracing of the significant impact on the industry by diversity comic readers. It might be in a Blatinx tween cosplaying Shuri at a Comic-Con, a Nerdino Expo, or a Black & Brown Comix Art Festival. No matter the approach, diversity fans, cosplayers, and readers of comics play an important role in the shaping of a diversity comics field (see also Danziger-Russell 2012; Nicholson 2017).

Diversity readers of comics have always been around actively supporting comics—and diversity comics especially. Contemporarily, more than ever the industry is paying attention to these shifts. As far as superhero comics go, in 2014, *Ms. Marvel* was Marvel's top digital seller and *Thor: The Goddess of Thunder* outsold the male-Thor comic by leaps and bounds. Of course, there will always be those upset by diversity comics and their readers. There was the recent controversy over the reasons for canceling titles such as *Gwenpool, Luke Cage, Iceman, Generation X*, and *America* that featured diversity characters and writers. While some fans (usually white and male) identified this as the outcome of poor sales, the reality tells a different story. These comics did well, selling upward of two hundred thousand copies, but of course they will never sell as well as the A-listers like *Batman, Spider-Man, The X-Men, Justice League of America*, or *The Avengers*. Moreover, there is a rise in the number of diversity readers who wait for the trade paperbacks. With the huge sales of the trade paperbacks of *Saga*, *Paper Girls*, and *Monstress*—many making it onto the coveted *New York Times* best-seller list—the single-issue comics sales as a measure of success is quickly becoming a thing of the past.

Indeed, I think of the tremendous momentum to diversify the comics industry—and not just in their very varied creative iterations (film, TV, web, print). Since 2014, when Sheena Howard was the first African American woman to win an Eisner, diversity has become somewhat more consistently recognized, and across all the award categories. The 2018 Eisner Awards ceremony was hailed by the mainstream press as the first Eisner Awards to fully recognize diversity in the comic book arts and industry. More awards than ever were given to women of color creators, including Marjorie Liu and Sana Takeda for *Monstress*, along with Emil Ferris for *My Favorite Thing Is Monsters*, Jillian Tamaki for *Boundless*, Taneka Stotts for *Elements*, and Roxane Gay and Alitha E. Martinez (with Ta-Nehisi Coates) for *Black Panther: World of Wakanda*. *Latinx Superheroes in Mainstream Comics* and John Jennings with Damian Duffy won for their adaptation of Octavia Butler's *Kindred*. Eisner Awards are a mirror in the road to the radical shifts that have been taking place in deep time to diversify comics around the world. Of course, gatekeeping continues, including the hate and vitriol of the alt-right-motored Comicsgate. With eyes wide open, diversity scholars and creators of color remain vigilant in our quest to create willfully realized intersectional comic book story worlds for the vital growth of world comics today and tomorrow.

18

Documentary

Christopher Spaide

"Documentary comics"? That phrase would have struck the earliest comics readers as a category error or an improbable pairing—the nonfiction art of *documentary*, a term developed by film critics, welded to *comics*, a medium popularly associated with the strange and outlandish. Even today, we might hear a dare muffled inside "documentary comics," as it contests the truth-telling claims of modern media (photography, sound recording, film, video) and finds actuality present instead within comics, those hybrid visual-verbal documents. But today's readers might find nothing questionable in the phrase "documentary comics." If they know Art Spiegelman's *Maus: A Survivor's Tale* or Lauren Redniss's visual nonfiction, Ben Passmore's viral provocation *Your Black Friend*, or testimonial webcomics uploaded worldwide, they have found some facet of documentary comics today—a flourishing pluralist tradition exploiting, if not expanding, the full promise of the medium.

From its original use in the early nineteenth century to its meaning in courts today, the adjective *documentary* has designated legal evidence in the form of written or recorded documents (as opposed to, say, oral testimony or physical evidence). Only a century later would *documentary* harden from adjective to noun and take on its contemporary generic sense. The Scottish filmmaker John Grierson introduced the term in a film review credited only to "The Moviegoer"; the coinage slips in, almost an afterthought. Appraising Robert Flaherty's second feature film *Moana* (1926), Grierson casually noticed that "*Moana*, being a visual account of events in the daily life of a Polynesian youth, has documentary value"—the value of documentary evidence, of recording a way of life, likely unfamiliar to Western audiences, in material, rewatchable form (1926). (Covertly, Grierson was also adapting a French term: *documentaire*, or travelogue.) In his 1933 essay "The Documentary Producer," Grierson glossed the "new art" of documentary (now a stand-alone noun) as "the creative treatment of actuality" (1933). Grierson's pithy phrase at once makes the boldest claims for documentary's material—nothing short of "actuality," in the form of evidence selected, presented, made visible—and acknowledges that documentary should not be mistaken for unmediated "actuality" itself. The documentarian, an agent not simply reportorial but "creative," presents actuality through a removed "treatment," a richly ambiguous word that suggests affective behavior, interpersonal care, aesthetic handling, and even a director's condensed summary of a film-worthy subject. Grierson's definition makes room for quasi-anthropological, furtively fictionalized work, including *Moana* and Flaherty's better-known *Nanook of the North* (1922), which captures several weeks in the life of an Inuk hunter and his family (with several sequences of that "life" artfully staged). Today, the term *documentary* has widened out to encompass many kinds of nonfiction films; indeed, for many viewers, studios, distributors, and prize-giving institutions, "documentary" and "nonfiction" may effectively be synonymous.

In its loosest application to comics, we might take *documentary* to border, even include, such nonfiction genres as memoir, biography, history, journalism, editorial, essay, op-ed, sex-ed, art and architecture criticism, educational comics, and even food writing. Whether we stretch out *documentary* that far or reserve the term for work that presents, frames, and manipulates evidence, the phrase *documentary comics* carries an apparent contradiction, best formulated as a question. How can comics—so artificial, so distantly removed from what it represents, the unmistakable product of paper and ink and pixels, of labor and cramped hands and exhausted minds—ever document "actuality"?

Curiosity, even cynicism, about comics' truth-telling capacity has gravitated toward its visual component: the image and its evident drawnness. What truth, what evidence, can drawing convey, especially when compared to photography and film, whose verisimilitude goes without question? As Hillary Chute observes, our standard usages betray tacit valuations: we say that we "take" a photograph, whereas we "make" a mark or a drawing (Chute 2016). Photography, in the conventional view, is an art of repository, seizing what's there in actuality for the taking (photons, stances, slices of reality); drawing is an act of making, *poesis*, imitating and supplementing "actuality." Yet we should be wary of the idea that photography transparently looks onto truth—like drawing, photography is a medium that is selective, perspectival, flattened, framed—and equally wary of the supposition that drawing, a creative act driven by one person's hand, impulse, and direction, has no purchase on actuality. If Flaherty's partly staged work broadens out our understanding of documentary's "creative treatment of reality," so should *The Sinking of the Lusitania* (1918), the earliest surviving animated documentary film, directed by the cartoonist Winsor McCay. Intertitles, spliced between footage of animators at work, explain the film's development and purpose: "Winsor McCay, originator and inventor of Animated Cartoons, decides to draw a historical record of the crime that shocked Humanity." "From here on," another intertitle announces, "you are looking at the first record of the sinking of the Lusitania" (1918). In McCay's time, the phrase "to draw a historical record" was not a misusage but a testament to drawing's

reach. In a manner undeniably stylized yet committed to the accuracies of sequence and scale, McCay's animation serves as an after-the-fact record for a historical event, lending itself (as "the first record" produced) to the stock of available actuality.

Comics' truth-telling capacity, then, rests on the presence and materiality of images—images framed within panels, placed in sequence, arranged on the page, collected and bound. But documentary comics works communicate through both images and words, two nonsynchronous registers of narrative, meeting and diverging, in parallel and all knotted up. It might seem useful to imagine a spectrum that orders documentary comics according to the forms of evidence they foreground, visual or verbal. Some documentary works grip us chiefly with images, rendered in meticulous detail or visceral force. Other works persuade us chiefly with words, aspiring to the breadth and depth of reportorial prose, meticulously transcribing dialogue, arranging data drawn from the archive or gathered in the field. At one extreme, we could plant Joe Sacco's twenty-four-foot-long wordless panorama *The Great War* (2013), which flaunts his vast visual scope while relinquishing the journalistic tools honed in his comics on crises in Palestine, Bosnia, and elsewhere. At another extreme, we could set certain pages by the writer-artist Lauren Redniss. *Century Girl* (2006), a biography of Ziegfeld Follies star Doris Eaton Travis; *Radioactive: Marie & Pierre Curie: A Tale of Love and Fallout* (2010); the essays on the weather collected in *Thunder & Lightning* (2015): all three of Redniss's books rival the best prose nonfiction for their immersion in labyrinthine archives, complete with extensive endnotes. At times, Redniss appears to forgo images entirely, crowding pages with carefully sourced prose.

This taxonomic exercise could clarify comics' extreme cases, but it fails to account for the myriad ways word and image can interact, counteract, or refuse to meet: the resulting consonances and dissonances are indispensable to these mixed-media documentaries. In Sacco's work, a single text box can shift the center of gravity of even the most compulsively detailed, attention-consuming image; he introduces text, variously, as caption, indication of time or location, explication, correction, dialogue, narration, lyric outburst, and sound effect. And Redniss's prose reacts one way with photographs, diagrams, and maps excerpted from the archive, another way with images she creates with antiquated printmaking techniques, and yet another way with nonrepresentational multimedia fantasia. Even unillustrated text, Redniss's books show, can be arrestingly visual. If one page of text comes in unshowy black on white, evenly spaced, margins justified, the next might be printed in the manner of concrete poetry, yet another visual element to be stylized and seen afresh.

Whether the evidence on display is verbal, visual, or some alchemy of the two, documentary comics make imaginative, vigilant use of a central element of comics: the panel. In one cool provocation among many in *Understanding Comics*, Scott McCloud proposes that (I re-create his ebullient typography) "THE PANEL *ITSELF*" may be "OVERLOOKED AS COMICS' MOST IMPORTANT *ICON*," even as its lacks both the "*FIXED OR ABSOLUTE MEANING*" of linguistic icons and the "*FLUID* AND *MALLEABLE*" meaning of pictures. The panel's meaning, McCloud suggests, is a function of time and space, dimensions the panel not only divides and measures but warps and relativizes, conflates and destroys; further, each panel asks us to consider both content (what's inside the lines) and context (what's outside it—further panels, layouts, pages, serials; McCloud 1993). In documentary comics, the mere act of paneling signals that this moment, this setting, is worth registering, remembering, reinscribing. In sequence, multiple panels can continuously reframe a subject, asking readers to consider a multifaceted subject from composite, shifting perspectives.

Temporalities jostle and space contracts and constricts in *Hostage* (2017), by the Canadian cartoonist Guy Delisle, best known for his first-person comics travelogues in China, North Korea, Burma, and Jerusalem. *Hostage* adapts the testimony of Christophe André, who, two decades earlier, then a French nonprofit organization (NGO) administrator working in the Caucasus region, was kidnapped by armed men; after three months in solitary confinement, he managed to escape. Delisle measures André's confinement according to calendrical time and daily activities as well as subjective paces—agonized heartbeats, pieced-together realizations, frantic second-guesses. *Hostage* maps, as best as a secondhand re-creation can, the repurposed bedrooms and basements where André was confined, but it also travels back to a France fashioned from André's memory and reverie. Whimsically, *Hostage* re-creates even the legendary battles of European military history, which André mentally reenacts to pass the time, situating his solitary condition within world-historical arcs.

Over time, in comics as in film, *documentary* may stretch out into an increasingly capacious term that no longer specifies a single genre, canon, or braid of intertwining traditions. Instead, we may think of *documentary* as a function—found across genres, throughout nonfiction and even in fiction, perhaps latent in any comics work—that looks for sources within textual archives or out in the field, turns to photographs for inspiration or reference, reproduces preexisting documents, collages drawing and text with other media, and preserves ephemera otherwise forgotten or lost. Innumerable comics that we would hesitate to call "documentaries," in whole or in part, nevertheless perform documentary work.

Take Richard McGuire's *Here* (2014), "the story of the corner of a room." *Here* takes to an extreme one hallmark of recent documentary comics: audacious traversal across time, juxtaposing unlike moments in adjacent panels, vaulting over years (or eras) in the gutters in between. Keeping his visual perspective absolutely fixed on that "corner of a room" (or, before and after the room existed, where the corner would be), McGuire draws a staggeringly expansive history of the town of Perth Amboy, New Jersey. Looking back, he draws famous neighbors (Benjamin Franklin's son), Native Americans in precolonial times, and even the Cretaceous period, with a triptych of enigmatic washes representing 3,000,500,000 BCE. On nearby pages, McGuire speculatively sketches the irradiated postapocalypse of 2313 CE, then the mutated, carnivalesque flora and fauna of 22,175 CE. Despite its shuffled sequence and idiosyncratically brazen scope, *Here* orbits a fictional, human core: for some readers, it may cohere as a twentieth-century family saga; for readers familiar with McGuire's life, *Here* works as autobiography, told through the still-recoverable history of his own family's home. Many pinnacles of documentary comics are works we tend to read as autobiography, works that filter world history through family history, focalizing massive political movements through the lens of personal witness. Recent studies of comics, disaster, and war have found the inextricability of documentary and autobiography, of historical scales and personal trauma, in works as diverse as Keiji Nakazawa's *I Saw It* (1972), an "atomic bomb manga"; Art Spiegelman's *Maus: A Survivor's Tale* (1980–91) and *In the Shadow of No Towers* (2004), about his father's experiences during the Holocaust and his own following the attacks of September 11, respectively; and Marjane Satrapi's *Persepolis* (2000 [2004]), a memoir of an Iranian childhood and young adulthood in the aftermath of the Islamic revolution (Chute 2008; Chute 2016; Earle 2017; Prorokova and Tal 2018).

If some documentary comics works aspire to record history at every scale (lived memory, the *longue durée*, the geological epoch), other works invest close, provisional attention to today, this moment, the improvisatory impulse—comics as journal, diary, news update, blog. Or a sketchbook: Gary Panter's *Satiro-plastic* is a facsimile of a "travel companion book" kept from December 1999 to November 2001, flipped through and filled in at random, without regard to chronology. Sightseeing in Oaxaca abuts views from Florida porches; doodles venting the spite and tedium of air travel ("DELAYED FLIGHTMARE," "REPULSIVE FOOD IN THE FRIENDLY SKIES") neighbor plein air sketches, drawn on a Brooklyn rooftop, of New York City on September 11—a day spent "watching in abject horror as the World Trade Center in Manhattan was attacked and pitifully and incomprehensibly disintegrated before our burning eyes, drawing" (Panter 2005). Panter's sketchbook suits his moment-by-moment attention—now lingering on cityscapes, now racing to depict evanescent smoke plumes; here confirming times in the margins, there posing unanswerable questions to himself. For other cartoonists, that level of attention is best accommodated by the web, by comics taking the form of linked pages, successive social-media posts, and livestreamed videos. Indeed, for reasons of audience and accessibility, for the near-instantaneity of publication and lack of impediments to reception, documentary work has proliferated on the web, a venue that combines the unprecedented range of digital technology with the oldest virtues of newspaper strips—seriality, brevity, transience, disposability (Mickwitz 2016).

Taken together, the most acclaimed documentary comics create an unlikely world atlas, an astonishingly diverse (if far from comprehensive) constellation of countries and cities, restricted neighborhoods and perilous borderlands: Auschwitz and Pyongyang, New Orleans during Hurricane Katrina and refugee camps on the Gaza Strip, Ground Zero and the Arctic Circle. One blossoming subgenre of documentary comics—what Nina Mickwitz has termed "the documentary of social concern"—records not (or not only) new places and moments but new subjectivities, lives yet to be fully written, drawn, and presented within panels (Mickwitz 2016). Even while carving out space for the particularity of memoir, these documentaries strive to faithfully present entire demographics and to render shared and systemic predicaments visible. Titles like *Epileptic* (David B.), *Pregnant Butch* (A. K. Summers), and *Your Black Friend* (Ben Passmore) all advertise an experience at once personal and representative. We might say their art documents bodies—queer bodies and racialized bodies and disabled bodies, some bodies rendered in photorealistic detail, other bodies clarified into icons—and allows cartoonists to remedy erasures, challenge caricatures, and represent their own lives as they could or should be seen.

Once we recognize the documentary function at play in more kinds of comics—indeed, once we realize that the documentary function is latent in any comics that materialize evidence on the page and screen—we can revisit once-familiar comics and better appreciate their truth-telling efforts. Alison Bechdel's *Fun Home* has been classified as many kinds of graphic narrative—the autobiography, *Künstlerroman*, coming-out story, or (to quote its subtitle) "family tragicomic"—but none entirely accounts for its obsession with a life's worth of documents or for its arduous reproductions from visual and textual archives. For every drawing of a person in *Fun Home*, Bechdel took a reference photo, herself her only model: in panels depicting her parents fighting, Bechdel posed as both her mother and her father; for a full classroom, Bechdel posed separately for each child. And every drawing of memory's physical, fragile detritus (handwritten and typed letters, diary entries, childhood drawings, adolescent doodles, and photographs, among other kinds of documents) was reproduced, redrawn, and retraced in Bechdel's own hand (Chute 2010). What better term for this—this care, this labor, this "creative treatment of actuality"—than *documentary*?

19

EC Comics

Nicholas Yanes

EC Comics was founded in 1944. While it lives on due to licensing deals and reprints, it largely ended by the mid-1950s as a publisher. Originally standing for Educational Comics before becoming Entertaining Comics, EC is known for groundbreaking horror and science fiction stories. EC also expanded into humor when it created *MAD Magazine* in 1952, a magazine that continues to be published as of 2020. However, EC's impact on the comics industry and its legacy are greater than just being another publisher with some still-relevant intellectual properties. In the world of comics studies, EC is often associated with issues of juvenile delinquency and censorship, while in the worlds of horror and humor, EC is often seen as a disruptive and influential brand that shaped the minds of many entertainment creators. In EC's short life, it impacted the foundation of the comic book industry and created a legacy that continues to inspire.

Despite its short life span, EC provides a unique insight into entertainment production in the United States. First, it embodied entertainment production adapting to American life after World War II and in the 1950s. Though this period is overly nostalgized by many, it was also a time in which American culture shifted from celebrating the defeats of our enemies abroad to being consumed with paranoia over the perceived spread of communism as well as the potential for rebellion against cultural conformity that forced us to look for and create enemies within. And few companies embodied the fear of the internalized enemy in the 1950s better than EC.

Second, EC's commitment to quality over quantity set a standard for producing to a niche audience companies would try to emulate for decades. William Gaines—the second and more significant owner of EC—understood EC's sales numbers would never allow his business to directly compete as an equal against larger publishers like DC Comics or Atlas Comics (Marvel's predecessor). However, the quality of EC's books—the combination of its art and socially aware writing—allowed it to find success with a comparatively smaller but more loyal customer base. In short, the story of EC is the tale of a short-lived brand that has continued to influence comic book companies, creators, and fans long after its demise.

Maxwell Charles Ginsberg's history in comics began long before EC was founded: from creating what some described as the first comic book for the Eastern Color Printing Company and describing himself as the "originator of the comic book in its present form" (Gaines 1942); to helping *Famous Funnies, Series I* (Wright 2001, 3) first get published; to cocreating All-American Publications. While All-American is now a part of DC Comics, it was the company that created iconic characters such as Sandman (1939), Hawkman (1940), Dr. Fate (1940), Hourman (1940), Atom (1940), Flash (1940), and Green Lantern (1940).

Despite overseeing such popular characters, M. C. Gaines wanted to bring educational values to his comic books. With this in mind, M. C. produced *Picture Stories from the Bible* and *Picture Stories from American History* (Jacobs 1973, 48). M. C. believed comics could educate people about history and the Bible so much, he wrote checks for $3,500 to religious organizations ("Publisher Shares Profit" 1943). Gaines was constantly fighting with All-American's cofounder, Jack Liebowitz. Gaines had enough of Liebowitz by 1945 and demanded Liebowitz buy him out. Liebowitz agreed. All-American and National Publications soon merged into what became DC Comics. M. C. left All-American with *Picture Stories from the Bible*, *Picture Stories from American History*, *Tiny Tot Comics*, and *Animal Fables* and a half-million-dollar buyout. Maxwell Gaines used this money to found the first incarnation of EC: Educational Comics.

In addition to what M. C. Gaines took from All-American, he also published *Picture Stories from Science* and *Picture Stories from World History* under EC. M. C. used Educational Comics to focus on his goal of teaching readers but soon realized not enough people were buying his books. He invested an additional $100K into EC and moved away from his educational mission by creating a superhero. This character was Moon Girl, and though similar to Wonder Woman, she wasn't popular and fell into the public domain from lack of use. M. C. wanted to turn EC's fortunes around but died before he could.

M. C. Gaines died on August 20, 1947, and left Educational Comics to his son, William Gaines. Bill Gaines knew his father never thought highly of him and found himself dealing with his father's death at the time his first marriage ended. In addition to these emotional strains, Bill Gaines had no experience running a business and now owned a failing company. Worse than ignorance, the Bill seemingly hated the business his father built. He once said, "In the beginning . . . , I hated the business so much that I visited the office only once a week to sign the payroll checks" (Geissman 2005, 12). The disdain toward his father's business was compounded by EC being $100,000 in debt. EC's problems were exacerbated because many at the company felt that William Gaines wasn't up to the challenge.

William Gaines's early leadership struggles came from his inability to figure out how he could succeed when his father, the man who created the comic book, failed to make EC a success. EC found success once Bill Gaines realized that the America M. C. envisioned was changing into a nation where young consumers wanted entertainment that embodied a sense of rebellion against authority figures.

At first, William simply copied better-selling comics. As Westerns became popular, Gaines commissioned titles like *Saddle Justice*, *Gunfighter*, and *Saddle Romances*. As crime comics became popular, EC produced *War against Crime!* and *International Crime Patrol*. However, aping other publishers was not working. Despite learning how to manage EC and moving beyond its original educational goals, Gaines was failing to make EC his own. This changed once Al Feldstein, a newly hired artist, encouraged Gaines to go in a direction that became the "new trend."

EC's *Crime Patrol* had poor sales, so Gaines allowed Feldstein the opportunity to use issues #15 and #16 to experiment with a horror story. Feldstein used this chance to write stories from what he titled "The Crypt of Terror." As such, *Crime Patrol*'s fifteenth issue contained a story that was billed from "The Crypt of Terror" and called "Return from the Grave!" The success of this experiment was the catalyst that turned EC from educational into entertaining.

"The Crypt of Terror" represented a different approach to storytelling for EC. Instead of large exposition blocks introducing readers to a story's premise, Feldstein began the story with the Keeper (an early version of the Crypt Keeper), functioning as a cross between narrator and host and inviting readers to not just read his tale but enter the world that he was depicting. These stories would always end with a macabre joke and an invitation for the reader to come back next issue. This tactic worked, and EC was soon publishing titles that leaned into horror or science fiction. In addition to "The Crypt of Terror" becoming *Tales from the Crypt* (1950), some other titles were *The Vault of Horror* (1950), *The Haunt of Fear* (1950), *Weird Fantasy* (1950), *Weird Science* (1950), and *Crime SuspenStories* (1950).

A key reason EC found success was that it produced stories that filled an ideological niche overlooked by other publishers. While most comic books in the 1950s told stories that enforced conformity in postwar America, EC bucked this trend and told tales about corrupt authority figures and institutionalized racism and challenged readers to question the status quo. EC never shared its exact sales numbers in the 1950s. Despite this absence, it is clear that the company's fortunes were turning around as its new stories found and grew a loyal audience. Gaines himself believed that the source of this loyalty came from how smart EC's stories were; as Gaines once said, "Our sales were never all that great, maybe half a million per issue. . . . *Superman* and *Crime Does Not Pay* sold 3 and 4 million an issue. But we always had the more intelligent kids. We always wanted to be small, and get the good craftsmanship" (Allen 1972).

William Gaines and others at EC believed that most of their consumers weren't children but smart teenagers and young adults. Lyle Stewart, EC's business manager, once stated that "millions of teenagers, servicemen and college students used to buy horror and crime comics" (Rutledge and Bart 1955). Reinforcing this is Feldstein's claim about EC's audience: "We functioned out of a presumption that our readers were at least fourteen, maybe thirteen, and older—up to adulthood, through adulthood. Mature readers, in terms of comic books" (Hajdu 2009, 239).

Regardless of how old EC's consumers were, the company acted to solidify its fans' loyalty. This was done by creating the EC Fan-Addict Club. The fee to join was twenty-five cents, and members would receive, as documented by Robert Warshow, "a humorously phrased

certificate of membership, a wallet-size 'identification card,' a pin and a shoulder-patch bearing the club emblem, and occasional mailings of the club bulletin." The club "tries to foster in the membership a sense of identification with this particular publishing company and its staff" (2001, 53). In addition to this club, Gaines provided autographs to fans who stopped by EC's office.

Despite the success EC found, it was on collision course with moral panics and shifting consumer habits. Politicians, parental organizations, scholars, and other authority figures had been criticizing comic books since the 1930s. These concerns failed to gain enough momentum to do any damage until Dr. Fredric Wertham. While many have demonized Wertham, it is important to remember that he was a prominent psychiatrist. He was a fellow at the National Research Council and a senior psychiatrist at the New York City Department of Hospitals. His research on the negative impacts of racism even helped change the nation's laws. This stemmed from working with the National Association for the Advancement of Colored People (NAACP) to examine the effects of school segregation on children; research that was cited in *Brown v. Board of Education*. However, Wertham is mainly remembered for his criticism of comic books.

In 1954, Wertham published *Seduction of the Innocent*, which argued comic books threatened America's youth. Wertham claimed that comic books inspired violence, drug use, homosexuality, un-Americanism, and fascism. Wertham was eventually called before the Subcommittee on Juvenile Delinquency. Wertham testified that all comic books were dangerous. Before the subcommittee, Dr. Wertham stated, "Crime comic books are comic books that depict crime and we have found that it makes no difference whether the locale is western, or Superman or space ship or horror, if a girl is raped she is raped whether it is in a space ship or on the prairie" (Senate

Committee on the Judiciary 1954, 82). Wertham presented a criticism of the industry that William Gaines wanted to counter. Sadly, Gaines did more damage than anyone intended. Gaines's testimony appealed to free-market principles, and he wanted to defend comic books by attacking ideologies that were critical of the medium's consumers. As Gaines said to the Senate, "The comic magazine is one of the few remaining pleasures that a person may buy for a dime today" (98). Gaines further argued his point by immediately asking, "What are we afraid of? Are we afraid of our own children? . . . Do we think our children are so evil, simple minded, that it takes a story of murder to set them to murder, a story of robbery to set them to robbery? Jimmy Walker once remarked that he never knew a girl to be ruined by a book. Nobody has ever been ruined by a comic" (98). This was a mistake because it assumed that free-market forces that represented citizen consumers were more important than the moralistic stances many took. Comic book creators who witnessed Gaines's testimony immediately saw it as a failure.

Gaines's testimony created such negative press, he invited other publishers to create an oversight authority to respond to criticism against comic books. The publishers who accepted Gaines's invitation hijacked the event and created a new industry organization, the Comics Code Authority (CCA), to undermine Gaines's company. One of the first rules of this new code stated, "No comic magazine shall use the words 'horror' or 'terror' in its title" (Comic Book Legal Defense Fund, n.d.). The code also targeted EC by requiring all stories to present "respect for parents, the moral code, and for honorable behavior [to] be fostered"; it also stated that "policemen, judges, government officials, and respected institutions shall never be presented in such a way as to create disrespect for established authority." In short, the CCA was born to destroy EC Comics.

William Gaines tried to bypass CCA's rules but found that distributors, newsstands, and other retailers would not work with EC. With sales dropping, Gaines announced in September 1954 that EC would drop five of its comics. Gaines replaced those titles with a line of comics called "New Direction"—these books being *Impact* (1955), *Valor* (1955), *Aces High* (1955), *Extra!* (1955), *Psychoanalysis* (1955), *M.D.* (1955), and *Incredible Science Fiction* (1955). The first issues of the "New Direction" titles were published without the Comics Code's seal of approval, and all of them failed to sell.

The breaking point for Gaines was not decreasing sales but the CCA's institutionalized racism when it rejected the EC story "Judgment Day." Written by Al Feldstein and drawn by Joe Orlando, "Judgment Day" is about an astronaut determining that a society of robots, which is segregated by color, is not ready to join a galactic organization. The story ends with the reveal that the astronaut is Black. This story was blocked by the CCA because of the Black character. This was the final straw for Gaines. He canceled all but one of his titles—the survivor being *MAD*.

While many comic book historians connect Wertham and the CCA to the industry's financial struggles in the 1950s, it is important to remember that comic books were already beginning to lose their place in popular culture. EC and others were unprepared for the shift in consumer spending habits that occurred in the 1950s. After all, the 1950s saw vast transformations of other media. Movies combated declining sales with the widespread usage of 3D movies and other new technologies to improve the theater experience. Also, increasingly automotive teenagers gravitated toward drive-in theaters, an experience that reached its peak in the late 1950s and early 1960s. Comics were also competing against entertainment completely free to consumers: television. The 1950s was when TVs became a standard part of the

American family as the number of televisions in the average US household increased dramatically: "By 1955 nearly three-quarters of American homes had [a television]. . . . As a cheap, accessible, and immediate form of audiovisual entertainment, television was unchallengeable" (Wright 2001, 181). So while Wertham may have loudly criticized comic books, television, films, and other popular entertainment played a role in disrupting the comic book industry's consumer base.

Even with these industrial and market changes in effect, EC's work would continue to resonate for decades. After Gaines canceled his comic books, he put all of his company's focus on building *MAD* into a success. *MAD* became a cultural icon and was even purchased by Warner Bros., meaning that William Gaines's *MAD* was under the same corporate roof that M. C. Gaines's All-American IPs were under. Not only would *MAD* inspire comedians such as Jon Stewart and Judd Apatow, but *MADtv*—a show based on the magazine—would launch the careers of Keegan-Michael Key and Jordan Peele.

Outside of *MAD*'s success, fingerprints of EC's comic books can still be found today. John Carpenter, Steven Spielberg, or other filmmakers have admitted to having been inspired by EC. Additionally, *Tales from the Crypt* was revived by Papercutz from 2007 to 2010, and Super Genius announced in 2017 it would publish new stories with the Crypt Keeper. Even outside of these revivals, many comic books have covers that pay homage to EC titles. So while EC's comics may have ended in the 1950s and William Gaines passed away in 1992, the ghosts of his creative works continue to inspire.

20

Fandom
Aaron Kashtan

In an episode of the popular television series *The Big Bang Theory* titled "The Bakersfield Expedition," three girls walk into a comic book store, and the exclusively male customers all turn around and stare until the owner scolds them, "They're just girls. It's nothing you haven't seen in movies or in drawings." This scene emphasizes the common assumption that comics fandom is an unwelcoming and sexist space. However, this assumption is only partly true, because comics fandom is a broader category, including but not limited to men who shop at comic book stores.

In the context of comics, *fandom* usually means a specific subcultural community: a group of people who are mostly white men and are united by their shared love of, primarily, Marvel and DC superhero comics. This fan community emerged in the 1960s, consciously modeling itself after the much older science fiction fan community, and is organized around institutions such as comic conventions, comic book stores, and fan magazines. Since the 1980s, members of this group are considered the primary audience for American comics. Yet organized comics fandom is much younger than comic books or comics themselves, and since its creation, it has coexisted with other audiences and other modes of comics readership. In the pre–Comics Code era, nearly every child in America was a comics fan. Thanks to the manga and graphic novel booms, comics are now reaching a level of mainstream popularity not seen since that era. Therefore, we need to echo Benjamin

Woo's question "Is there a comics industry?" (2018b) and ask whether there is such a thing as comics fandom anymore.

Comics fandom, in the narrow sense, may be defined as a community of people united by their common interest in comics and their active participation in activities such as writing about comics and attending comics conventions. In this sense, comics fandom is consciously patterned on the much older phenomenon of science fiction fandom. Sci-fi fandom originated in the 1920s, when magazine editor Hugo Gernsback started publishing fans' letters in his magazines along with their mailing addresses, allowing fans to write letters to each other. This allowed fans to form a community, resulting in practices such as fanzines and fan conventions. Sci-fi fandom provided the model for other fandoms, including comics fandom as well as television fandom, which is the standard example in academic fan studies (Bacon-Smith 1991; Jenkins 1992; Coppa 2006).

DC editors Julius Schwartz and Mort Weisinger were early members of sci-fi fandom and followed Gernsback's practice of publishing readers' letters. Some sci-fi fans were readers of comics as well, and the first comics fanzines date from the 1950s. These fanzines were often devoted to EC Comics, which consciously cultivated a fan community with its Fan-Addict Club, as Marvel would subsequently do in the 1960s and later. However, the organized comics fan community is considered to have been founded in the early 1960s by Jerry Bails and Roy Thomas, who published the pioneering fanzine *Alter Ego*. While not active sci-fi fans themselves, Bails and Thomas were aware of sci-fi fandom and used it as a model for the community they sought to create. Comic book conventions, as distinct from sci-fi conventions, were first held in the mid-1960s (Schelly 1995). Direct-market distribution originated in the following decade,

and by the 1980s, comic book stores had replaced the newsstand as the primary distribution channel for comic books and had become gathering places for fans (Beerbohm 2000). Although underground comics played a major role in the rise of the direct market and thus of comics fandom, comics fans' privileged texts are mostly Marvel and DC superhero comics.

To be a member of a fan community is to be an active participant, not simply a passive follower (though see Gray, Sandvoss, and Harrington 2007 for other definitions of fandom). For example, sci-fi fans in the narrow sense are not just people who enjoy reading science fiction but people who engage in fan activity (or "fanac"), such as organizing conventions and publishing fanzines. Nearly everyone in the developed world watches TV and movies, but media fans also write fan fiction, create fanvids, and attend conventions. Thus comics fans are distinguished from other comics readers because they take an active role in reading comics, and their comics fandom is a significant part of their lives. However, comics fandom is often more passive than sci-fi or media fandom. Comics fans are likely to express their fandom not by writing fan fiction or publishing fanzines (although the latter do exist) but by hanging out at the comic shop, attending comic conventions, and collecting old comics as well as related memorabilia such as original art. While sci-fi and media conventions are usually fan-run, comic conventions are often run by professionals, since they are spaces for buying and selling comics and for meeting celebrities, and therefore they attract far larger audiences than other types of conventions. Conversely, comics fans make up a larger portion of the readership for comics. Over the course of the 1970s and 1980s, comics readership contracted to the point where active fans were the primary audience. Marvel and DC comics explicitly cater to people who attend conventions and visit the comic book store weekly, whereas, for example, most people who read a Harry Potter book will never attend a Harry Potter convention.

Organized comics fandom has mostly negative connotations. Comics fans are stereotyped as fat, bespectacled misfits and comic book stores as dingy man caves that exclude women and minorities. These stereotypes have been promulgated within comics by texts like Evan Dorkin's *Eltingville Club* and in society at large by *The Simpsons* and *The Big Bang Theory*. Because of the negative valences of fandom generally and comics fandom specifically, some comics scholars who are also fans have sought to deny their fan identity and separate their scholarship from their fandom (Smith et al. 2011), though this is becoming less common. The alternative comics community's very name indicates that it defines itself by comparison to normative comics fandom.

The limited body of scholarship on comics fandom tends to assume that normative comics fandom is the primary readership for comics and that this fan community is mostly straight, white, and male (Pustz 1999; Healey 2009). Several types of critical work are necessary in order to complicate our understanding of comics fandom. First, we need to explore other historical fan communities. Normative comics fandom was not the original readership for comics and was not the primary readership until the 1980s. Rather, its rise to dominance resulted from the contraction of newsstand comics sales and the disappearance of genres like romance and funny animal comics. Due to these developments, the direct-market comic book store became the primary sales outlet for comics, and superhero comics, the privileged texts of comics fandom, became the dominant genre.

In earlier periods, comics fandom couldn't have existed as a cohesive community because there were too many comics readers. In the 1940s, 95 percent of American boys and 90 percent of girls read comic books (Lopes 2009, 22)—to say nothing of comic strips, which were perhaps the nation's most popular mass medium—and different readers read different kinds of comics. Historical readerships other than normative comics fandom need more attention (though see Gabilliet 2009; Beaty, Woo, and Sousanis, n.d.). Even after superhero comics rose to dominance, other comics communities still existed, including underground and alternative comics readers. Even within normative comics fandom, some subcommunities were more diverse and accepting than others. For example, the 2008 San Diego Comic-Con International included a panel on "50 Years of Gay Legion of Super-Heroes Fandom." Comics fandom is also not a purely passive activity. Fan labor, such as fan fiction and fanzine publishing, has been a significant phenomenon in the comics fan community and deserves more scholarly attention than it gets.

A second necessary critical project is to account for contemporary transformations in comics fandom. In the 1980s and 1990s, comic books were mostly walled off from other segments of the entertainment industry, which allowed comics fandom to exist in isolation. This subsequently became impossible thanks to media convergence and transmedia storytelling, which integrated comics into larger media franchises (Jenkins 2008a; Johnson 2013; compare Steinberg 2012). Superheroes are no longer the exclusive property of normative comics fans; far more people watch Marvel Cinematic Universe films than read Marvel comic books. Marvel and DC have sought to capitalize on their characters' new audiences by publishing comics that appeal to readers other than normative comics fans—for example, *Ms. Marvel* and *Batgirl* (Landis 2016). This push for "diversity" has prompted hostile reactions from enfranchised fans, including a semiorganized Comicsgate movement based on the notorious Gamergate harassment campaign, thus further damaging the reputation of organized comics fandom (Kashtan 2018b). Media convergence has also transformed comic conventions, originally privileged spaces of normative comics fandom, into giant transmedia spectacles. When I first attended Comic-Con in 2002, I was able to buy a four-day pass on the day the show began. Since then, Comic-Con has been taken over by Hollywood, becoming a venue for publicizing new films and TV shows, and has become a household name (Salkowitz 2012; Bolling and Smith 2014). The entire event now sells out as soon as tickets go on sale, and many comics fans and dealers have been priced out of attendance. Comic-Con has also become a gathering place for communities very different from normative comics fandom—for example, Twilight fans—and this development has drawn hostile reactions from the comics fans who formerly dominated the event. Comic-Con's visibility has led to a glut of comic conventions and fests that sometimes have only a tangential connection to actual comics.

A contemporaneous phenomenon is the rise of new comics readerships that often have little contact with normative comics fandom. The manga boom of the 2000s demonstrated that girls were an untapped audience for comics (Brienza 2016), leading American book publishers to start developing their own graphic novel lines, and the readership for young adult and middle-grade graphic novels is now larger than the readership for comic books. Meanwhile, thanks to the mainstream literary success of texts like *Maus* and *Fun Home*, graphic novels now have a significant adult readership and are widely reviewed and taught in colleges, even in classes not devoted to comics. Webcomics have a wide and diverse audience that is difficult to survey accurately, and platforms like ComiXology have made comics available to people who cannot or will not visit comic book stores. As a result, comics fandom has moved away from its privileged location of the comic book store and has been severed from its connection with comics collecting and speculation, although webcomics fans still often buy their comics in physical form (Kashtan 2018a). The new comics readerships enabled by the internet are generally ignored by the comics fan press, which still tends to assume that normative comics fandom is the primary audience for comics. More work is necessary to understand who is reading comics today, what they do with the comics they read, and how their fan activity differs from normative comics fandom.

A final important question is whether "comics fandom" even exists anymore as a single identifiable phenomenon or whether it ever did. The comics fan community, in the narrow sense, is organized around a canon of texts that all fans have in common. Any normative comics fan can be assumed to have read *Watchmen* or Claremont and Byrne's *The Uncanny X-Men* run and to recognize references like "I did it thirty-five minutes ago" or "Okay, suckers—you've taken yer best shot! Now it's my turn!" In France and Japan, such a normative comics canon does not exist, or is much less specific, because there are too many different types of comics for different types of readers. For example, in Japan, people of all genders and ages read manga, but they don't all read the same manga. If there is a central canon of comics that everyone is supposed to have read, it is only a very loose one. Thus the French and Japanese languages have words—*bédéphile* and *otaku*, respectively (Kitabayashi 2004)—for a person who is interested in comics to an unusual degree—or, in the case of the latter term, to an excessive degree. Reading comics is a normal activity, but *bédéphiles* and *otaku* are people who make comics a significant part of their lives. Similarly, in America, it might be better to stop thinking of "comics fans" as a single category and to develop new terms to distinguish between different ways of reading comics.

21

Fantasy
Darieck Scott

What you read and see on the page is often fantastic, and the structure of the storytelling comics engage is fundamentally informed by fantasy. In comics, anything can happen: Visitors from other planets fire lasers from their retinas and lift buildings with their bare hands. Invincible, beautiful warriors are shaped from clay, and nerdy scientists are transformed into green-skinned behemoths and balletic pugilists who swing from New York City skyscrapers. Civilizations are abundant throughout the universe, and not one but many other-than-human races share the earth with us—mutants, water-breathing Atlanteans, Eternals, Deviants, gods old and new, immortal Amazons, mole people. Beagles lead rich, linguistically mediated fantasy lives; cats plot world domination; raccoons perform spectacular burglaries; impossibly gorgeous and overendowed women and men enjoy endless orgasms; space gods rove the universe eating planets; robots build their own families and establish their own polities; and businessmen and magicians travel into alternate dimensions unbound by euclidean geometries and walk on winding pathways of crayon-smudged color. Due to comics' serial production—generally appearing as ongoing stories paced by intervals, whether daily, weekly, monthly, quarterly, or yearly—action and occurrence are elongated, elaborated, as well as condensed and abbreviated. Time moves backward as well as forward, as the story happens not once but as many times as it's read, and the sequence may be read in or out of order, whether in linear narrative or in jarring non sequitur, perceived at a page-length glance or panel by panel. Whatever was seen to "happen" in the story before is revised, rewritten, redone, and undone.

More so than its closest cognate media, which also summon into quasi-existence the scenarios of imagination; more so than cinema, which is limited by the technologies of its special effects and the human bodies portraying its characters; more so than fiction or literature, which rely on the letters of carefully selected words and those words' ever-slippery signification—comics enjoy the near infinity of possibilities of an utterly elastic structure. Whatever can be *drawn* within the conventions of panels—as well as across and beyond them—no matter the tenuousness of the images' claim to realist reference or representation, can by its very suggestiveness rather than its mimetic depiction suspend disbelief. This then is a description of how comics are fantastic in content as well as fantastic in structure. This then is also how we can see comics as a privileged expressive *form* for fantasy—fantasy understood as the imaginative construction of what-is-not, of nonreality.

Might we also think of the obverse proposition, less apparent to the experience of reading a comic but perhaps revealed by analyses of the process of reading comics? Such a proposition might read, *The content of fantasy in the modern world of readers is shaped by comics. Fantasy is a form of expression that privileges comics.* These are assays of a relationship between comics and fantasy that sees them not only as connected or analogous but as deeply informing one another, as coconstitutive. Comics are the fantastic stories or fantastically (i.e., nonrealist) structured stories of their creators, which in the hands and minds of comics' readers also become templates for readers' fantasies, individually experienced and collectively (yet combatively and unharmoniously) worked on and elaborated, in the letters pages of comics, in online forums, in the sharing of fan art, in comics conventions, and so on. Even in the large—and, not insignificantly, more readily studied—group of comics that aim toward high degrees of representational realism, such as memoir comics, comics about war and disaster, documentary comics, biographical comics, comics that explicitly describe/explain/educate (comics that chart the effects of capitalist neoliberalism, for example), the demands of comics form always privilege imaginative redrawing of actual people and events in a labile representational mode that fabricates and *invents* figures for the readers' engagement.

This keyword essay theorizes the both-and-between interpenetration of comics and fantasy. We might call the essay's object of inquiry comics/fantasy, or fantasy/comics. We can theorize comics/fantasy according to the insights we can glean from addressing comics narrative form: fantasy as a psychic state or psychological creation, fantasy/comics as exploring the possibilities and limits of the real, and comics/fantasy as speculative, utopian, and charged, in often obscure fashion, with political valence.

Common to each of these facets of the relationship between comics and fantasy—narrative form, psychic and psychological state and product, and speculative or utopian politics—is a common-sense (and therefore always somewhat obfuscating and misleading) understanding of fantasy as the jejune relative of fact and truth, the disreputable product of petty desires that can receive no other judgment than "unrealistic." The perception of fantasy as wish fulfillment is one of the primary accusations historically levied against modern comics, especially its core genre, superhero comics: here, it is blithely and with considerable self-satisfaction said, we see "nothing more" than the paper-thin fulfillment of (male) adolescents' dreams of invulnerability and power and universal adoration, at best a pressure gauge or a release valve for barely concealed horny fantasies, the products of a soon-surpassed stage when biology overwhelms the finer faculties.

And indeed a powerful motor of reading comics is the engagement of wishes, if by wishes we mean the imaginary conjuration of what is not actually present. This wish summoning inheres in comics form. There is a particular kind of subjective encounter necessitated by comics form, where, as Scott McCloud succinctly maps it, the reader must supply the connective action, reason, and movement that is not on the page but only indicated by the lines displayed upon it, the imagination of what happens *between* panels as well as what *moves* within the stationary, nonanimated panel itself. McCloud's seminal nomenclature for this process is "closure"—the comics reader mentally *closes*, as it were, the gap between the panels (McCloud 1993). The reader contributes to the action and the reason for the action, and these actions and reasons obviously must take as many different forms as there are readers of a given comic. This closure is guided, to be sure, by the cues of the lines drawn in the panels and the accompanying and sometimes explanatory text, but the connective tissue is *not there* on the page and must be supplied from the readers' own knowledge and imagination.

McCloud and all comics scholarship that follows him focus on the reader's supplement of meaning and movement directed by the sequence of image-text representations. But it's reasonable to suppose that the supplied closure—which, after all, ultimately cannot be limited by what is laid out on the page—follows or is in the nature of the readers' *wishes*. Here then we can also bring focus to subcreative processes, generations of meaning that occur in response to the sequence of image-text representations but also wholly out of its published sequence: the act of fantasizing by generating fragments of story, imagined undrawn images, as representations of possibility at most suggested by but not cordoned off by or foreclosed by—and even in defiance of—what is on the page and in the story. Generations of queer readers or those inclined to read queerly can testify precisely to such forms of wish-fulfillment closure, wherein the shift between the coup de grâce punch that sends the villain to his just deserts and the "Later . . ." caption of the next panel in an adventure of, say, the Legion of Super-Heroes, the guys and gals of that assemblage of youthful heroes enjoy pairings and polyamories evidently not in the least undreamt of (put "gay fan art" prefaced by any superhero's name—but especially Batman—in your image search engine, and see these very wishes transformed into their own joyously rendered erotic drawings). If McCloud's comics studies' reader works *between* panels and *within* panels, we can also theorize comics reading that uses that work as a trampoline surface from which to leap—and perhaps with the comic book powers to transcend gravity bequeathed us within and between the representational elements of the initiating fantasy—never to return to the earth where it began. Here then reading is not only an intersubjective encounter with images in conjunction with text but also indistinct from the fantasizing that occurs beyond the text though initiated within it.

Thus it is possible to view comics/fantasy certainly as providing the templates or the content of imaginative mental play—again, played out individually and collectively. But we also can intimate that comics/fantasy provides an education *in* desire: where desire is one of the primary modes (if not *the* mode) of establishing a sense of self (the self that, in psychoanalytic theories as in other theoretical accounts, is in any case by its nature in large part chimerical and might well be described as a fantasy).

Comics' use of and participation in fantasies that help fashion their readers' selves has long been recognized as a fundamental aspect of reading comics—usually as an evil or a social peril. Elsewhere in this *Keywords* volume, you can find a description of Dr. Fredric Wertham's powerful insistence that comics contributed to juvenile delinquency and sexual perversion. While Wertham's judgment of the outcomes of reading has been and should be challenged (one can easily see that Wertham's perverted delinquent is just a tendentious way to describe someone queer), his divining of the *process* of comics reading is not without merit. Frantz Fanon, the Black Martinican psychiatrist and activist-theorist of blackness and antiracist revolution, devoted two pages of his 1952 *Black Skin, White Masks* to a discussion of how "weekly comics for the young" plays a principal role in the inculcation of white supremacy and racialized self-perception in their readers (Fanon [1952] 1984, 124). Even if both Wertham and Fanon wrote about a period when comics reading was more universal than it now is, their observations still resonate for the narrower readership of the contemporary moment and arguably also for the much larger audiences that thrill to comics images and narratives in cinema, television dramas, and animation. Both track an interface between the text-image of comics and the readers as giving shape to, as well as answering, wishes.

The idea that this interface involves *identification* is assumed in both accounts—the explicit proposition being that the reader identifies with (for Wertham, the covertly queer) Batman and (for Fanon, the clearly white-as-dominant-race) Tarzan. But we might view reading comics as performing a subtler function, as being less clearly a site of imaginary mimesis wherein reader and comic book figure are matched one-to-one. Rather, we might see identification operating by (1) identifying what fantasy is in relationship to—as distinct from—reality and (2) identifying what to desire and what kinds of desire to nurture, wherein the reader accumulates touchstones for self-perception and self-definition.

The greatest fantasy, perhaps the ur-fantasy, is to transform oneself into another, fantastically better self. Reading many kinds of comics, but especially the core genre of superheroes, fits this wish beautifully. This being that is transformed by fantasy, this not-you-but-You, will probably be wealthier—think Bruce Wayne (Batman), Tony Stark (Iron Man), T'Challa (Black Panther), and Richie Rich—and anyway, do Thor or Hawkman ever worry about money? Probably this You will be considered universally beautiful, will be ultraintelligent and ultrainvulnerable to all the hurts and emotional wounds of life as a social being, may be able to teleport vast distances; read minds; create, destroy, and resurrect by fiat.

The ego-fluffing, grandeur-delusion trajectory of such fantasies is clear enough. But their potentially political facets should be equally apparent. Such politics can range across the spectrum. One persistent criticism of the male superheroic figure is its availability to the kinds of masculinist and white-supremacist iconography and narration that underpin fascism. The splash-page images of powerfully muscular figures drawn as male and white and attired in versions of the American (or Canadian or British) flag would seem to confirm this reading. Indeed, a recent story line in *Captain America* mined such implications for dramatic effect, transforming the earliest and arguably paragon character of what would become Marvel Comics into the sleeper agent of a fascist organization bent on Fourth Reich–like world domination. But this story arc was not popular among many fans and generated considerable controversy online (though truth be told, most story arcs have that effect): Captain America was, after all, created to fight fascism in the fantasy world of comics and could be seen on the cover of his first issue in March 1941 pummeling Hitler himself with a vicious right hook to the face. A similar if less directly politicized description can be made of 1939's Superman; it is now fairly commonly agreed among comics historians that Superman's escape from a world on the brink of destruction to adopt America as home and, eventually, fight for "the American way" was the character's creators' Joe Shuster and Jerry Siegel's fantasy reimagining of Jews' harried flight from Hitler's Europe.

Comics' political valence is also evident in superhero comics' constant celebration of difference or freakishness as a ready-made metaphor for any number of otherwise degraded departures from societal norms, especially following the explosion of new comics characters at Marvel in the 1960s. The fantasy aspects of the medium of comics have lent themselves to the depiction of a vast array of nonnormative expressions of gender and sexuality—from the most metaphoric (in hyperbolic camp visuality or the metamorphosing of human bodies into forms that put into question traditional gender norms, etc.) to the most literal (the actual depiction of queer bodies and erotic attachments).

The underlying premise in comics that anything that can be drawn can be believed taps into the productivity of human capacities for fantasy. Thus the formal character of comics—the idea that you can have indefinite iterations of a single story that never reproduce a single trajectory—lends comics as much to utopian imagination as to culturally narrow and idealized imagery. As Thomas Waugh notes, writing about gay male erotic comics in *Out/Lines*, the power of pornographic comics is precisely opposite to the indexical and documentary pretenses of pornographic photography and film (where, as Linda Williams has established, a chief formal principle has been to document—from a heterosexist male perspective—women's sexual pleasure and orgasm): "Graphics offer a richer spectrum of fantasy than do indexical images like photographs, often in inverse proportion to their importance as documentary evidence" (2002, 20). Moreover, "the graphics usually have a utopian dimension," and "in some sense, non-indexical eroticism can be more utopian than the indexical variety" (20).

The fantastic in comics unlocks a great richness of representational possibility, with a corresponding wealth of fecundity for critical attention. It should not be entirely surprising, given that we know the relationship between representation and what's "real" to be confoundingly and irrepressibly blurred, that the following description of Black art by philosopher Achille Mbembe is nearly on the nose as a description of comics/fantasy too. Black art, Mbembe writes in *Critique of Black Reason* (2017), "is a form of art that has constantly reinvented myths and redirected tradition in order to undermine them through the very act that pretended to anchor and ratify them. It has always been an art of sacrilege, sacrifice, and expenditure, multiplying new fetishes in pursuit of a generalized deconstruction of existence precisely through its use of play, leisure, spectacle, and the principle of metamorphosis" (174).

22

Feminism

Yetta Howard

Feminism as a concept has an all-at-once fraught and productive relationship with comics as a medium for the political domains associated with gender and sexual difference. In the context of comics, feminism comes to describe a set of approaches that seek to contest the exclusionary status of women and/or female or feminized social subjects in graphic forms and narratives. Such resistance to predominantly sexist and patriarchal attitudes applies to the very question of characters embodying feminist beliefs as much as it applies to creators and assumed readers. The putative consumer of comics has been historically conceived as male, especially the "fanboy," the geeky male reader obsessed with the particularities of characters or who harbors a fanatical approach to a narrative or franchise. But the figure of the fanboy does not neatly correspond with dominant masculinity. Instead, the passive act of reading—and passivity as a feminized "trait"— associated with an attachment to comics as well as comics' word-image qualities perceived as infantilized or as subordinated textual forms reflects a difference of reading as a feature of the genre regardless of the gender and sexual identity of the comics reader. If we are to think about comics reading as a gendered form of reading, then its confluence of words and images signals a nonnormativity of visual signifiers that engenders a critique of dominant modes of textual engagement. Nonetheless, until the debut of *Archie* in 1941 and other teen-themed and romance titles that aligned with the midcentury construction of the teenager, female characters were largely absent or peripheral and were created with the adolescent male reader in mind (Robbins 1999). Functioning as gradual feminist interventions in the longer history of male-focused comics production and reception, female characters, whether cast as liberatory, villainous, or otherwise, presented—and continue to present—nuanced approaches to locating feminism's representational parameters within the complexities of the genre.

When considering the larger stakes of characters embodying feminist perspectives, we need to begin with Wonder Woman, possibly the most recognized female comic book character and certainly the most well-known female superhero. Her embodiment of exaggerated strength reflects feminism's broad possibilities while addressing the longer trajectory that a politics of difference followed from the Second World War to the present day. When William Moulton Marston (pseudonymously Charles Moulton) debuted the Wonder Woman character in 1941, he did so in ways that attend to contemporary, if anachronistic, perspectives of her overt feminism and the conspicuous queerness of her desires in the scope of the comic's narratives (Robbins 1996; Halberstam 2017). One widely discussed site of queer erotics in the Marston *Wonder Woman* comics was their emphasis on fantastical moments of bondage and submission (Berlatsky 2015). For example, Noah Berlatsky discusses *Wonder Woman* #18 from 1946, in which a minister at a wedding party turns into "pink ectoplasmic ropes of phallic goo" and binds everyone, including Wonder Woman, who proceeds to stretch the goo because it cannot be broken (2015, 16). The scene positions *Wonder Woman* to be read as working against a heteronormative script (the context of the wedding), using erotically repurposed BDSM imagery (pink "ropes") to battle oppression through the lens of

a feminism invested in autonomous sexual expression (stretching as circumvention). Such temporal endurance and modification are valuable in that one iteration of mass culture's investment in feminism in this case can be usefully traced in the investment in comics-to-film adaptation. Unmistakably timed after Donald Trump's election, this took the form of the 2017 Hollywood blockbuster action film *Wonder Woman* directed by Patty Jenkins. But the question of where to identify the character's simultaneously transitory and lasting representation as feminist in the film pertains to tracking what some scholars have suggested as missed opportunities to live up to—or even a betrayal of—the radical potentials of her Amazonian roots (Halberstam 2017; Penrose 2017). Perhaps, then, the film's version of the character should be thought about less as a full encounter with patriarchal realms that dictate unequal social and material conditions and more in terms of the promise of her influence in the domains of the popular. As Ramzi Fawaz (2017a) writes, "Her name alone should remind us that she is a *wonder*, an enchantment, a fantasy of what woman can be, not a realistic portrait of the heterogeneity of actual women."

Wonder Woman's creation was coterminous with J. Howard Miller's poster image creation for Westinghouse Electric, the comics-art graphic that was eventually dubbed "Rosie the Riveter." Named "Rosie" and given the wartime-specific occupation of "riveter" after Norman Rockwell's illustration of the emancipatory figure (Honey 1984), Miller's World War II–era propaganda poster illustration features a white woman with a red handkerchief wrapped around her head, presented midmotion rolling up the sleeve on her blue-collar shirt (with the Westinghouse badge embroidered on her collar) to reveal her flexed right-arm muscle. Resignifying a typically masculine-inflected class-determinate pose, the image is highly identified by the large dark-blue speech balloon looming over her head containing the shouted slogan "We Can Do It!" Here, the formal qualities of comics—the large speech balloon and cartoon illustration itself—solidify a commonly recognized feminist "character" of Rosie the Riveter and thus situates comics aesthetics as a vehicle for historically resonant articulations of female labor independence beyond the reference to the large number of women who took industrial and manufacturing jobs during the Second World War. By the 1980s, the transformation of Miller's image into the Rosie figure became ubiquitously associated with feminist political praxis, and many revisions and parodies of her iconic status persist, including the Women's March cover of the February 6, 2017, issue of the *New Yorker*—a magazine read for its cartoons as much as its articles—featuring Abigail Gray Swartz's painting of an African American Rosie the Riveter wearing a pink pussy hat. The cover reflects renewed investments in antisexist politics in the wake of would-be first female president Hillary Clinton's loss. The feminist periodical history of these comics contexts can be traced to the first issue of *Ms.* magazine in 1972, which includes an image of a King Kong–sized Wonder Woman walking briskly, overpowering the (sexist) environment around her with a large banner that reads "Wonder Woman for President" directly below the magazine's masthead; she reappeared in her supersized state on the covers of *Ms.*'s fortieth- and forty-fifth-anniversary issues, looming over Washington, DC, among feminist activists in the fall 2012 issue and fiercely by herself in the fall 2017 issue, crossing her forearms with her iconic metal cuffs, looking directly at the reader alongside the text "Resisting Persisting," which adorned the cover (Spillar 2017).

If we then consider the political fantasy that Fawaz (2017a) discusses in dialogue with Rosie's insistence that "we can," we arrive at an instructive juncture that encompasses grappling with the subordinated status of woman-, female-, and feminine-identified social subjects while contending with a minority discourse of comics and sequential art that is attuned to the vectors of difference that can exist in the range of available graphic textual forms and content. In other words, the question of who falls under the "we" signifies a feminism that may be defined as exclusionary as much as it is inclusive. Such negotiations with antiessentialist coalitional politics are observable, for example, in the ways that underscoring ethnicity and sexuality contributes to a shared sense of inequality that marks the instability of the feminist "we," which all at once applies to readers, characters, and creators of comics maintaining feminism's intersections. Deborah Whaley's (2015) analysis of Jackie Zelda Ormes's midcentury Black-cultural-front *Candy* comic for the *Chicago Defender* and the early millennium creation of the Ormes Society animate such considerations. In displaying Black defiance of monolithic whiteness that exists across the lines of feminism, class, and erotic presence, "Candy resists the asexuality of the Black domestic in the popular imagination" (Whaley 2015, 48), and her influence extends to examining the inclusion of Black women artists in comics creation itself. Contrastingly, andré carrington (2016) has shown that despite the wide visibility of the Black female superhero Storm from *The X-Men*, "the character represents Black women while negating the proposition that Black women's lived and historical experiences and ongoing creativity are the conditions of possibility for representations of Black women in media" (91).

Indeed, characters and their creators such as those of Candy and Storm emerge divergently in their embodiments of difference and open up multiple approaches to navigating the relationship between feminism's necessary inconsistencies—those pertaining to varying emphases on race, sexuality, and other bodily or social conditions—and the dynamic heterogeneity of comics' visual-narrative qualities. Moreover, competing perspectives associated with sexual libertinism in the history of feminist thought find fertile arenas in popular as well as underground titles, particularly for inquiries into the vicissitudes of gendered desire and violence. When investigating the transformation of Jean Grey into the Dark Phoenix through the lens of demonic possession, Fawaz (2016) has written that this narrative connects "the superhero's loss of self-possession with a loss of control over one's sexual and gender identity" (205), and rather than be regarded as critiquing uninhibited forms of desire, the Dark Phoenix becomes a searing commentary on the commodification of difference in the 1980s. Similar to the role played by Phoenix's straddling the spaces between narcissistic pleasure and others' pain (Fawaz 2016, 213) in locating arguably controversial yet politically palpable brands of feminism's margins, Rebecca Wanzo (2018), in her analysis of Melinda Gebbie and Alan Moore's underground graphic text *Lost Girls* ([2006] 2018), theorizes how its recasting of canonical female characters such as Alice from *Alice in Wonderland* via queer and adolescent sexualities is "uniquely positioned to articulate what can be created by the seeming irreconcilability between pleasure and pain" (352). Addressing concerns central to feminist aesthetics broadly construed, such contexts exhibit comic art's limitations and possibilities when situated within oppressive structures at both the representational and authorial levels. Drawing on lived experience in primarily underground graphic texts, Chute (2010) reminds us that "today's readers of graphic narrative may not know how hard-won the opportunity was to visualize non-normative lives of women in an aesthetically engaged format during the significant period when comics shifted from the strictly commercial to the politically and artistically revolutionary" (26). Comics created by women, whether autobiographical or not, have become imperative ways to engage with the risks that come with challenging dominant systems of artistic and narrative practice.

Accordingly, collaborative efforts by women's underground comix collectives of the 1960s and 1970s into the 1980s brought into relief feminist creative independence and becomes a salient context for exploring the radical sexual politics and contestations of creative norms within the history of male-dominated underground comix creation. Spelled with *x*, comix distinguished themselves from comics for children and openly displayed X-rated material (Sabin 1996, 92) such as psychedelic drug use and sexually explicit material while expanding the domains of the form. Comix were mainly sold at head shops and were firmly ensconced in the era's various countercultural modes of circulation and distribution. While these comix presented important directions in the radicalization of graphic art beyond the confines of the mainstream, they were, for many, tone-deaf to the effects of putatively violent, sexist imagery and the exclusionary atmosphere of the largely male comix scene. In response, female artists and writers created titles of their own, but these comix were by no means less explicit and included narratives of menstruation, abortion, nondominant bodies, and sex-positive themes. Unapologetically depicting feminist sexual politics no matter how controversial, some of such comix embraced "unfinished" styles as a resistance to a patriarchal sense of cartoon "mastery," while others reinscribed recognizable feminist figures and adopted titles designed to offend mainstream audiences, feminist or otherwise. Trina Robbins's cocreation of the first all-female-authored comix anthology, *It Ain't Me, Babe* (1970), features a cover adorned with its subtitle, *Women's Liberation*, next to the bold-red word *Babe* from the title emerging centrally from the page, leaving behind its trace. Importantly, the cover includes iconic female comics characters such as Olive Oyl from *Popeye* the Sailor, Wonder Woman, and Sheena from *Sheena, Queen of the Jungle* angrily marching with purpose, some with their fists in the air, all with politically auspicious frowns on their faces. Following this was the collectively run *Wimmen's Comix*, along with titles such as Joyce Farmer and Lyn Cheveley's *Tits & Clits* series and *Abortion Eve*, Mary Wings's *Come Out Comix*, Lee Marrs's *Pudge, Girl Blimp*, and the sex-themed *Wet Satin* series. *Wet Satin* presented a particularly striking double standard when it came to allowable sexual expression. According to Robbins (1999), "The printer insisted that the male sex book, *Bizarre Sex*, was satire, while *Wet Satin* was serious and therefore objectionable" (97). *Tits & Clits*, too, was singled out: the bookstore owner selling it was arrested, and Farmer and Cheveley hid copies of the first issue for four years before releasing the subsequent issues (Pilcher with Kannenberg 2008). While continuing to resist logics of subordination and censorship that far exceeded their narrative contexts, these forms of feminist self-expression reflect tensions within feminism and its various receptions rather than merely dismantle uniform political perspectives organized around questions of difference.

As underground comix mirrored second-wave feminist politics of sexuality and notably addressed debates around pornography that defined the sex wars of the 1980s, the legacy of these comix is detectable in counterintuitive investments in identificatory modes of negativity that characterize queer, racialized, and transgressive feminisms from the 1990s to the present, such as Jennifer Camper's *Rude Girls and Dangerous Women*, Roberta Gregory's *Bitchy Bitch* and queer counterpart *Bitchy Butch*, Diane DiMassa's *Hothead Paisan: Homicidal Lesbian Terrorist*, Julie Doucet's *Dirty Plotte*, and experimentally unclassifiable graphic novels underscoring ethnic and trans embodiment such as Erika Lopez's *The Girl Must Die: A Monster Girl Memoir* and Edie Fake's

Gaylord Phoenix. As strange bedfellows, comics nevertheless have good chemistry with feminism's ever-renewing status as an always incomplete project, ultimately allowing us to expand our understandings of their dually prolific visual-textual vocabularies: the medium's refusal of allegiance to words or images exclusively thus exemplifies a dismantling of a patriarchal adherence to binaries upholding inequality while opening up the multiplicities of minority narrative forms distinguishable instead as a dialectical relationship between feminism and comics—the feminism *of* comics itself.

23

Form

Scott Bukatman

I've little to no use for any writing about comics that doesn't engage with the fact that it is, before and after all, a *comic* that's being examined and not a short story, movie, or TV show. This is true of all media—I'm unrepentantly dedicated to the specifics of a given medium—but has a heightened relevance when it comes to comics, where formal properties are so evidently on display. To be clear, the "form" of a comic is composed of elements of individual style (visual and literary) and the materiality of the comics object (whether physical or digital).

To consider the form of a novel is to emphasize language, structure, and authorial style, but the materiality of most non–comic books is largely *im*material, at least insofar as it conveys an author's intentions. Books and e-readers have their own physicality, but the conditions of that physicality are typically not under the writer's jurisdiction. Book size, whether the covers are hard or soft, the quality of the paper, font design, and size—such choices are instead the purview of the publisher; in the case of works in the public domain, numerous variations of the "same" book proliferate, without significantly altering the impact of, say, *Oliver Twist*. Meanwhile, the e-book can be reformatted by individual readers. The work survives these various translations, more or less intact.

Comics, though, can't be translated. I'm not referring to the words; the problems of translation are, as with other wordy media (fiction, film scripts, essays),

problematic but surmountable. But a comic is more than words; it's typically a concatenation of words and images, organized with specific intent. It might be, upon reprinting, up- or downscaled, recolored, or collected into a new volume of some sort, but the fundamental layout, proportions, saturation, and page count are retained. Andrei Molotu has reminded me that newspaper comics were designed to be reformatted for the spatial needs of particular newspapers and that there are instances of book-length comics reformatted to fit the needs of a smaller volume. These exceptions prove my point: they are actually deleterious to the impact of the comic.

The choices available to cartoonists include all the variables that define style in writing, along with the variables involved in producing an image and even the variables involved in reproducing an image. So word choice as well as the amount of (or even the presence of) text; clear lines or dense hatching; panels or no; black and white or color (Which colors? How many? How saturated?); print or online (If print, scale and weight? Glossy or matte finish? If online, what's the relation of "page" size to screen size?); a four-panel strip, or a never-*ever*-ending saga, or anything in between—these variables multiply exponentially, which poses significant challenges for scholars.

Having written about film and comics, comics seem to me the more challenging medium. The cinema has its own set of variables: film length, narrative structure, film stock, palette, naturalistic or spectacular, and so on. But the materiality of the medium is largely shared among filmmakers; cinema is predicated upon a camera that works pretty much the same way for every filmmaker, lenses that focus the image just this way and no other, and a rectangular screen shape (digital cinema has, thus far, tended to mimic its celluloid forebears). Experimental filmmaker Stan Brakhage once proposed or demonstrated a litany of ways to work against these givens, including filming through ashtrays or gluing moth wings to the film strip, but the lengths to which he needed to go only underscores the determining power of those cinematic parameters, no matter whether technological or conventional.

Other visual arts—painting, illustration, printmaking—have their fair share of variable elements; decisions that each artist makes are perhaps constrained by the requirements of print or gallery space but are generative of rich, ongoing diversity and complexity. And yet the mystery of the complexity of comics abides; perhaps it's that fecund concatenation, the intersection of narrative and aesthetic decisions, that makes it unique.

To be sure, not all comics creators exercise control over all of these parameters—the current artist on, say, *Batman* already operates within given parameters of page size, paper choice, color, and, to some degree, action. But even within those parameters, that *Batman* comic can accommodate very diverse visual styles. Neal Adams imported a brand of realism from melodramatic comic strips that used such tools as expressive lighting and nuanced body language and gave readers a more adult Batman grounded in a plausible reality. Michael Allred embraced the pop sensibility of the 1960s TV series and produced a rather more (metaphorically and physically) weightless experience. And narratively, the gritty realism of Denny O'Neil's scripts (many written for Adams) fit Batman just as comfortably as Grant Morrison's later psychedelic, metafictional fantasias.

Creators working beyond the realm of commercial comic book production, though, are confronted with an even greater set of variables, including, as mentioned earlier, the scale of the book (its heft and length), the weight and gloss of its pages, and the legibility of its system (this is what leads Thierry Groensteen to contend that each comic constitutes a system of its own). Panel size and placement contribute to the pace and rhythm of a comic—evenly spaced, similarly sized panels create a metronomic regularity; the interruption of a larger panel can slow the eye and alter the tempo. Page grids of six to nine panels are easier for novice readers to navigate than jagged labyrinths that complicate the mapping of a proper reading sequence.

It might take a few minutes to get a handle on a film's style or a few paragraphs to recognize literary style, but a comic announces itself at a glance. The world of the comic is immediately available. Walt Kelly's warm, even cuddly depiction of Pogo's Okeefenokee Swamp (with its gracefully curled tree trunks and Disney-sweet Rackety Coon Chile) is a world away from the haunted bayou inhabited by the more monstrous Swamp Thing as rendered by Stephen Bissette and John Totleben (where those same trunks ensnarl and tangle), and readers understand that before even reading a word. In a moment, the parameters of the universe begin to be established; reading protocols and horizons of expectation begin to emerge. The cartoonish reality of *Pogo* presents a comedic world where bodies will bounce rather than break, while *Swamp Thing*'s world looks more consequential—a precarious reality constantly on the verge of being overrun by mysterious and malevolent forces.

Comics critic R. Fiore has written on the pleasurable experience of reading comics, which is "the experience of inhabiting the subjective world the cartoonist creates. . . . The cartoonist doesn't merely describe a tree, he determines what trees look like. And so with every person and object in the cartoonist's world." Comics are good at world building, which goes beyond the structure and design of fictional universes in which the stories occur, but also what Eric Hayot calls "aesthetic worldedness"—the cohesion of its various formal and material elements. Such aesthetic worlds are never complete—readers are called upon to "complete" these worlds based on their own knowledge of what it is to *be* in a world: to be hurt, to drive a car, to wear something itchy. Comics creators decide how much, or how little, detail to provide; how immersive, or not, the reading experience is to be; and what the reader must bring to the act of reading to perform this act of completion. Scott McCloud has famously emphasized the degree to which the reader has to "complete" a comic, by which he meant the connections and inferences we must make across panels, but it's true in this larger (and more interesting) sense as well.

And so form, the aesthetic and material in combination, is fundamental to what a comic is and to the experience of the world that it builds. And it must be understood as more than just the signifier for the effective conveyance of a referential element usually called "content" or "meaning."

This form-content divide is both artificial and reductive. Cinema is regarded as a primarily storytelling medium, and indeed, narrative cinema is a dominant mode. Films were initially a single shot, less than a minute in duration, but this novelty soon gave way to multishot works connected by a narrative. This perhaps demonstrates that storytelling was cinema's destiny, but it's also possible that film narrative emerged to permit a more sustained immersion in the spatiotemporal exploration that is the experience of cinema. The myriad ways that comics present movement fueled genres involving hyperkinetic funny animals and superheroes, while its strengths in manipulating time and presenting subjectivity later permitted the explosion of comics autobiographies and memoirs. Content and form intertwine and are interdependent.

David Mazzucchelli's *Asterios Polyp* (2009) is one of the few works that truly merits that underthought label of "graphic novel" and easily illustrates the specific affordances of the comics form. The book itself has the heft of a weighty novel—a somewhat oversized 344-page hardcover. It's telling that there has been no English-language paperback edition; this is clearly the version that Mazzucchelli envisioned, and there is no other. The story is, in many ways, a typical New Yorker story—a jaded academic learns how the real people live and begins to get his emotional life together—but aspects of the story are presented in purely pictorial terms. Mazzucchelli deploys an extensive formal vocabulary, rooted in caricature, to give each character a unique set of visual motifs and associations. The protagonists, the theoretical architect Asterios and his sculptor lover Hana, are drawn differently: the rigidly intellectual Asterios is depicted in flat profile facing one way or the other, and the lines are brittle and stiff; the practicing artist Hana is presented with softer lines and feathering, giving her a textured softness that, metaphorically, suggests that she has greater depth. Each has their own associated color, and when their relationship blossoms, their palettes bleed into one another. Asterios's word balloons are boxy, like narrative captions, and the lettering is similarly blocky. Hana's balloons are all sinuous curves, the lettering of her words more akin to handwriting.

The contrasts between them are presented graphically, allowing the reader easy access to their respective psychologies and attitudes. Style is expressed as part of their very condition of being; the self is projected onto the very surface of the page. In a film, the nuances of performance might allow for something similar, but in this work about two willful artists struggling to navigate one another, graphical contrasts, overlaps, and bleeds prove uniquely suitable to the ideas of the work.

Issues of form merit more focus from comics scholars in the United States. That such scholars tend to cluster in departments of English or communications, neither of which tends to emphasize visual analysis,

FORM SCOTT BUKATMAN

nudges scholarship—whether overtly or covertly—in the directions of narrative or cultural studies. Emphases on the language of the script, the semiotics of superheroic characters, and a preference for more literary "graphic novels" marks enough comics scholarship as to make it a cause for concern. The study of superheroes easily lends itself to issues of identity, whether secret or culturally marginal, and the ongoing shifts in superhero (and audience) demographics and diversity provide rich material for such work. Further, when media that the academy continues to regard as "lesser," such as comic books (to say nothing of superhero comic books), are under the microscope, the pressure on scholars to demonstrate both seriousness and "critical distance" exerts a magnetic pull.

In the resulting scholarship, issues of form are often subsumed by more content-based study. When authorship is considered, it's almost inevitably the writer (Alan Moore, Chris Claremont, G. Willow Wilson) that is positioned as the auteur rather than the editor or artist. There are plenty of exceptions, and more all the time—see recent works by Ramzi Fawaz, Hillary Chute, and Charles Hatfield, to take but three examples—nevertheless, the word and the expression of cultural identity are still overrepresented in comics studies.

And yet I'll admit that one can overvalue medium and form. I once regarded the garishness and exhibitionistic tendencies of superheroes as exemplifying the possibilities of comics. But contemporary audiences of an exponentially greater magnitude and inclusivity quite appropriately regard superheroes as primarily cinematic and televisual. As thousands have noted before me, CGI has made it possible for superhero films to provide perceptually convincing digital spectacle that (almost) matches the visual imagination that Jack Kirby displayed half a century and more ago. The opulence of Wakanda's architecture and costumes in *Black Panther* (Coogler 2018) was perhaps more glorious on-screen than it ever was on the page, and while the 1978 *Superman* promised that we would "believe a man can fly," more recent films deliver ever-more compelling and plausible corporeal spectacles. And the characters shuttle between or among media, accruing meanings along the way that exist (or come to exist) independent of the media that birthed them.

Superheroes, then, have become interesting in ways that are detached from comics' particularities and peculiarities; it could be useful or even (gasp) desirable to study the genre without considering the form and materiality of comics. But then we should distinguish between a field of study that takes superheroes as its primary object, and comics studies, that retains an interest in medium specificities and possibilities.

To do comics studies (and do I have to add "IMHO"?) means grappling with form—as a producer of meaning, as a vehicle for spectacle, as generative of a strangely intimate experience of reading, and as an enriching engagement with aesthetics (which can often be its own reward). What's central to comics is the experience of reading them. And that experience is defined by form: that irreducible confluence of the materiality of the object being read, the properties of style and organization—visual and narrative—deployed by artists and writers, and the events that occur in the world of, and the world that is, the comic.

24

Funnies

Joshua Abraham Kopin

For most of the twentieth century, readers in the United States associated comics not only with the comic book and the graphic novel but also with the comic strips in the "funnies" section of their daily newspaper. The funny pages were an essential aspect of twentieth-century US popular culture, serving as the home for many of the most famous fictional Americans: they were where the Yellow Kid explored Hogan's Alley and the Katzenjammer Kids got into trouble, where Nemo dreamed his little dreams and Krazy Kat fell in love with Ignatz Mouse, where Walt found Skeezix on his doorstep and Blondie married Bumstead, where Nancy and Sluggo got into trouble and Lucy van Pelt pulled the football away from Charlie Brown, where Calvin and Hobbes rode their wagon down the hill and Huey and Riley Freeman fought suburban complacency.

Although they have been marginalized by academic comics studies' project of redeeming the form by elevating it through the superhero comic book and the graphic novel, the funnies represented comics' dominant distribution strategy for the medium's first decades and retained significant cultural currency until the turn of the twenty-first century. They are an essential but underexplored dimension of comics history and culture, an important space of encounter for immigrants and citizens, children and adults, and comics and America's other lively and popular forms. The funnies evolved out of the Sunday supplements that newspapers in New York and elsewhere began to produce in the 1890s but that are particularly associated with that period's circulation wars between Joseph Pulitzer's *New York World* and William Randolph Hearst's *New York Journal*. These supplements, in turn, were influenced by fully illustrated newspapers that had appeared after the Civil War and by the humorous (that is to say, comic) magazines, like *Punch* and *Judge*, that were popular in the late nineteenth century. Alongside steep price cuts, Pulitzer and Hearst attempted to boost the number of papers they were selling by integrating elements from those other periodicals and experimenting with new color printing technologies. It was in the pages of the Sunday supplements that R. F. Outcault, a technical illustrator formerly employed by Thomas Edison, developed the Yellow Kid, a bald boy in a yellow smock whose adventures in the fictional Irish American neighborhood Hogan's Alley made him the medium's first major star. Although Outcault was once called the inventor of the comic strip, his work was influenced by magazine illustrators like A. B. Frost and developed alongside the comics of peers like Frederick Burr Opper and Rudolph Dirks. Together, these artists and others transformed the nineteenth-century political cartoon and comic sequence into the comic strip as we understand it today.

Even as the conventions and expectations of the form shifted, however, it was always in dialogue with other ones. Sunday supplements featured all manner of prose stories and illustrations, and although Outcault was among the first to use recurring characters, sequential images, and the word balloon in combination, most of his "strips" that featured the Yellow Kid were actually large tableaus. These half- or full-page single-image illustrations, crowded with words and figures, depicted the alley's children running chaotic races, playing lawless games of baseball, and participating in national politics, as when they welcomed the Chinese diplomat Li Hung Chang, at the time on a tour of the United States, to the neighborhood in the fall of 1895. The comics influenced other emerging forms too. The film industry, in particular, turned to them for inspiration (Gardner 2012): films based on Opper's Happy Hooligan character began appearing as early 1899, with film versions of Hogan's Alley and Dirk's *Katzenjammer Kids* appearing in 1903 (Crafton [1982] 1993).

A decade after the first appearance of the serial comic strip in the Sunday supplements, episodes of strips also began to consistently appear in daily newspapers. This development ultimately led to a division that persists to this day. Many newspaper comic strips are published in two separate formats: a one-tiered black-and-white strip of a few panels, usually no more than four, during the week and on Saturday, with a longer strip, multitiered and in color, appearing in an expanded section on Sunday. Preceding the appearance of the daily strip, and in the early period of the dual-format schedule, the Sunday strips occupied whole pages in the supplements, a practice that continued for a few decades before they began to shrink at midcentury (LeFevre 2017). At the same time, distribution strategies that likewise persist to the present were being developed. The funnies quickly moved out from New York, with Hearst distributing his Sunday sections to cities around the country, and comic sections began appearing in papers in Philadelphia and San Francisco. Eventually, syndicates like the Newspaper Feature Syndicate (owned by Hearst) and the King Features Syndicate evolved, selling strips to newspapers across the country and allowing cartoonists to develop into national stars (Walker 2004).

The early strips were largely episodic, used recurring gags, and were connected by their title and supporting characters and consistent structures: Opper's Happy Hooligan tried to do the right thing, but his actions are always misinterpreted; R. F. Outcault's Buster Brown always got himself into some kind of trouble and resolved

to learn from it at the end; Winsor McCay's Nemo never failed to wake from his dream. Serial narrative appears in the funnies in the 1910s, and while the daily recursivity of the funny animals, demon children, and domestic comedy that had dominated the early period of newspaper comics continued to appear, alongside them emerged strips in the action and adventure (sci-fi, Western, crime, medieval fantasy, etc.) and dramatic (romance, melodrama) genres that thrived on linear, if stilted, movement forward through a plot. The word *funnies*, then, much like the word *comics*, is a little bit of a misnomer; Buck Rogers, Prince Valiant, Dick Tracy, and Brenda Starr all appeared in the funny pages alongside Charlie Brown and Krazy Kat. Even the comedy strips sometimes got in on serial pleasures, however; the early years of Charles Schulz's *Peanuts*, for example, feature Charlie Brown and his friends growing up into slightly older kids before settling into the ages they would remain for four more decades, while in Frank King's *Gasoline Alley* (begun in 1918), Gary Trudeau's *Doonesbury* (begun in 1970), and Lynn Johnston's *For Better or for Worse* (begun in 1979 and concluded in 2008), characters change, age, and die (LeFevre 2017).

If the funny pages encompassed many different genres, it is the subgenre of the gag strip starring a young character—sometimes called the "demon child" strip—that is perhaps their most enduring cultural legacy (Hatfield 2011). Because funny strips featuring children as main characters and emphasizing them as individuals in their own terms have been popular for the whole history of newspaper comics, their characterization reveals a great deal about strip audiences (or, at least, newspaper publishers' perceptions of those audiences), especially in the first half of the twentieth century. Some of comics' earliest high-profile characters were immigrant children: both Outcault's Yellow Kid and Dirks's Katzenjammer Kids appear to be forces of chaos within rigid ideals of US nativism because they take the cultural forms of the United States and alter them to suit their own needs. After the turn of the century, these strips were joined by satires of the urban upper class; Outcault's Buster Brown and Winsor McCay's Nemo operate as repeated fantasies of escape from the strictures of adult expectations. Similar strips followed: the children in Percy Crosby's *Skippy*, Harold Gray's *Little Orphan Annie*, and Nancy's takeover, with Ernie Bushmiller's assistance, of what had once been her aunt Fritzi Ritzi's strip all center on children navigating utterly incomprehensible adult worlds.

Despite the overwhelming presence and influence of the child character in the funnies, the notion that comics were exclusively for children emerged much later and is related to the extreme popularity of the magazine-formatted comic book at midcentury. Newspaper comics, which, because of their size and modularity, can be enjoyed by two people at the same time or even be split up and shared, instead functioned as a meeting place where children and adults could participate in each other's worlds (Sanders 2016; Hatfield 2011). The importance of the "demon child" comic strip is especially clear in the context of the funnies as shared space; there, comic strip kids lived mental and physical lives familiar to grown-ups, the iconic emptiness of childhood allowing adults to examine those lives as if they were alienated from them. The imagination required to make this process work both attracted children to the otherwise adult world of the newspaper and presented the opportunity for adults to approach the very serious and very real concerns of childhood with the same gravity that they approached their own.

The funnies as a deeply subversive space of generational encounter reached a benchmark when Charles Schulz premiered Charlie Brown and the rest of the *Peanuts* cast in 1950. Schulz's suburban world was largely void of adult presence, a conceit that both allowed adults to see themselves especially clearly in the world of the comic strip and points to the deeply flawed but growing perception that comics were for children that remains with us today. The demon child formulas continued to appear in various updated modes throughout the rest of the twentieth century and into the twenty-first, with Bill Watterson's *Calvin and Hobbes* and Black preteens Huey and Riley Freeman in Aaron McGruder's *The Boondocks* emerging as worthy, if short-lived, successors.

The wide distribution of newspapers and their whole family appeal made the funnies one of the most important popular art forms in the twentieth-century United States. After World War II, a spate of scholarship on the funnies posited that they were the second most widely consumed popular form in the United States, after television, and suggested both that they were a kind of folklore, serving as the shared stuff of US culture and influencing it via the generation of idioms (White and Abel 1963), and that they were reflective of US culture and therefore useful for the social scientific study of it (Berger 1974). Outside of a few early scholars, however, the "new comics studies" has instead largely focused on the superhero comic book and the graphic novel at the expense of the study of the funnies (Hatfield 2011), potentially because of their indisputably popular, rather than literary, appeal. Ignoring the funnies, however, means significantly mischaracterizing the breadth of comics' significant influence on culture, language, and other popular and literary forms, particularly in the nineteenth and first half of the twentieth centuries. This dearth of scholarship is likely worsened by the recent decline of the daily newspaper and its especially ephemeral qualities conspiring to keep primary sources unavailable. As reprint collections of early strips proliferate, however, and as comics studies continues to grow, the funnies represents an emergent field that significantly bolsters the claim for comics' importance in the cultural history of the United States and that does so without having to resort to reproducing misleading cultural hierarchies.

25

Gender

Ian Blechschmidt

The comics medium is obsessed with gender—perhaps because it is also a medium obsessed with bodies. Sometimes it is the bulging biceps of a hypermasculine hero that is the focus of the comics panel. Other times, it is the body, in all its messy, disruptive glory, as in the underground works of Julie Doucet (Kohlert 2012). And other times, bodies in transition are the focus. These might include real bodies, as in Julia Kaye's autobiographical account of gender transition, *Up and Out*, or imaginary and metaphorical, as in countless stories of mutant superbeings. Whatever the focus, as a medium that relies on the rendering of bodies in space—and all the gendered markers and performances that such rendering requires—comics can't *help* but be about gender and the bodies on which they are inscribed.

Many people who study sequential art turn to the theories of Judith Butler to understand the medium's potential for exploring gender, because a number of ways she theorizes gender map onto the unique ways that comics tell stories. She argues, for example, that gender is a process of repeated performances of gendered "stylizations" of the body, not the outward expression of some inherent quality. As Darieck Scott and Ramzi Fawaz point out, Butler's now-classic description of gender as "a kind of imitation for which there is no original" (1993, 313) also "characterizes the comic strip form" (Scott and Fawaz 2018, 202). Comics rely on images in sequence to tell stories, meaning that characters in comics and their bodily "stylizations" are pictured over and over, which can both reinscribe and challenge our ideas about what those stylizations can and should look like.

Butler also questions whether a person's gender—indeed, a *person*—is ever a complete or unified "self," arguing that identity is far more fluid and multifaceted than we often believe ([1991] 2006, 23). The comics medium seems ideally suited to capture this idea because its images in sequence are forever presenting multiple versions of a character's "self" without necessarily resolving the character into a single, stable whole. Comics' own instability allows it, then, to capture the instability of gender. It also allows the medium to capture gender's *intersectionality* with other aspects of identity and experience, such as race or class, owing to the fact that it is always presenting a multifaceted image of a given character without prioritizing any of them as the "real" one. It is this combination of features—the repeating images of characters' bodily performances, the refusal to claim an original or "natural" referent for those stylizations, and the kaleidoscopic representation of characters' "selves"—that gives comics such a profound ability to abstract, dissect, iterate, and reiterate gender performance (*as* performance) and has made gender such a rich topic for both artists and scholars working in and on the comics medium.

Elizabeth El Refaie makes the important point that no bodies exist independent of the concepts that we use to make sense of them: "Our bodies do not constitute a pre-discursive, material reality; rather, they are constructed on the basis of, and marked by, social and cultural assumptions about class, gender, sex, race, ethnicity, age, health, and beauty" (2012b, 58, citing Butler 1993; Waskul and Vannini 2006). A drawing of a body in a comic necessarily includes markers of these assumptions. "If a character is drawn with breasts or without

breasts," Krista Quesenberry argues, "with long hair or with a beard, then the character's gender identity is assumed based on the presence or absence of those gender-encoded physical features" (2017, 418). The images that make up comics, then, can be thought of not as images of bodies per se but as repeated visualizations of these markers and of the "cultural meanings" *through which we understand* gendered bodies, categories, and subjectivities.

Comics thus has the potential both to reinforce these meanings and to challenge them. For some, many comics have historically been reliable and powerful enforcers of the gender status quo. This is a charge sometimes leveled against superhero comics, a genre often (but erroneously) treated as synonymous with "comics" themselves. "Without a doubt," Adilifu Nama notes, "superheroes have played a significant role in presenting idealised projections of ourselves" (2009, 133). Some have pointed out that such projections have composed the repeated iterations of very exaggerated markers of *gender* ideals. Jeffrey Brown provides an example of this line of thinking in his work on comic book masculinity: "Classical comic book depictions of masculinity are perhaps the quintessential expression of our cultural beliefs about what it means to be a man. In general, masculinity is defined by what it is not, namely, 'feminine', and all its associated traits—hard not soft, strong not weak, reserved not emotional, active not passive" (1999, 26–27). And these characteristics are highlighted in the often-hypermuscled bodies of male superheroes. "Modern female characters," on the other hand, according to Brown, "are so thoroughly eroticized that it is near impossible to find a superheroine or villainess that is not defined primarily by her sex appeal" (2011, 77).

Gender has also been a factor in who gets to live up to superheroic ideals. Female characters, for example, have frequently been relegated to supporting roles in superhero comics, mirroring the more passive social roles to which patriarchal norms would see them relegated. (Anyone not conforming to the male/female binary is typically left out of the story altogether.) An extreme example of this is the phenomenon known as "fridging." This term was coined by comics writer Gail Simone to describe her observation "that in mainstream comics, being a girl superhero meant inevitably being killed, maimed or depowered" (1999). The word itself derives from a scene in a 1994 issue of *Green Lantern* in which the title character discovers that his girlfriend has been killed and her body stuffed into a refrigerator. Rather than focusing on the trauma experienced by the victim, the scene focuses on the (male) protagonist's sense of grief and loss. As Gray and Wright note, "The idea of 'fridging' women in comics became a shorthand for the way female characters, and by extension female fans, found themselves sidelined by the industry" (2017, 266).

And yet there are countless examples of comics being used to undermine those same tendencies and the cultural logics that underwrite them. For one thing, many artists have used the comics medium to lay claim to public space for people who have historically been kept out of it because of gender norms and stereotypes. One example is the long-running anthology *Wimmen's Comix*, which committed to publishing work by all female-identified artists (and was run by a rotation of female-identified editors) who had trouble getting published on account of their gender. Comics are unique in the way they claim such space, owing to their constant attestation to the presence of their author(s). Hillary Chute refers to comics as a type of "handwriting" that perpetually foregrounds the creator's presence, style, and ownership over the textual space (2010, 11). In the case of autobiographical comics, this effect is compounded by the fact that the creator literally appears in public on the page. When Kaveri Gopalakrishnan draws the "battle stance" she uses to avoid unwanted attention on public transit ("blank/stern face," "stiff arms," etc.), she is not just narrating a moment from her life; she is also reclaiming her "basic space" (as she puts it) for herself and for others whose movement through the world is often limited by gendered norms, expectations, and even violence.

Comics do not need to be autobiographical to claim space for historically marginalized people. According to Sheena Howard, the comic book series *Cyberzone* features a Black, lesbian superheroine, Amanda Shane, who "productively deepens representation of Black queer women" (2018, 7). Howard identifies many ways that the comic does this. One example is the portrayal of Shane's relationship with her girlfriend, Chela, which "does not neatly fit into the stereotypical mold of one hyper-masculine female who is partnered with a submissive-feminine partner" (8, citing M. Moore 2006, 120). In this and other ways, *Cyberzone* is an example of comics that claim public space for communities who are often misrepresented or simply not represented at all.

Countless other artists have also used the comics medium to explore the limits, costs, and (il)logics of hegemonic gender norms through their work. The title character in Chris Ware's *Jimmy Corrigan: The Smartest Kid on Earth*, for example, confronts the "idealised projections" of adult masculinities presented in his childhood superhero fantasies as the flabby, balding, painfully ordinary real-life versions—embodied by himself and his father—fail to live up to them. Kukhee Choo analyzes how some shojo manga (Japanese comics historically associated with female audiences) complicate traditional notions of gender through their blending of various gender markers. She points to, for example, some series' depiction of male characters with "feminine" features ("pretty faces, slender bodies . . . graceful mannerisms" [2008, 291]) and of female characters who embody "both the traits of a mother-like caretaker and an independent sexualized girl," traits previously kept rigorously separate in Japanese media (2008, 293). A graphic novel like Edie Fake's *Gaylord Phoenix* challenges the historical (and, as the comic shows, inadequate) logic of gender boundaries and binaries altogether, as the title character undergoes a profound journey of healing in an ever-transforming body that never resolves into a stable collection of exclusively masculine- or feminine-coded bodily traits.

Fake's work brings to mind Butler's questioning of the very concept of a stable, single identity, on which many assumptions about gender are based. "The 'coherence' and 'continuity' of 'the person,'" Butler argues, "are not logical or analytic features of personhood, but, rather, socially instituted and maintained norms of intelligibility" ([1991] 2006, 23). For Butler, the single, contiguous self is a fiction, and comics represent the self in a way that resists that fiction. Ramzi Fawaz has done extensive work to show this tendency in superhero stories from the "Silver Age" of comics, which was roughly inaugurated in the early 1960s with the emergence of Marvel Comics as a powerhouse of superhero comics publishing; he argues that these comics present a queer reimagining of previously dominant ideas about gender: "The visual instability of the superhero's body across time and space negated the figure's previous iconic status as a seemingly invulnerable masculine body by proliferating countless permutations of the superhero that refused to cohere into a unified image or physiology" (2016, 18). Superhero bodies can stretch, like Mr. Fantastic's, become invisible, like Sue Storm's, or be made suddenly and simultaneously powerful and monstrous, like the Thing's. The gender performances represented by such images are constantly changing across and within panels, highlighting and even celebrating their instability

and flexibility and thus the instability and flexibility of gender itself (Fawaz 2016).

Even if they are not depicted with superheroically mutable bodies, characters in comics are depicted multiple times (sometimes dozens or hundreds) across multiple panels and pages, from different angles and perspectives, making it difficult to think of any single image as a contiguous, "real" version of that character. This is compounded by comics' layered temporality. Comics may depict a character at multiple points in time on the same page or even in the same panel, such as when a protagonist is pictured in the "past" while they narrate their story in the "present" through caption boxes. When Zeina Abriched combines a verbal narration of an event with an image of herself as a child experiencing that event in *A Game for Swallows*, two different iterations of her "self" that existed at two different times appear on the page at once. This technique—which can also be seen in other graphic memoirs like *Persepolis*, *The Arab of the Future*, *Fun Home*, *One Hundred Demons*, and any number of others—"establishes a temporal structure in which multiple selves exist graphically" within the same visual field (Chute 2010, 140). In such a temporal structure, no gender (or any) performance can stand as a representation of the stable, unified self, since multiple versions of the self are equally present and active on the page. In comics, the "past" self is no more or less real than the "present" or the "future" self. The self that conforms to normative boundaries of the body is no more or less real than the one that exceeds them. Gender is represented as multiple, multifaceted, and forever incomplete.

Perhaps this is why so many comics explore how gender interacts with other axes of identity and experience *also* tied up with bodies—like race, ethnicity, and class—recognizing that the raced or classed self is similarly no more or less real than the gendered self and that indeed none of these is really separable. In Gene Luen Yang's *American Born Chinese*, when Jin is advised by a schoolmate to stay away from a (Caucasian) girl he likes because he is Chinese American (and "she has to start paying attention to who she hangs out with" to preserve her social status [2006, 179]), he is "learning what it means to be a man" in the United States, where "Asian masculinity [has been] feminised . . . emasculated," and stereotyped (Oh 2017, 21). Through her "defiant pin-up aesthetic," Jackie Ormes's Candy character both "positions Black women in . . . [an] aesthetic usually associated with white pin-up femininity" and "engages in a larger class discourse aimed at solidifying the dignity and pride that fine adornments might bring to those disadvantaged by color and class" (Whaley 2015, 53). When heroic Isaiah Bradley—one of several Black men to don Captain America's star-spangled uniform before Steve Rogers in the series *Truth: Red, White, and Black*—struggles with his mistreatment by his own government, he lays bare the complicated relationship between race, masculinity, and citizenship in the United States (Wanzo 2009). And Muslim American superhero Kamala Khan / Ms. Marvel not only saves Jersey City; she "helps to construct a narrative about Muslim women that is anti-colonial, feminist, and liberational. [Superheroes like her] are individuals whose control of their own bodies challenges the colonization of female bodies that is embedded in the history of Islam and the West, while also establishing a feminist voice that is unapologetically Islamic" (Arjana 2018, xx). In the realm of comics' infinite and unstable representational possibilities, comics artists and scholars continually learn more about the medium's capacity to tell stories about complex characters with multifaceted, ever-shifting gender identities.

As Sheena Howard puts it, "Often, our reality shapes our imagination, but our imagination should not be limited by our reality" (2018, 5). Comics are sometimes criticized for reinforcing gender stereotypes but can just as easily represent ways of imagining and understanding gender performance that falls *outside* of or even explode those same norms. They can also combine and layer gendered images in ways that challenge or even destabilize taken-for-granted ideas about what constitutes gender. It is perhaps in this combination of representational capacity and representational instability that both artists and scholars have found the greatest potential for exploring, confronting, and reimagining our ideas about gender and how it shapes people's experience.

26

Genre
Shelley Streeby

Genre is a loaded word for comics studies in the United States, as it has been for studies of mass and popular forms since the industrial and print revolutions. On one hand, genre is an indispensable term in scholarship that focuses on comics as a genre of literary, popular, mass, and visual culture and sequential art. Genres such as superheroes, crime, humor, children's, romance, war, memoir, and others are central to comics history. On the other, this keyword is still often used pejoratively to situate comics as low and suspect within hierarchies that distinguish genre-marked cultural forms from "literature" and others with more cultural capital. In the last twenty years or so, however, comics have risen within cultural hierarchies—partly because of the publication of graphic novels and other kinds of comics in more expensive formats with cultural prestige—that experiment with genre and can be understood in relation to realist codes that privilege the representation of everyday life and allied forms of memoir and autobiography. Experimenting with genre and engaging comics readers' multigenre literacies is not a recent phenomenon, however, and this has long been a strength of the form. And while the mark of genre has historically been stigmatizing, the translatability of genre across cultural forms is surely one of the biggest reasons for comics' continuing significance in global popular culture.

Genre is defined by capitalist marketing strategies and categories, choices made by individuals and teams of creators within constraints, and the activity of readers. The historical disdain for comics as a low form marked by genre partly derives from its emergence within industrial contexts of production and its status as a commodity in an emerging mass culture. The nineteenth-century history of US comics is also strongly shaped by changing configurations of whiteness, race, nation, citizenship, colonialism, empire, gender, and class. In the US, the mass-circulation lithographs, story papers, and illustrated newspapers and magazines of the print revolution of the 1840s, which coincided with the industrial revolution in northeastern US cities, ongoing settler-colonial violence against Indigenous people, and the US-Mexican War (Streeby 2002), are one important beginning point. In the 1850s and 1860s, sequential graphic narratives in the war, news, and history genres were also prominently featured in oversized illustrated weeklies such as Frank Leslie's Illustrated Paper, which extensively covered the US Civil War, the Indian Wars, and sites of "new empire." Such sites include Hawaii and Cuba—both of which provide pictorial narratives of city life, immigrants, and race that extended and transformed the cultural work of earlier "mysteries of the city" and frontier literature.

Late nineteenth-century comic strips such as The Yellow Kid (1895–98), which featured tableaux and graphic narratives of slum life starring a New York City Irish American street urchin, connect to earlier mysteries of the city literature, urban reporting, and pictorial city and empire narratives while also illuminating shifting boundaries of whiteness in this period. The original publication contexts for the strip were mass-circulation daily newspapers known for fanning the flames of imperialism: Richard F. Outcault's character originally appeared in Joseph Pulitzer's New York World and later during a circulation war was induced to move to industrial and media magnate William

Randolph Hearst's *New York Journal*. Strips about the globe-trotting adventures of the mischievous German Katzenjammer Kids (1897–2006) were also staples of mass-circulation daily newspapers and Sunday supplements. By the early 1900s, Hearst was marketing booklets composed of comics reprints starring some of the most popular comic strip characters of the day. These early comic strips and comic booklets appealed to adult and younger readers alike with genre stories of boys' hijinks, small-town and city life, imperial adventure, and funny animals such as George Herriman's *Krazy Kat* (1913–44).

The 1930s was an important flashpoint in the emergence of the comic book as a distinct genre separate from the newspapers, illustrated magazines, and other periodicals in which they had formerly been embedded. Even as comic books became a distinct form of culture and the superhero genre became ascendant, however, many other genres coexisted within the pages of early comic books. This encouraged readers to both develop cross-genre literacies and connect to longer histories of genres such as science fiction, Western, crime, sports, humor, and imperial adventure in nineteenth-century paper literature, dime novels, pulp fiction, and early cinema. All of these genres, along with funny animals and more, appeared in Dell Publishing's *Famous Funnies: A Carnival History of Comics* (1933), a historically significant multigenre compilation of previously published strips that was distributed by Woolworth's. This landmark comic book was soon followed by the monthly periodical *Famous Funnies* (1934–55), distributed by the massive American News Company and sold at newsstands across the United States, which also featured multiple genres including humor, funny animals, boys' hijinks, adventures, sports, war, history, and science fiction and introduced the character Buck Rogers.

Although comics genres are often imagined as discrete, the promiscuous mingling of genres is more common throughout comics history: comic books often contain multiple stories and genres within their pages, while individual stories and story arcs frequently engage multiple genre codes. This is true, for instance, of the superhero comics that became popular after the 1938 introduction of Superman in *Action Comics* #1, published by Detective Comics, the precursor of DC. While a colorful image of a caped Superman's hypermuscular body holding a villain's green car in the air famously appears on the cover and a "startling adventure" about "the most sensational strip character of all time" leads the issue, the comic book also contains Westerns ("Chuck Dawson" and "Tex Thomson"); crime, mysteries, and imperial adventure stories ("Master Magician Zatara," "South Sea Strategy," and "The Adventures of Marco Polo"); a humor story ("Sticky Mitt Simpson"); a sports story ("Pep Martin"); and more. The inclusion of stories representing several different genres within superhero titles continued in the late 1930s and early 1940s as new superheroes such as Batman (1939) and Captain America (1941) emerged. *Detective Comics* #27, which introduced the "Amazing and Unique Adventures of The Batman" on the cover and in the lead story, also included the humorous tale of Tenderfoot, a boy soldier; the adventures of "Steve Saunders, Ace Investigator and the Killers of Kurdistan"; a Western starring "Buck Marshall, Range Detective"; the story of Flatfloot Flannagan, a funny Irish cop; Sax Rohmer's "The Mysterious Doctor Fu Manchu"; and other stories of diverse genres featuring white boys and men as the leads. The first issue of *Captain America Comics* similarly featured a cover image of Captain America punching out Hitler, which illustrates a pivotal scene in the lead story, followed by one about Hurricane, a Greek God who returns to Earth to fight his ancestral enemy Pluto, and another featuring the white lead character Tuk Caveboy in "Stories of the Dark Ages."

As these examples suggest, while a diverse array of genres appeared within early superhero comic books, despite the abundance of funny animals and female humans in minor roles, most of the featured characters in and the imagined audience for these comics were white boys and men. During this era, "the creative potential" of the superhero genre was "mitigated," as Ramzi Fawaz (2016) puts it, "by the superhero's affirmative relationship to the state" (7), since "with rare exceptions the defining characteristic of World War II superheroes was an invulnerable male body whose physical strength functioned as a literal bulwark against threats to the nation's borders and ideological values" (8). In other words, manhood and the state were mutually reinforcing in most early superhero comics, as superheroes confronted villains who were imagined as threatening national boundaries, ideals, and norms—a dynamic that could easily become racialized when the nation was imagined as white. And while relationships between gender and genre in comics are complex, and girls and women have always found ways to participate in a mass culture that is not primarily aimed at them and to enjoy boys' stories as well as female-marked genres, there were relatively few of the latter in the early twentieth century.

All of this changed during the 1940s with the arrival of *Wonder Woman* (1940); *Archie*, which prominently featured female teenage characters Betty and Veronica; girl detectives and journalists such as Brenda Starr; and romance comics of the post–World War II period, such as Captain America cocreators' Joe Simon's and Jack Kirby's *Young Romance* (1947), which was soon followed by *Young Love*, *Young Brides*, and other similar titles. Publishers aimed these romances not only at female but also at nonchild audiences. On the cover of *Young Romance*, Crestwood Publications and the Simon-Kirby team prominently inserted

under the title the tagline "Designed for the More ADULT Readers of Comics." A few years later, Fawcett Publications hoped to capitalize on Black women as comics readers by offering three issues of the comic *Negro Romance* (1950), which featured Black women and men as idealized romantic protagonists and was the result of the collaboration between white editor-writer Roy Ald and Black illustrator Alvin Hollingsworth.

This appeal to adult readers and creative teamwork with an array of genres continued in the post–World War II period until 1954, when the Comics Code Authority (CCA) was created by the Comics Magazine Association of America as a self-regulatory move after Senate hearings in which genre comics were demonized as a threat to children (Hajdu 2009). At the center of this moral panic was EC Comics, originally Maxwell Charles Gaines's Educational Comics, which included Bible stories and histories for children and teachers. After Gaines died in a motorcycle accident, his son Bill took over the company, which he renamed Entertaining Comics and made famous for genre comics such as science fiction, Western romances, war, and especially crime and horror. Under Gaines's watch, EC also published "preachies," which Quiana Whitted (2019) characterizes as "social-protest comics" that drew on "the conventions of EC's signature genres to confront racial prejudice, religious intolerance, anti-communist rhetoric, and other forms of social discrimination" (x). Whitted argues that rather than being an impediment to complex thinking, in the "preachies," the "so-called clichés and constraints of genre ultimately served as an important conduit for EC to disrupt normative assumptions about race and ethnic identity and to complicate relevant notions of patriotism, tradition, safety, and authority in the process" (xi). In these ways, genre was an important tool for comics oriented toward social justice in the Cold War US.

Although the constraints of the CCA ultimately forced EC out of business, Whitted suggests the company "inspired new generations of comics creators, particularly those associated with underground and alternative comics" (23) in the 1960s and 1970s as well as later independent comics creators such as Lynda Barry, Alan Moore, and Daniel Clowes. Direct market distribution, beginning in the early 1970s, would allow creators and companies to bypass the regulatory norms of the CCA and experiment with forbidden genres, overtly aim for adult readers, and include more explicit sex. A little earlier, the mid- to late 1960s Silver Age of comics was notable, Deborah Whaley explains, for its "modern break with the confines of the Comic Book Codes, its expansion into television and animation, and its expansion of the superhero genre" (75). When Eartha Kitt replaced Julie Newmar as Catwoman in TV's *Batman*, for instance, the character gathered "deeper meanings and expanded interpretations of race, gender, and sexuality" (75), challenging "notions of space and blackness in the popular imagination and the confines of social relations of racial apartheid and segregation in the United States" (76). At the same time, new superhero comics such as Marvel's *The X-Men* broke with earlier genre codes by emphasizing what Fawaz calls a liberal "cosmopolitics" (2016, 23) nonnormatively embodied by often multiracial teams that sometimes included women. Thus readers did not have to wait for the arrival of underground comix and alternative comics to experience renewed appeals to young adults and older people and new ways of playing with genre to question dominant social hierarchies and structures during the 1960s and early 1970s.

Graphic novels of the 1980s and 1990s restored some prestige to the lowly comics genre of popular culture by incorporating a valued literary term and privileging "realist" genres such as memoir, biography, history, and journalism. Throughout comics history, however, realist and nonrealist genre codes have coexisted to a greater extent than is generally acknowledged. The classic work of cartoonist Jaime Hernandez is one among many significant examples in the recent history of comics of the coexistence and creative juxtaposition of realist and nonrealist genre codes within a single title and body of work (Streeby 2017); his Maggie stories from the long history of *Love and Rockets* mix scenes of everyday life and quotidian spaces and places with fantasy and science fiction, among other genres. Not surprisingly, readers of comics have also long been and still are adept at developing multigenre fluencies and moving between realist and nonrealist genres.

In *Speculative Blackness: The Future of Race in Science Fiction* (2016), Andre Carrington gives audiences special power when it comes to defining genre. Carrington suggests that "it is in the shared, contested space of the audience that the artifacts of the genre's production are translated into use." Carrington examines how Marvel Comics superhero Storm "appears in stories shaped by Afro-Asian, Afro-Native, and diasporic connections that reconfigure the genre traditions she draws into conversation in *X-Men*." He also explores how fan letters in *Icon*, one of the 1990s comics published by Black-owned Milestone Media, stage an encounter between the genre conventions of superhero comics and "the genre conventions that shape other popular representations of Black Americans." Throughout, Carrington emphasizes that "whole segments of society experience genre traditions in different ways according to their sense of how these mediations pertain to their lives and the lives of others." In other words, instead of imagining genre in terms of a "collection of fixed meanings" imported from other texts, Carrington suggests comics studies scholars should understand genre as "mediating a variety of lived conditions as well as fantastic possibilities conceived from multiple vantage points" and operating across multiple media. This means reckoning with the creative work of genre activated by different kinds of comics readers and viewers despite industrial constraints inside and outside the United States, across multiple platforms, including film, TV, games, and internet forms of digital comics.

27

Graphic Novel
Tahneer Oksman

In a now well-cited interview, Art Spiegelman, creator of the Pulitzer Prize–winning *Maus*, a two-volume memoir-in-comics recounting his parents' experiences of living through the Holocaust, once famously explained that he had been interested in making a comic book that would require a bookmark (Juno and Spiegelman 1997). Sometimes referred to as the father of the graphic novel, Spiegelman has nonetheless admitted to a beleaguered acceptance of the increased circulation and popularity of a term that he, and other cartoonists, have often seen as troubling. "The Faustian deal is worth making: it keeps my book in print," he admitted in a more recent interview (Mitchell and Spiegelman 2014, 24). Indeed, the history of the keyword *graphic novel* is a contentious one, as evidenced by the extent to which it has been variously claimed, defined, or disavowed—as everything from a medium, a genre, a marketing term, a movement, a format, and a form to a way of reading. These discrepancies point to misapprehensions and complexities surrounding the term as well as the ideological and historiographical implications of such categorizing and naming.

The term *graphic novel* famously graced the cover of Will Eisner's *A Contract with God and Other Tenement Stories* in 1978, and it was largely through this usage that the term became popularized. Eisner employed it as a way to describe his work of short stories about tenement life in 1930s New York in order to appeal to a trade book publisher and, he hoped subsequently, an audience beyond the world of already avid comics readers. While some, including Eisner himself for a while, attributed the neologism to Eisner, comics historians have evidenced how the term had been evoked at least over a dozen years earlier (Hatfield 2005; Kunka 2017a). In the mid-1960s, fanzine writer Richard Kyle deployed the term, along with "graphic story," to distinguish a different kind of comic book from the majority of those in circulation at the time, one with a so-called serious, or at the very least what could be seen as forward-looking, artistic or storytelling ambition (Harvey 2001; Kunka 2017a). The term was then used by editor and publisher Bill Spicer in his *Graphic Story Magazine*, a sophisticated fanzine published in the late 1960s through the mid-1970s (Hatfield 2005). For Eisner, the term was primarily meant to differentiate the content and tone of what he was composing from the broader comics market and especially from works presumably aimed at young audiences or those trading primarily in humor or satire. As a marketing strategy, the term has had an outsize influence on what would eventually become an overhaul in the production and distribution of many works of comics by the turn into the twenty-first century; one of its immediate effects was to increase the cost of many comics publications for individual consumers (Hatfield 2005; García 2015). In addition to his part in catalyzing such seismic shifts in the industry, Eisner is perhaps best remembered for the ways in which he experimented with formal conventions of comics storytelling, including most notably a restructuring away from a fixed grid to more narrative-driven arrangements of the comics page or pages. He outlined many of his innovative narrative techniques in his 1985 work, *Comics and Sequential Art*, a book widely seen as the first English-language attempt to appraise and codify the properties of comics (Sabin 1996).

The era of the graphic novel is generally said to have started more or less in England and in North America in the 1970s and 1980s, with other important principal works published around then, in addition to Eisner's, including (though not limited to) Justin Green's forty-two-page-long autobiographical work from 1972, *Binky Brown Meets the Holy Virgin Mary*; Spiegelman's aforementioned *Maus*, published in book form as two volumes in 1986 and then 1991; writer Frank Miller and illustrators Miller and Klaus Janson's collected miniseries riffing on the story of Bruce Wayne, *Batman: The Dark Knight Returns*, published in 1986; and writer Alan Moore, artist Dave Gibbons, and colorist John Higgins's *Watchmen*, a series reimagining the superhero myth and collected in a single volume in 1987 (Sabin 1996; Chute 2010; Baetens and Frey 2015). As a number of scholars and practitioners have argued, this supposed turn to the graphic novel was actually more of a return. First, it was a return to the albums heralded by the generally accepted progenitors of the medium, such as Swiss teacher and caricaturist Rodolphe Töpffer (1799–1846). Töpffer's early nineteenth-century, self-described *histoires en estampes*, which were fictionalized, humorous, character-driven stories composed in comics and eventually printed and consumed internationally, have long been recognized as the original "comic strips" (Kunzle 2007; García 2015). Second, the so-called development of the late twentieth-century graphic novel can be understood as a revival of sorts, a rekindling of an investment in comics by adult audiences, who had been the principal readers of comics in the nineteenth century, from humor magazines popularized in Europe to widely admired North American newspaper strips (Sabin 1996; Groensteen 2009; Baetens and Frey 2015). Other commonly cited forbearers to what we now think of as the "graphic novel," whether based in content, form, style, audience, or a mix of these elements, include, as some examples, Belgian-born Frans Masereel's woodcut wordless novels, published beginning in the late 1910s and soon followed by American Lyn Ward's woodcut wordless novels, including his best-selling *Gods' Man*, which came out a week before the 1929 Wall Street crash; Arnold Drake, Leslie Waller, and Matt Baker's then-racy "picture novel," *It Rhymes with Lust*, an illustrated pulp noir published in 1950; editor and cartoonist Harvey Kurtzman and publisher William Gaines's highly influential humor magazine, *MAD* (later, *MAD Magazine*), launched in 1952; and Japanese cartoonists Shigeru Mizuki, Tatsuo Nagatmatsu, and Yoshihiro Tatsumi's *gekiga*, a term coined in 1957 that can be translated as "dramatic pictures" (Eisner [1986] 2008; Hajdu 2009; Mitchell and Spiegelman 2014; García 2015). While all of these various publications can be seen as crucial influences in what would later come to be collectively known as the "graphic novel," other critics have emphasized that whether in terms of length, subject matter, audience, or aesthetic, the so-called graphic novel has existed over the course of the history of comics. Rejections of the notion of the graphic novel as something *novel*, or new, are thus often based in large part on frustration with how the contemporary moment in comics is often separated from a longer, complicated, global, and diversified history and is also often evoked in a way that suppresses and localizes a more dynamic and complex present.

Early rejections of the term in the wake of its increased and more prevailing usage in the late 1980s and early 1990s emerged most vocally from cartoonists themselves, including those whose works are hailed as foundational. Many regarded the term suspiciously, as definitionally vague or confusing, as a commercial invention, and, perhaps most urgently, as potentially damaging to a medium that had for so long flourished not only despite but also quite likely because of its regularly having been considered an "outsider art" that can, in Spiegelman's words, "fly below [the] critical radar"

(quoted in Sabin 1996, 9; Hatfield 2005). Spiegelman's objections to the phrase, like those of many invested in the medium, generally acknowledge that while it may have useful, practical implications, it is neither accurate nor precise, and perhaps most damagingly, it seems to suggest, or reinforce, a hegemonic framework for accepted ways of telling stories (Witek 2007; Spiegelman and Ware 2014). Many from within the field thus find *graphic novel* to be an elitist, misleading bid for legitimacy. Some argue that the term and its attendant status implications potentially even mask problems of cultural illegitimacy that continue to affect the world of creating, distributing, and reading comics and, more broadly, the power dynamics behind various forms of cultural capital (see Pizzino 2016).

In addition to such arguments against the contemporary use of *graphic novel* as problematically portentous and historically misleading, many have rejected the term for its semantic inaccuracies. For some, *graphic novel* has been introduced as a corrective to the more widespread word *comics*, which suggests humor where often there is none. *Graphic novel*, in turn, highlights the supposedly more sophisticated literary and visually artistic nature of a certain kind of work. Nonetheless, as scholars like Catherine Labio have pointed out, with this phrasing, *graphic* serves as a modifier to *novel*, making the focal point words over images and reinforcing the false notion that visuals, or pictures, are somehow "easier," less sophisticated, and potentially even dangerous in comparison with words (Mitchell 2004; Labio 2011). This phraseology points to a broader problem in discussions of comics, which is that the literary element is often emphasized over and above the visual element instead of a recognition that the two, word and image, when both present, function together to form what Thierry Groensteen and others have recognized as a "language" or "system," one that, as Hillary Chute has observed, has its own internal grammar and logic and can be considered both externally and internally "dialogic" (Groensteen [1999] 2007; Chute 2015).

Perhaps even more distressing for some is that the word *novel* suggests fictional output in addition to a certain requirement of length, seriousness of subject, and physical properties (book format). Scholars and cartoonists have come up with, or brought credibility to, alternative terms, some broadening out and some narrowing the scope of the genre or genres, autobiographical and otherwise, referenced therein. A small sampling of these includes "comic-strip biography," "comic-strip novel," "graphic narrative," "autographics," and "graphic storytelling" (Brown 2003; Clowes 2005; Chute and DeKoven 2006; Whitlock 2006; Heer and Worcester 2009). Many of the best-known works of what is thought of as the contemporary graphic novel are nonfiction. These include Marjane Satrapi's two-volume *Persepolis*, published in 2000 and 2004, an autobiographical story of growing up in Iran during and after the Islamic revolution. The critically acclaimed best seller was turned into an animated film in 2007, with a cast including the well-known French actress Catherine Deneuve, and it was nominated for and received a number of prestigious awards. Similarly, Alison Bechdel's best-selling *Fun Home*, a 2006 work recounting her childhood with a closeted father, was adapted into a musical in 2013, whereby it gained even more recognition and acclaim. Though many practitioners who have helped usher in this era of the graphic novel, from Chris Ware and Charles Burns to the Hernandez brothers and Jessica Abel, have often traded in rich, fictional forms of comics storytelling, the ubiquity of nonfictional texts in the more popularized comics landscape is an additional complication that has invited serious inquiry and also reinforced the importance of carefully scrutinizing questions of terminology (see Chaney 2011a).

Despite these limitations, by now many working in the field embrace the term even as they acknowledge it as confusing or even, like Eddie Campbell, "disagreeable" ("The *Drawn & Quarterly Manifesto*" [2003] 2015; E. Campbell [2004] 2010). As a movement and a popular term, *graphic novel* has come with benefits, including the expanded inclusion of works of comics into institutions of learning, like high schools, colleges, and libraries; the increased share of graphic narratives into the broader book and bookstore market; their inclusion in literary and scholarly conversations and analyses; and the generally improved attention, in various media outlets, brought to the sphere of comics as a storytelling form. As the audience for comics has grown, so too have its practitioners and critics slowly diversified to include, for example, more people of color and more women (though as many continually and rightly point out, comics still have a very long way to go). As Diane Noomin expressed in her own interview in the late 1990s with Andrea Juno, "It's very frustrating to just have your work sold in comics stores. You know it'll only sell a small amount. You know a huge section of the population won't see it. And you know almost no women will see it" (Juno and Noomin 1997, 181–82). By leading new audiences to the wide world of comics, fresh and unexpected ways of playing with, manipulating, thinking about, and discussing comics have also emerged. Perhaps this is why it is no surprise that, for all of their hesitations and misgivings, it is those most invested in comics who have been at the forefront of such broadening marketing strategies. Spiegelman, along with other comics visionaries including Chris Oliveros and Peggy Burns (then working at DC Comics), successfully lobbied the book industry in 2003 to make "comics and graphic novels" an officially recognized subject category (Rogers and Heer 2015). The inclusion of "comics" alongside "graphic novels" suggests a continued awareness of the problematics surrounding each term individually, while it also reflects an acknowledgment of the marketing potential of *graphic novel* as both alluring and capacious.

As recent histories of the graphic novel make clear, the term is inarguably linked to a significant historical shift. The increased familiarity of the term marks a period brought on by a variety of forces—cultural, aesthetic, technological, political, and economic—that needs to be more fully studied, explored, and prodded if we are to fully understand where comics have been and where it is going (see Lopes 2009; García 2015; Baetens and Frey 2015; Baetens, Frey, and Tabachnik 2018). Ultimately, as Charles Hatfield has judiciously pointed out, "we ignore the term at our peril" (Hatfield 2005, 29). Rather than discount a term that has taken hold, we might instead more carefully track its history and usage. To sidestep it would suggest willful ignorance in the face of a changing cultural landscape, however difficult and tangled that terrain.

28

Gutter

Christopher Pizzino

Over the past two centuries, printers and bookmakers have used the term *gutter* in a range of ways. Initially it referred to a grooved device that minimized accidental marks in letterpress printing (Savage 1841, 307–8). Subsequently, it named the small segment of a page behind the seam in a book's binding (Jacobi 1888, 55); later still, it referred to the seam itself (Darley 1965, 114). All these meanings have some association with efficiency and management of excess or waste, probably echoing the term's origins in architecture and civil engineering. Such echoes are perhaps still heard in the term's most widespread usage in publishing today. *Gutter* now names the blank spaces between printed columns, which shorten lines of text to facilitate rapid scanning.

Because gutters arrange and pace reading experience in spatially specific ways to keep our attention flowing, it is easy to see why the term has become the name for spaces separating panels in a comics sequence. Upon first encountering the whole of a comic strip, page, or book, we see immediately how it is divided into parts for our reading attention—usually by the blank space of gutters. When comic book artists discuss their creative process in making a strip or page, there is little talk about gutter placement—or about gutters at all; the focus is on panel shape, layout, and page design. Among comics scholars and theorists, however, the gutter is a notable and sometimes controversial subject.

Scholarly ideas about the gutter have tended toward one of two positions. The first holds that the gutter is simply an unremarkable convention with self-evident usefulness for readers and creators alike. As we will see in the case of French comics theory, this perspective is compatible with the idea that gutters might direct readers' attention in more than one way. The second idea is that, in being an absence or lack on the page, the gutter plays a special role in readers' engagement with comics. The difference between these positions can often be stark, and ongoing debate between them is to be expected—although, as will shortly appear, the first position has produced stronger evidence. At the same time, the overall disposition of the debate sheds light on the cultural status of comics and comics studies, suggesting how and why scholarly interest in the gutter has proceeded along certain lines.

In English-language comics studies over the past quarter century, the idea that the gutter has particular power as absence or lack has been especially prominent thanks to its most well-known advocate, comics creator and theorist Scott McCloud. In "Blood in the Gutter," the third chapter of his groundbreaking work *Understanding Comics* (1993), McCloud argues that the gutter profoundly affects the reader's imagination. His memorable example is a simple two-panel sequence, the first panel showing a man with a raised ax threatening another man with death, the second showing a skyline and a loud scream. These two images, each a separate scene, can be perceived as one story through closure, "the phenomenon of observing the parts but perceiving the whole" (63). McCloud asserts that while many forms of closure—for instance, the perception of photographs as representations of reality—may be automatic, "closure in comics is far from continuous and anything but involuntary!" (68). The gutter, the visible gap between panels, is crossed by active visions seen only in the mind's eye.

On this point, McCloud is profuse and insistent, if not entirely clear. Because they are separate, static

images, "comics panels fracture both time and space, offering a jagged, staccato rhythm of unconnected moments. But closure allows us to connect these moments and mentally construct a continuous, unified reality" (67). McCloud is confident this mental construction requires conscious effort on the reader's part. Discussing his central example, he addresses the reader directly: "I may have drawn an axe being raised . . . but I'm not the one who let it drop or decided how hard the blow, or who screamed, or why. That, dear reader, was your special crime, each of you committing it in your own style" (68). McCloud does not precisely establish "where" or "when" this mental crime takes place. In his example, readers must see the second panel—presumably without imagining anything specific "in" the intervening gutter—and then backtrack to imagine what has not been shown. Regardless of its precise workings, McCloud sees the gutter as the guarantee that comics sequences are open to reader engagement, and that such engagement—filling in what gutters omit—is specific to the comics medium.

It is no accident that McCloud's central example is a murder. Depicting a scene associated with crime and horror—the genres most despised by anticomics crusaders of the mid-twentieth century—McCloud evokes the specter of comics' low status in US cultural history. Thus he challenges a central assumption of much anticomics discourse: that readers of violent comics images are passive victims. Asserting that the reader is the creator's "equal partner in crime," McCloud values the static quality of the comics image, cut off from its neighboring images by blank gutters, as precisely what stimulates reader activity (68). Further, he implicitly argues against the inferiority of comics images relative to film, a medium with much higher cultural prestige. Thus McCloud attempts to redeem the gutter as evidence of the medium's unique power and of the comics reader's special agency.

As a component of McCloud's overall project of combating the marginalization of comics, this redemptive reversal is understandable. Certainly it has inspired similar arguments concerning the power and significance of comics as a "low" medium. For instance, Jared Gardner (2012) has asserted a connection between "comics' inability to escape the *cultural* gutter" and "comics artists' living in and experimenting with the *formal* gutter, both literal and metaphorical, that defines the narrative apparatus" (xii). Not surprisingly, the gutter has become a way to link comics to a variety of intellectual traditions concerned with the marginalized, the oppressed, the repressed, and the unrepresentable. Discussions of the gutter have claimed that comics have a special relationship to, for example, Lacanian conceptions of selfhood and perception as dispersed and unstable (Ault 1997, 2000, 2004), Derridean and Deleuzian conceptions of difference as open-ended and transformative (Pitkethly 2009), queerness as subversive and disruptive (Gregory 2012), and the gothic as a discourse of displacement (in this context, it can be designated a "crypt," with Derridean and other overtones; Round 2014). In short, the gutter is a reliable site for new theories of comics, or at least for new connections to existing theories from various disciplines.

But such energetic intellectual investment in the gutter does not necessarily shed light on the process of reading comics. The many voices arguing for the importance of the gutter in comics studies often assume, but have actually done little to verify, McCloud's conception of the gutter as a key stimulus for readers' imagination and agency. Cognitive science, meanwhile, has produced a significant body of research on how comics reading, as mental activity, actually functions. This research suggests that McCloudian ideas of how gutters work are incorrect—which, as we will consider in conclusion, might indicate that theoretical investment in the gutter reveals more about the disposition of comics in academic study than it does about the intrinsic workings of the medium.

Leading this new area of research is linguist Neil Cohn, whose studies have made decisive strides in establishing that we read comics in much the same way we process verbal discourse: as language. Cohn has challenged a number of claims in *Understanding Comics*, not least its ideas of how temporality works on the comics page. McCloud posits any given panel as a moment taken from a putative temporal whole, only some of which appears in a comics sequence—while, prompted by the "staccato" rhythm of visual presence and blank gutters, the reader imagines more of the timeline (1993, 67). Cohn, however, effectively argues that panels need not encapsulate moments as such and that they can represent different kinds of "fictive time" or "event states" that we conceptualize in various ways (2010, 131–34). Further, our conception of a comics narrative is decisively shaped by a process of grouping or "chunking" panels together as "constituencies" that reflect an unconscious grammar of comics reading (2010, 133–44). In this model, gutters separating panels do not give a reader's imagination free play to construct what is not shown any more than spaces between words in a printed sentence loosen the reader's mind from grammatical understanding.

Several studies led by Cohn have furthered this line of investigation, but perhaps the most important, in relation to the gutter, is a 2014 study of how readers process comics sequences that disrupt ordinary reading practice. Using electroencephalography (EEG), this study demonstrates that blank panels inserted into a comic strip, momentarily halting the reader's absorption of the narrative, prompt brain responses that are similar to the effects of clicks or static inserted into a verbal utterance. The type and intensity of such reactions vary according to the placement of the blank panels, and these variations confirm some of the ways readers process constituent groupings of panels. Such findings are only possible if ordinary blank spaces between panels—gutters—in a given sequence are not processed as disruptive presences in the same way that a full blank panel is when inserted into the same sequence. A clear implication of this study is that readerly perception *normalizes* and then effectively *ignores* gutters in the process of distinguishing and grouping panels.

If this is the case, then gutters do not—or do not immediately—invite the mind to imagine what is not shown in a sequence. Like spaces between printed words, gutters simply segment elements that readers mentally group as constituent structures, enabling anticipation of what will appear in upcoming panels (much as we might anticipate what has yet to be heard in a spoken utterance). And such anticipation, as evidenced by EEG, is only possible and consistent if readers are most immediately focused *not* on what is *absent* from a comics sequence but on *what is present*, or *will be present*, in the sequence itself. This would also explain why less conventional gutters (or no gutters at all, in the case of a comic with panels separated only by a line) do not strike us as markedly different from more typical ones. In a sense, Cohn demonstrates, we are always reading *past* gutters or other devices for separating panels, joining visible parts to construct larger wholes. As suggested earlier, McCloud seems to indicate this very point, and then to ignore it, in his own central example (Cohn 2010, 135). Discussing this same example, Cohn notes that while readers may infer a murder McCloud does not depict, the inference is nevertheless encouraged by what *is* shown—the scream—which we connect to what is visible in the

previous panel rather than to an unseen, imagined event (136).

Of course, it is possible to take account of Cohn's discoveries while believing there could be aspects of comics reading, and of the gutter, not accounted for by the reader's reliance on constituent panel groupings. The brain's immediate focus on what is or soon will be visible in a comics sequence could certainly coexist with other mental activity and phenomenological experience related to what is not (or, in the process of reading experience, is no longer) shown, and perhaps the gutter could be part of what stimulates such activity. Alternately, we might consider additional ways, as yet unexplored in Cohn's line of research, that gutters function in relation to the panels that are present around them.

Contemporary French comics theory might point the way here because it resists absence-oriented understandings of the gutter while allowing a variety of approaches to it. In *The System of Comics* ([1999] 2007), perhaps the most influential French theoretical work of recent decades, Thierry Groensteen asserts, "Reading a comic, I am here, then I am there, and this jump from one panel to the next (an optical and mental leap) is the equivalent of an electron that changes orbit" (113). Groensteen's understanding of each panel as a kind of valence, from which the eye is perpetually moving on to the next valence, treats what is visible to the reader as the whole of a comics narrative, much as Cohn does. But because Groensteen sees comics as spatiotopical—that is, as a system consisting of places (panels) existing in the same space (a page/book)—he is interested in aspects of comics reading separate from the constituent structures Cohn discusses and in various roles gutters might play in nonstandard vectors of reader attention. Discussing the routes a reader's eye might take through a page, Groensteen notes that "when . . . gutters are arranged as vertical continuations of each other [i.e., as a grid] . . . other routes are open to the page than the horizontal of the strip: a vertical route, or even, in the style of the checkerboard, a diagonal route"—obviously routes not encompassed by Cohn's analysis of reader attention to small linear sequences (67). The significance of such vectors of attention, facilitated by gutters, has yet to be investigated in full.

Cohn's approach is based on cognitive science, while Groensteen's is more or less aligned with semiotics; the substantial differences between them cannot be addressed in full here. But considering them together, we can turn back to absence-oriented theories of comics with a skeptical yet sympathetic eye. It is rather counterintuitive to approach a medium so rich in pictorial presence and plenitude as if it derives its true power from what it does not show. But valorization of the gutter, we should recall, arises in the context of a centuries-old discourse that is iconophobic, to use W. J. T. Mitchell's (1984) term, that has long associated visual images with deception and seduction—and that has certainly shaped anticomics discourse. The surplus of meanings ascribed to the gutter in the wake of McCloud probably derives not from observable practices of comics reading (or making) but from the fact that comics are still suspected of lacking cultural and intellectual substance. Indeed, given the medium's history of marginalization, perhaps the question of the gutter as absence and the resulting connections to theoretical discourses concerned with such questions are inevitable.

Moreover, it is likely no accident that *both* the intellectual focus on the gutter as an absence *and* the linguistic research that challenges this focus have arisen in places where comics have been decisively marginalized, and most visibly in the US. McCloud's validation of the gutter as generative and Cohn's validation of comics as a language seem ideally designed to oppose notions of comics as worthless, unhealthy, and obscene. Of course, this should remind us of what *gutter* has long meant in culture at large—and of how decisively the association of comics with waste, filth, and delinquency has influenced comics studies thus far.

29

Industry

Gregory Steirer

In academic parlance, the word *industry* refers to a broad set of business-related practices, including financing, marketing, distribution, sales, and (usually nonartisanal) production. Perhaps surprisingly, *industry* has not been a particularly important word in comics studies, nor have the practices to which it refers had much of a discursive life in the field. There are two reasons for this, the first of which has less to do with comics themselves than with the methodological demands associated with studying industry—demands that tend to require the research tools of social-science disciplines. The second has to do with the comics industry itself and the ways in which its differences from other media industries have effectively precluded the development of a strong trade press (i.e., a network of professional news publications written specifically for working members of an industry). In what follows, I discuss each of these reasons in turn, but I also offer suggestions for how comics scholars might more closely attend to industrial practices in the future.

Before I do any of these things, however, it is worth discussing in greater detail what media industry research looks like and why the knowledge it generates can be valuable even to scholars whose work is rooted in the more traditional, text-based research paradigms usually associated with the humanities. In their 2009 overview of media industries scholarship, Jennifer Holt and Alisa Perren identify eight interrelated "themes and concerns" that drive industry research; of these, three—because they are the most general—are also the most important:

- the relative power and autonomy of individual agents to express divergent political perspectives, creative visions, and cultural attitudes within larger institutional structures;
- the means by which the relationships between industry, government, text, and audience can be conceptualized; . . .
- the aesthetic, cultural, economic, and social values associated with the media industries and their contents. (3)

In practice, individual works of industry scholarship tend to pursue these themes by examining the ways particular aspects of a specific industry are shaped by such "institutional" or "infrastructural" phenomena as government regulation, trade policy, financing, managerial structure, monetization strategy, and technological change. The inaugural Media Industries Conference of 2018 thus witnessed papers on such topics as the ecology of gray-market internet television distribution, the fight for residuals by Hollywood unions, and the marketing strategy employed for Nintendo for its miniconsoles (but regrettably no comics industry scholarship). Such work has not only been useful for revealing the complex network of business, labor, and legal institutions upon which different kinds of media texts depend; it has also helped produce new models for understanding textual aesthetics that do not depend on high theory, hermeneutics, or new historicism but can still generate insight as to where style comes from, how genres evolve, how authorship is produced, and even how textual interpretation itself can be primed or constructed by extratextual forces (such as marketing and distribution).

In comics studies more specifically, a robust body of industrial-oriented research might include studies of comic book distribution; labor practices, policies, and mobility; licensing practices and the impact of intellectual property law; company organizational structures; and the economics of retailing. With respect to distribution, for example, comic books have historically depended on a wide variety of distribution pathways. Of these, newsstand distribution (dominant from the 1930s until the 1970s) and direct distribution to comic book stores (begun in the 1970s and constituting what is called in the United States the "direct market") are the most well known, and much comics scholarship has been attentive to their importance. Zoom in a little closer, however, and the world of comics distribution raises a host of questions that would benefit from more industrially oriented research. How, for example, did the system of newsstand distribution work in practice, given the highly concentrated structure of the distribution syndicates in the US and the fact that comics were treated on the distribution and retail ends as print periodicals, forced to compete for space with glossy and pulp magazines alike? Some market participants have even suggested that the US system was so inefficient and stakeholder incentives so misaligned that in key respects the system *did not work* in practice and that the newsstand sales data scholars rely on may be faulty (Beerbohm 1999). How might we then better treat this data?

Similar questions might be asked of other modes of distribution. Before Diamond Comics Distributors monopolized direct-market wholesale in 1996, how did wholesalers compete on price and service, and how did this competition shape publication practices, marketing opportunities, and comic book store retailing? And what of the many other distribution pathways: promotional giveaways, direct-to-consumer subscriptions, big-box stores, libraries, bookstores, comic book conventions, and a host of digital platforms—not to mention that of comic *strips*?

As the example of comics distribution demonstrates, industrial topics tend to spill over single categories so that the would-be scholar might find herself forced to attend to retail economics, corporate marketing practices, digital-rights-management infrastructure, or even freight regulation in order to make sense of the particular industrial institution she is studying. Although this is without question one of the difficulties of industrially oriented research, it is also what makes such research so useful and exciting: at its best, industry work not only illuminates a specific phenomenon but also reveals the complex interdependencies that constitute the medium.

Of course, undertaking industry work is not easy—especially for scholars whose research paradigms are informed by the values and methods of humanities disciplines. As Michelle Hilmes has argued, "A media industries focus points directly to those aspects of cultural production in the twentieth century and beyond that most trouble the humanities-oriented categories of coherence and analysis so central to our understanding of culture itself: the author, the text, the reader" (2009, 22). Media industries research tends to dissolve traditional categories, substituting shifting and often provisional networks of human and nonhuman actors for seemingly "solid" entities such as *Watchmen* (a graphic novel), Roy Thomas (a writer), or Image Comics (a publisher). The epistemological framework of media industries research thus arguably has more in common with that of sociology than it does disciplines relying upon close reading and formal analysis, such as literary studies.

Epistemological difficulties, however, are only part of what makes comics industry research difficult. Equally challenging are the particular research methods

INDUSTRY   GREGORY STEIRER

and subject competencies that such research requires. Some training in finance, economics, law, and human-subject research is usually necessary for serious studies of industry—especially those involving interaction with workers, managers, or regulators. Unfortunately, doctoral training in most humanistic disciplines typically includes no coursework in these areas, let alone training in business norms pertaining to communication/textual production, technology use, budgeting, or management. Would-be comics industry researchers might thus feel unequipped to navigate institutional review boards, conduct ethnographic research, or negotiate access to human subjects and business documents. These challenges are not insurmountable, however, and with enough time and energy, interested scholars can develop the skills they need, whether by collaborating across disciplines, attending training workshops, consulting colleagues, or immersing themselves in the copious literature that exists on industry-research methodology.

The question then remains why so few comics scholars have yet to develop these skills—or, inversely, why so few media scholars who possess them have used them to study comics. The answer is that the comics industry is in many respects different from other media industries, and the most telling marker of this difference is the industry's absence of a strong trade press. In contrast to other media industries, where a robust, competitive trade press abets research into industrial issues (often also serving as source material), trade coverage of the comics industry is anemic, with serious, in-depth reporting on industrial issues usually confined to that of the more general business press, such as *Forbes* and *Businessweek*. Although a host of comics "news" sites and magazines exist, including that of Bleeding Cool and the *Comics Journal* (which from the 1970s through the 1990s sometimes served some of the functions of a trade journal), they differ substantially from journals in other industries with respect to their reporting resources, their missions, their scope, and their tone—with all of them aiming primarily at fans rather than industry professionals. In the absence of a strong trade press, the discursive construct that is the comics industry has thus long been both emptier, semantically, and less familiar, conceptually, to academics and journalists than that of the film industry or the music industry.

There are several important reasons that such a press has not developed, and it is worth reviewing them here so as to further account for the relative dearth of comics industry research. First, the comics industry has long lacked traditional industrial associations of the kind that help structure and organize other industries. There exist no unions or guilds (though some artists might count themselves members of the Graphic Artists Guild—a much broader industry group), no publisher associations, and no lobbyists that specifically serve the industry. Although a retailer association, ComicsPro, has been active since 2004, it is quite young and represents only direct-market retailers—an important but gradually shrinking portion of the retail market.

Second, based on almost any metric, the comic book industry, at least in the United States, has for many decades been very small compared to that of other media industries. Compare, for example, the number of specialty comic book stores in 2017—somewhere close to 3,200 (counting Canada), most of which are small mom-and-pop stores or parts of tiny regional chains—to that of bookstores and movie screens: 23,750 and 40,246, respectively (counting only the United States; Gearino 2017). Or the total sales revenue generated by comic books in 2016: $1.085 billion (including specialty stores and book stores) versus $24.5 billion for video/computer games and $11.4 billion for movie tickets

(Griepp and Miller 2017; Siwek 2017; Faughnder 2017). The audience size for any single comic book is also comparatively minuscule: for many years, the print run for all but a handful of comic book issues each month has been between two thousand and ninety thousand copies. This is a fraction of the audience achieved for most television shows, films, and video games. Of course, the comics industry has not always been so small; at various points in its history, print runs for individual books have exceeded a million copies. Even during such boom times, however, its economic footprint has been dwarfed by that of other media industries. For this reason, in many important policy and economic contexts, the comics industry does not meaningfully exist at all: formal studies of economic output, productivity, and labor routinely ignore it, as do governments and lawmakers (excepting the brief hysteria surrounding child delinquency in the 1950s). The industry's small size has also meant that there has been little funding available for the development of robust data-collection practices. Some important metrics, such as sales-to-consumers (or "sell through"), for example, remain uncollected today.

Third, the recent explosion of comic book intellectual property (IP) licensing deals and the integration of comic book publishers into media conglomerates have tended to blur industrial lines, making it hard for both would-be trade journalists and industry scholars to identify what the comic book industry actually is. Should it be restricted to the business of making and selling comic books? Or should it consider the myriad of other media that utilize comic book IP? Almost half of the wholesale offerings by Diamond Distribution currently consist of toys, games, clothing, and other nonprint material. And this is to say nothing of the theme park rides, films, television shows, and product advertisements employing comic book IP, which bypass the traditional comic book retail market entirely and are often overseen by corporate divisions that have little interaction with or understanding of comic book production. The single comic book trade journal/service, ICv2, thus bills itself not as a comics-industry trade at all but rather as a trade devoted to "the business of geek culture"—a business label that, at least for now, has even less currency among actual business stakeholders than that of the "comics industry."

To recap, the comics industry lacks a strong trade press, is relatively disorganized or unstructured, is small, and may not even really be organized around comics at all. These differences from other media industries, however, are precisely what makes it such an intriguing—if frustrating—area for future comics research. Indeed, because the comics industry's contours have been (and continue to be) so vaguely defined, it is a particularly attractive research area for comics and media scholars interested in macrocultural questions, institutional sociology, and transdisciplinary or mixed research methods. Media studies scholars working on convergence, transmedia, and digital culture have thus focused on industrial questions that touch upon comics (Johnson 2013; Clarke 2012; Steirer 2014; Perren and Steirer 2021), while scholars working on fandom have increasingly taken up questions of comics retail and consumption (Woo 2018a; Cox 2018). Because such scholarship reproduces rather than tames the messiness of its research object, it typically makes visible the multiple connections among comics and other media products, businesses, and social and economic institutions. In doing so, it demonstrates the potential for comics industry research to complicate, in productive ways, how we as comic scholars read and interpret comics as aesthetic and cultural objects. But perhaps more importantly, it also extends the scope and impact of comics studies itself, situating it within broader scholarly conversations and concerns and building bridges between it and a wide array of other academic disciplines.

30

Ink

Stacey Robinson

As a graphic designer professor, one of the first lessons I teach my students is that a logo should be able to function perfectly in "black and white." I compare good design, specifically a good logo, to one of my favorite things in the world—my mother's pound cake. With no frosting and additional flavoring, my mother's pound cake has become my first lesson in foundational design in regard to function and form. After that, all other flavorings are additional accents. Arguably, it may make the cake preferable, but it doesn't make it taste or function better. Comic book storytelling is a form of sequential art and graphic design. And just like my mother's pound cake, sequential storytelling should function without the addition of color. Telling a story in black and white requires a strong penciler and an inker who can add three-dimensional depth to the flatness of the comic page. Fundamentally, telling a story in sequence requires a series of skills. It is often said by comic industry professionals that the best inkers are also pencilers because they can interpret the penciler's page and therefore know what the drawings are supposed to look like.

Initially, the purpose of inking a comic page is to make it visible for the scanner. In those earlier days, inkers did little more than trace the already established pencil lines, making them dark enough for the film emulsions to capture the details. At that time, photographic films and emulsions were not as sensitive as they are in contemporary times. Scanners needed a solid black image to capture the details. Scanning and printing technology has since evolved in recent years, allowing for better scanning of pencils to create a high-quality image for print publishing.

As graphic design, the comic page has to navigate the novice reader through the journey to the next page. A good design allows the reader to venture innately through the story, one panel at a time. Words on the comic page most times are designed with devices called speech bubbles, which are strategically placed to lead the reader from one panel to the next panel. Reading a comic book requires a different type of legibility than reading other literature, and inking is essential to helping readers venture through the sequential narrative.

Since those early days of comic publishing, inking has become more than tracing penciled lines. Inking is its own art form and has become an element of design. When done well, inking advances the story and the reader's experience through experimental techniques, styles, and processes. Techniques like "spotting black," where solid black inked areas are strategically placed on the page to direct the reader, add weight, heavy light, shadows, and so on to the scene.

In his 2006 book *Making Comics*, Scott McCloud writes, "If you're just starting out, you might want to try as many tools as possible, in case your perfect match is out there somewhere." I couldn't agree more. When I first began inking regularly, I invested in a number of inking tools. I began as many artists do—with Micron brand disposable pens. They were and still are very inexpensive. They also offer a control that works well with my drawing style. As my skill level grew, I ventured into using brushes and different inks. Some inks only adhere to the surface of the paper. This didn't work well for me, because for comics, it is common to erase the pencils after the page is completely inked. If the inks are not soaked into the depth of the paper, then the eraser will remove some of the inks as well as the pencils, leaving transparent lines.

My preferred inking tool has become the watercolor brush. I watercolor and ink-wash with the Winsor & Newton Series 7 Kolinsky Sable Pointed Round #3. But I brush-ink my foundational lines exclusively with the Scharff Series 3000 Kolinsky Red Sable Fine Line #3. I also use a variety of other tools such as old toothbrushes and white acrylic paint for creating different effects—for example, when making star clusters. I thumb my finger over the lightly paint-applied bristles of the toothbrush, flicking the paint onto the page. The sporadic paint creates a variety of drops that resemble stars of different sizes and distances. I also repeat this technique to create tighter clusters and lightly dip my bristles in water to create more washed-out-looking stars.

In *Drawing Comics Lab*, Robyn Chapman (2012) states, "The nib offers both precision and versatility, which has made it a mainstay of the cartoonist's toolbox for more than a century! Because nib holders are held much like regular pens, the nib is often the first varsity-level inking tool new cartoonists try out." The quill pen has a split tip that holds ink, allowing variable lines through applying slight pressure. Disposable pens are also lower-budget inking tools that pro and novice inkers use. They tend to require a lot more time as the tip does not allow for varying line width using a single stroke. The best quality disposable pens offer is their precision. Because of this, many times they are also used with rulers for inorganic objects like buildings. Disposable brush pens are also inexpensive choices for the beginning cartoonist. Some brush pens come with refillable ink chambers, which allow for continued use once ink reserves are exhausted. There are many tools and techniques used by veteran cartoonists. Some veteran inkers use a razor blade to lightly scrape the inked areas to pull the white of the paper under the inks, which then produces a scattered-line effect.

In *Drawing Comics Lab*, Steve Bissette adds, "Never throw out a brush—brushes that no longer have a proper drawing point are always useful for effects, textures, or laying down large areas of ink." Additionally, there are also different strategies for inking. Two different approaches are used: "pushing" or "pulling." Placing your brush at the nearest point to you and stroking in an outward direction is called pushing. Beginning the brush at a point farther away and moving the stroke toward you is called pulling. There is no correct way, only a preferred way. I find myself using both approaches. There is also no correct way to hold a brush.

Comic artist Shawn Martinbrough uses a minimalist approach to creating comic pages and crafts his designs with solid black shapes as silhouettes that add a film noir aesthetic to his creations. In his book *How to Draw Noir Comics: The Art and Technique of Visual Storytelling*, the veteran comic artist talks about the power of suggestion by using ink to block the surrounding areas of the figure, leaving the interior form to the imagination of the reader.

The *DC Guide to Inking Comics* is a seminal book for cartoonists. In it, author and artist Klaus Janson writes, "A common question among beginner inkers is when to use a specific tool. After years of practice and concentration the artist should be able to adapt any tool to any requirement. For example, hair should look like hair whether you use a brush or a pen. . . . Use the nature of the inked object as a guide to which tool you use." He uses the example of the hard metal of the pen point, which might be best used for inking hard or metal shapes like cars, buildings, and so on.

Regardless of your inspiration, the best way to learn to ink is to practice over copies of professional artists' penciled pages. One other practice technique I recommend is drawing with a brush instead of with a pencil. This requires a level of confidence. I tend to do this when making my abstract and nonobjective art. When inking with a traditional watercolor brush or digital stylus, I always warm up first before I begin inking directly on my penciled work. I ink a page of practice strokes that will end up in the trash. I practice my dry-brush techniques with pushing and pulling. I begin with a thin and light stroke and build up to a larger one within a single stroke.

As technology over the last several decades has advanced, so has the need for inking comics. Many comics are not inked traditionally anymore. Inking has become more of an aesthetic rather than a necessity. Inking has become increasingly more digital in its process. Several new digital software packages and technology devices have allowed for the faster completion of inking projects. Therefore, deadlines potentially can be met quicker. Currently, inking has become arguably more of an aesthetic than a need for many publishers, depending on printing methods. Traditional inking with brushes and pens, for example, can now be completely done with digital hardware like the Wacom Cintiq and the iPad Pro and software like Adobe Photoshop and Procreate. Digital inking requires using a stylus, a device that works like a digital pen and allows for no drying time, no mistakes with smearing wet ink, and clearing up those areas. Additionally, brush tips are available digitally with the click of an icon on the computer screen. I'd even argue that many times, it's difficult to tell the difference between traditional and digital inked lines.

Inking is as much a conceptual way of thinking about the production of comics as it is referring to the actual practice of inking—putting pen to paper or stylus pen to screen. Here, from the vantage point of an artist, I have demystified the process for those who wish to draw comics and for those educators and learners who wish to have a better understanding of what it means, in practical terms, to produce part of the artistry of comics. For the former camp, there are many books for the beginning cartoonist to reference, including *How to Draw Comics the Marvel Way* by Stan Lee and John Buscema (1978), the entire *DC Comics Guides* series, *Comics and Sequential Art* by Will Eisner (1985), and *Writing and Illustrating the Graphic Novel* by Daniel Cooney (2011), to name a short few.

31

Latinx
Isabel Millán

Following the 2016 shooting in the Orlando Pulse nightclub, where the majority of patrons and victims were Latinx, Marc Andreyko initiated the *Love Is Love* (2017) comic book anthology to benefit survivors. When Hurricane Maria struck Puerto Rico in September 2017, two comic book anthologies were published in support of disaster relief and recovery for the island: *Puerto Rico Strong* (Lopez et al. 2018) and *Ricanstruction: Reminiscing and Rebuilding Puerto Rico* (2018), featuring superhero La Borinqueña. While the term *Latinx* is relatively new, it demarcates a multifaceted category that includes identities, histories, cultural productions, academic fields, and niche markets, affecting how one might classify or characterize Latinx comics. Within our contemporary lexicon, *Latinx* (noun) may refer to (1) individuals born or residing within the United States of Latin American descent regardless of gender expression or, more specifically, (2) gender-nonconforming individuals born or residing within the United States of Latin American descent. Within the US, Latin America is usually understood as any of the countries or territories south of the US—including Mexico, Central America, South America, and the Caribbean—that speak Romance languages such as Spanish, Portuguese, and French. Debatable exceptions include English-speaking countries such as Jamaica, Belize, or Guyana or Dutch-speaking countries such as Suriname. Puerto Rico is also unique in that it is currently a US territory or commonwealth, which

situates it within a subliminal space between other Latin American countries and the United States.

Latinx overlaps with and is also distinct from *Hispanic*, *Latino*, *Latina*, *Latina/o*, *Latin@*, or other pan-ethnic terms that range in usage or popularity depending on geopolitical space and time (see Serrato 2011; J. M. Rodríguez 2014; Vargas, Mirabal, and La Fountain-Stokes 2017). If applied as an umbrella term, *Latinx* encompasses specific communities within the US such as Chicano/a/xs or Mexican Americans and Cuban Americans. While each designates a unique country of origin or ancestral descent, these are not homogenous categories. Instead, they should also be understood as the result of colonialism and struggles for independence with nuanced and often contentious relationships to Europe, slavery, and Indigenous nations of the Americas. Although *Latinx* is usually understood as US specific or Western centric (see María DeGuzmán 2017), it may also apply to individuals of Latin American descent within Canada or other places outside of Latin America.

In contrast, the term *Hispanic* derives from an emphasis on the Spanish language and excludes individuals within the US from non-Spanish-speaking countries in Latin America such as Brazil whose official language is Portuguese. Although formal Spanish dictates that *Latino* includes everyone regardless of gender, the term is marked as masculine or male because it ends in *o*. Terms such as *Latina/o* and *Latin@* attempted to incorporate women; however, they still fall within a gender binary. Presently, *Latinx* serves as a gender-neutral umbrella term for individuals of Latin American descent, although it runs the risk of being seemly all-inclusive without paying specific attention or homage to transgender and nonconforming individuals, communities, or political struggles (see R. Rodríguez 2017), nor does it account for all the descendants of Indigenous populations across Latin America (see Blackwell 2017).

For scholars invested in the field of comics studies, major debates include determining not only who is Latinx but what are Latinx comics. Unlike cultural productions such as single-authored novels or paintings created by one artist, comics are often collaborations between multiple creators (e.g., authors, illustrators, inkers, colorists, and graphic designers). Each individual brings their unique style, perspective, and lived experiences to these collaborations. What qualifies a comic as Latinx? Is it the character? The major themes within the story line? The writer? The lead artist? The target audience? Only one of these characteristics must be met to qualify or all? Creators, editors, publicists, consumers, award selection committees, or scholars decide whether a comic is Latinx (see Aldama 2010, 2016, 2018), and they are undoubtedly shaped by our current climate as well as our understanding of what constitutes a comic. Expositions such as the Latino Comics Expo, which was founded in 2011 by Ricardo Padilla and Javier Hernandez, also function in deciding which comics are Latinx based on who participates and which comics are showcased. Similarly, the comics industry, whether independent presses or mainstream ones such as DC Comics and Marvel, also plays a major role in determining which comics fall under the rubric of Latinx. Lastly, as consumers, fans help shape the market. For the purpose of this essay, I will primarily focus on comic strips and comic books or graphic novels that depict Latinx characters or were produced by Latinx writers and artists.

Gus Arriola, born in 1917 in Florence, Arizona, is often credited for creating the first Latino or Mexican American / Chicano comic strip, *Gordo*, which was nationally syndicated, appearing in over two hundred newspapers from 1941 to 1985 (Harvey and Arriola 2000). Set in Mexico, it followed the life of Gordo, whose name translates to "fat man." Over the course of the comic strip, Gordo went from farmer harvesting beans to tour guide for US citizens visiting Mexico. Arguably, although Arriola was Latino, Gordo was not. Arriola was a US-born Mexican American, whereas Gordo was born and lived in Mexico. Had Arriola decided to migrate Gordo to the US, then he, too, would be Mexican American or Latino. Instead, Arriola deliberately chose not to, stating, "People at the syndicate wanted to bring [Gordo] up here to make it more popular. I couldn't do that. Up here, he would have been a second-class citizen. In Mexico, he was in his home ground. He could be anything, do anything. But up here he would be restricted. So I never did" (quoted in Aldama 2009, 124). Thus the question becomes, is *Gordo*, the comic strip, Latinx? One may argue that although the main character is not, he was created through the US Latino lens of the writer and illustrator for a primarily US audience. In 1999, Arriola received the Sparky, or the Charles M. Schulz Lifetime Achievement Award. Upon presenting the award, Mark Burstein proclaimed, "Gus imparted a subtle education about Mexican-Chicano culture and folk traditions that remains in the psyche of many readers" (Harvey and Arriola 2000, 3).

Whether responding to or contesting earlier Latinx stereotypes, Latinx comic strip creators include Ivan Velez Jr., *Adam* (1982) and *Planet Bronx: The Will of the People* (1992); Deborah Kuetzpalin Vasquez, *Citlalita: La Chicanita Super Hero* (1998); and Hector Cantú and Carlos Castellanos, *Baldo* (1998) and *Chica Power!* (2010). Recognized nationally first as a Disney critic and then as a cultural consultant on Pixar's *Coco* (2017), Lalo Alcaraz's career began with cofounding the comedy sketch troupe Chicano Secret Service, creating the zine *Pocho*, and producing editorial cartoons for *LA Weekly* as early as 1992, which ultimately led to his syndicated strip, *La Cucaracha* (2002; R. C. Harvey as quoted by Alcaraz 2004, 5).

Expanding from comic strips, Latinx comic books first appear in the late 1970s. Margarito C. Garza, a Texas judge, created *¡Relampago!* in 1977, which starred the character Marcos Zapata, who with the assistance of La Bruja Mendoza becomes a superhero (see Garza 1977; Fernández Rodríguez 2015, 116). The 1980s witnessed the emergence of the Hernandez brothers, three brothers whose collaborations include *Love and Rockets* (1981–present) and *Mister X* (1984). Jaime, Gilbert, and Mario Hernandez recall growing up with comics in their home, similar to their mother, who also collected them during her youth. Mario, the eldest, would purchase and share comics with his younger brothers, all of whom eventually began sketching their own characters and story lines (Sobel and Valenti 2013). This led to the now legendary *Love and Rockets*, which was self-published in 1981 and then republished by Fantagraphics in 1982. Two of its more popular subseries or story lines include "Locas" (exploring a queer relationship between characters Maggie and Hopey set in Los Angeles, California) and "Palomar" (featuring Luba and set in a fictional Central American country). On the one hand, *Love and Rockets* centered on queer and Central American characters, but on the other hand, these were narratives created from a putatively straight male, US-centric perspective. For example, the lesbian or bisexual women often played on male sexual fantasies, and the Central American characters lacked regional specificity. Yet the end of the 1980s was also when Ivan Velez Jr. created *Tales of the Closet* (1987), a comics series that featured many queer youth of color and openly addressed HIV/AIDS. As an out, gay Latino of Puerto Rican descent, Velez wanted to "make heroes for people who look like most of the people in the world, and that's a different viewpoint from the middle-class suburban viewpoint" (1994, 7).

The following decade produced the next generation of Latinx comics. Andrea M. Guadiana published a graphic novel titled *Azteca: The Story of a Jaguar Warrior* (1992). Three years later in 1995, PACAS, or the Professional Amigos of Comic Art Society, was established as a support network. Its cofounders included Carlos Saldaña, Richard Dominguez, Jose Martinez, and Fernando Rodriguez. In 1990, Saldaña self-published *Badd Burrito* featuring Burrito, the sarape-wearing donkey, and friends such as Torito, the bull. Richard Dominguez created *El Gato Negro* (1993) and *Team Tejas* (1997), both published by Azteca Productions. As PACAS continued to hold network gatherings and meetings, its members expanded to include Steven Conrique-Ross, *Chesty Sanchez* (1995); Javier Hernandez, *Daze of the Dead: The Numero Uno Edition* (1998), *Maniac Priest: The Genesis Edition* (2014), and *El Muerto Resurrection* (2016); Rafael Navarro, *Sonambulo* (1996) and (as the artist) *Guns A'Blazin'!* (written by Mike Wellman, 2016); Michael S. Moore, who collaborated with Richard Dominguez on *Team Tejas* and, in 2004, created *El Gato Negro: Nocturnal Warrior*; and international member Oscar González Loyo of Mexico. As evidenced by the PACAS cofounders, most of its members were men whose depictions of women were often hypersexualized, passive, or on one extreme or another of the virgin-whore dichotomy and were dominated by the male gaze. Thus the women in PACAS, such as Martha Montoya (*Los Kitos*, 1995) and Sandra Chang (*Achilles Storm*, 1990, and *Akemi*, 1995), stood out—in particular, Laura Molina, who also served as secretary and treasurer for the organization.

In 1996, Laura Molina self-published *Cihualyaomiquiz, the Jaguar*. The title highlighted Linda Rivera, a Chicana feminist from East LA who was also a law student fighting for civil rights and social justice and against hate. Her superhero name, Cihualyaomiquiz, translates to "woman ready to die in battle" in Nahuatl (Aztec language). Molina created Cihualyaomiquiz in response to the lack of Latina characters, hate crimes, and the discrimination backlash from California's Proposition 187 and immigration debates: "The country had taken a hard turn to the right, pushing toward something dark and violent. . . . You had to take a political stand because of the overt racism that you faced every day. . . . I've always been interested in pop culture, so I decided to go with the comic book" (quoted in Aldama 2009, 211).

Since the beginning of the twenty-first century, there appears a plethora of independent- or smaller-press comic books and graphic novels that fall under the Latinx label because of either their creators or their characters. Whereas earlier decades were dominated by Mexican American or Chicanx creators and characters, the 2000s brought about a greater diversity of Latinx artists, including Isis Rodriguez, Frank Espinosa, Graciela Rodriguez, Liz Mayorga, Rhode Montijo, Wilfred Santiago, Anthony Oropeza, Anthony Aguilar, Joe Quesada, and Christian Ramirez, among numerous others.

Unlike independent Latinx comics, mainstream companies such as DC and Marvel are often driven by marketing and sell to specialized niche markets. My overview of mainstream US comics includes those produced by DC and Marvel during the Golden Age (late 1930s to mid-1950s), Silver Age (mid-1950s to 1960s), Bronze Age (1970s to mid-1980s), and the Modern Age (mid-1980s to the present). When considering this periodization, one must ask, For whom? There was little golden about classic comics depicting predominately all-white characters and created by all-white production teams of mostly heterosexual men.

DC Comics first began as National Allied Publications in 1934. It was named after *Detective Comics*, the series that introduced Batman. DC's first Latino characters were introduced in the early 1940s: Rodrigo "Rodney" Gaynor (the Whip) and Anthony Rodriguez (Big Words). Decades afterward in 1975, Hector Anaya was introduced as the White Tiger in Marvel Comics; he is depicted as Nuyorican and Afro-Latino. The numbers rise during the 1980s with characters such as Paco Ramon (Vibe from Detroit), Yolanda Montez (Wildcat from Gotham), Jose Delgado (Gangbuster), Amelinda Lopez (Touch-n-Go), Gregorio de la Vega (Extraño), and Rafael Sandoval (El Diablo from Dos Rios, Texas). Of Montez, one might ask, How do US race and ethnicity logics configure within a fictional city such as Gotham? Although fictional, it is still imagined within the US border. Extraño, of Peruvian descent, was also gay and "flamboyant." Responding to the AIDS crisis, he contracts HIV and is killed off.

Then in 1992, DC Comics introduced Renée Montoya, who initially is a police officer and then a homicide detective in Gotham City until she becomes the Question. She is of Dominican descent and is a closeted lesbian until she is outed and disowned by her Catholic family. Gradually, she takes ownership of her multiple identities. In 1993, DC Comics introduced Bane. He was raised in a prison located on a fictitious island within the Caribbean. He then moves to Gotham to challenge Batman. Overall, Bane is quite clever and speaks English, Spanish, Portuguese, and Latin. WildStorm (DC Comics) introduced Hector Morales, a.k.a. Powerhouse, of German and Argentinian descent, in 1995. His clone status brings about another dilemma about the relationship between DNA and race, ethnicity, citizenship, and identity. In 1996, Kyle Rayner, a Mexican American, became the iconic superhero Green Lantern. Also, that year, Hero Cruz, who is Afro-Latino and gay, was created. Interestingly, in his own body, he is gay but holds the superpower to take on the sexuality of others when inhabiting their bodies. In 1996, Alejandro "Ally" Sanchez became Firebrand. He is Cuban American and differently abled. In 1997, Hector Ramirez becomes Wildcat, and in 1998, Esteban Rodrigo Suarez Hidalgo emerges as El Hombre.

Marvel did not begin introducing Latinx characters until much later than DC, and most were sidekicks or secondary characters. Marvel introduced its first Latina character in 1981, Bonita Juarez, or Firebird, from New Mexico. In 1982, Roberto "Bobby" da Costa appeared as Sunspot, of Afro-Brazilian descent. In 1983, Amara Aquilla, or Magma, was introduced. Amara is from Nova Roma, a fictitious Roman colony in Brazil's Amazon rainforests, and trains under Charles Xavier. In 1985, Antonio Rodriguez, or Armadillo, was introduced. In 1989, La Bandera was introduced, a Cuban American who grew up in Florida. In 1990, Miguel Santos, the Living Lightning, was introduced, a character who will eventually come out as gay. In 1992, Miguel "Mig" O'Hara was introduced, who took over the mantle of Spider-Man in the year 2099. O'Hara is of Irish and Mexican descent. The next year, Roberto Velasquez, a.k.a. Bantam, from Puerto Rico, was introduced. In 1997 Dr. Cecilia Reyes was introduced in the pages of *The X-Men*. She is Afro-Latina and is of Puerto Rican descent. In 1999, Manuel Diego Armand Vincent debuts as Junta and Maya Lopez as Echo (and later becomes Ronin). She is Native American and Latina as well as deaf. Whereas DC had more (albeit minor) characters in prior decades, Marvel has dominated the 2000s with not only Latinx sidekicks but also Latinx leads with their own series. This can be attributed in part to the increased number of Latinx writers, artists, and editors at Marvel (e.g., Joe Quesada and Axel Alonso).

DC Comics characters created since 2000 who are either Latinx or Latin American include the following: Andrea Rojas as Ácrata, who is of Mexican descent, was introduced in 2000. Also that year, the Súper Malón team from Argentina appeared. They include Cachiru, La Salamanca, El Yaguratte, Cimarron, El Lobizon, Pampero, El Bagual, and Vizacacha. In 2001, Alexander "Alex" Montez became the character Eclipso, and

Pamela, or Menagerie, and her twin sister, Sonja, were introduced. All three are Puerto Rican. In 2004, Lorena Marquez became Aquagirl, and in 2006, Jaime Reyes became the Blue Beetle. In 2008, Marguerita "Rita" Covas became Tarot, and Chato Santana first appeared as El Diablo. In 2011, Miguel Jose Barragan, a.k.a. Bunker, was introduced. He was born in a small town in Mexico and is Catholic and gay (R. Rodríguez 2016). In 2013, Rhonda Pineda became Atomica, one of several villains of Earth-3, whereas on Earth, Armando Ramon became Rupture and Jessica Viviana Cruz took over the role as the new Green Lantern.

Marvel's more nuanced Latinx characters appear after 2000. In 2003, Robert "Robbie" Rodriguez appeared as El Guapo. In 2004, Anya Sofía Corazón debuted in her own series as Araña and eventually as Spider-Girl (Millán 2016). In 2005, we meet Victor Mancha, who is an android built from Ultron and Marianella Mancha. That year, Marvel debuted a group known as the Santerians (Nama and Haddad 2016). In 2006, Marvel introduced Maria Vasquez as Tarantula as well as mixed-race Antoñio "Tony" Stark as Iron Man. In 2008, Yo-Yo Rodriguez as Slingshot from Puerto Rico was introduced. In 2009, Black and Latino Victor Alvarez appeared as Power Man, and in 2011, Alejandra "Angela" Jones as Ghost Rider, Ava Ayala as White Tiger, Miles Morales as the Afro-Latino Spider-Man, and America Chavez as Miss America. These last two characters have proven controversial among mainstream audiences.

Miles Morales stars in the film *Spider-Man: Into the Spider-Verse* (2018) and challenges Spider-Man's presumed whiteness (Nama and Haddad 2016). On the other hand, Miss America's sexuality is explicitly depicted as queer. Written by Gabby Rivera, queer Latina author of the novel *Juliet Takes a Breath*, America is from Maltixa, "a planet on the outskirts of the Utopian Parallel." She is described by Professor Douglas as the "daughter of two mothers. Raised in the utopian parallel. Mothers sacrificed lives to save the multiverse. With powers imbued by the demiurge, [she] left utopia for worlds that needed saving." In the first issue, she references punching a Nazi and then time travels and, indeed, punches Hitler. America attends Sotomayor University, where she takes courses such as "Intergalactic Revolutionaries and You" in the Department of Radical Women and Intergalactic Indigenous Peoples (n.p.). Marvel continues to add Latinx characters with their introduction of Ana Cortés in 2014 as Lady Deathstrike from Bogota, Colombia, and Robbie Reyes as the next Ghost Rider.

As a whole, this sampling of Latinx characters is not necessarily meant to depict linear progress, nor is it all-inclusive. Additionally, many of these can be faulted for their own continued reproduction of stereotypes as well as not being fully accountable to all the nuances within the umbrella term of *Latinx*. We still need more Latinx characters who are also Black, Asian, Middle Eastern, and Indigenous and of diverse religious and spiritual backgrounds, with differently abled bodies and who encompass an array of genders and sexualities, including those who are gender nonconforming, trans, queer, poly, pansexual, asexual, and intersex, and who are from multigenerational and mixed-citizenship status families and communities. It may be that *Latinx* cannot fully capture all of these, and we may need to find other terms in the future. For now, *Latinx* provides us with a malleable term from which we can expand, contest, or completely shatter as we attempt to decide who is Latinx and what constitutes Latinx comics or Latinx comic studies.

32

Love and Rockets

Enrique García

Love and Rockets is an anthology comic book series created by the collective known as Los Bros Hernandez and published by Fantagraphics since 1978. Most of the stories in the series have been created by siblings Gilbert and Jaime Hernandez, with some minor contributions by their older brother, Mario Hernandez. The title *Love and Rockets* reflects the concept of the series in which the artists provide an intertextual and postmodern narrative. This comic book's intertextuality lies in how Los Bros link and play with signifiers, meanings, and cultural references to establish a literary parody. Both siblings apply this parodic "genre deconstruction," mixed with a Latinx (Mexican American) point of view, to stand in opposition to—while also lovingly sharing the signifiers of—the US comic book industry and the hegemony it typically represents. Postmodern art is typically associated with post- to mid-twentieth-century narratives that decenter the point of view and styles of institutions in power during the modernist age, and *Love and Rockets* is one of the seminal alternative and postmodern comic books published in the United States. The Hernandez brothers' creativity, innovation, disruption, inclusivity, and independence, along with the title's longevity, make this one of the most celebrated comic books in the American industry.

The series contains numerous stories, but the most important are arguably Gilbert's "Palomar" and Jaime's "Locas" stories, which many readers also read as graphic novel collections. *Graphic novels* can be defined as comic book narratives with more pages than the usual serialized books (thirty-two pages). Sometimes, the stories in a graphic novel are reprinted collections of monthly comic books or daily newspapers, and other times, they have new and original material. Gilbert and Jaime's new material is usually introduced in *Love and Rockets* comic books and then is collected in larger *Love and Rockets* graphic novels.

The Hernandez brothers self-published the first issue of *Love and Rockets* in 1978 and sold it at comic conventions until they submitted a copy for review to the *Comics Journal* (Aldama 2009, 184). They were expecting negative criticism because that journal always gave harsh reviews, but editor Gary Groth offered to publish the title while maintaining the artists' independence (Groth 2013, 32). This first issue included Gilbert's story "BEM," where he introduced an earlier version of his popular character Luba, one of the main characters in Gilbert's "Palomar" saga. It also included "Mechan-X," where Jaime's most popular characters from the "Locas" saga appeared for the first time. Both stories were exciting sci-fi adventures that fit the comic book genre conventions of the time, but from the onset of the series, the brothers deployed intertextual devices that parodied white masculinity, empowered their Latina heroines, and explored queer elements that were far ahead of their time. For example, in Gilbert's "BEM," Luba first appears as a sexualized object while a monster is on its way to destroy a fictional Latin American country. In turn, Jaime's Maggie is introduced in "Mechan-X" as a clumsy bisexual mechanic in a futuristic American setting. However, as these stories progress, both Latina characters save the world from apocalyptic destruction while the "white male" protagonists (that would have been the saviors in traditional American comic book adventures) are portrayed as neurotic and incompetent (García 2017; Streeby 2017). Los Bros had the freedom to publish this type of story because they had complete financial and editorial independence as well as the support of a prestigious institution such as the *Comics Journal*.

The type of independence achieved by Los Bros Hernandez in *Love and Rockets* can be traced back to the works of comic creators Harvey Kurtzman and Robert Crumb. Kurtzman was well known in the 1950s for his work in EC Comics, specifically *MAD*. In this particular comic book (which later became a magazine), Kurtzman parodied the comic book industry's corporate characters and, using self-reflexive devices, attempted to familiarize the audience with many narrative and industry conventions (e.g., "Superduperman"). Kurtzman later moved to *Playboy* magazine, where his stories could indulge in more overt sexuality and adult themes, thus subverting the self-censorship embraced by the Comics Code Authority. As a result, he set the path for the underground comix movement in the 1960s and 1970s, which involved artists such as Crumb, who continued to satirize and parody the prudish nature of the mainstream through self-publishing in comic magazines such as *Zap Comix* (Sabin 1996, 92). These new underground comix were distributed in alternative stores that sold records and drug paraphernalia and that did not have to submit to the Comics Code standards to be able to physically distribute works not sanctioned by the code. Charles Hatfield has observed that "comix did pave the way for a radical reassessment of the relationships among publishers, creators, and intellectual properties, a reassessment that was to affect even mainstream comics in later years" (Hatfield 2005, 418–21). This freedom, however, led to brilliant but controversial material that occasionally displayed racist and misogynist tendencies. For example, Robert Crumb has recently garnered some criticism because of his depictions of rape in comics such as *Fritz the Cat*.

Gilbert and Jaime also have pushed the boundaries of sexuality in *Love and Rockets* and have created material that can be subversive to hegemony but still offensive to certain audiences. The difference is that the brothers provide their characters with ethnic, female, and queer perspectives that differ from the approach of Anglophone creators such as Kurtzman and Crumb while continuing their subversive traditions and merging other influences, such as the ideas of the anarchist LA punk movement that were popular with Latinx creators from Gilbert and Jaime's generation. Scholar Michelle Habell-Pallán (2005) discusses in her book *Loca Motion* how for Chicano artists, deploying punk sensibility and attitude was an early step in a broader engagement with the world at large (46). She also mentions how filmmaker Jim Mendiola praised *Love and Rockets* as an example in which "youth of color made the punk scene in their image and changed it themselves" (73).

Both Gilbert and Jaime are well known for their respective "Palomar" and "Locas" sagas, published for the most part in *Love and Rockets*. Gilbert's "Palomar" story began as the collective story of a small town in a fictional country in Central America. Following the tradition of nonexistent countries, often used as a device in US comics, Gilbert actually avoids using Mexico as his setting because he has never lived there and does not feel comfortable depicting that country's reality (García 2017, 80). In a way, his fictional "foreign" town serves as a metaphor for his Mexican American barrio in Los Angeles and the people who grew up alongside him. The characters of Luba and her half sister Fritz are arguably Gilbert's most popular characters; however, their sexuality can be controversial because it is very graphic and could be perceived as a male pornographic fantasy. Certainly not every reader will be comfortable with some of his choices, which range from depicting rapes to extravagant sex. However, Gilbert also provides

complex character development and brilliant aesthetics that can engage the reader with issues related to queer sexuality and its disruption of heteronormativity. For example, in "Poison River" (published 1989–93 in *Love and Rockets* vol. 1 and now collected in *Beyond Palomar*), Luba has a romantic love square with Fermin, a mobster who used to be a musician; Blás (his gay friend); and Isobel, a former exotic dancer who is trans. Even though the story has many of the extravagant aspects of a crime story, Gilbert develops and depicts all of these queer and gendered identities with a lot of compassion and empathy. Their queerness is never "othered" or "vilified," and open-minded readers can bond with these particular characters. One of the interesting visual twists in the story is that Isobel is initially drawn following "female" visual conventions, so the reader is led to think that they are consuming a traditional heteronormative love story. In a later chapter, Isobel is revealed to have a trans identity, and this changes how the story is interpreted. This type of liberatory storytelling was important in the twentieth century for the comic book medium and industry, which have been limited in these controversial topics by the influence of the Comics Code and the dominance of companies focused on mostly bland superhero narratives.

Gilbert has created many great stories in *Love and Rockets*, but the two most famous are "Human Diastrophism" (where a serial killer is unleashed in the town) and "Poison River" (which reveals Luba's origin in a complex story that rivals any masterpiece of US and Latin American literature). In the second part of his career, Gilbert moved Luba and her family to live close to her sisters in Los Angeles. As Luba's neighbor and friend Pipo makes a fortune in the United States with her business companies, the "Palomar" story setting becomes more about the characters' decadent life in the US, their inclusion into the US bourgeoisie, the LGBTQ+

identities of many of Luba's female family members, and the bizarre B-movie acting careers of Fritz (Luba's stepsister). This period of Gilbert's career is more intertextual, self-reflexive, and less accessible for some of his audience, which is why some readers are nostalgic for the original "Palomar" stories that were grounded in a small-town setting. The original "Palomar" stories always contained bizarre/surreal narrative devices, but Gilbert's new stories set in the US require a deep knowledge of the history of the characters in the original "Palomar" setting, a better understanding of the complexities of LGBTQ+ life, and also a complex grasp of the double meanings of the conventions of horror, science fiction, and other genres that he explored through made-up film adaptations featuring his female character Fritz. Robert Crumb himself has said he preferred Gilbert's early work when he was writing/drawing about a "bunch of guys" (Groth 2004, 55–56), but I still think his narrative evolution into exploring female sexuality and its effects on genre performance is brilliant, and readers should appreciate that he is willing to change his storytelling without being afraid of losing readership or critical acclaim. Some of Gilbert's stories have been more successful than others because it is not always easy to catch all the meta references, but his willingness to experiment is precisely what makes his art so attractive.

Unlike the "Palomar" saga, which was initially set outside of the US, the "Locas" universe, created by Jaime Hernandez, follows the lives of several Latinx characters such as Maggie, Hopey, Penny Century, and a large diverse cast of characters living in Los Angeles and other settings in the United States. Maggie's original stories were sci-fi punk parodies, but Jaime eventually shifted the narratives to more realistic and comedic melodramas where the characters face tough situations growing up. There are many famous story lines in the "Locas" saga. For example, "The Death of Speedy Ortiz" explores the death of one of Maggie and Hopey's friends in the barrio and the violence and trauma that young Latinos were experiencing in LA at the time. Another famous segment, "Flies in the Ceiling," portrays the controversial issue of abortion from Isabel's (one of Maggie's friends) perspective through innovative abstract imagery depicting psychological trauma. Additionally, stories like "Wigwam Bam" portray the split between Maggie and Hopey, depicting realistically how different Latinx experiences in the United States can affect a longtime friendship. Finally, the more recent story line "The Love Bunglers" explores traumas of the past such as the divorce of Maggie's parents and her brother's sexual abuse. Although sometimes Jaime's characters look and act similar to the ones found in *Archie* comics, the story lines in Jaime's "Locas" universe function as liberating tools for many readers who have experienced these issues but never saw them represented in the industry's dominant genres. Many of these controversial topics have begun appearing more frequently in mainstream comic books in the past few decades. Examples include Peter David's 1990s run in *The Incredible Hulk* and its depiction of the AIDS epidemic and the recent inclusion of diversity characters in Marvel and DC comic books such as America Chavez (2011) and Naomi (2018), respectively. Still, Jaime, along with Gilbert, was one of the first authors to break ground in the industry with a continuous narrative, and his goes all the way back to 1978.

Gilbert and Jaime's characters grow older in their respective series, and their age is visually represented in the art of the comics as their bodies decay. However, the main difference between the two brothers' work is that Jaime has a tighter continuity with the characters. In his stories, Maggie is still the protagonist, and the setting typically remains the same, while Gilbert moved the setting of his stories from the fictional Palomar to the United States and shifted protagonists in the different phases of the "Palomar" saga. Two elements that both artists have shared in their respective story lines in *Love and Rockets* are their avoidance of thematic closure after their characters assert their queer identities (Saxey 2006) and the shifts from fantasy to realism to fantasy again, which is why many readers have tied their narratives to Latin American magic realism. In numerous interviews, both Jaime and Gilbert have claimed that they have not read authors such as Gabriel García Márquez. They have, however, certainly acquired some intertextual literary techniques from other sources.

Love and Rockets continues to be published today in its fourth incarnation. It was originally published as a black-and-white magazine, but changes in the publishing and collecting aspects of the industry have forced the creators to alter this format. In the second version of the series, Los Bros Hernandez changed the comic book to the traditional smaller format because readers were complaining that the magazines did not fit into their comic book boxes. Then in the third incarnation of the series, they changed the format to original graphic novels that were over two hundred pages long because they realized that many customers did not buy the single issues and were waiting for the collected editions instead. This decision was important for their work to gain more initial distribution in bookstores around the country. However, in the last incarnation, they returned to the original magazine format while also making the stories available in digital reader applications such as ComiXology. Having a digital distribution alongside the printed edition gives titles a wide distribution, especially in states where bookstores and comic book stores are sparse or where the series' topics would be considered controversial. With *Love and Rockets*, Los Bros Hernandez have made several important contributions to the US comic book industry, such as providing a model for creative independence, defiantly writing diverse stories to counter Eurocentric and heteronormative whiteness, and creating two epics with runs of over thirty years that has provided readers with characters that, unlike many mainstream superheroes, can mature and grow emotionally. Their work is in the pantheon of the greats such as Alan Moore, Will Eisner, Denys Cowan, Osamu Tezuka, Marjane Satrapi, Rumiko Takahashi, Alejandro Jodorowsky, and others.

33

Lowbrow

Sean Guynes

In November 2018, centrist comedian Bill Maher sparked a furor among comics fans after penning a short piece claiming, "I don't think it's a huge stretch to suggest that Donald Trump could only get elected in a country that thinks comic books are important." Even if sarcastic, the tone of the piece and its title, "Adulting," showcased Maher's frustration with the idea of taking comic books—a children's medium—seriously. He lamented that "some dumb people got to be professors" by writing theses about comics, a cultural shift that took place "some twenty years or so ago" when "adults decided they didn't have to give up kid stuff." Unsurprisingly, this outrage piece ignored both the substance of scholarship produced on comics and the historical shifts occurring in comics creation that, ironically, made them anything but a children's medium in the eyes of most public commentators. In fact, every few months since the mid-1980s, a new opinion piece has claimed that comics are finally for grown-ups. They reference a growing awareness of "serious" graphic novels among literati, academics, and book reviewers and suggest like Maher that before the advent of (largely autobiographical) graphic novels, comics—whether the newspaper funnies, romance or superhero comic books, webcomics, or evangelical religious tracts—were simple entertainment for simple people: the usual suspects of popular culture consumption.

At stake in discussions of whether comics are for kids or adults—or whether there are some comics that are decidedly "adult" on account of their narrative or artistic "seriousness"—is a question about comics' cultural status. As Maher's claim demonstrates, comics have long been considered *lowbrow*, belonging to a cultural status denoting intellectual or aesthetic inferiority in comparison to the supposedly more accomplished "art" of *highbrow* culture. As Lawrence W. Levine has noted, the concept of *lowbrow* originated in the United States in the early 1900s, roughly twenty years after *highbrow* came into popular usage. These terms labeled "types of culture" and pointed to quintessentially American concerns about producing American art that continued the supposedly superior artistic traditions of white European civilization (Levine 1988, 221). The lowbrow was distinguished from highbrow art, literature, and music by its mass popularity, its industrial production, its affordability to the lower classes, and (often) its production by poor and working-class whites. In addition to being classist ways of taxonomizing culture, the concept of *brow* was also racist, since the level of brow referenced by the concept referred to racist beliefs that the shape of the skull (notably the height, thickness, and prominence of the brow) determined traits associated in the eugenic and phrenological "sciences" with intellectual capacity and criminality (Levine 1988, 221–25).

In the United States, the highbrow/lowbrow divide determines much of the political landscape of culture. Although the high-/lowbrow hierarchy has constantly shifted across the past century, marking a series of ideological investments in the meaning and status of cultural works and practices, the categories themselves are significant for how they demarcate and contest beliefs about cultural value, our concerns about who makes and owns culture, and our constant preoccupation with who consumes it, why, and how. Unsurprisingly, much scholarship on popular culture, especially among cultural historians, has focused on it as the domain of uneducated and working-class people (Denning 1987; Rabinowitz 2014), women (Enstad 1999; Radway 1984), people of color (Acham 2004; Lhamon 1998), and/or children (Kline 1993)—in other words, everyone *not* an educated, middle- to upper-class white man. In doing so, much popular culture scholarship has had to take on the widespread public (and academic) juxtaposition of popular culture's artistic quality and intellectual depth with that of art or literature proper; in many cases, scholars of popular culture have pointed to the shaky ground on which the high-/lowbrow distinction stands.

Like dime novels, pulps, and mass-market paperbacks, comics have long been understood as lowbrow. This cultural-artistic status has proved a significant barrier both to the average adult's ability to discuss comics in public without invoking the stereotype of *The Simpsons*' hyperbolically unattractive, sexless, and misogynist Comic Book Guy and to the development and acceptance of comics studies as a legitimate field of inquiry. Though comics scholarship emerged out of comics fandom and journalism in the 1980s at precisely the moment that the general public began to "take comics seriously," the study of comics has been plagued by the medium's lowbrow association and was built on the (often strikingly defensive) premise that comics are in fact quite smart. Any account of *lowbrow* as a keyword for comics studies must necessarily deal with it as a problem in comics history, a social factor that must be understood in its specificity for each study of a given comics, and beyond that as a problem for the field itself. Lowbrow is dealt with—usually only in passing and almost never with direct reference to the word itself—in nearly every study of the subject and follows the seemingly necessary defense modeled in nearly all studies of popular culture (Fiske [1989] 2011; Freccero 1999; Gans 1999; Strinati 1995). In the past few years, comics scholars have become increasingly skeptical of

the need to "defend" comics as a worthwhile subject and have turned their attention to how conceptions of comics' status manifest in comics scholarship (Pizzino 2016; Singer 2019).

As this overview suggests, and as the essays in Smith and Duncan (2017) attest, for decades the key barrier to studying comics was their historical imbrication in and emergence from the popular culture scene. Although the genealogy of comics *can* be drawn to a range of art-historical accomplishments such as the Egyptian hieroglyphs, the Bayeux Tapestry, and the early nineteenth-century cartoons and caricatures of Rodolphe Töpffer (Kunzle 2007)—most of which, at present accounting, can hardly be considered lowbrow—comics' history over the past one hundred years was closely aligned with mass publishing and the media industries. Because of preferences within the academy for singular works of art, intellect, and cultural brilliance—for example, in the tradition of the Great American Novel (Buell 2014)—comics were denigrated for decades in the public and academic eye. Some of this preference was zeitgeist-driven reactionism to moral panics in nations such as the United States, Britain, Australia, and Sweden, where comics were associated with childhood delinquency and sexual deviancy (Beaty 2005; Hajdu 2009; Nyberg 1998). And while the success of creators like Art Spiegelman, Marjane Satrapi, and Alison Bechdel has brought comics to a wider audience and into the classroom, the past two decades have also seen comics dragged in popular (and scholarly) writing as a result of the medium's increasing synonymy with the superhero genre, thanks to a massive transmedia adaptation industry driven by Marvel and DC Comics.

Early work in comics studies was in much the same position as early film studies or science fiction studies, having to justify the artistic quality and intellectual depth of the medium and defend comics' worth as objects of study. Often, this was accomplished by pointing to the artistic genius of individual comics creators and to specific works of comics art, particularly those collected in or originally conceived of as *graphic novels*. The term *graphic novel* (Baetens and Frey 2015) is typically applied in order to add the artistic weight of *graphic* and literary seriousness of *novel* to the otherwise undignified *comic* (too synonymous with humorous newspaper strips), *comic book* (closely linked with superheroes), or *comix* (with links to countercultural vulgarity and underground indie-chic alike). Take, for example, Witek's (1989) book on comics as historical narratives, in which his chapters focus on a single great work by a single comics luminary produced outside of the mainstream comics industry and the superhero / science fiction / horror genres (e.g., Spiegelman's *Maus*, Harvey Pekar's *American Splendor*). As Beaty and Woo (2016, 5) have noted, comics studies established a canon of "plausible texts" around which the field developed; these texts—particularly Spiegelman's *Maus*, Bechdel's *Fun Home*, Satrapi's *Persepolis*, a handful of work by cult-status alternative comics creators like Chris Ware and Charles Burns, and two narratively contained, genre-deconstructing superhero comics (Moore and Gibbons's *Watchmen* and Miller's *Dark Knight Returns*)—became the center of a growing field of study by the mid-2000s.

Although the growth of comics studies confronted the problem of comics' lowbrow cultural status, particularly in the US and British contexts (the Franco-Belgian and Japanese traditions are considerably different), and ensured that comics were now widely taught, the lowbrow problem remained in the form of the separation of those comics worthy of scholarship from those that failed to make easily plausible texts—for the most part, serialized mainstream genre comics. For example, despite the historical significance and artistic and narrative complexity of DC Comics' *Crisis on Infinite Earths* limited series (written by Marv Wolfman with art by George Pérez), it has remained out of the scope of most comics research because the intelligibility of the comic relies on decades of prior story lines involving hundreds of characters; as a result, it is also virtually unteachable. Other comics that have been historically influential, such as Frank Miller and Klaus Janson's run on *Daredevil* in the late 1970s and early 1980s (a mainstream superhero comic) or Stan Sakai's *Usagi Yojimbo* (an indie samurai / funny animal comic), to take two examples, occupy complex production histories with regard to the interrelation of the series to a larger comic book universe—the distribution across multiple publishers and likely dozens of individual comics—or are otherwise difficult to access (because of either the cost of collected editions or the difficulty of access to original copies).

In contrast to serialized genre comics, texts like *Maus* and *Persepolis* could arguably be saved from the biases of popular culture and its mass appeal by referring to them instead as singular works of artistic greatness. Moreover, the need for plausible texts gives primacy to comics that can be taken as singular texts (either stand-alone graphic novels or complete story lines no longer than a few issues of a comic book series) in regularly available editions that can be cited by a groundswell of scholars. It is unsurprising, then, that much of the transformation with regard to the cultural status of comics has come in the form of our terms of reference for the medium. What comics are called has become an especially important signifier for brow level and the medium's acceptance in literary criticism. The deployment of the terms *graphic novel* and *graphic narrative* and their use as legitimizing technologies in the fight against the medium's lowbrow associations are symptomatic of what Beaty and Woo (2016, 5) describe as comics' "poorly developed critical infrastructure," a situation that has led to comics scholars developing a vocabulary drawn from film, literary, and art theory that "ennoble[s] the comic book by stealing fire from the better-established art form." Despite all the good that this new vocabulary and growing institutional acceptance of comics has wrought, the old ties between the medium and its cultural status, as well as an increasing awareness of comics' narrative complexities, have posted comics at the boundaries of literary, film, media, and cultural studies (Pizzino 2016)—not yet fully accepted but enticing scholars who have typically immersed themselves in the discourses of highbrow art to dabble with the lowbrow.

Recent years have seen a tentative shift away from disciplinary constraints that once either made the study of comics impossible or required scholars to perform contortions in defense of their texts. The number of academic journals and university presses devoting space to comics has exploded as our cultural moment militantly erodes highbrow/lowbrow distinctions and as popular culture becomes an increasingly fruitful area of inquiry. The defenses of comics in the introduction to monographs have become shorter or disappeared altogether in the past five years alone. Meanwhile, the longtime distinction between comics and art (Beaty 2012), though still a productive space for historical and aesthetic concern, has slowly withered. It's worth noting, of course, that this situation is context specific. The cultural status of comics has been a more significant concern in US and British scholarship as a result of the heavy influence in those countries of the Marxist tradition of cultural studies through the Frankfurt and Birmingham schools and their protégés in the US. In Francophone scholarship, however, the cultural status of comics has played little role in comics studies, which has tended to focus on the formal functions of comics art, in part because comics enjoy higher cultural regard in France and Belgium than they do in the US and UK. Comics are not considered of equal artistic/cultural value everywhere, and as such, the various linguistic and national traditions have their own stories to tell about comics' relation to art.

This discussion of the keyword *lowbrow* and its relevance to comics studies also invokes the growing description of *middlebrow* (Radway 1997; Rubin 1992) as a concept that mitigates the binary historical tension between high and low. Middlebrow arose to describe the culture of a growing middle class at the turn of the nineteenth century and throughout the twentieth century, when new levels of consumption created a shared sense of cultural and class values in the form of upmarket paperback fiction, quality television shows, and intelligent (but not "art") cinema. A term like *middlebrow*—or Peter Swirski's (2005) *nobrow*, which denotes the seemingly dissolution of brow categories in some spaces of cultural production and reception—better describes the changing historical dynamics of culture, industry, and consumption in the wake of the emergence of more complex economic strata, especially the upper-middle class in postwar America. Alternatives to high-/lowbrow are of increasing importance to comics studies, since following the growing recognition of comics as (sometimes, provisionally) "adult," the medium has become a more significant touchpoint for broader studies of culture, such that comics are now easily found alongside literature and film in certain studies—for example, those of periods or issues in cultural history (e.g., Barzilai 2016, 145–85; Chute and DeKoven 2012; Strub 2011, 15–21). The growth of newspaper and upmarket magazine sections devoted to comics reviews and criticism, the inclusion of scenes from *Maus* in *The Norton Anthology of English Literature*, and the longlisting of a comic for the Man Booker Prize in 2018 are all signs of cultural shifts in the status of comics that have led nearly all to utilize the term *graphic novel* and that have marked comics as intended reading material for the fantasy of the college-educated middle-class American.

We might consider lowbrow the field-defining problematic for comics studies, especially in the US and British contexts. At stake in the status of comics as a lowbrow (or not) form is whether comics can be studied—in other words, whether comics studies can exist within the present institutional terrain of the humanities—since it seems not to be a question worrying those using comics in many other fields, like communications, education, and medicine, and if so, how it should persist in its interstitial relationship to more well-established areas of inquiry. This volume and others like it (e.g., Aldama 2018) suggest that comics studies is alive and well, though some still turn their noses up at anything but the middlebrow-sanctioned graphic novel. Lowbrow status remains a significant issue for us in comics studies, but it is also an opportunity. If the field turns its attention to how the discursive terrain of brow levels and especially to scholars' fear of being connected with the lowest of lowbrow cultural forms—that is, with the basest of mainstream comics, with the romance boom of the 1950s, with the franchise comics that have kept companies like Dark Horse and IDW afloat, with the mega-best-selling superhero melodramas of the 1990s, with the outrageously ostentatious "event" comics that enforce crossover reading of Marvel and DC series, with the evangelical tracts of Jack Chick—our field stands to gain a lot. Recognition of lowbrow status at the level of methodology—that is, taking account of the ways in which the cultural status of our objects of study impact our selection of and approach to texts—will create a comics studies open to the generic vastness, artistic inventiveness, industrial depths, awesome capacity, and more holistic history of our subject.

34

Manga
Adam L. Kern

Reports of the death of manga are greatly exaggerated.

True, physical sales of what is universally (though problematically) defined as "Japanese comics" have dropped alarmingly in recent years, at least in Japan. In the first decade of the twenty-first century, total annual sales of manga books and magazines decreased roughly from over 500 billion yen ($4.5 billion) to about 300 billion yen ($2.7 billion). This is not surprising, given that manga has become somewhat overshadowed by other media, particularly animated film (anime) and digital gaming.

Yet slumping sales of manga belie the fact that interest in manga may actually be on the upswing. Until recently, works were produced and consumed in what might be described as the "manga pyramid," consisting of (1) a base of amateur fare, a fraction of which was submitted directly to publishers, though most of which consisted of self-published minicomics or "zines" (*dōjinshi*) circulated among acquaintances or at comics conventions (*komikon*); (2) a middle strata of works that, while crafted primarily by professional artists, were test-driven in a slew of manga magazines, or *mangashi* (e.g., Kōdansha's *Young Magazine* launched the now-classic series *xxxHolic*, *Be-Bop High School*, *Ghost in the Shell*, and *Akira*); and (3) an apex of works that, having come up through the ranks, were collected into dedicated paperbacks (*tankōbon*), as with *Sailor Moon*, *Naruto*, and *One Piece*. The logic of this pyramid no doubt projected manga into the wider pop culture industry as a whole too, with blockbusters crossing over into video games and anime but also live-action cinema, action figurines, and other forms of mass merchandizing.

Lately, however, digital technology seems to be turning this pyramid on its head, changing both the conditions of creation and the reception of manga. Readers are increasingly consuming works online through countless websites, even those that are not punctiliously legal. Although reprehensibly robbing artists of their livelihood, some of these sites nevertheless provide a platform for widely read "fansubs" (unofficial translations) of works—into English, Chinese, and many other languages—that otherwise might never be read outside Japan. The manga industry begrudgingly tolerates this practice, since aggressive legal action would risk both alienating consumers and turning off the spigot from lucrative foreign markets.

The industry may even one day come to embrace it. After all, successful works and artists are routinely assimilated into the very fabric of mainstream manga, the most conspicuous example being the phenomenon of boy love manga known as *yaoi* (*yah-oh-ee*). Starting out as queer underground parodies (a bit like gay Batman and Robin?) of mainstream manga aimed at young women (shojo), *yaoi* has become a major—if not *the* major—subgenre in its own right. Be that as it may, although statistics for illicit websites are hard to come by, ultimately the decline of sales in physical manga would seem to be exceeded by increases in surreptitious online readership.

It might also be argued that manga represents the very heart of the Japanese pop culture industry. Indeed, the industry could probably never afford to allow manga to expire. Comics are, after all, far cheaper and less risky to produce than most of these other widely disseminated pop culture media. The rule of thumb has long been that three-quarters of all anime start out as

manga, for instance. Many of the most successful pop culture characters who, having crossed over from one medium to another within the complex media mix of twenty-first-century Japan, trace their roots back to manga, like Goku from the *Dragon Ball* franchise. Tezuka Osamu's Iron-Arm Atom (*Tetsuwan atomu*) migrated from minor character to blockbuster star in manga magazine stories during the 1950s. *Atomu* then made the leap, in January of 1963, into the first major animated TV series in Japan. Almost immediately, NBC had syndicated an American version of the series, called *Astro Boy*, airing it on national TV beginning in November of that same year. (No doubt the English title allowed the series to sidestep the inconvenient truth that the character, harnessing atomic energy for good rather than evil, implicitly suggests a moral superiority over the US bombing of Hiroshima and Nagasaki.) One reason that Tezuka is hailed as the "god of manga," then, probably has to do with Japanese pride that the local boy made it big overseas. Conversely, other popular characters find a comfortable nest in manga. Pikachu of the Pokémon franchise, who started out in life as a video game character, is perhaps among the most famous.

Moreover, manga has been flourishing in recent years *outside* Japan. Manga is broadly consumed in the Americas (not the least of which in Canada and Brazil) and Europe, particularly in Germany, France, Australia, and the UK, which is undergoing a bit of a Japan boom in contemporary times—as evidenced by megaexhibitions at the British Museum on the woodblock artist Hokusai, erotic art (*shunga*), and, most recently, manga itself. In the United States, there was even a stretch during the first decade of this century (at the same time sales in Japan were slumping) when manga represented the fastest-growing segment of the *American* publishing industry. Likewise, manga are progressively being read in Africa, South Asia, and the Middle East.

All things considered, then, manga represents the largest, most profitable, and arguably most influential of the major comic book traditions worldwide, dwarfing its Franco-Belgian and Anglo-American rivals—including the recent spate of Hollywood flicks mining superhero comics for material. Even more significantly, however, Japanese comic books may represent the most *venerable* of the world's great comics traditions. About a century prior to the advent of the British and American comic book industries (sometime during the mid- to late nineteenth century, depending on one's definition), the Japanese began mass-producing woodblock-printed comic books that constituted a major center of the emergent pop culture industry in its day. These woodblock-printed comics, which came into full swing during the mid-eighteenth century, undoubtedly represent the first major comic book industry in world history. Whereas the forerunners of Euro-American comics (illuminated manuscripts, Englishman William Hogarth's illustrated stories, the wordless graphic novels of Flemish artist Frans Masereel's [1889–1972], among others) had limited circulation, the woodblock-printing industry of eighteenth-century Japan—which also produced the world-famous *ukiyoe* ("pictures of the Floating World" of kabuki actors and pleasure quarter courtesans)—produced comics in vast quantities that could be sold for a pittance, thereby almost immediately reaching a significant slice of the Japanese urban population. This population enjoyed a far greater level of basic literacy (the ability to read the Japanese syllabary rather than the more advanced Chinese graphs) than its Euro-American counterparts.

Collectively known as *kusazōshi* (pronounced *coo-sah-zoh-oh-she*), these woodblock comic books consisted of one to three ten-page softcover pamphlets (*zōshi*) of rag paper. While interior pages were printed using black ink, frontispieces sported colorful cover art.

To reach the masses, works were written in an easy-to-read calligraphy, known as the "grass" (*kusa*) script. (One puckish author punningly observed that these works were in such high demand that when sold, their ink was still wet and "stinky," or *kusai*.) Early genres (late *otogizōshi*, *akabon*, *kurohon*, and early *aohon*), popular from the first half of the eighteenth century, were intended for a mass readership with rudimentary verbal and visual literacies. Story worlds were prototypically drawn from children's fables, fairy tales, folk stories, kabuki and puppet plays, celebrated events from history, and classic works of literature. Later genres (late *aohon*, *kibyōshi*, *gōkan*, and *yomihon*) hijacked the simple-looking format and visual idioms of these earlier genres to produce works of remarkable sophistication that might be considered the graphic novels of their age.

One genre in particular, the *kibyōshi* (key-byoh-she), so called for its "yellowed covers," occasionally used its whimsical stories to mask deeper sociopolitical satire to such extent that some of its luminary creators ran afoul of the authoritarian military government. A best-selling *kibyōshi*, like Santō Kyōden's (1761–1816) *Edo umare uwaki no kabayaki* (*Playboy, Roasted a la Edo*, 1785), was printed in three editions of approximately ten thousand copies per edition. With book clubs and lending libraries extending the reach of individual titles, approximately 5 percent of the population of Edo (present-day Tokyo) is believed to have perused *Playboy*, making it not only one of the most widely read texts in its entirety up to that point of Japanese cultural history but also a work to rival today's greatest megahits on the *New York Times* best-seller list, which typically reach only 1–2 percent of the American public. During the three decades of its heyday, the *kibyōshi* averaged approximately one hundred titles per year—about one title every three and a half days. No wonder the sheer volume of works spawned critical reviews (*hyōbanki*) to guide readers in their purchases.

Accordingly, these comic books were central to the media mix of their time. Authors engaged in product placement, actively promoting real-life kabuki actors, courtesans, geisha, various kinds of business establishments, hairstyles, cure-alls, reading pills, and so on. Authorship itself became reconceived as a vendible commodity that could be "placed" within works. Kyōden, for instance, in addition to advertising his tobacco shop and its paraphernalia, concocted the fictional character of the comic book creator Santō Kyōden, who makes cameo appearances in many stories. Similarly, comic book characters hopped from one story to another, leaping off the page into other media, particularly *netsuke*. These miniature action figurines were attached to purses and tobacco pouches—not unlike the innumerable manga and anime characters who dangle from cell phone straps as plastic figurines today. Some characters materialized within designs on hand towels and clothing, as with Enjirō, the comic hero of Kyōden's *Playboy*. And Tofu Boy (*Tofu Kozō*), a comic hero endowed with the special power of disrupting any situation merely by dropping his serving tray, became a mainstay of shop signs on tofu stores, a veritable Hello Kitty of his day.

Accordingly, such uncanny resemblances make it tempting to jump to the conclusion that modern Japanese manga can trace its roots back directly to these eighteenth-century woodblock-printed comic book genres. The real story, however, is more complicated. It turns out that what we think of today as the modern Japanese manga actually resulted from the comingling of two distinct comic book cultures during the late nineteenth century: the Indigenous tradition of woodblock-printed comic books that came into full swing during the eighteenth century and the Euro-American political and editorial cartoons that entered Japan during the second half of the nineteenth century. Not long after the earliest Western-style comics were published in Japan, in Charles Wirgman's (1832–91) magazine the *Japan Punch* (1862–87), a profusion of Japanese humor magazines followed suit with what might best be described as hybrid Japanese-Western cartoons. The earliest included *Marumaru chinbun* (est. 1877) and *Nipponchi* (est. 1874), the title of which playfully combines *Nippon* (Japan) and *ponchi* (punch).

Japanese pioneers who combined these two traditions included Honda Kinkichirō (1850–1921) and Okamoto Ippei (1886–1948). In 1895, Imaizumi Ippyō (1865–1904) applied the term *manga* to his one-panel Western-style Japanese cartoons within his book *Ippyō manga shū* (*Ippyō's Manga Collection*). Kitazawa Rakuten (1876–1955) titled his widely popular comic strip *Jiji manga*, appearing in the humor magazine *Jiji shinpō* from 1902 on. Rakuten was perhaps the first Japanese artist to work for a Western comics magazine, *Box of Curios* (under Frank Arthur Nankivell, 1869–1959). Rakuten also developed one of the earliest recurring female protagonists in Japanese comic books, Tonda Haneko (1928 onward). Rakuten's humor magazine, *Tōkyō pakku* (Tokyo puck, est. 1905), circulated in China and Korea as well as Japan, arguably making it the first Japanese manga publication to be widely sold abroad. Thus somewhat paradoxically, even though the term *manga* goes back to woodblock comic books, the modern manga as a genre traces its roots back to the comixing of those comic books with Western comics.

Simply put, manga has always-already been *transnational*. For this reason, it may be best to rethink the common-sense, long-standing, and pervasive definition of *manga* as "Japanese comics," where "Japanese" refers to works produced and consumed in Japan by Japanese people for Japanese people, in the Japanese language, and in an instantly recognizable Japanese visual idiom.

This average-person-off-the-street definition unfortunately tends to obscure the complicated transnational history and nature of manga, potentially even subordinating manga to Western comics.

After all, the oft repeated phrase "Japanese comics" surreptitiously implies *Japanized* comics, as though manga were merely a cheap imitation of "real"—meaning Euro-American—comics. According to accounts in the popular Western media, the modern Japanese manga begins with Tezuka, whose debt to Disney (and other Western animators and cartoonists) is emphasized. Similarly, just over a dozen years ago, *Wired* magazine ran the article "How *Manga* Conquered America." This title provocatively suggests that Japan beat "us" at our own game. The Japanese may have lost the war, in other words, but they won the battle of the comic books. Lurking beneath the surface of such accounts is the long-standing and loathsome Orientalist stereotype of Asians as talented imitators rather than original geniuses in their own right. This stereotype has regrettably underwritten most Western accounts of the Japanese postwar "economic miracle," in which Japanese commercial success is attributed to cheap and perhaps even illegal imitations (think "transistor radio" here). To the extent that Japanese comics predate Euro-American counterparts, it is curious that comics are not defined as Western manga. The inevitable imitations among Western comic book creators, for that matter—inevitable, because all art is by definition promiscuous—are never framed in terms of a putative tendency among Anglo, American, and Franco-Belgian people toward mindless imitation. For instance, it may come as a shock to many fans of the blockbuster *bande dessinée* series *Les Aventures de Tintin* (which began publication in 1929) that Hergé partially modeled his globe-trotting boy reporter Tintin and his trusty canine sidekick Milou (Snowy) on a Japanese predecessor

launched a half dozen years earlier: *Shō-chan no bōken* (The adventures of Shō-chan), which Kabashima Katsuichi (1888–1965) and Oda Nobutsune (1889–1967) began publishing in 1923. Their manga series related the adventures of the globe-trotting boy reporter Shō-chan and his trusty rodent sidekick, Risu (Squirrel). Why is it that, in the context of the East-West binary, inspiration is downplayed or ignored for Western creators but vilified and demonized for Easter creators?

In conclusion, I would suggest that manga be more generatively thought of as Japanese-*styled* comics. Although the distinction between this definition and "Japanese comics" is admittedly subtle, there are at least three main advantages. First, it acknowledges the origins of modern Japanese manga as having been deliberately *styled* from these two comics cultures. This, in turn, allows us to avoid Orientalist and binary notions of Asians (versus Westerners) as superb copyists rather than originary geniuses in their own right. Second, it significantly allows works to be considered manga even if they are *not* written, drawn, or read by Japanese people for Japanese people in Japan. This allows manga to be regarded as a style that can be learned and practiced by anyone around the world, thereby allowing German manga to be included as well as contemporary Japanese comics, for that matter.

Many comics around the world are produced in this manga style. A case in point is Sakai's *Usagi Yojimbo*, a beautifully illustrated, long-running series set in Japan during the age of shoguns and featuring a samurai warrior named Usagi who happens to be a bunny rabbit (*usage*). Yet Sakai is really Stan Sakai, an American-based artist. Some comics are even created, billed, sold, and consumed as "authentic" manga even though they are *not* produced in Japanese for Japanese by Japanese. There are even works that are deliberately marketed as Japanese manga in translation that turn out to have been originally composed in German, French, English, and other languages under a Japanese pseudonym, as though the works were really "only" a translation of a Japanese manga original that in fact does not exist.

In a sense, then, the problem with defining manga as "Japanese comics" is that many manga are not really Japanese in the common-sense understanding of the word but are always styled after what people *imagine* to be Japanese. I would even argue that Japanese creators of manga are in their own way reimagining Japanese-styled antecedents. Defining manga as Japanese-styled comics allows us to conceptualize it as a style of comics that anyone with enough talent can master. Ultimately, the term *manga* has become a kind of prestige label that benefits from the illusion of Japaneseness, when in fact manga not only are often the product of transnational production—printed in Hong Kong and colored in South Korea, for instance—but were never uniquely "Japanese" in the first place. The point is not that manga must be "purely Japanese" to be authentic; rather, anyone can, theoretically, learn how to produce an authentic Japanese-styled manga regardless of their national, linguistic, or cultural identity.

Third, by situating manga in a global, transhistorical, transnational perspective, this definition may help promote a deeper understanding of *all* comics. I am advocating that we consider the term *comics* nation neutral, meaning that we speak of Anglo-American-styled comics and Franco-Belgian-styled comics, as well as Japanese-styled comics, in order to acknowledge that all comics are styled after antecedents that have been affected by global flows. In the final analysis, comics have always been a worldwide medium. To regard comics as inherently Euro-American is to accept the terms of Euro-American colonialism, whereby American superhero comics and Franco-Belgian *bande dessinée* are exalted as a kind of cultural capital over other comics traditions, even those that are larger, more profitable, more influential, and more venerable.

The conviction here is that comics—the comixing of words and images, often to tell a story—is a major mode of *human* communication that spans historical time as well as cultural, linguistic, and national divides. This trend can only become more important with increased globalization. If comics studies is to advance, then, it must at the very least include a transnational awareness of the greatest comics tradition in the world—a tradition whose trajectory from eighteenth-century woodblock-printed comic books to modern Japanese-styled comics was always already itself transnational in the first place.

35

Memoir

Joo Ok Kim

Memoir, as a genre, asserts the significance of memory and personal experience. Derived from the French word *mémoire*, the closest English meaning translates to "memory." The genre bears a relationship with autobiography yet does not imply the totalized history of a singular lifetime, as in the case of autobiography. Instead, memoir creates possibilities for an excerpted, nonlinear timeline and experience for the author. Graphic memoir, in particular, can represent life experience in fragments, thus disrupting normative temporality: panels suspended in time, infusing the reading moment with urgency or a sense of belatedness. Encircled by "memory," "history," and "autobiography," the genre yields a unique approach incorporating elements from these categories (Yagoda 2009). Further, memoir prioritizes affect and feeling, ranging from the author's relationship to occasions of historical significance to the quiet details of personal experience, concerns the genre shares with queer theory. Indeed, queer theorists have observed such everyday moments as yielding "the understanding that utopia exists in the quotidian" (Muñoz 2009); as seeking "low theory in popular places, in the small, the inconsequential, the antimonumental, the micro, the irrelevant" (Halberstam 2011); and as offering an "archive of familiarity and incongruity, of things and situations that are utterly mundane, mainstream, predictable . . . yet have somehow managed to remain unthinkable in both normative and queer cultural contexts" (Tongson 2011). As such, it perceives what cultural studies scholar Raymond Williams (1978) theorized as "structure of feeling," the "specifically affective elements of consciousness and relationships: not feeling against thought, but thought as felt and feeling as thought: practical consciousness of a present kind, in a living and interrelating continuity."

This centering of affect, while deep with critical possibility, has at times been mobilized against the genre. Thus memoir is a particularly contested form, its significance as a critical mode questioned because of its necessarily subjective positionality. Critics often deem memoir narcissistic or self-indulgent, feminized, bereft of objectivity and authority. Yet as feminist scholars such as Ann Cvetkovich (2012) have demonstrated, "Memoir has been an undeniable force in queer subcultures, where it has been an entry point into the literary public sphere for working-class writers, the backbone of solo performance, and a mainstay for small presses." As with the memoir, comics have evolved through a blending of genres, particularly under the historical conditions of comics' material production. Shelley Streeby (2017) historicizes an alternative genealogy charting the affinities among comics, science fiction, and fantasy in her work on *Love and Rockets* (the Hernandez brothers), observing that "the history of comics and the history of science fiction and fantasy are in many ways inseparable, since they emerged from the same world of sensational newspapers, dime novels, and pulp magazines of the late nineteenth and early twentieth centuries." As a mode within comics, itself a cultural form that has historically been devalued as not meriting serious inquiry, the graphic memoir occupies what has been a doubly marginalized terrain in arts and literature (McCloud 2000; Royal 2007; Aldama 2010; Whaley 2015; Fawaz 2016; Chute 2017). At the same time, given its proximity to memoir itself as a more legitimated genre, the graphic memoir has garnered relative scholarly acceptance compared to the academic reception of other comics genres.

Contemporary graphic memoir, especially in the genre's inquiry into trauma, family narratives, war, displacement, and the violence underwriting these phenomena, visually and verbally articulates such thematic complexities and nuances. Comics invite formal and structural play, expanding narrative possibilities and allowing for the reader to improvise reading practices. The memoir has been theorized as an ensemble or "outlaw genre" (Quinby 1992; Kaplan 1992), employing what Gillian Whitlock (2006) has coined "autographics," "the specific conjunctions of visual and verbal text in [graphic memoir], and . . . the subject positions that narrators negotiate in and through comics." Some of the most recognized graphic memoirs refashion the genre further still: Marjane Satrapi's *Persepolis* ([2000] 2004) is "the story of a childhood," Alison Bechdel's *Fun Home* (2007) is "a family tragicomic," and Thi Bui's *The Best We Could Do* (2017) is an "illustrated memoir." The proliferation of naming practices suggests the graphic memoir's pliability for disrupting generic conventions, formally significant for perceiving the fracturing aftermaths of trauma, violence, war, and displacement.

The graphic possibilities for simultaneously representing multiple subjectivities suggest the comics memoir's utility as a vehicle for witnessing and for testimonial. The partial perspective of comics, often criticized for centering the subjective, instead lends authenticity to the narrative (Haraway 1988; Smith and Watson 2017). The graphic memoir thus enjoys an important role as a popular medium that reaches publics that might not otherwise be able to access narratives of historical trauma and violence, especially in the complex, layered presentation of the verbal and visual. On the other hand, precisely due to many graphic memoirs' attention to violence, war, and displacement, the genre's popularity in the global literary landscape may also work to uphold the human rights regime. Scholars have critiqued the amnesiac operations of Euro-American human rights discourses, which have obscured global legacies of colonialism, legacies that continue to reverberate yet remain unaddressed (Williams 2010; Melamed 2011; Atanasoski 2013; Hong 2015; Lowe 2015). And so the mobilization, circulation, and political value (in particular the state's selective endorsement) of graphic memoirs must be considered as the broader context in which they are received. To offer one example, Christine Hong (2015) has traced the creation and reception of Miné Okubo's illustrated memoir *Citizen 13660* (1946), for which Okubo was "faced with the challenge of visually rehabilitating both the 'enemy alien' on the home front and the enemy in the Pacific as democratically inclined subjects capable of thriving in settings conditioned by the strictures of US militarism." Key officials in the War Relocation Authority who read *Citizen 13660* as faithfully documenting the rehabilitation of Japanese American subjects lauded Okubo's visual memoir for its "authentic" portrayals of internment camp life. Such incongruous readings affirmed the state's presumed democratic, assimilationist rationale for racialized incarceration (Hong 2015).

The graphic memoir also transnationally mediates both content and distribution. While graphic memoirs such as Art Spiegelman's 1986 *Maus* appeal to English-language publics, of particular note is the international reception of the genre. Scholars have marked the tension between the reception of local comics within the Middle East, for instance, and the global market's specific interest in the autobiographical memoir (di Ricco 2015). The critical and consumerist attention to graphic memoirs internationally is also significant, since autobiographical comics "account for many of the foreign works translated into English" (Mazur and Danner

2014). As well, the graphic medium may potentially record what is otherwise technologically prohibited, whether in the Japanese internment camps, as a work-around to the memoir as a banned form in Iran, or as the court sketches of Guantanamo military tribunals (Hong 2015; Smith and Watson 2017; Hamlin 2013). While the history of Japanese manga is itself a long study (and its own keyword), Tessa Morris-Suzuki's (2005) analysis of Japanese historical comics suggests the possibility of the genre serving as a nationalist, allegorical memoir for creators such as Kobayashi Yoshinori. Other scholars have considered how the memoir as a comics form is mediated through colonialism—for instance, in the case of Korean comics (Mazur and Danner 2014). Through this lens, Park Chan-wook's film adaptation of *Oldboy* (2005), from the Japanese manga, carries remarkable resonance as an adaptation of a colonialist medium. So too does Thi Bui's *The Best We Could Do* (2017), which negotiates the formal elements of French and US comics as she narrates the transgenerational traumas of the Vietnam War in her family.

If the graphic memoir is intimately tethered to affect, it merits a return to Williams's concept of the "structure of feeling," in which perhaps the genre could in fact theorize a visual "structure"—replete with grids, gutters, and dialogue bubbles—*for* feeling. The possibility of the graphic memoir and comics at large to grasp what Williams describes as that which lingers "at the very edge of semantic availability" could offer one entry point for thinking about the paired publication of Ta-Nehisi Coates's *Between the World and Me* (2015) and his launch of *Black Panther* in 2016, mediating his own relationship to superhero comics in his youth. Queer theorist José Esteban Muñoz (2009) lingers on his relationship with characters like members of the Fantastic Four and X-Men and Spider-Man, "real people with problems. Their powers were more curses than blessings. The

Fantastic Four were a dysfunctional family, the X-Men had a certain genetic difference that made them social pariahs (like theories of the gay gene that I do not buy), and Spiderman [*sic*] was a fucked-up teen. The Surfer was an alien exiled to Earth, always longing to return to his homeland. For me, a Cuban who grew up in Miami, where I was always told I was living in exile from my homeland, the Surfer's mythology resonated." In this genre, so vividly constituted by superheroes—in particular, queer yearning for and dreaming with the fantastic and the quotidian—perhaps the popularity of graphic memoir comes as no surprise, for the graphic memoir creates its own universe populated with "outlaw" subjectivities, taking the retrospect and transforming it into horizon, into possibility not foreclosed by its own past.

36

Nostalgia

Blair Davis

In the beginning, life was pure experience, and processing, and comparison, and the determination of likes and dislikes, pains and pleasures, revulsions and adorations. Lifelong comics fans know from a very young age which images, sounds, smells, and textures are the ones that we would devote the rest of our lives to. We can still vividly recall both the scent and the feel of the newsprint of our childhood comics. In turn, our adult encounters with comics are forever tempered by the spectral sensations of youth. When we're nostalgic for bygone times and experiences, there's often an implied distance between the present moment and an earlier era—between the surface upon which we now tread and the foundational layers that prop up our current age. We refer to mental dalliances in the past as nostalgia, as a longing for the departed and the ephemeral. Nostalgic tendencies are perhaps little more than the process of mourning those moments that can never be returned to, those memories that grow blurrier at the edges with the successive passing of years, and those emotions that proved so seminal to the ways in which our identities were shaped.

Devotees of comics are commonly characterized as being endlessly attached to the heroes they grew up with—"perhaps as an attempt to reconnect with their childhood experiences," argues Carol Tilley (2018). Comics fans, creators, and scholars alike regularly bring these nostalgic tendencies with them to the titles they read, create, and analyze. While comics fans are often represented as suffering from Peter Pan syndrome in television shows like *The Big Bang Theory* and *Comic Book Men*, few comic book readers escape the seductive draw of nostalgia entirely: conventions, specialty retailers, and online sales offer increasingly easier ways to access the most memorable comics from our past. Nostalgia is also difficult for creators to avoid, between their own affinities for drawing inspiration from childhood-favorite story lines and characters and constant industry efforts to rebrand classic characters and continuities. Scholars can often be the worst offenders of all in their clinical efforts at dissecting the corpses of their youthful passions with a pathological devotion.

There's a certain sickness to being a die-hard comics fan that we all have to reconcile when coming to terms with the comics of our formative past. Psychologist Douwe Draaisma notes that historical scholarship on the phenomenon of nostalgia in past decades described how it "can lead to illness and psychological harm" (2013, 134). Even the word itself betrays medical origins, as a seventeenth-century Swiss doctor named Johannes Hofer coined the term *nostalgia* to describe extreme states of illness stemming from prolonged homesickness. Hofer took the "Swiss dialect word Heimweh (homesickness) and 'translated' it into Greek. From *nostros*, homecoming, and *algia*, pain, he derived the word 'nostalgia'" (Draaisma 2013, 135).

Along with this pain and sickness, some also equate nostalgia with an obsessive intensity when it comes to comics readers. In *Demanding Respect: The Evolution of the American Comic Book* (2009), Paul Lopes ties the rise of organized comics fandom (and comic book collecting in particular) to nostalgia desire. Lopes argues how journalists began "suggesting a certain fanaticism on the part of these fans," even referring to them as "cultists" (95). He cites a *New York Times* article from 1973 that posits, "Comic book collecting has been growing slowly but steadily since the series of nostalgic waves began in the middle 1960s. Today, serious—not to say obsessive—collectors who analyze stories, criticize artwork and even examine the staples have created a full-fledged market" (96).

In turn, fanzines like *Alter Ego* and *Comic Art* allowed (overwhelmingly male) fans a forum for celebrating and analyzing older comics, the former started by Roy Thomas before he began a long career as a writer for Marvel and DC Comics. Many, if not most, comics creators started off as fans, often bringing to their work a nostalgic fervor for the books they read growing up.

For many creators, nostalgia can be a muse whispering in their ear. Others see it as a siren beckoning only destruction. It can be the angel or the devil on your shoulder, urging you to revisit your own favorite comics, characters, and story lines of the past as you work on new material—the voices offering words of either caution or encouragement (depending on your perspective) about drawing upon the past for inspiration.

Many creators talk about nostalgia in negative terms while still succumbing to its lures. In *Give Our Regards to the Atomsmashers! Writers on Comics* (2004), Jonathan Lethem describes his favorite childhood comics as "a realm of masturbation, of personal arcana," and as a "private communion with our own obscure and shameful yearnings" (12–13). He pays tribute to the "mad genius" of writer Steve Gerber, whose character Omega the Unknown Lethem revamped for Marvel in 2007 (16).

Nostalgia can also serve as a driving force for creators working independently of mainstream publishers. In *Forging the Past: Seth and the Art of Memory* (2016), Daniel Marrone chronicles how acclaimed creator Seth's work (such as *It's a Good Life If You Don't Weaken*, *Clyde Fans*, and *Wimbledon Green: The Greatest Comic Book Collector in the World*) is regularly driven by issues of memory and nostalgia. In turn, Marrone asks, "Could the ostensible prevalence of nostalgia in many of the popular and critically acclaimed comics be more than a mere trend or coincidence? The abundance of memoirs, period pieces, carefully researched chronicles, and otherwise historically inflected work—to say nothing of the longing for a lost home that defines superheroes as familiar as Superman and Batman—seems to suggest that comics as a medium might be particularly suited to wrestling with nostalgia" (3–4).

While Seth and other independent creators often focus on their nostalgia for bygone eras and places, many of the top writers at Marvel and DC Comics draw inspiration from the comics they read growing up. In writing *Ultimate Spider-Man*, Brian Michael Bendis acknowledges that his youthful love of *The Amazing Spider-Man* played a significant role in how he approached the new series: "A lot of my stories stem from a classic Spider-Man story" (quoted in De Falco 2004, 230).

Marvel's line of Ultimate books was one of many attempts since the start of the twenty-first century at Marvel and DC to refresh or reboot their comics line. At DC, this trend includes such event titles, story lines, and corporate directives as *Infinite Crisis* (2005), "One Year Later" (2006), "Earth One" (2010), *Flashpoint* (2011), *The New 52* (2011), "Zero Year" (2013), and "DC Rebirth" (2016). Marvel has kept pace with such efforts as "The Heroic Age" (2010), "Marvel Now!" (2012), "All-New, All-Different Marvel" (2015), and "Fresh Start" (2018). Many of these initiatives draw on the long history and continuity of familiar characters, often attempting to undo recent changes and hearken back to the origins of popular heroes in the effort to tap into readers' nostalgic tendencies. Geoff Johns described the "DC Rebirth" event as a process of "bringing the characters back" while at the same time "moving them forward." He labeled this process not as an attempt "going backwards or being regressive" but as delivering a "tonal shift" to "give back that sense of hope and optimism" that was present in the earlier years of these characters (quoted in McMillan 2016).

Other writers view nostalgia with caution, hesitant that it can breed stagnation rather than creative rebirth. In *Supergods* (2012), Grant Morrison describes the comics industry in the late 1970s as an era in which "superheroes were in the doldrums. Many of the mavericks had moved on, and an air of listless nostalgia was all that remained. Journeymen turned out competent work to a safe house standard that rarely broke new ground" (170). Superhero comics, he says, were "running in place, like the Flash on a cosmic treadmill that took him nowhere but back to where he was, as a trail of afterimages, fossilized empty gestures now drained of relevance to anything but their own arcane, synthetic continuities" (170).

But as writers have been drawing more heavily on past story lines and continuities in the last two decades, Morrison describes a different trend that emerged in American comics since 9/11, particularly at Marvel: "The emphasis veered away from escapist comical fantasy, nostalgia and surrealism toward social critique, satire and filmic-verité wrapped in the flag of shameless patriotism and the rise of the badass-motherfucker hero. The formal experimentation of the eighties and nineties had bred out a powerful strain of streamlined Hollywood-friendly product that came road tested and shorn of rough edges" (335). These rough edges are marked by the very "synthetic continuities" he despised in earlier decades but that other writers like Geoff Johns have made a career out of revamping and rebooting. Nostalgia left untempered by critical reflection can offer pleasant enough distractions, but it poses considerable problems for the study of media texts. In his book *Mediated Nostalgia* (2014), Ryan Lizardi writes that "contemporary media nostalgia engenders a perpetual melancholic form of nostalgia as opposed to a comparative, collective or adaptive view of history" (2). He argues that "narcissistic nostalgia" relates to "individualized pasts that are defined by idealized versions of beloved lost media texts pumped up with psychic investment to a level of unreality" (2). More dangerously, if those "individualized pasts" add up across fandom, creative practice, and scholarship to become a predominantly male recollection of comics history, the result is what Ellen Kirkpatrick and Suzanne Scott call "the construction of (literally 'man-made') boundaries and oppositions" for how comics are studied and understood (2015, 121).

Narcissism and melancholy aren't the best starting points for approaching objects of critical study. But film critics have often faced the challenges of dealing with nostalgia in their reviews. And many acknowledge the role that it plays in their work: Richard Schickel described being "haunted" by the films of his youth as he began his career as a film critic (1999, 4), while Jonathan Rosenbaum wrote of the "unconscious programming that helps to mold every set of tastes"—that "dirty old nostalgia," he says, which can prove unshakeable (1980, 3).

These are evocative words: *dirty, haunted, melancholic, nostalgia*. So while comics studies has come into its own as a discipline in recent years, many scholars still fear the close study of their favorite childhood texts (lest the result become a mere exercise in unfettered personal nostalgia). Film theorist Christian Metz has said, albeit ironically, that "to be a theoretician of the cinema, one should ideally no longer love the cinema and yet still love it" (1982, 15).

Is the same true of comics, then, which most scholars come to as longtime fans? Is it better to "just be friends" with the formative comics of our early years so as to approach them with a necessary measure of critical distance, to love them but not be *in love* with them? Metz says of film theorists that it's important to have "loved" film "a lot" but to also approach the medium after having "detached oneself" so that you can later begin the process of "taking it up again from the other end, taking it as the target of the same scopic drive which had made one love it" (1982, 15). The same can be argued of comics.

Navigating the divide between fan and scholar comes with many pitfalls and potentials when academics confront the role that nostalgia plays in their own work. Comics scholars must recognize that the objects of study that consumed us in our formative years often still haunt the corners of our critical faculties (and that the inherent subjectivity of nostalgia can potentially sidetrack us from considering how readers of different genders, racial and cultural backgrounds, sexualities, and age ranges consume and interpret those same objects of study; see Streeby 2018). If we want to overcome the nostalgic homesickness that can problematize studying the media objects we grew up with, we must balance the methods used in examining comics—moving beyond formal and textual analysis to consider questions of culture, industry, and audience. Nostalgia may represent a specific pinpoint on the map for each and every student of the media, but there are still ways of charting the larger terrain.

37

Panel
Matt Silady

In our best estimation regarding the history of comics, the panel existed long before the page (and long before the written word, for that matter). Let's imagine our ancestors huddled closely around a fire. They stare at a cave wall lit only by the warm, flickering light of the flames.

To our right, we hear, "I'm hungry. Let's hunt."

To our left, "Naw, hunt later. Let's rest."

And then there's us, in the center, speaking after a deep sigh, "I don't know. I think I'm going to scrape this dirty stick on that wall and draw a story about my day."

The first cartoonists were not worried about the size or shape of the panel. Page layout, gutter spacing, and all the quirks of modern comics were far from their minds. It was not until much later that we started thinking of the panel as a box in which to put all our things. Before long, cartoonists were lining these boxes up to create classic comic strips, stacking them in tiers to make six- and nine-panel grids, and experimenting with complex visual architectures in order to bring intricate, nuanced fictions to life on the page.

All these years later, though, the panel is still nothing more than space. It is a space to make marks, a space to think, and a space to create. In comics, the panel serves as the basic unit of measurement. And yet it is of indeterminate size and shape. Panels exist with or without borders. With just a little help, they can tell a story on their own or play well with others. A panel can be as big as a mural on a four-story brick building or as tiny as a dot on the head of a pin. When it comes to understanding the way the panel functions in comics, it can be useful to think outside of the box or to forget about the box altogether.

The Panel as Portal

Perhaps instead of defining panels by a particular shape or size, it is more important to discuss some of the things comic panels can do. Cartoonist Lynda Barry describes her experience of reading Bill Keane's *The Family Circus* as a child: "I didn't love *The Family Circus* because it was funny. I don't think I noticed or cared about that part at all. I loved the very world of it, a world that I could watch through a portal edged in ink every day when I opened the newspaper. It was a circle I wanted to climb through" (2008, xii). Barry depicts herself flopped on the carpet with the newspaper funny pages spread out before her. Actively ignoring the captions, Barry views each individual comic as a way to travel to a place and time as real and tangible as another room in her house only a few steps away: "For me, a comic strip is a place that seems to be ongoing. If you look through these circles, you'll see a place that brought a lot of comfort to me as a kid" (xiii).

Barry's observation about the way comics can serve as a telescopic portal helps us avoid thinking of the panel as a frozen moment in time. The single panel is moving, both physically and emotionally: "Comics are a place to go. They gave me a 'meanwhile' and an 'elsewhere.' They are a form of transportation for the shut-in kids who need to see life in other worlds" (2008, xiv). Even more so, when paired with dialogue or narrative text, the panel resists collapsing into a snapshot. Rather, it represents an ongoing world as alive as Barry's own. In a fanciful reversal, Barry imagines the point of view of Keene's ageless family glancing back out through the

panel only to see Barry's face pressed close to the circular portal, gazing back in (xii). For comics, the panel is asked to do many things. When serving as a small passageway from one world to another, it is fully activated when the reader is engaged. As a space, as a portal, or in any other of its roles, the panel is never alone.

The Panel as Relationship

The importance of the panel's inherent connection with the artist, the reader, and the cultural context in which it is viewed has caused some trouble for those seeking a working definition for comics over the years. Initial efforts fell victim to the impulse to isolate single-panel cartoons from long-form comics and other related styles of visual art. Taking the lead from Will Eisner's seminal work *Comics and Sequential Art* (1985), Scott McCloud considered comics to be "juxtaposed pictorial and other images in deliberate sequence, intended to convey information and/or to produce an aesthetic response in the viewer" (1993, 9). This definition cites panels in sequence as the foundational building blocks of the comic form. Accordingly, McCloud keeps a single-panel gag strip at arm's length from the world of proper comics while his bespectacled avatar warmly issues a challenge: "If anyone wants to write a book taking the *opposite* view, you can bet I'll be the first in line to buy a copy!" (21). Fortunately, it doesn't take an entire book to bring political cartoons, illustrated *New Yorker* covers, and even Lynda Barry's love of *The Family Circus* back into the fold.

Sequence is just one of many attributes associated with the panel. The particular importance of sequence to the medium and its prominent position in these early definitions can be attributed to the frequency with which sequence is employed in comics through the connection of one panel to the next. The desire to privilege sequence as the driving force behind comics makes sense because it does preoccupy much of the cartoonist's attention while constructing a page. Much of comics magic comes from placing the panel in sequence, as Ivan Brunetti points out: "As with moments in time, each panel exists, in a latent state, in all the other panels—a mutually inclusive whole" (2011, 50). And yet sequence is just one attribute of comics rather than the defining feature of comics themselves.

Beyond sequence, other attributes such as story, dialogue, narration, word balloons, sound effects, gutters, and emanata (those wonderful worry lines emanating from a character's head) begin to round out the list of metaphoric devices employed when making comics. Why not define comics based on any of these other reoccurring elements? Take the representation of time as space in the gutters between panels, for example. Because of the frequency with which this device is utilized, it might suggest another useful way to define comics right alongside sequence. Limiting comics to a time-based narrative art, however, leaves out the possibility of exploring the abstraction of the panel in works like those featured in 2009's *Abstract Comics*, edited by Andrei Molotiu, where the panel itself becomes the actual subject of the piece.

For example, *Border Suite* by Billy Mavreas utilizes the visual conventions traditionally associated with the square boxes that surround comics panels as its means of expression (Molotiu 2009, 201). Mavreas plays with the shape, size, and fidelity of the panel borders to evoke various feelings and a particular mood. In more traditional narrative comics (anything from *Batman* to *The Walking Dead*), the panel border can also take on a life of its own. The border often transmits its own message independent of (or in cooperation with) the illustration it contains. Imagine a cartoonist drawing someone on Rollerblades clumsily crashing into a tree. Instead of containing the image in a simple box with clean, thin lines, the artist tilts the square askew and renders it with a jagged, ink-splattered stroke. The reader views the image of the crash while decoding a second layer of meaning from the border telling them the impact was sudden and disorienting. The relationship between the panel and the panel border is as important as any in comics.

To get to the actual heart of comics, it turns out, we need only begin with the panel and its relationship to the world around the panel. A panel simply never stands alone. By its nature, the panel is either connected to another panel, altered in some way by text, or ever changing in its meaning based on each viewer's interpretation of its content. Thanks to the latter two of these relationships, groundbreaking single-panel "cartoons" by Jackie Ormes and Gary Larson are as much part of the comics family as monthly superhero adventures and book-length graphic novels. Scott McCloud actually creates an excellent example of a single-panel comic in *Making Comics*. While demonstrating the concept of interdependent text-to-image relationships, he illustrates an image of a woman crying as she speaks into a phone. Above her, a speech balloon captures the heartbreaking complexity of her predicament as she bravely replies through her tears, "I'm so happy for you" (2006, 140). In spite of its perfectly realized narrative and dramatic punch, measured by Eisner's and McCloud's definitions of comics as sequential art, this would not be considered a comic at all. In their view, it is only a single panel with text.

But this is all one needs to make a great comic: a panel and a relationship. Odds are this relationship is most likely with another panel. There is also a very good chance the relationship is with text. And one can be assured, in every instance, there is a relationship between the panel and the reader. With this in mind, we start seeing comics everywhere. If you've ever spotted a decade-old issue of the *New Yorker* in a doctor's office, by simply glancing at the illustrated cover, you are reading a comic. It is a comic whose meaning shifts from viewer to viewer. The cover serves as the panel. The panel serves as a space for visual art to enter into a relationship with the reader. Through that relationship, the art is turned into a story. From the first cave paintings to this afternoon's doodle on a napkin, once a piece of visual art exists, it is comics.

For some, this inclusive definition of comics is problematic. For the panel, it is a liberation. Thierry Groensteen suggests, "In the face of these developments, what remains of traditional definitions of comics? Nothing more than the sharing of a space for inscription or display—in other words, the apparatus, the 'plurality of images in solidarity'" (2013, 14). From roadside billboards to illustrated instruction manuals, comic panels are everywhere. As a result, there are more cartoonists and a greater audience for comics than ever before. And while some of those readers are still poring over old, dusty bins of back issues in a comics shop, most are sharing memes with a simple click of a touchscreen. Each meme, a comic made of borrowed visual art in relationship to its user-generated text, is remixed and reworked as it is passed along from one reader to the next. With extraordinary velocity, reader becomes producer as the comic is remapped with new and unexpected meanings along the way. By establishing the relationship between the panel and the world around it as the binding force behind all comics, the discussion shifts from "Is this a comic?" to "Is this comic any good?" or "Does this comic move me?" or "Can this comic change the world?" The latter questions inevitably evoke much more interesting discussions than the first and speak to the real power of the panel.

The Panel as Thinking

In some respects, a reader may view the panel only as product rather than process, as it is the result of thoughtful, painstaking (and sometimes, painful) cartooning. A cartoonist outlines and scripts, considers sequence and relationship, and then thumbnails with stick figures through a process of trial and error until the exact architecture of a page is worked out. Pencils are scribbled and smudged and refined on smooth Bristol board until the careful application of ink transforms the illustrations into a finished page. The panel is a thing we can point to as something someone made.

For the cartoonist, the panel itself can be a way of thinking and processing the world: "Cartooning is entirely an art based on the archeological digging of one's own visual memory. . . . When you draw something on the page, you're looking at it and then there's this sort of reciprocity loop or something going on in your mind when you are seeing something and reacting to it. And before you know it, you're drawing a corner of a room that you haven't thought about in a certain number of years" (Ware 2015). Structurally, comics mimic memory: "In comics, an individual panel is read as both a discrete parcel of information as well as a link in a greater chain" (Karasik and Newgarden 2017, 119). Instead of seeing the panel as a hand-drawn storage device set to capture a fleeting moment, it can be viewed as a means to process memory as it is created. Even for the reader, the comic panel can simulate the experience of memory: "A comic doesn't come with a running time" (Gravett 2013, 54), and therefore "the fragmentation of time in comics also enables us to freeze and meditate on fleeting events, deepening our appreciation of the ephemeral" (48).

With panels serving as space to engage with memory and as portals to transport the reader, they also provide us with a way of thinking: "Comics are primarily neither drawing nor writing, but they are, in some respects, like simple machines, designed to communicate swiftly and efficiently and with all working parts laid bare" (Karasik and Newgarden 2017, 23). These simple machines can provide cartoonists the opportunity to process the world through the lines on the page. Eleanor Davis's striking *You & a Bike & a Road* serves as an account of her solo interstate bicycle trek. With its organic, borderless panel structure, Davis's pencil traces her journey in real time. We see her make marks on the page, cross them out, and begin again (2017, 2). The panels, separated only by undulating tributaries of space, seem to have more in common with our first comics, the cave paintings, than the carefully planned layouts found in any recently published superhero adventure. There's a thrilling immediacy clinging to each mark as if Davis is figuring out how she feels about what she is drawing at the very same moment she places pencil to page: "This is one of the ways in which comics seem to embody our associative, fluid thought processes, whereby at any moment our thinking, our attention, can be in the present, the past, and the future. Flicking back and forth through the pages, it all becomes the now" (Gravett 2013, 62).

The panel's relationship with the cartoonists is a give and take. Its creation requires more than the placing of content within a frame. It requires a dynamic, evolving conversation between memory and image and thinking as an act of creation on the page. For the reader, a similar level of participation is required. McCloud calls the act of making meaning out of the relationship between panels creating "closure" (1993, 63). Creating closure may involve assessing whether a single second or a million years pass in the space between panels or noting a thematic connection between the image in one panel and the next: "Comics, in fact, is a medium that involves a substantial degree of reader participation to stitch together narrative meaning" (Chute 2017, 22). It is in this moment when the reader decodes the cartoonist's intended relationship between panels that the comic comes alive once again.

The Panel as Comics

The panel provides comics with both its structure and its meaning. Through its relationship with other images, text, and the reader's cultural context, the panel becomes comics. The panel is the volume in which we fill our stories and shape our ideas. It is in relationship with the artist and allows the cartoonist the opportunity to experience the world in a transformative way. More often than not, the panel is a simple square among many others on a page. Comics were our first form of visual communication, and they are the most ubiquitous form of communication today. And right at this moment, the panel is any space that holds the very next mark you make.

38

Pornography

Justin Hall

Comics have a long and complicated relationship with pornography. Comics have long been associated with the lowbrow and potentially harmful, a cultural space also inhabited by pornography; both have seen censorship, regulation, and book burnings on large scales (Hajdu 1999, 7). Of course, comics are a medium, while pornography—by which I mean art and storytelling intended to arouse sexual excitement—is a genre; it is their intersection, however, that is of particular interest to me, where the unique language of comics creates stories that both engage and expand erotic imaginations.

The illustrative nature of comics makes the medium a powerful vehicle for erotica. While photographic pornography assumes the existence of actual people in front of the camera, illustrations do not; there is a voyeuristic element to the former lacking in the latter. The consumers of a video are immersed in the artistic experience created by the director, editor, and film crew, but more likely they feel engaged by the actors on the screen, while the readers of an erotic comic are turned on by the fantasies that are conjured entirely from the creativity and craft evident on the page.

This immersive quality of an illustrative storytelling medium can be used to push stories and visual elements into the realm of the fantastical, what Darieck Scott refers to as "parallel realities of cooler sexier realness" (2014, 192). Erotic comics can experiment wildly with content well beyond the reach of the limited budgets of porn films: alien worlds, impossible sex devices, monsters, and so on. They can exaggerate the physical characteristics of the characters to the edge of realism and beyond, giving them enormous genitalia or breasts, perfect abs, or copious body hair. The illustrative nature of comics also allows for certain ways of viewing sex unattainable for a camera or the naked eye; erotic manga artists such as Gengoroh Tagame often show a penis ejaculating into an orifice by illustrating an anatomical cross section or remove the insertive partner from the picture, thus allowing for an impossible full-body view of the receptive partner in the midst of sex. In *Why Comics?*, Hillary Chute sums it up: "A visual technology that can make the unseen concrete and easily conjures the improper, there is something *illicit* about drawing" (2017, 113).

Drawings allow for a metaphorical distancing between the reader and the act of sex being depicted, and this distance, in the hands of a skilled cartoonist, is malleable in arousing and fascinating ways. This in turn allows for more entry points for a diversity of readers into a specific pornographic work. For example, Colleen Coover's erotic magnum opus *Small Favors* (2017) only features sex between women but has a loyal fan base that extends to straight people and even gay men. Through her engaging line work, character designs, and conceptual storytelling, Coover invites all readers into an empathic understanding of her erotic desires in a way that would be nigh impossible with film. She allows readers to see the objects of her attraction through her eyes; they are turned on by her pornographic imagination as opposed to being turned on simply by its object. As Alan Moore said about the erotic graphic novel *Lost Girls* that he created with Melinda Gebbie, "What we're talking about here is purely the human sexual imagination. We're not talking about sex: We're talking about the sexual imagination" (quoted in Shindler 2006).

In her landmark essay "The Pornographic Imagination" (1969), Susan Sontag makes the claim that the goal of the pornographer is to create flat and interchangeable characters in order for the readers to have room for their own sexual responses and that this creates an emotional disconnect: "What porno-literature does is precisely to drive a wedge between one's existence as a full human being and one's existence as a sexual being—while in ordinary life a healthy person is one who prevents such a gap from opening up" (58). While I disagree that this is a necessary condition of any medium of pornography, erotic comics in particular offer a platform from which to refute this assertion. The most important "gap" on the comics page—that of the gutter—is not a locus of "disorientation [and] psychic dislocation" (47) but rather one of engagement and creativity. The gutter represents a place of great power and potential for erotic cartoonists, as it is where the readers are encouraged to insert their own pornographic imaginations.

Comics are a more interactive medium than film or animation; the readers use their own creativity to move the characters from their positions in one panel to their positions in another, thus creating their own tableaus and their own moments of sexual fantasy. While there are, of course, edits done in pornographic film, the viewers are not encouraged to ruminate on what happens within those moments; in fact, the actors take breaks, hydrate, and move into other positions while the crew rearranges the cameras and lighting, something of which the viewers are at least unconsciously aware and that most probably does not sexually excite them. The task of erotic cartoonists creating a dynamic and engaging sex scene, however, is to choreograph a dance between their erotic imaginations and that of the readers using precisely those moments of transition; this level of engagement belies the idea of pornography necessarily creating disorientation in the reader.

Sontag writes, "The arousal of a sexual response requires [emotional flatness]. Only in the absence of directly stated emotions can the reader of porn find room for his own responses" (1969, 53). Applying that concept to visual pornographic media, there can certainly be profound sexual interest and arousal generated by depersonalized pornographic imagery; simply watching close-ups of genitals in action, for example, is often extremely compelling, and of course there is an artistry to portraying that well. Reader identification in pornography, however, can go far beyond simply imagining one's own body fitting into the imagery of two other bodies engaging in sexual acts or fitting oneself into a sexual situation involving flattened character types or sexual "everymen." Sex, like all other human endeavors, is given meaning by its context, and the most compelling and complex art about sex takes that into account.

One need only look at the differences between two stories in *The Passion of Gengoroh Tagame* (2013), an English-language collection of short stories by the great master of Japanese erotic comics to whom I referred earlier, to illustrate this. "The Country Doctor" is a tale of a young doctor arriving at a rural Japanese town that engages in an ancient tradition where the men of the town "marry" a given man who will then have sex with all of them. He becomes, in effect, a sex surrogate for the overworked local wives, girlfriends, and even boyfriends, and the result is a number of emotionally positive, consensual group sex scenes. The other, "Arena," posits an underground mixed martial arts competition where the contestants are secretly given a military drug designed to enhance their strength but also their sexual appetite; the fights result in the winner brutally sexually dominating the loser. It's a tale of sexual humiliation and loss of consent. Both stories are exciting for different reasons, and readers will gravitate to one or the other depending on their mood or inclinations. In each, Tagame beautifully illustrates men having sex with each other; in both, there are arousing images of genitals and penetration. The stories' narrative intentions, however, are completely different; readers are drawn to each of these stories precisely because of their emotional contexts, not in spite of them.

Pornography is perhaps the only genre with an implied and associated action; while Sontag argues that physical changes can accompany the reading of nonerotic works, making masturbation not such a distinct phenomenon (Sontag 1969, 45), others such as Magnus Ullén (2009) make the claim that masturbation is, in fact, a unique mode of reading. Ullén argues that even when not masturbating to porn, it is assumed that the material will be used by the consumer in a "preparatory phase of masturbation which may not entail actual self-stimulation of the genitals but involves cognitive stimulation in which such physical stimulation is . . . always already implied."

This is, however, a reductive view of the complex, profound, and mysterious nature of the erotic imagination. Pushing the boundaries of how readers conceive of sexuality and providing them with new road maps to erotic stimulation are not only simply for masturbation (though that can be a worthy goal in and of itself, of course) but also for inspiration for all the other modes in which sexual creativity is used, from partnered sex to artistic production to the ways in which we relate to one another through the dynamics of power, seduction, and cooperation. Often implied in such arguments is also a simplistic and condescending assumption of the artistic goals of the creators of pornography. Sexual stimulation is certainly the defining goal of pornography as a genre, but other artistic intentions can exist alongside and be intertwined with that purpose. As Alan Moore states, "There's no reason why it shouldn't be arousing and yet also be talking about important issues, about serious human things" (quoted in Shindler 2006).

The main challenge of pornography is not its focus on one of the most fundamental of human experiences nor its ability to handle multiple themes at once in emotionally complex modes but that it is so often poorly executed or hobbled by the baggage of a sex-negative, misogynist, queer-phobic, and racist culture. We need to encourage the artistic production of talented creators like Tagame, Coover, Moore, and Gebbie and add to the growing body of pornographic comics that stimulates, engages, and challenges.

39

Print

Carol L. Tilley

In 1951, at the near peak of comic book sales in the United States, the two Goss high-speed rotary newspaper presses at Spartan Printing and Publishing, a new facility in southern Illinois, printed six million forty-eight-page comics a month ("Sparta Plant" 1951). The presses at Spartan required thirty-five thousand pounds of cyan, yellow, magenta, and black inks each month to keep up the demand for the four-color "funny books." Spartan Printing was not exceptional: it was one of a series of presses across the United States that contributed to the one hundred million new comic book issues that were printed and then distributed to shops throughout the country. About a hundred employees at Spartan ensured that those copies of *Archie*, *Dick Tracy*, *Black Cat*, and other titles were trimmed, bound, and loaded onto trucks headed for a post office in St. Louis, Missouri (O'Keefe 2006).

When one considers *print* in relation to comics, a first image might be of those offset lithographic printing presses like the ones at Spartan, which were the dominant means of the physical production of comics. But *print* is more than that physical production. *Print* is liminal, signifying elements of not only comics' physical production but the medium's communicative and cultural production as well. *Print* can summon the act of physically creating comics, but it may as easily refer to the *print* medium that incorporates much of the semiotic image-text—"an inseparable suturing of the visual

and the verbal" (Mitchell 1995, 95)—that is comics as well as the creative/economic/reception networks that form comics' print culture. *Print* is not only liminal; it is also symbiotic: the production format of the printed comic (and this includes the variety of digital possibilities) is inexorably linked to its circulation and reception. The physical and social technologies that facilitate the material production of comics and the popular print cultures in which people engage comics are inexorably linked. Thus to understand comics and *print*, one must interrogate the press and its products as well as the "relationships between people and objects" (Raven 2014, 228).

Print has long had both popular and etymological associations with writing, words, and published texts. Subsequently, in comics studies and two of its most closely related disciplines, literary studies and book/print culture studies, textually focused scholars have dominated the conversation (Hayles 2002; Kashtan 2018a). Thus works on stories, themes, authorship, and similar word-focused topics abound, making Ong's (1986) proclamation about the imperiousness of literacy and its tools true here. In recent years, the admonitions of scholars such as bibliographer Donald McKenzie (1999) and art historian W. J. T. Mitchell (1986, 1995)—all of whom work outside the realm of comics studies proper—have spurred comics scholars to move beyond words to focus on broader material, sociological, and semiotic issues.

As the close association between print and word continues to break and scholars feel encouraged to explore more catholic issues around the intersection of print and comics, historian Robert Darnton's (1982) model of the communication circuit is a pragmatic starting point. Within book history and print culture studies, Darnton's model is central to conceptualizing disciplinary boundaries, although at the time of its publication, his model was intended to shake book historians free from deep but narrow silos. Darnton's model proposes that for each book, authors, publishers, printers, distributors, sellers, and readers, along with suppliers and binders, compose an interdependent circuit. Beyond individual actors, a variety of broader social, political, legal, economic, and intellectual phenomena shape the circuit. Whether a comic is formatted as a printed book, a complete periodical or a smaller unit of one, a digital multimedia text, or in some other manner, to understand it as print requires the application of Darnton's circuit model or some similar culturally holistic approach. Sydney Shep's (2010) model of the situated knowledges of book history is an example of such an alternative and one that has found purchase in comics studies (Jacobs 2020).

To illustrate how Darnton's approach can inform the sorts of questions one might ask about the intersection of comics and print, consider this example. Ten-year-old Ann Fujisue of Honolulu appears in a grainy newspaper photo published in a 1953 article in the *Honolulu Advertiser Sun* (Boyer 1953, 13). The article profiles six girls in total, each photographed individually with a comic book. They were all participating in activities at the Richards Street YWCA and prompted to talk about comics and "how they would handle the comic-reading problem when they get to be parents."

Wearing a pale short-sleeved dress and a Mona Lisa smile, she is looking up at the camera while holding a copy of *Little Dot* #1 (Harvey Comics, September 1953) near her face. Ann, who wants to be a nurse, reports, "I like to read Little Lulu for the jokes, and Dick Tracy for the kind of crime I can understand. But I don't like most crime comics because I don't know quite what they're doing. I get about three comic books a week from my parents. They pick them out for me. I like it that way

because there's all kinds of comics and some might be good. When I'm a parent I wouldn't want the kids to read crime because it has all kinds of bad stuff like killing" (Boyer 1953, 13).

Ann's photograph and brief statement, individually or in the context of the whole article, provoke numerous questions. One might ask, for instance, about the specific titles Ann mentions and shows: Who created, wrote, illustrated, colored, and edited comics featuring Little Lulu, Dick Tracy, and Little Dot and under what economic conditions? Were these characters typical for comics produced by their specific publishers? Comics publishers generally? At what frequency were comics featuring these characters published? Where were these comics printed? Were Ann's beloved *Dick Tracy* comics printed at Spartan Printing in Illinois? How did they travel from the printer to Hawaii? What specific technologies enabled the printing of four-color comics such as these?

Questions about the distribution and sales of these comics include the following: Where were these comics sold (e.g., a newsstand, a drugstore)? How many different comics titles were available for purchase? Under what conditions did the newsagent (i.e., retailer) select titles to stock? How were they displayed? What was the return rate (i.e., what percentage of displayed comics went unsold and were returned) for these titles compared with the broader selection of comics? What geographical area and publishers did the distributor represent?

Questions arise about readers and purchasers (the latter is more certain, since we cannot always know whether having a book in one's possession is an indication of having read it) such as the following: What proportion of comics—generally as well as these specific titles—were sold to adults? To children? How many comics did purchasers tend to buy at once? Did purchasers tend to buy only comics, or did they also buy other printed materials such as magazines or paperbacks? Why did purchasers make the selections they did? Was the purchaser the only person who interacted with / read the comic after leaving the store? If there were other readers, who were they? Was it common for a ten-year-old girl to read three comic books a week? What did the purchaser do with the comic ultimately (e.g., sell, trade, gift, store, throw away)?

And, of course, broader social, cultural, political, and economic factors lend themselves to questions: Why would a newspaper ask young girls about their comics reading? Why did Ann mention crime comics specifically? What was the "comic-reading problem" that in part spurred this article? Did the interviewer have difficulty finding six girls who read comics at the Richards Street YWCA? Why were the girls at the YWCA? Were they friends? Did they share comics or talk about them with one another?

When we break *print* free from a too-strong association with the verbal, not only can we more readily ask questions about issues such production, materiality, and circulation; we can also ask questions about print culture that connect comics to popular and participatory cultures. Media theorist John Fiske (1989) views popular culture as the ways in which people make meaning from the artifacts of mass culture, while Henry Jenkins (Jenkins and Carpentier 2013) suggests participatory culture as a social, mentorship-based approach to creative engagement with the world.

In short, the intersection of print, popular, and participatory cultures allows us to investigate what I often shorthand as *people doing things with comics*. At this intersection, we ask questions such as the following: What did a comic mean to its readers? A particular reader? In what ways did the comic allow the reader to participate in a greater social network of readers? How did readers remix or repurpose particular comics? Did readers use comics in ways perhaps unintended by their creators and publishers (e.g., as tools for learning to draw, as material to decorate personal spaces, as instructional texts in formal settings)? It is this intersection where, as a scholar, I garner some of the most interesting insights about *print* and comics, including ways in which young people have historically used comics as a spur for political action (Tilley 2015), social critique (Tilley 2016), civic engagement (Tilley 2014), and artistic production (Tilley 2019).

Comics scholar Ernesto Priego (2010) offers a useful reminder of the importance of *print* and materiality in understanding comics: "The physicality of comics has remained central to its identity as a system of communication, and any discussion of the medium's future in a cultural context that assumes that all information can be digitized needs to take this into account. The variety of printed comics formats and the accompanying differences in binding, page shape, number of pages, volume, weight, type of paper and covers, etc., has consequences that go beyond the intratextual, and define other practices framing the processes of reading and reception" (159).

Although *print* must move beyond its technological association with presses, paper, and physical objects in order to include the consideration of web-based and other digital comics, whether born native or retrospectively converted, comics scholars remain mindful of the impact comics' different material containers have on the questions we ask, the theories we pose, and the insights we glean. Engaging with pixels on a screen may exclude a creator, publisher, distributor, or reader from sensations such as feeling the sticky roughness that accompanies touching one's fingers on newsprint or experiences such as browsing shoulder to shoulder at a local comic book store. Yet the broader questions of print culture studies such as the political economies of their production, how these comics circulate, and what people do with these texts apply here even though the objects at the focus of these concerns may lack analog expressions.

40

Queer

Ramzi Fawaz, with Darieck Scott

There's something queer about comics. Whether one looks to the alternative mutant kinships of superhero stories (the epitome of queer world making), the ironic and socially negative narratives of independent comics (the epitome of queer antinormativity), or the social stigma that makes the medium marginal, juvenile, and outcast from proper art (the epitome of queer identity), comics are rife with the social and aesthetic cues commonly attached to queer life. Moreover, the medium has had a long history as a top reading choice among those "queer" subjects variously called sexual deviants, juvenile delinquents, dropouts, the working class, and minorities of all stripes. Despite this, comics studies and queer theory have remained surprisingly alienated from one another. On the one hand, comics studies' tendency to analyze the formal codes of sequential art separately from social questions of sexual identity and embodied difference has often led to a disregard for a nuanced queer and intersectional critique of the comics medium. On the other, the prevailing assumption that mainstream comics (i.e., the superhero genre) embody nationalistic, sexist, and homophobic ideologies has led many queer theorists to dismiss comics altogether or else to celebrate a limited sample of politically palatable alternative comics as exemplars of queer visual culture. In this logic, "Queer zines yes! Superhero comics no!"

This alienation—at times even antagonism—evinces a failure of recognition in the current development of scholarship rather than a true gulf between the foundational questions and concepts of the two fields. The conceptual and historical intersections of queer theory (and sexuality more broadly) and comics culture in both its visual and narrative production and its fan communities are rife and rich. At every moment in their cultural history, comic books have been linked to queerness or else to broader questions of sexuality and sexual identity in US society. In the 1930s and 1940s, *Wonder Woman* visually celebrated S/M practices and same-sex bonding between women, metaphorized through the image of the chained, shackled, or bound submissive; in the late 1940s and early 1950s, crime and horror comics presented what was arguably the most antisocial critique of postwar domestic life outside of noir cinema, spectacularizing forms of violence, gore, and criminality that radically upended the ideals of nuclear family harmony and the sublimation of desire in material goods; in the late 1950s, *MAD Magazine* elicited affective pleasure in the satiric critique of the nuclear family and its blatant refusal of the Cold War security state; in the 1960s and 1970s, Marvel Comics revitalized the superhero comic book by infusing its art with the visual politics of gay and women's liberation while the independent comics art of R. Crumb and the *Wimmen's Comix* collective brought a radical sexual politics to the visual culture of comic books; and from the 1960s to contemporary times, gay, lesbian, and queer culture has taken up comics as sites of sexual pleasure, such as in the graphic sex narratives of Tom of Finland and the cartoonists inspired by him, many of whom testify to beginning their cartooning by tracing and imaginatively redrawing the male figures they encountered in superhero comics. These latter crosscurrents now flow strongly in both directions, as evidenced by the recent proliferation of explicitly LGBTQ+ characters and scenarios in contemporary comics, from the X-Men's Legacy Virus (a spectacular metaphor for HIV/AIDS)

to the lesbian Batwoman and the gay Green Lantern. Moreover, the ubiquity of the medium—comic books being among the most mass-produced and circulated print media of the twentieth century—alongside its simultaneous stigmatization as the preferred reading material of a small slice of so-called immature youth and social outcasts models Eve Sedgwick's now-classic formulation of queerness as both a universalizing and minoritizing discourse: comics end up in the hands of nearly everybody, but comic book readers are a niche (i.e., queer, nerd, outcast, weirdo) group; anyone and everybody could be queer, but actual queers are a minority group in the larger culture.

As this broad sketch of comics' queer attachments suggests, rather than needing to be queered, comics themselves "queer" the archive of American culture. Encounters between queer theories and comics studies potentially offer broader historical assessments of how the literary medium of comics, and its larger aesthetic and production history, might be understood as a distinctly queer mode of cultural production that has functioned *as* queer history rather than its serialized supplement. When we understand the history of sexuality and the history of comics as *mutually constitutive*, rather than merely reflective or coincidental, we can gain insight into the ways that the comic book medium's visual structures not only lend themselves to questions of sexuality and sexual identity but have also taken shape historically in response to transformations in the history of sexuality.

Among the questions we might begin to consider when we explore what is distinctly queer about comics—and what aspect(s) of comics represent and give meaning to queerness—are the following: How might a medium made up of the literal intersection of lines, images, and bodies capture the values of intersectional analysis? How does comics' attention to the visual orientation of images in space model a conception of sexual orientation—especially in relation to race and gender—since all of these are coordinates of embodied being not truly "present" on the two-dimensional page but signified and referred to by combinations of text and image? How might the medium's discontinuous organization of images map onto disability's discontinuous relationship to heterosexual able-bodied existence? How might the medium's courting of marginal and outsider audiences allow for the formation of queer counterpublics? How do the comics medium's formal properties provide material analogies for or creatively materialize and literalize seemingly formless experiences of nonnormative erotic desire, pleasure, and intimacy?

These questions only begin to scratch the surface of productive encounters between comics studies and queer studies, but they suggest a synthetic approach to comics that considers the medium's queerness as opening out into a variety of formal and narrative experiments that have attempted to deal with the problem of being literally and figuratively marginal or "queered" by social and political orders.

In the interest of developing some of these links, we map three of the primary sites where we see queerness as a social/affective force intersecting productively with comics as a medium. This initial mapping functions merely as a starting point for identifying those locations where queerness—understood variously as a social force, a complex network of erotic and affective ties, or an entire shared culture—appears intimately bound up with the formal and narrative capacities of the comics medium.

First, the status of comics as marginal literature and art and the assumed immaturity of its audiences (associated with childhood or arrested-adolescent fantasy) situate comics as an outsider medium that elicits attachments from perceived social delinquents, outcasts, and minorities. Comics readers and fans construct their relationships to these texts on the basis of the medium's marginality and often their own sense of disconnection from the expectations of normative social life. Comic books are a medium that thus hails counterpublics. Per Michael Warner, "A counterpublic maintains at some level, conscious or not, an awareness of its subordinate status. The cultural horizon against which it marks itself off is not just a general or wider public but a dominant one. And the conflict extends not just to ideas or policy questions but to speech genres and modes of address that constitute the public or to the hierarchy among media. The discourse that constitutes it is not merely a different or alternative idiom but one that in other contexts would be regarded with hostility or with a sense of indecorousness" (2002, 56). Comics counterpublics are shaped in large part by the development of a variety of alternative—and often egalitarian and grassroots—forms of sociality between readers, creators, and textual content, including fan clubs, letter-writing campaigns, zines, and comic conventions. What psychologist and anticomic crusader Fredric Wertham presciently captured in his derision of the homosexual undertones in Batman and Robin in the mid-1950s was the same queer spirit that he would later celebrate in his embrace of comic book fan communities and their egalitarian practices in the 1960s and 1970s; both comic book content *and* fan culture ran an ongoing critique of normative social relations that exhibits itself in comic books' visual content and its solicitation of nonnormative counterpublics.

Second, the expansive representational capacity of the medium queers it. As a low-tech medium primarily composed of hand-drawn images, the representational possibilities of comics vastly outrun those of other media, requiring little to no special effects or technical equipment in its most classical sense. (It might be said, too, that this low-tech quality makes comics either fundamentally democratic or especially available to democratic practices.) Both the protocols of writing/drawing and reading comics dictate that anything that can be drawn can be believed—often if not most times with little or no attention to verisimilitude between what's represented on the page and what we perceive in the three-dimensional world beyond the page. This has made the medium especially effective as a space for the depiction of an array of fantastical characters, worlds, and social interactions (among humans, mutants, aliens, cyborgs, and other "inhuman" figurations). The fantasy aspects of the medium have historically lent themselves to the depiction of a vast array of nonnormative expressions of gender and sexuality—from the most metaphoric (in hyperbolic camp visuality, the metamorphosing of human bodies into forms that put into question traditional gender norms, etc.) to the most literal (the actual depiction of queer bodies and erotic attachments).

Such figures are possible to read as refractions of social and political possibilities: a perhaps unexpected example of comics' refractory fantastic can be found in *The Fantastic Four*, Marvel Comics' first commercial hit during the company's renaissance in the early 1960s. In that series, the three male characters' physical mutations ran up against and undermined their ability to embody normative masculinity even as their commercial dominance and fan response presented them as exemplars in a tradition of representation whose post–Wertham Comics Code Authority brief was to produce heroic masculine role models (Fawaz 2016, 66–88). Instead, the heroes were freaks: Mr. Fantastic's pliability was a sign of "softness," the Thing's rocky body rendered him fundamentally androgynous, and the Human Torch's flaming body functioned as both a figure of hypermasculinity as well a visual signifier of the "flaming" homosexual of Cold War America. The extraordinary transformations that made them "super" and "heroes" also unraveled their traditional performance of gender and sexuality, or as Fawaz suggests, such unraveling might even productively be seen as a necessary part of how it was possible to *think* heroism (for putatively straight, white, male, educated cultural producers) on the cusp of the vast social changes coalescing under the signs of the civil rights movement and later the New Left and antiwar movements, Black Power, second-wave feminism, the sexual revolution, and gay liberation.

Third and finally, the unpredictability of serial narrative/narration and the visual structure of comics as a set of sequential panels that repeat, but always with a difference, suggest that comics are *formally* queer. Just as the underlying premise in comics that anything that can be drawn can be believed taps into the productivity of human capacities for fantasy, the formal character of comics—the idea that you can have indefinite iterations of a given story that never reproduce a single trajectory—helps clarify the ways that fabulation underwrites our realities in decidedly queer ways.

Here for definitions we can turn to Saidiya Hartman's description of the practice of critical fabulation:

> "Fabula" denotes the basic elements of story, the building blocks of the narrative. A fabula, according to Mieke Bal, is "a series of logically and chronologically related events that are caused and experienced by actors. An event is a transition from one state to another. Actors are agents that perform actions. (They are not necessarily human.) To act is to cause or experience and event." . . . By playing with and rearranging the basic elements of the story, by re-presenting the sequence of events in divergent stories and from contested points

of view, . . . [critical fabulation] attempt[s] to jeopardize the status of the event, to displace the received or authorized account, and to imagine what might have happened or might have been said or might have been done. (2008, 11)

What's potentially queer about comics' fabulation and thus the formal relation comics bear to queer politics? Take two fundamental conceits of queer theory: In what is perhaps the most oft quoted line from the inaugural moment of queer theory, Judith Butler claimed that "gender is an imitation for which there is no original" (1993, 313). Only second to this then-revolutionary statement might be Eve Sedgwick's first axiom for queer studies that "people are different from each other" (1990, 22). Though both theorists first formulated these claims to describe the instability of gendered and sexual identity, their statements describe the operation of comic strip form exactly. As a serialized medium, comics proliferate images that imitate both material or embodied experience and previous images or copies in a sequence; this proliferation underscores the limitless differences produced between an ever-expanding range of images and the figures and worlds they depict. Simultaneously, the sheer number of images, texts, and characters the medium produces renders claims to originality superfluous, as does the presentation of mutant, monstrous, or altogether fantastical characters that have no "original" form in everyday life. Perhaps more than any other literary or cultural mode, then, comics self-consciously multiply and underscore differences at every site of their production. Each iteration of an image, an issue, a story line, or a world has the potential to disrupt, comment upon, or altogether alter the flow and direction of what has come before: in this sense, comics function, to borrow from Sara Ahmed (2006), as queer orientation

devices, productively directing readers toward deviant bodies that refuse to be fixed in one image or frame, toward new desires for fantasy worlds that rebel against the constraints of everyday life, and toward new kinds of counterpublic affiliation among readers who identify with the queer, deviant, maladjusted form called comics.

Each of these areas of nexus is rich unto itself and allows scholars working at the intersection of queer theory and comics studies to talk about a range of things—from the cultivation of rarified fan communities, to the production of queer intimacies between readers and fantasy characters, to formal and representational feats that lend themselves to being articulated to the depiction of nonnormative or queer orientations to the world. Such conversations allow us to see comic strip seriality anew not merely as the accumulation of drawn images in sequence but as the unfolding of thrilling and unpredictable desires into an indefinite future, very much like queerness itself.

41

Race

Jonathan W. Gray

As comic book writer Ta-Nehisi Coates remarked in 2015, "Race is the child of racism, not the father. And the process of [representing] 'the people' has never been a matter of genealogy and physiognomy so much as one of hierarchy" (7). Coates's observation foregrounds the ideologies that led to the construction of a racial caste system in Western society, one that established whiteness as the normative and unmarked default with blackness serving as its often deviant obverse (with other racialized groups falling somewhere in between these two poles). Any examination of racial representation in US comics must keep this history in mind, as US culture in general—and comics in particular—continues to be shaped by the racial classifications that support and sustain white supremacy. Further, since the rise of comic books depended on twentieth-century modes of mass production and distribution, racial representation in the medium often served to (re)inscribe and disseminate contemporaneous understandings of racial hierarchy via its display and consumption in the marketplace.

The ideology that produces racial representation in US comics derives in part from the eye-catching illustrative practices that flourished during the post–Civil War period in the nineteenth century—especially during the "circulation war" waged by newspaper magnates Joseph Pulitzer and William Randolph Hearst. During this period, Thomas Nast, the so-called father of the political cartoon in the United States, often aligned civic virtue with racial phenotype to establish a seemingly natural visual order of things, a commonplace understanding of a given racial group's worthiness for citizenship. This is perhaps clearest in Nast's December 9, 1876, *Harper's Weekly* cover, titled "The Ignorant Vote—Honors Are Easy" (see figure A.4), which featured an illustration of a barefoot Black man wearing a straw hat, flashing a vacuous smile, and sitting in the pan of a balance scale labeled "Black" across from a scowling and simian-visaged man in an Irish country hat, shabby cutaway jacket, and knickers in a scale marked "White." Nast labeled the arm of the scale supporting the Black figure "South" and the opposite arm "North," making the implication clear: allowing uneducated Irish immigrants in the North to vote imperiled the social order there in much the same way that enfranchising formerly enslaved men threatened the social hierarchy in the South. This illustration alluded to the still-in-dispute 1876 presidential election and anticipated the infamous Compromise of 1877 that awarded Republican Rutherford B. Hayes the presidency after he promised to withdraw Union soldiers from the South. Black voters provided the margin of victory for Hayes, whom *Harper's* supported, but the withdrawal of Northern troops enabled the establishment of Jim Crow by allowing revanchist whites to suppress Black voting rights in the South until the 1950s. Nash reified commonsensical anti-Black stereotypes by drawing an equivalence with a group of supposedly unassimilable immigrants—Irish Catholics—justifying discriminatory practices that would limit each group's access to political power. (Interestingly, Notre Dame University's "Fighting Irish" football mascot incorporates the same Irish country hat, cutaway jacket, and knickers that Nast used to denigrate the Irish.)

The illustrative practices of the editorial cartoons fathered by Nast would continue in the popular comic strips and comic books that emerged during the Great Depression, in part due to the exclusion of Black creators from the industry. It's telling that the most accomplished Black cartoonist during this period, the New Orleans creole George Herriman (a particular favorite of Hearst), passed for white and that his most famous creation, the groundbreaking comic strip *Krazy Kat*, featured an elaborate and surrealist visual narrative that never explicitly engaged with issues of race. Hal Foster's *Tarzan* comic strips—based on the best-selling adventure novels by Edgar Rice Burroughs—offered one of the earliest representations of Africans in a popular newspaper comic strip. But these illustrations included such perfidious stereotypes as an African chieftain clad in a grass skirt and headdress with a bone through his nose. The influence of these images was vast, for, as Frantz Fanon recalled about encountering such images during his youth in Martinique, "in comic books the Wolf, the Devil, the Evil Spirit, the Bad Man, the Savage are always symbolized by Negroes or Indians; since there is always identification with the victor, the little Negro, quite as easily as the little white boy, becomes an explorer, an adventurer, a missionary 'who faces the danger of being eaten by the wicked Negroes'" ([1952] 1984 146). Fanon's observation about the illustrations he encountered in the 1930s in a Francophone Caribbean nation demonstrates the ubiquity of these kinds of images in the West and its colonies and supports the revolutionary thinker's claim that one can only adequately represent people of color by challenging the logics that produce and justify racial hierarchy. Scholars interested in racial representation in comics must attend to these histories when investigating the complexities surrounding the reproductions of hierarchy.

Another way to engage with issues of race in comics—one that involves assessing the US history of empire and immigration—would be to trace the legacies of the so-called yellow peril. From the late 1930s through the end of the Vietnam War, comics offered stereotypical representations of an implacable East Asian threat to the West, exemplified in the ubiquitous figure of Fu Manchu. Often rendered in the court uniform of the Qing dynasty with yellow skin, long pointed nails, slanted eyes with all-white or all-black irises, sharp teeth, and the long mustache that has become affiliated with his name, Fu Manchu represented the inexorable threat of the Orient. Asian American creators such as the Chinese American cartoonist Gene Luen Yang have attempted to complicate this tradition in works such as the *Shadow Hero* and *American Born Chinese*, and scholars might place these more modern renditions in conversation with the earlier images in order to trace changes in East Asian representation.

Attitudes toward people of color evolved rapidly during the Cold War period, thanks to the civil rights movement domestically, the decolonial movement in Africa, and the perceived threat of communism spreading throughout Asia and across the globe. Despite this, pejorative illustrative practices proved surprisingly resilient. Thus in the 1960s, a decade marked by sit-ins; the eloquence of Martin Luther King Jr.; the assassinations in Mississippi of Medgar Evers, James Chaney, Andrew Goodman, and Michael Schwerner; and the enactment of several pieces of landmark civil rights legislation, popular illustrators such as Robert Crumb and Will Eisner offered images of Black Americans that trafficked in stereotypes established by Nast and Foster. While neither illustrator evinced the outright hostility toward Black citizenship that informed Nast's work, their enthusiastic embrace of nostalgic plantation imagery—and how cherished and highly sought after that work remains to this day—demonstrates how the hegemonic logics that govern the illustration of race remain resistant to social change.

In the post–civil rights era, representing race has become simultaneously a question of artistic codes—how to properly depict so-called minorities—and a question of political sensibility as the social valiance of race continued to evolve. Yet even this more tolerant period produces a wide divergence of mimetic practices. Commenting on her own representational practice as an illustrator who works primarily in black and white, Alison Bechdel (1998) noted that she has "never used any kind of shading to differentiate the skin color of my African-American characters. . . . A lot of white cartoonists . . . used shading as the only way of indicating that a character was black. They would basically draw a white person, give them curly black hair, and fill in their faces with grey shading. So I tried to convey my characters race by focusing on their features." While this comment seems to represent both an artistic and a political choice, later in the same passage, Bechdel confesses that she finds the meticulous use of shading employed by other artists "prohibitively labor-intensive," undermining its salience as an injunction from a celebrated cartoonist about how to "properly" represent racial difference. Indeed, Bechdel notes that Howard Cruse, another queer white cartoonist who works primarily in black and white, "creates an incredibly rich palette of skin tones, shading even his white characters with a delicate cross-hatching. But assuming I could find the extra time . . . that level of fine detail isn't consistent with my drawing style" (70). Bechdel's comments here reveal how progressive-minded artists might arrive at different techniques for depicting race after carefully thinking through how to balance their commitment to accurate and affirming representation with their illustrative style. As Bechdel's discussion reveals, there's no single way to present the realities of race in comics.

The post–civil rights period also produced a proliferation of Black characters, particularly at Marvel and DC Comics, the two dominant US-based publishers of the period. Between 1966 and 1974, Marvel Comics introduced the Wakandan ruler Black Panther, the Harlem-based social worker the Falcon, the Kenyan mutant X-Man Storm, and the falsely accused ex-con Luke Cage, four Black superheroes that brought much-needed diversity to the Marvel Universe and remain popular to this day. DC followed suit by introducing a Black member of the Green Lantern Corps named John Stewart, the bioelectric high school teacher Black Lightning, and the technohero Cyborg between 1972 and 1980 in an attempt to match their competition. In more recent years, both Marvel and DC have built on the precedent established by John Stewart by introducing racialized iterations of previously established characters. This "reskinning" has resulted in two African American Iron Men (James Rhodes and Riri Williams), a Chicano Blue Beetle (Jaime Reyes), a Pakistani American Ms. Marvel (Kamala Khan), a Chinese American Atom (Ryan Choi), an Afro-Latino Spider-Man (Miles Morales), a Lebanese American Green Lantern (Simon Baz), a Korean American Hulk (Amadeus Cho), and a Congolese Batman (David Zavimbe), among many others. This creative direction has been criticized as pandering by those who prefer the original iterations of these characters and as reinscribing the centrality of the white archetypes by those calling for even greater diversity in comics. Less remarked upon is the reality that contemporary comic creators are loath to offer their original intellectual property to Marvel (owned by Disney) or DC (owned by Warner Brothers) in perpetuity and so choose to reinvigorate preexisting characters rather than lose control over their own ideas. The convergence of these issues of marketplace, audience, intellectual property, and race offers rich ground for scholarly inquiry into a creative environment unique to comics published in the United States that remains largely underexamined.

However, while superhero comics have diversified over the last fifty years, comic creators—both those laboring at DC and Marvel and independent writers and cartoonists either self-publishing or working for smaller, more creator-friendly publishers like Image, Dark Horse, Fantagraphics, Drawn & Quarterly, and others—remain overwhelmingly white and male. Comparing the winners of the Harvey Awards—the US comic industry's highest honor—for best writer and best cartoonist (which is to say, the figure that best balances the duties of writer and artist) between 1988 and 2016 with the winners of the Pulitzer Prize for Fiction over the same period provides one important metric to assess inclusion, since college instructors are more likely to include critically acclaimed books on their syllabi: There were fifty-six possible winners of these two Harvey Awards over this twenty-eight year period, which included exactly two creators of color—the cartoonist brothers Gilbert and Jaime Hernandez, creators of the celebrated *Love and Rockets* series. Over the same period, there were twenty-eight possible winners of the Pulitzer Prize for Fiction, a group that included seven different authors of color, among them Toni Morrison, Jhumpa Lahiri, Junot Diaz, and Viet Thanh Nguyen. Indeed, the most prominent contemporary writers of color working in mainstream comics today, such as Coates, Eve Ewing, Nnedi Okorafor, Marjorie Liu, and Saladin Ahmed, established themselves as writers in other fields before being invited to write comics, while independent creators such as Ron Wimberly, Jeremy Love, Jerry Craft, and Kyle Baker fail to attract the critical attention reserved for their peers.

Comics scholarship has to this point been dominated by a diacritic formalism that directs undue attention to the logics that inform the marks on the page while granting less attention to the politics of what is represented there. The work of W. T. J. Mitchell on the image offers one way to engage both. In *Picture Theory*, he calls for the modern interlocutor to partake in

a postlinguistic, postsemiotic rediscovery of the picture as a complex interplay between visuality, apparatus, institutions, discourse, bodies, and figurality. It is the realization that *spectatorship* (the look, the gaze, the glance, the practices of observation, surveillance, and visual pleasure) may be as deep a problem as various forms of *reading* (decipherment, decoding, interpretation, etc.) and that visual experience or "visual literacy" might not be fully explicable on the model of textuality. Most important, it is the realization that while the problem of pictorial representation has always been with us, it presses inescapably now, and with unprecedented force, on every level of culture, from the most refined philosophical speculations to the most vulgar productions of the mass media. (1995, 16)

While there are numerous studies of visuality and the institutions that make comics publishing possible, the investigation of race in comics demands more attention be paid to both the discourse and the bodies—the persons represented within the images as well as the ways that an audience might receive those images. The bodies represented in comics shape meaning in important ways, and scholars of the medium must not avoid this reality in a misbegotten attempt to avoid producing readings that some may find controversial. A fearless engagement with the various permutations of race in comics will enrich our understanding of the multivalent ways that images implicate us in their address even as they circulate as material and digital images.

42

Reader

Frank Bramlett

The notion of a "comic book reader" can be explored from many different perspectives. This essay will focus on two approaches in particular. First, a comic book reader is a person who makes meaning from a text by engaging with the visual and linguistic codes in a comic. Second, a reader is a person who constructs her or his readerly identity by engaging in a wide range of possible sociocultural practices. These two aspects of the concept of reader apply not only to comics but also to readers of newspapers, academic journals, and novels, among others; however, the process of reading comics means recognizing that comics are a semiotic system relying on a wealth of visual and linguistic resources. While comic book readers are variously defined by institutions and groups in societies at large, it is also within comic book communities that definitions of reader are established.

In this essay, I address print comics in English because of limitations of space and because most scholarship has been published about reading print comics. Less is known about the way readers read webcomics, but there are some features of webcomics like alt text and hidden comics that differ significantly from a print comic (Bramlett 2018, 75).

Reading the Visual Codes in Comics

Comics are primarily visual texts consisting mostly of drawn images. Readers engage with comics by examining the spatial relationship of images and unpacking their meaning. People who read comics have to know how to interpret an array of elements, like the panel, the speech balloon, and sound effects. Readers also have to understand that the relationship between panels is most often sequential, meaning that the action in one panel comes before the action in another panel. However, they understand that comics often manipulate the sequential relationship of panels and that they should adjust their understanding of time and sequence in order to make sense out of the images. We might think of panels and speech balloons as visual containers; they are specified areas on the page that hold limited amounts of information, and readers have to figure out how each individual container relates to the other visual containers on the page and be able to read page to page, making connections between containers across panels and over the course of many pages.

In the study of visual semiotics, images are described in terms of their logical and meaningful relationship to the objects they refer to outside the text: "An image is an *icon* if it bears a similarity or resemblance to what we already know or conceive about an object or person. . . . An image is a *symbol* when it has no visual or conceptual connection to an object or person" (Harrison 2003, 50). In comics, the vast majority of images (i.e., the contents of panels) are icons. Readers encounter these images and read them as part of the "real world" outside the comic or, in many circumstances, understand the logic of the constructed world inside the comic. In any case, the images—even if they depict fantasy or alternate realities—must be read and interpreted by the reader.

In figure A.3., taken from *Saga* (2014), the reader has to make sense out of these two panels. The reader sees four adult characters but has to determine the situation, the actions, the facial expressions, and the gestures in order make meaning out of these images. Taken out of the context of the comic book, it is difficult to determine the fullest meaning possible. However, seeing these two panels in the greater context, a reader would be able to understand that these four characters are facing each other: Alana and Marko, an interspecies alien couple, are standing close to each other, with Marko's body turned slightly to his right, positioning him at a right angle to Alana. Together, Marko and Alana face Marko's parents, with Barr standing slightly in front of Klara, his right shoulder partially obstructing the reader's view of Klara's left shoulder. (Readers also see a baby in Marko's arms, and with context, we know the gender of the baby as well as some of her physical traits that prove important to the narrative later.)

Additionally, readers note the background, which helps position the four characters. Marko and Alana stand with the starry night sky behind them, and Marko's parents stand with their backs to the interior of the room, a stairway leading to an upper level visible behind them. Although there are elements of these two panels that are considered fantasy (humanoids with horns, humanoids with wings), readers draw on their knowledge of the world they live in to make sense of the constructed world inside the comic.

Reading the Linguistic Codes in Comics

The majority of comics that use language employ speech balloons to represent spoken dialogue. There is sometimes additional language to indicate sound effects or to communicate information about the social context; this is often referred to as ambient language, the language found on signs or newspaper headlines or even T-shirts.

To make meaning out of a linguistic text, a reader "predicts what is coming next" and "infers what is not explicitly in the text" (Goodman 2014, 83). We do this by drawing on all "language levels," including sounds/spelling, word forms, and sentence structure, as well as word meanings. Further, readers make meaning out of texts using knowledge of discourses and genres by comparing information in the text with the readers' "existing knowledge of the language and the world" (83). As readers progress through a text, they "are both confident of the sense they are making and tentative about the possibility that the text may contradict their expectations" (83). In other words, as readers make predictions about what is coming, their meaning-making strategies include confirming their understanding. In those instances when readers find their progress slowed or stymied, they "correct themselves when they recognize that they . . . are not making sense. They do this by regressing visually to gather more information but they may also regress mentally by reprocessing the information they have" (83).

Linguistic reading embraces the complex blending of language on the one hand and writing system on the other. Italian, Portuguese, German, and Swedish are all separate languages, but they use essentially the same writing system, derived from the Roman alphabet. Linguistic reading is the cognitive processing of written alphabetic symbols into a linguistic code so the brain can decode the symbols to create meanings from the text. In English, the letter *f* has the phonetic value of [f]. On the other hand, there are imperfect correspondences between a written alphabetic symbol and a phonetic value. For example, the combination *th* represents a single sound in the word *think* but a different sound in the word *this*. Vowel sounds can be particularly thorny in English—for example, the written letter *a* corresponds to a range of vowel sounds: the different vowels in *hat* and in *arch* as well as the first syllable in *ashore*.

The details of writing systems can be complex, but research shows that readers do not examine every feature of every symbol: "The eye does not need to see every word or every feature. . . . 30% or more of words in a text are not fixated. The brain uses the most useful graphic cues to form its perceptions" (Goodman 2014, 83). When we write words, we write each individual symbol, but when we read words, we read them holistically, allowing our eyes to glide along very quickly, slowing down if there is a problem with legibility or comprehension. Becoming a literate reader in any language takes years of reading instruction and practice, and the complexities of learning how to read comic books should not be underestimated.

Figure A.3. demonstrates a number of strategies for displaying linguistic codes. The speech balloons contain dialogue: Marko introduces his wife, Alana, to his parents. The speech balloons contain different languages—Marko's mother is speaking a language that is rendered with blue ink, which along with obvious spelling differences indicates different linguistic codes. Even if the reader does not understand Klara's words, her facial expression signals displeasure with the situation. The bottom panel also has uncontained language, which is produced by Hazel, the adult narrator of the comic.

In order to understand the comic, readers must attempt to decode "foreign" language, especially given that the codes are only sometimes translated. In these instances, some readers might skip over the codes they do not know, but some readers will try to read them and infer their meaning based on contextual cues in the panels. Readers also decipher linguistic codes in the context of social identity and power relations based on race, age, and socioeconomic status, among other factors (Gartley 2017).

Reading Comics in Educational Settings

When comics are used in schools, they are most often associated with children and adolescents who are reluctant or weak readers on the one hand and second-language learners on the other hand. Comics are used because they are assumed to be easy to read (they have more pictures than words) and use limited vocabulary. Educators also assume that comics can be fun to read and thus may appeal more to students who are reluctant to read other kinds of texts. Likewise, comics are thought to be good learning tools for second-language learners because they exhibit everyday vocabulary in the visual context of a dialogue between characters.

Most research conducted on comics in the classroom consists of interview studies in which teachers, parents, and students express their opinions and attitudes toward comics. In a few cases, these studies aim to investigate the impact of reading comics on language and particularly vocabulary development. A 1948 study, published in the journal *Elementary English*, attempted to discern the impact that comics have on the learning of vocabulary in elementary schoolchildren (Sperzel 1948). The author conducted an experiment with three groups of students: a control group (group 1), who did not read comics, and two experimental groups—group 2, who read comics freely with no further requirement, and group 3, who read comics freely but kept a vocabulary journal to record which vocabulary was important to them. At the end of this study, all three groups showed no significant differences in vocabulary development. The study concludes that reading comic books neither improves language significantly nor interferes with language development.

More than fifty years later, scholars are still wrestling with the notion of the comic book reader and whether language development is affected by comic book reading. For example, in a study of comic book culture and language learning, English-language learners (grades 5, 6, and 7) report that they took pleasure in reading *Archie* and that they believe *Archie* comics are excellent resources for improving their English (Norton and Vanderheyden 2004). This study examines the opinions of teachers and students about reading comics; they do not measure the impact of reading comics on literacy development, vocabulary development, or grammatical accuracy.

Reader Identity and the Comic Book Experience

Being able to read a comic book successfully means reading both language and image, but it can also have implications for reader identity. When readers become interested in a particular comic book genre, they often consider themselves "fans." But fans aren't limited to genre only. There are fans of particular characters, like William Moulton Marston's Wonder Woman or Charles Schulz's Snoopy; or particular worlds, like the world created in Neil Gaiman's *Sandman*; or sprawling intersections of characters and story lines in the DC and Marvel universes, created through a corporate structure combining the talents of many individual writers and artists.

Here I will use the term *reader-fan* to distinguish a reader of comics from a fan who creates their fan identity using sources of information other than comics (like movies, television shows, and online forums). Fans signal their participation in a fandom in multiple ways. In the past, readers of comic books wrote letters to publishers, and these letters helped establish and maintain the identity of fans and of fandom generally (Gordon 2012). But readers and fans are not always the same thing; reader-fan identities exist across communities that have similar interests (Pustz 2016). Readers may participate in fandom by creating clubs or participating

at their local comic book stores. Some fans attend conventions, where fans come together to celebrate their favorite comics or comics makers. A subset of fans also projects their fan status by dressing up as characters, a practice widely known as cosplay (from costume play).

People from outside comics communities may view comic book reader-fans rather neutrally, but there is a long tradition of casting reader-fans in a less than friendly light. Even before superhero comics became famous, critics cited comics for their negative impact on children's language (Bramlett 2016, 386–87). By the mid-twentieth century, politicians and tastemakers leveled accusations that comics had negative influences on children's mental health and promoted juvenile delinquency among other social ills, and as a result of political and social pressure, the comics industry began to self-regulate its publications by following the Comics Code (Nyberg 2016, 25–27). Even though the Comics Code ended in 2011, there remains "the persistent public perception of comics as a 'juvenile' literary form" (32). In the twenty-first century, the comic book is enjoying an improvement in its public image in the US because of scholarly research and university syllabi, among other factors (32).

In some cases, reader-fans have harmed their own reputations with hostile behavior directed toward other fans, most commonly occurring when "chauvinistic fans seem to be afraid of losing their 'boys-only' club" (Pustz 2016, 272). The terms *fanboy* and *fangirl* have a range of positive and negative connotations, but without question, most of the hostility has come from male fans "resistant to the idea of increasing numbers of women becoming involved in comics fandom" (272). Increasingly, reader-fans have "influence over the [comics] industry" in part because of economic power (274). Readers have aligned against the toxicity of chauvinistic fans and demonstrate this unity in social media venues as well as physical venues such as comic cons. Readers and reader-fans contest the very notion of what it means to be a comics reader, and that struggle will undoubtedly continue. See Kashtan (this volume) for more on fans and fandom.

What counts as a comic book reader changes depending on fan communities, sometimes resulting in very difficult relationships based on gender, race, and sexuality. But reading comic books is also an individual activity, where a reader may read a print comic at home or use a digital tablet while traveling to read digital comics. Reading comic books is a perennial interest for educators, and comics will for the foreseeable future be used in a wide range of educational contexts. The definition of what it means to be a comic book reader will doubtless expand in the future to encompass a wide variety of reading habits and technologies.

43

Sequence
Barbara Postema

"The comic image finds its truth in the sequence," writes Thierry Groensteen in *The System of Comics* ([1999] 2007, 114). Individual comics images may not mean much. In fact, in isolation, they can often seem ugly or banal. But working together with their surrounding images to form a sequence (or even multiple sequences), these individual panels come alive and start to move, progressing the narrative of the comic. For this reason, Will Eisner (1985) dubbed comics "sequential art," making the sequence the key defining aspect of comics. Certainly, the sequence of images as it appears in comics sets the form apart from (most) other visual or textual forms, as neither literature nor film share this feature. This is what makes comics "a form of reading," as Eisner elaborates (7). Instead of reading words and sentences, in comics, readers decode sequences of images in panels: Eisner writes, "The rendering of the elements within the frame, the arrangement of the images therein and their relation to and association with the other images in the sequence are the basic 'grammar' from which the narrative is constructed" (39). He is describing the basic apparatus of comics here: pictures, panels, frames, gutters, and pages. Panels and their placement on pages are not random or accidental: in them, the sequence becomes the vehicle by which images transfer narrative. As Scott McCloud has pointed out in his formulation for a definition of comics, images in comics are in a "deliberate sequence" (1993, 8).

Groensteen and other Formalist theorists (mainly from France and Belgium) have elaborated on the means by which this deliberate sequence is formulated, explaining the apparatus by which comics force images to create meaning in sequences. The signifying power that turns individual images into sequences and thus action, meaning, and narrative comes from the way images in comics are spread across the page in panels: they are separate—kept at a slim distance from one another through panel borders and gutters—and yet are visible together on the page, *in praesentia*, as Groensteen puts it ([1999] 2007, 18), which creates iconic solidarity. Iconic solidarity, individual images standing together on the page, creates the circumstances that, as Ann Miller has summarized, allows the sequence as a succession of panels to transform into sequence as narrative, so that the reader can transition from a tabular reading of the page to a linear reading of the story (154). The operations underlying this process are layout and breakdown. The layout entails the use of the space of the page: the size and shape of the panels and gutters and how they are distributed across the page. The breakdown determines what goes inside the panels to fill the available space, translating the planned narrative into a series of images, from the creator's point of view and the reader's point of view, offering visual fragments for assembly into a story line while one is reading the comic. During this process, the panels offer key moments—moments with the duration of a blink of an eye up to several minutes depending on the amount of dialogue included in the panel or duration implied in other ways. The panels are brought into conversation with one another through what Groensteen calls the "forced virtual" of the gutter, a known unknown where readers are invited to fill in what was skipped based on the evidence of the panel before and after: in "reading"

the gutter this way, it no longer represents empty space on the page or a break between panels—instead, the gutter represents gaps in the narrative that the reader is invited to fill. Groensteen identifies three planes of meaning in comics reading: (1) the individual image conveys a wealth of information for the reader to observe and identify; (2) panels and their neighbors invite the reader to look for links and relationships, the beginning of interpretation; but only (3) the sequence produces "global meaning" ([1999] 2007, 111), and specifically narrative meaning, since "comics narration is essentially founded on the articulation of images within a sequence" (2013, 85).

Of course, sequences in comics do not necessarily convey narrative. Andrei Molotiu has discussed ways of reading comics for dimensions other than narrative, and with his term *sequential dynamism*, he suggests ways in which comics can be read for movement and flow that have nothing to do with story lines, where sequentiality is divorced from temporality (2009, 88). Instead, such abstract sequences suggest visual collisions of, for example, shape, texture, and direction, divorced from the temporal dimension of change over time. While this kind of reading is imperative in reading abstract comics, it is a kind of reading that can also be applied to narrative comics by giving preference to elements of page design and panel composition that are (perhaps) unrelated to the narrative. In his discussion of several pages from Stan Lee and Steve Ditko's *The Amazing Spider-Man* series, Molotiu invites readers to disengage themselves from the linear, narrative-driven reading of these pages, which show Spider-Man as he engages his adversary, the Green Goblin, opting instead for a tabular reading, which can lead to the perception of visual symmetries across the page, and iconostasis—the whole page as a global image—even as panels are participating in a sequence (94–95): such a reading of the panels across the page, filled with movement lines and swaths of webbing, allows the reader to take in the composition as an abstract visual rather than a narrative sequence. Like the rabbit-duck illusion from *Fliegende Blätter*, the comics page can in some cases be read as both a single, large image and a series of small sequential panels. Several examples of this can be found in Neil Gaiman and Dave McKean's 1988 miniseries *Black Orchid*, where, for example, panels showing a progression of close-ups of Black Orchid's features, on the first page of chapter 2, can simultaneously be read as a full-page image of her face (figure A.5). The leaf making its way down the six vertical panels suggests time passing as the leaf falls to the ground. But these six panels also capture Black Orchid's face, altogether showing her in a close-up or, read as a sequence, suggesting a drawing into focus on her face.

Sequences in comics can be of any length, though in his three planes of meaning, Groensteen implies they need to be longer than three panels to reach full narrative potential. Thus one could read the panels on a single page or a two-page spread as a sequence, a sequence limited by the field of vision and peripheral vision. On the other hand, one can delimit a sequence as all those panels participating in a single scene, perhaps encompassing several pages. Sequences may be formally bounded by chapter breaks, or finally, we could take a complete story arc, or all the pages between front and back covers, as a sequence.

Alan Moore and Dave Gibbons's maxiseries *Watchmen* plays with all the possibilities of the sequence, creating an alternate history version of the 1980s, nightmarishly similar to the real 1980s but with a status quo dependent on the powers of certain superheroes rather than on the nuclear standoff between the US and the USSR. A meticulously crafted work, the twelve sections build carefully toward the climax of the narrative, making the work as a whole singularly coherent and thus a strong example of a stand-alone graphic novel, once it was completed and published in a collected volume. The visual echo of the first and last panels, encapsulating a smiley-face icon, emphasizes the sense of sequence encompassing the entire series. From the start, the twelve single issues functioned as chapters, each a sequence with its own title and its own individual character, often signaled by particular choices in dominant colors or types of panel transitions, in terms of formal or visual cues. *Watchmen* demonstrates that sequences are often nested or overlapping, with the possibility of panels participating in more than one sequence simultaneously or a sequence that includes cover images. Like *Watchmen*, *Black Orchid* uses sequences that mimic cinematic effects to create transitions between scenes. In *Watchmen*, the remediated effect is the zoom, in or out, while in *Black Orchid*, sequences capture the effect of a fade from one scene to the next. One page ends with a color burst from a gun being fired, for example. The burst of color is picked up in the first panel on the next page, but the next two panels of the sequence reveal that the colors now belong to a tropical fish in an aquarium, as the scene has changed.

While the combination of adjacent panels into readable sequences is a major source of meaning in comics, it is important to be aware of another way in which panels cooperate, forming what Groensteen has called the series or the network. As discussed, panels that are in close proximity to one another on the page, or perhaps across page turns, allow for a linear reading that supports narrative momentum. Besides the connections to adjacent panels, these panels may also reverberate with, reach out to, and create connections with other panels within the work, linked by repetitions of shapes, objects, colors, or other means. These connections work visually and create a network of meaning at the level of theme or motif rather than narrative. Groensteen calls this type of connection braiding ([1999] 2007, 147). Groensteen's own example is *Watchmen*'s smiley face (155), which appears not just in the form of the yellow button but also as a crater on Mars, among other apparitions. In Jessica Abel's (2008) *La Perdida*, a souvenir Día de los Muertos skeleton performs a braiding function, representing main character Carla's fascination with and experiences in Mexico but also suturing flashbacks to the main story line and offering foreshadowing (discussed in Postema 2013, 113–15). Through the braiding function, the series of panels can even help clarify how to read sequences, as in Ray Fawkes's fragmented narrative *The People Inside*, where the page layout creates interrupted sequences representing a number of different relationships. Readers have to attend to visual cues to understand which of the panels on the page and across several pages form the continuing sequence, creating an even more challenging way than usual of trying to piece together a linear reading from fragmented—and in this case discontinuous—panels. Thus sequence and series in comics, though very different concepts, work together intricately. Braiding can serve several functions, including the suggestion of themes and motifs, but the sequence is the driving force of comics narration, providing the means to create an evolving story out of still images.

44

Seriality
Osvaldo Oyola

In the realm of comics, seriality is easily understood as stories published in installments or successive parts arranged in a series—an approach common to television shows, films, and Victorian novels. This sequential accretion of issues and volumes of particular series of comic books or strips (especially in, but not limited to, superhero story publication), however, highlights the complex range of possibilities that exist for ordering and understanding the narratives broken up and reimagined along that sequence. Seriality has four primary aspects that pervade comics and that can be put to use in conceptualizing how they are organized, arranged, and understood. These include how seriality influences the shape of the narrative, its relation to capital and industrial production, the "openness" of a serial format that fosters ongoing reader engagement, and seriality as a metanarrative, or overarching long-form account, of the publishing history of a title or character.

First, seriality shapes the ongoing narrative. The experience of reading a serialized comic varies depending on the style and frequency of the gap between individual issues or strips and how that organizes the individual stories or portions of stories present in each of those installments. These styles can be categorized as "continuing, cliffhanging, episodic, nonlinear, non sequitur and so on" (Szczepaniak 2014) and develop rhythms for storytelling that vary both within and between particular manifestations of the comics medium. For example, consider the serial format of a daily newspaper strip that has a unified narrative or thematic focus in the black-and-white strips during the week and leading to the longer Sunday color strip (e.g., *Doonesbury* et al.). This example is very different from the typical monthly serial format of mainstream superhero comic books published by Marvel and DC or the irregular intervals for ongoing alternative comic series like Daniel Clowes's *Eightball* (1989–2004) or the Hernandez brothers' *Love and Rockets* (1982–present), which have indeterminate gaps between issues. The narrative is shaped further by the indefinite length of most serial comics. "Indefinite" is used here both in the sense of having no predetermined length save that applied by unpredictable market forces or creators' personal lives but that must inevitably end and in the possibility of presumably going on "forever" (even canceled or completed titles are often revived years later [Klock 2002]). Some scholars also point to identifiable forms of seriality within the confines of an individual comic book issue or strip that frame the narrative. Consider Thierry Groensteen's description of a "series" as a "succession of continuous or discontinuous panels" (as opposed to a "sequence" that is always contiguous) as part of his "system of comics" (2009) or Jason Dittmer's assertion that even an individual panel's ambiguous and flexible relationship to time "narrating a range of events" in a single frame provides readers the opportunity to "produce temporal order in the scene" (Dittmer 2014), suggesting elements of seriality within the single comic image. In this sense, seriality is embedded in every scale of comics' visual and narrative form, within a single panel, between aggregate panels, and across pages, issues, or entire volumes.

The interruptions or gaps in an ongoing serial narrative serve to heighten the potential affective pleasure of reading a serial text through the anticipation of seeing the plot or characterization unspool overtime. However, this pleasure is connected to the second element of seriality: serialization as emerging from the logics of industrialization and capitalism. The popularity of newspaper comic strips in the early and mid-twentieth century meant they were commodities for publishers in their pursuit of maintaining loyal readers of these ongoing stories and increasing circulation. This relationship to capital means that the serialized form is vulnerable to publisher notions of what best serves their place in the market rather than the artistic concerns of the creators. This relationship can lead to the perspective that serials serve a fundamentally conservative end (Dittmer 2007), primarily by positioning readers as passive consumers that, in the words of Roland Barthes, are only concerned with the "articulations of the anecdote" (i.e., the need to know "what happens next"; Eco 1994; Barthes 1975). This notion—that the story's possibilities are second to the market for it—is especially tied to the major superhero comics franchises that hinge upon the so-called illusion of change. Such comics require "a narrative world that resembles our own," thus ensuring that protagonists are fighting to maintain a conservative status quo that resists a radical reimagining of that world, serves as a kind of commodified foundation for selling the characters and narrative, and remains within a broad notion of "ideological legitimacy" (Dittmer 2007, 2014). This perspective highlights the tension between the sense of time moving forward (and how that necessitates change) with the notion that the popular franchise characters must be consumed in such a way to remain "inconsumable"—that is, they must remain recognizable in form and in character to remain a lucrative commodity (Eco 1972).

The third element of seriality to consider in understanding these staggered narratives is the openness of the form. Angela Szczepaniak makes use of Umberto Eco's notion of "the open work" to consider how the possibilities for critically engaged readings are not limited to only avant-garde or experimental texts; she demonstrates that resistance to closure is part of an ongoing serial and provides an opportunity for that kind of speculative reading. In this view, the gaps between panels, strips, and issues provide a space for readers to regularly reevaluate and reinterpret the narrative. Furthermore, the potential for a network of parallel serial texts intermittently intersecting with and shaped by each other's events creates a narrative complexity that verges on the incoherent and is frequently referred to in comics circles as "continuity" and/or a "universe." The openness and "continual renewal" (Szczepaniak 2014) of the ongoing serial provides opportunities for readers to engage with and reorder a narrative according to their own needs and perspectives. As Szczepaniak reminds us, "Not every serial text will exploit the critical possibilities of this openness," but this opportunity for renewed engagement between installments emerges from the constant deferment of closure in relation to the narrative rhythms built into particular staggered structures. It also allows readers to foreclose some possibilities by downplaying or ignoring particular developments or iterations of a character or contributions by a creative team to construct their own understanding of that character.

The iterative approach to seriality—that is, that any given version of a character at a particular moment in time appears distinct from previous versions despite being part of the same timeline—leads to the collapse of time with the broader serial structure and undermines the concept of causality, making it difficult (if not impossible) to determine the order of events by narrative alone (Eco 1972). Eco's writing about Superman serial comics of the 1940s, 1950s, and early 1960s (as a stand-in for the entire superhero genre) explores how the iterative approach to seriality creates an "oneiric climate" that undermines a sense of narrative order altogether. Instead, a form of dream logic allows contradictory variations of stories to coexist, eschewing causality and ignoring a sense of the history of the serial's events. In other words, in the stories of this time, past events (as recent as the previous month's issue) were frequently ignored for the sake of the needs of the current story. Some scholars (Jenkins 2008; Ndalianis 2009) challenge Eco's claims by pointing to creators' focus on continuity and transmedial incarnations of characters and stories from serial comics common to superhero comics since the mid-1960s. Marvel Comics (and later Superman's home company, DC Comics) would build stories through attention to an established past and considering their influence on potential futures. Others, like Marc Singer (2013), claim that particular story arcs, runs by specific creative teams, or even whole swaths of continuity overseen by editorial mandates have displaced the single issue as the iterative basis for serials. In the comics Eco examined, he saw writers and artists "pick[ing] up the strand again and again" in issue after issue, but in contemporary caped crusader comics, the returned-to strands are longer segments set apart by varying forms and lengths of serial gaps. The most common form of gap is the "soft reboot," which establishes a new starting point and/or status quo for a long-established character without wholly erasing past events. Consider Spider-Man's supporting cast: within the same continuous narrative, Flash Thompson, high school bully to Peter Parker, has fought in the Vietnam War in the 1960s and the Iraq War in the 2000s without appreciably aging. Each iteration of his experience of war allows for the creators to both make use of this association of the character to war and shift that relationship to war and the trauma of veterans in regards to the contemporary social context in relation to particular wars. The character can then develop in ways that both rely on causality (his experience of war and home-coming) and eschew it (there is no way he could actually serve in both wars if serial characters in that universe existed in linear time).

Of course, some comic serials do allow their characters to age over the course of decades in something close to real time. Strips like Alison Bechdel's *Dykes to Watch Out For* (1983–2008) and *For Better or for Worse* (1979–2008) and comic book magazine series like the Hernandez brothers' *Love and Rockets* (1982–present) have characters visibly age and change, as do their settings. *Gasoline Alley* (1918–present) is the longest-running current newspaper strip. A legacy strip written and drawn by Frank King, Bill Perry, Dick Moores, and Jim Scancarelli, the aging of characters, both generally and individually, has slowed, frozen, or caught up to the present, depending on the creator's needs. Despite these series running against the more common timeless quality of many comic books and strips, the scaling quality of time in serials in conjunction with the necessary gaps in their telling nevertheless point to the endless possibilities for reframing and inserting events within the chronology that provide new ways to understand character identities while remaining within a recognizable skein of time passing.

Numbering comics issues and categorizing them into dated volumes is a legacy from their periodical origins, but numbering or dating issues, strips, or collections does not necessarily clarify or define a unified order for reading and understanding a serial narrative. The gap between the issue numbers or dates themselves, the multiplicitous retroactive reordering of segments of the narrative, and the gap made possible by virtue of the individual relationship of a reader to a series (which can lead to multiple gaps of several installments in a run) ensure this nonlinear reality despite the numbering. These gaps (both personal to an individual's collecting and as part of a series' publishing history) can be so large as to essentially make numbering arbitrary (and the recent adoption of so-called legacy numbering by comics companies like DC and Marvel further confuse and highlight the lack of linear order of the serial). Thus *The Amazing Spider-Man* #58 from 2003 is simultaneously designated #499 of the volume that began in 1963 because of the editorial choice to rejoin these narrative portions in one series and eventually dropped the newer numbering scheme. This confusion is in part constructed by the multiple appearances of characters in the parallel serial narratives of a "universe." Even ordering individual comics issues by publication date does not ensure a proper "order," as editorial notes at the beginning of issues might sometimes alert readers that "the events of [that] issue take place before [insert issue title and number]," whose events might influence the narrative portion about to be read.

Simultaneously, however, numbered serials do provide a broad framework for understanding years or even decades of long-ongoing narratives, even if a particular issue number may not always provide a foolproof mode of ordering a series to be read without more context. Numbering ostensibly becomes a marker of time, a quick reference for understanding where in an ongoing serial a particular story or part of a story takes place and when it was published and a context for making sense of those narrative installments. The seriality of comic books creates an interchangeable metanarrative of publication history that allows the fan expert to categorize different eras or iterations of a series or character via a numbering shorthand.

All of this suggests that comics provide a material example of the ironic lack of a foundational and linear order in serials. In some sense, the recursive reordering of a serial narrative that calls on the longtime or intermittent reader to contextualize the individual installment echoes the reading practice of the individual comics page in doing the same with each discrete panel (see McCloud 1993), demonstrating how the reader does this kind of conceptual work at different scales both intermittently and simultaneously. Comics provide a way to conceptualize how the very framework of the serial creates the discontinuities that require reimaging and rescripting the very sense of causality—why and how events unfold in a particular way but also the fact that they could have unfolded otherwise and commonly do. At first glance, the serial publication of comics stories should seem straightforward, especially given the tradition of numbered issues based on linear order and date of publication or collecting strips into numbered volumes, yet the tensions between (1) the accreted forward-moving development of a story; (2) the nonlinear development of character, setting, and plot through continuity and its retroactive reframing of events; and (3) creative attempts to produce seemingly coherent brand identities for long-standing characters who must remain even slightly recognizable to present and future fans in order to maintain sales make the serial nature of comic books infinitely complex and confusing. Serial characters change over time in a two-step-forward, one-(or more)-steps-back pattern that makes the accretion of that change alternately visible and invisible as a reader zooms out of or in on the overall serial at their particular point(s) of engagement. By its very nature, long-form serialization creates the discontinuities that drive the need to retcon—or retroactively revise, edit, or transform—the existing continuity or history of a character and their fictional world, as the framework of past events not only limits narrative possibilities for creators but creates multiple opportunities for mistakes and omissions that require addressing due to the ongoingness of the medium. For example, Jaime Hernandez explains in an interview how a mistaken reference to the number of his protagonist Maggie's siblings led to his scripting *The Love Bunglers* in part to explain the missing brother (Kunka and Royal 2017, 21). Furthermore, the very passage of time creates new opportunities for recontextualizing past events to drive current and future turns in the narrative or characterization. It is certainly possible that early in the days of ongoing serialized comics, creators assumed readers would ignore discontinuities or simply not be interested in comics long enough to notice them—outgrowing the medium—but as the back-issue market and later the reprinting of collected editions became more prominent, discontinuity became more difficult to ignore; as a result, identifying and suggesting explanations for those discontinuities became a feature of reader engagement.

Despite its surface forward-moving accretion of story, serialization actually points to the flexibility of narratives. This flexibility reflects lived experience, not through coherence or reliance on causality, but both through the potential for multiple simultaneous understandings of historical events (historical to both the serial and the real-world events it incorporates as markers of time) and through its production of identity. In other words, serialization highlights how identity is not a unified notion emerging from a singular origin but is positionally reframed (and thus reconstructed). This open-ended multiplicity of identity engendered by seriality has its ultimate political ramifications in the reimagining of characters and retelling of stories that ameliorates the underrepresentation of racial and sexual minorities in comics. This is accomplished through not only the inclusion of such characters but also seriality's ability to provide multiple points of view on the same or linked events, taking advantage of its backward-looping but forward-moving structure to challenge and re-present accepted events and preempt the calcification of canons. Furthermore, as Ramzi Fawaz (2018) suggests, this feature of seriality allows for conceptual considerations of difference that do more than merely represent the reality of difference but invite readers to imagine radical heterogeneous collectivity.

45

Southern

Brannon Costello

The US South has historically loomed large in North American comics. Beginning in the early twentieth century, newspaper strips such as *Li'l Abner*, *Barney Google and Snuffy Smith*, and *Pogo* circulated many of the classic tropes of what Kathryn McKee and Deborah Barker (2011) have termed the "Southern imaginary," a concept they define as "an amorphous and sometimes conflicting collection of images, ideas, attitudes, practices, linguistic accents, histories, and fantasies about a shifting geographic region and time" (2). These strips forwarded an idea of the South as a pastoral setting for the misadventures of comical rustics (Inge 2012). Another facet of the Southern imaginary familiar from comics is the idea of the South as a place of horror, depravity, and violence: think of Graham Ingels's vision of the decaying plantation home that shelters two murderous brothers (until it doesn't) in the classic EC Comics horror tale "Horror We? How's Bayou?" (*Haunt of Fear* #17, February 1953) or the stereotypical voodoo sorcerer Black Talon who menaces Marvel's superheroes in the Louisiana swamps (see, for instance, *The Avengers* #152, October 1976).

Indeed, these representations of the Southern imaginary are *so* familiar that they hardly seem worthy of attention, their meanings easily taken for granted. As literary and cultural critics, however, we should always be leery of such putative transparency, of taking our assumptions for fact. "The Jungle Line," originally published in *DC Comics Presents* #85 (September 1985) and written by Alan Moore, with art by Rick Veitch and Al Williamson, slyly riffs on such assumptions. In this tale, Superman is exposed to a rare Kryptonian fungus that he knows will drive him insane with rage before killing him. In order to find a quiet place where his inevitable rampage will not spark further violence, he "ma[kes] for the one place in America with no indigenous super-humans" (9). In other words, "the Man of Tomorrow is heading South to die" (1). Superman turns out not to be quite right about his destination: the Swamp Thing is there, and he uses his powers to help Superman survive, albeit without the delirious Man of Steel's knowledge. Of course, the Swamp Thing is not exactly the sort of square-jawed, well-coiffed superhuman Superman has in mind, and the story ultimately allows Superman to persist in his misperception about the region, returning to Metropolis confident that the ultramodern city is the appropriate setting for superheroes such as himself. Ian Gordon (2017) has argued that Superman is an especially durable icon of American values (3–14), and thus it is no surprise that in "The Jungle Line," he represents a conventionally American attitude toward the South, confident in his narrow preconceptions about the region and oblivious to its realities.

This story features many of the contradictory notions of the South that dominate the popular imagination. It is associated with backwardness, the past, and death, as well as with the monstrous and inhuman, embodied in the Swamp Thing. And yet it is also depicted as a place of succor, care, and kindness, a teeming natural environment in which the rage-inducing ills of the modern world can be soothed away. In grappling with these contradictions, we would do well to be a little less dense than Superman. Given the increasing prevalence of representations of the South in contemporary comics—in blockbuster series like *The Walking Dead* (2003–present); in popular independent titles such as *The Goon* (1998–2015), *Wet Moon* (2004–present), and *Southern Bastards* (2014–present); and in graphic memoirs such as Howard Cruse's *Stuck Rubber Baby* (1995) or GB Tran's *Vietnamerica: A Family's Journey* (2010)—comics scholars would benefit from engaging with recent scholarship in Southern studies, a field that has turned away from a long history of shoring up the idea of Southern exceptionalism. One direction that this critical work has taken is recontextualizing the US South beyond its national boundaries and viewing it instead as complexly situated within a broader hemispheric world, emphasizing connections and affinities with the Caribbean and Latin America, including, as Jon Smith and Deborah Cohn note, the common experience of "New World plantation colonialism" (2004, 2). Another avenue for critical reconsiderations of the region has led scholars toward critical interrogations of the ways that fantasies of Southern exceptionalism operate within discourses of US nationhood. Jennifer Rae Greeson (2010) has argued that the South functions as "an *internal other* for the nation, an intrinsic part of the national body that nonetheless is differentiated and held apart from the whole" (1). As Joseph Crespino and Matthew Lassiter (2010) write, our understanding of American history has long been dominated by a "simplistic dichotomy between southern backlash and American progress, an intractable region alternately deviating from and dominating an otherwise liberal nation" (7). According to Michael Bibler (2016), contemporary Southern studies is interested in "how the fantasy of exceptionalism denies the region's genocidal histories, and, in a different sort of denial, enables the nation to project everything negative about itself onto its regional other" (154). Thus American exceptionalism relies on the exceptional South—"the exception to the exception," as Sylvia Shin Huey Chong puts it (2016, 314).

Discourses of American exceptionalism have been central to certain types of comics narratives and to comics studies, especially with regards to the superhero genre, with its plethora of flag-draped characters. Jason Dittmer (2013) argues that superheroes can be seen as being not merely "reflections of" but rather "co-constitutive of, the discourse popularly known as American exceptionalism" (10). Stories that transplant the character type that Dittmer terms the "nationalist superhero" (3) to the South offer a useful but still underexplored site for exploring the function of superheroes in exceptionalist nationalism. In these stories, the recontextualization of the nationalist superhero within the region that embodies all the nation has disavowed can often produce revealing frictions and dissonances. Take Will Shetterly and Vince Stone's independent series *Captain Confederacy* (1986–88, 1991–92), for instance. An alternate history tale in which the Confederate States of America successfully seceded from the Union, *Captain Confederacy* chronicles the present-day Confederacy's evolution to racial equality, spearheaded by the replacement of a white, male Captain Confederacy with a new hero—Kate Jackson, a Black woman. Although, as Tara McPherson and Dittmer have argued, the series is ostensibly antiracist (McPherson 2003, 144–45; Dittmer 2013, 177–78), it struggles to balance its progressive tendencies with a lingering attachment to the symbols and icons of the Confederacy, staging awkward sequences in which a Black woman, clad in the Confederacy's stars and bars, opines that the flag on which her costume is based means different things to different Southerners, so that it should not necessarily be read as a symbol of racism. In order to promote a "potentially progressive" image of a "postracial Confederacy" (Dittmer 2013, 178), this patriotic hero obscures and downplays the horrors of slavery and positions them as something from which a nation can move on without an honest accounting. In

their overt (not to say deliberate) clumsiness and historical ignorance, these scenes call attention to the ways in which patriotic superheroes like Captain America or Superman enable a similar convenient amnesia about US history.

Other comics that have taken the superhero into the South have grappled with these issues, including the Atlanta-set *Southern Knights* (1982–93); the "Captain America No More" story line that ran through *Captain America* from 1987 to 1989, in which Steve Rogers's iconic New Deal liberal was replaced by a reactionary Southerner (Costello 2012); and *The American Way* (2006) and its sequel *The American Way: Those Above and Those Below* (2017–18), which examine the cultural upheaval that follows the introduction of a government-sponsored Black superhero in the civil rights era. Although these projects approach the problematics of the "Southern superhero" from various angles and with varying levels of deftness, taken together, they indicate that to "Southern" the superhero is paradoxically to emphasize the processes of disavowal, imaginative containment, and official forgetting central to the construction of a national identity.

While works such as those previously described tend to be formally conventional, however thematically rich, the comics medium is well suited to challenging limiting constructions of the South and its relationship to the nation. In our introduction to *Comics and the U.S. South* (2012), Qiana Whitted and I drew upon McPherson's compelling description of the "lenticular logic" governing representations of the South, in which images of Black and white Southerners are both visible, but only one at a time, so that the connections between them are obscured (McPherson 2003, 26; Costello and Whitted 2012, x–xi). We might see the relationship between nation and region as operating in a similarly lenticular fashion, with the belated and benighted South always positioned as an alternative to—never a part of—the liberal nation. As Leigh Anne Duck (2006) has noted, this contrast is often expressed temporally, with the "backward South" forever out of step with "the rigid temporal norms of the nation" (12). Yet as Whitted and I argued, drawing on discussions of the comics form by Thierry Groensteen and Charles Hatfield, the comics medium, with its ability to blend journalistic observation and subjective perception, to mix realist representation with caricature, and to present a multiplicity of temporal and geographical locations simultaneously, is well suited to refuting such logic (Costello and Whitted 2012, xi; Groensteen [1999] 2007; Hatfield 2005; see also Chute 2016; McClancy 2018; Cutter and Schlund-Vials 2018).

Among the contemporary cartoonists who have made effective use of comics' formal properties in depicting the South are Nate Powell and Jeremy Love. Powell's *Any Empire* (2011) is an ambitious, disorienting blend of fantasy and reality that examines the ways in which jingoistic nationalist narratives shape the lives of a group of young Arkansans. Love's *Bayou* (2009, 2010) follows a young African American girl, Lee Wagstaff, who must negotiate a magical-realist netherworld populated by figures of Southern legend and folklore and by monstrous figures who threateningly embody elements of racist discourse, such as the flesh-hungry Jim Crows or the corrupting caricature the Golliwog. In essence, as Whitted (2012) puts it, *Bayou* represents Southern history "as a microcosm of competing fictions the reader is forced to negotiate" (208). Love weaves in images of the official documents of 1930s Mississippi: newspaper articles depict Lee's father as a depraved monster, and a young lynching victim based on Emmett Till is depicted in the style of the once-popular lynching postcards. Such artifacts shape and limit their intended readers' imaginations, explaining what they can know

and how they should know it and instructing them in the unspoken laws of power. Lee, on the other hand, is on the search for another story. Her goal is to find Br'er Rabbit, the keeper of all the stories in the world, in the hopes that she can find an alternative narrative, one that will help her spare her father from the noose. She is searching for a way of telling the tale of Mississippi, the South, and the United States that will enable new possibilities—new images, new vocabularies, new futures. As Whitted writes, *Bayou* "effectively challenges the notion of the South as a closed, unified narrative by manipulating the presentation of African American history and memory through speculative genres" (209).

It should be no surprise that speculative genres such as science fiction, horror, or fantasy that dare to imagine the world as fundamentally otherwise are powerful tools for challenging settled ideas about the South. Depictions of the South in comics, whether they are affectionate or hostile, tend to rely on a set of idioms and conventions that do not always give full voice to the richness and variety of the disparate lives and locales that the regional label is meant to cover or that insist on a spurious and indeed insidious distinction between nation and region, miring the reader in regimes of knowledge that enable the United States' exceptionalist fantasy by perpetuating a vision of the South's otherness or abjection. Moreover, as Sharon Holland (2016) notes, these qualities have become firmly attached even to putatively progressive constructions of "the South," including in the way some critics deploy the concept of the "Global South." Although, as Robert Dainotto argues, many writers envision the Global South as a means of imagining affirmative political affiliation among disparate groups and regions oppressed by the predations of globalized neoliberal capitalism (41), Holland contends that too often the concept seems to mark "a negative human condition from which the term

South can never recover," such that "the South remains the stepchild of human beings' narrative of overcoming, of their will to progress" (167). Lee's quest in *Bayou* seems to be aimed at refuting such reductive formulations, acknowledging the particular horrors of the US South's history but also finding in that history opportunities for revision and renewal. A similar motivation animates Tim Fielder's Afrofuturist comic *Matty's Rocket* (2017), whose first collected volume chronicles the life of an African American sharecropper's daughter, depicting the Mississippi Delta in the 1920s as not only a space of fear and privation but also a launching pad for a voyage beyond the stars into a life of new possibilities. It is a work consistent with a vision of the South as, in Jarvis McInnis's words, "a place where new futures are being articulated every day" (2015, 18) and with LaRose Davis's call for critics to turn their attention to developing "theories of southern potentiality that look to the future" (2016, 192). As comics scholars grapple with representations of the South, we would do well to take characters such as Lee and Matty as not only objects of study but also examples for our own critical practice, acknowledging the power of old ways of knowing the South but refusing to be limited by them.

46

Speculation
andré carrington

Speculation names the faculty through which we allow comics to defy the laws of nature and reveal the rules of reading. Comics share a queer kinship with speculative fiction—that is, the genres of science fiction, fantasy, and horror—but speculation means much more to comics than the tropes they have in common with other media. Totemic figures like Flash Gordon, Asterix, Little Orphan Annie, and Astro Boy emerged in comic strips, and their stories have fashioned the medium into a venue where the print and visual cultures of disparate societies entertain flights of fancy. Speculative fictions featuring time travel, magic, horror, mystery, and technological wonderment took up residence in the popular imagination alongside the romance, the Western, and the superhero adventure in the interwar period that gave rise to the critique of mass culture, and they have been a mainstay of the medium ever since. In "The Myth of Superman," semiotician Umberto Eco (1972) surmised that the modern comic strip managed to overcome the risk of absurdity inherent in the way the superhero's life accumulates spectacular moments on a weekly or monthly basis by exploiting the oneiric (or dreamlike) quality of the experience of reading. The sui generis temporality of narrative makes it utterly unnecessary to reconcile the representation of the passage of time within a story with the quantity of time elapsed in the act of deciphering a text. Particularly in serialized comics, readers can experience the suspense of following a plot to its conclusion over any number of installments, only to see a new story wash it away like the waters of Lethe until it reemerges, half-recognized, in flashbacks and allusions. From the surreal landscapes of *Little Nemo in Slumberland*, which embedded childlike wonder alongside racist caricature in a world of infinite depth, to *Krazy Kat*, a reverie with seemingly endless self-reinforcing permutations, to the ageless adventures of Wonder Woman, Batman, and Archie, the medium of comics eludes realism even when its themes are mundane and its visual style aspires to verisimilitude. Plausibility notwithstanding, images of places, persons, and events that might take years to traverse in reality coexist via juxtaposition in comics, just as they might appear fractions of a second apart on video or separated by as little as a punctuation mark on a printed page.

Comics also convey lessons about speculation as a property of commodity exchange in the capitalist system of production. Analysts observe multiple markets in comic books: a primary or readers' market in which initial purchases of comics take place, a collectors' market in which consumers accumulate extant comics and exchange them for others or for money, and a speculators' market that assigns prices to old and new comics alike based on their potential to increase their monetary value in the future (Wyburn and Roach 2012, 310). As a mass-produced object for consumption, the comic book or comic strip derives its economic significance from the money involved in making it available for sale and from its exchange value (its cover price, for instance) to a much greater degree than artistic interventions in more prestigious forms. When speculating about the value of comics in financial terms, it is instructive to observe how the primarily commercial valuation and attendant intellectual devaluation of comics coincide with principles of "cultural capital" that make rarefied art objects priceless while defining ubiquitous objects of popular culture in terms of price

(Brown 2001, 67–70). The more fully a work in the comics medium attains the properties of fine art—serious rather than trivial subject matter; painstaking, artisanal execution by an individual commissioned creator rather than assembly-line production by a waged team, for example; and exclusive availability to a limited segment of the public rather than retail distribution—the more it accrues the aesthetic value associated with exemplary works in other art forms. Thus employing the term *graphic novel* to identify a comic within a single volume that sustains a narrative over a number of pages approximating the length of fifty thousand words of print evokes the aspirational status of the novel as a form of fiction writing: a magnum opus akin to a symphony or a feature-length film.

Prestige and popularity influence the compensation realized by participants in the production of comics, the ranks of whom include salaried executives, marketers, and shareholders; artists and technicians whose livelihoods depend on inconsistent work-for-hire engagements; and well-paid, sought-after stars who may also produce creative work in other media. The future marketability of ideas and images originating in comics also affects the conditions under which they circulate as intellectual property. In the forms of anticipatory hype, cult following, and media buzz, speculation about the possibility that the work they produce for comics might be licensed to produce lucrative movies, toys, and games informs the contracts governing the employment of contemporary comic creators and the career paths available to newcomers.

In addition to monetary remuneration, comics may obtain a return on the investment involved in their production and purchase in the form of critical acclaim. Critics engage in speculating about the value of comics by reviewing them and adjudicating prizes (the Ignatz and Eisner Awards, the Grand Prix de la ville d'Angoulême), but consumers can be just as influential in determining the fortunes of the comics they read. At the end of the twentieth century, vintage comic books became a viable investment. Publications like *Wizard* magazine and the *Overstreet Comic Book Price Guide* made it possible for collectors to track the value of comics without regard for their contents (Salzberg 1983, 71). The first appearance of a beloved character in a particular issue of a series (the antihero Wolverine's debut, for instance, in the 181st issue of *The Incredible Hulk*) could confer higher resale value to an otherwise unremarkable text (Alleyne 2003; Kasilag 2003). A complete print run of a limited series might fetch the kind of premium attained by a complete set of baseball cards, and nonsequential issues might reenter circulation together as the constituent parts of a newly cohesive subset of works representing the oeuvre of a respected industry veteran or up-and-coming talent. Conflicting modes of visual distinctiveness operated as determinants of price as well. Color, paper quality, and demand for the work of a few bankable artists have always been cost centers, but at the height of comic book speculation in the 1990s, publishers began to use novel materials in comic book covers such as iridescent plastic and metallic ink to increase the purchase price and perceived collectability of their new output. Prices rose, wages lagged, and opportunities for conspicuous consumption and market watching proliferated as the collectible comics bubble inflated and collapsed, recapitulating the logic of speculation in other commodities.

Whether they make up investment vehicles, cheap entertainment objects, masterpieces of artistic heritage, or assemblages reconfigured by disparate reading/viewing publics, comics are mercurial. The interdependence of pictorial and verbal signs in comics—along with the axiom that anything that can be thought can be drawn—makes the interpretation of comics as much of an art as a science. Readers make inferences about the relationship between elements juxtaposed on the comics page to form impressions and reach aesthetic judgments about the form in ways that seem intuitive, but comprehending what comics mean and how they work is as complex as understanding literacy itself. We could say that at the level of semiosis, as well as in the aggregate, as a mass communication phenomenon, comics are the subject of speculative inquiry. Investigating the functions of individual comics' imagery and the discursive and material processes they demonstrate are speculative practices, making the enterprise of comics studies, in an important sense, a speculative endeavor.

Speculation takes the assurance that comics can be about anything as the grounds for asking, What are comics like? One way to generate answers is to speculate about how comics are like and unlike other media. Using science fiction and fantasy (or romance, or memoir) as a test case illustrates that positing tentative associations between representative examples of a genre in comics and its literary, cinematic, and theatrical counterparts can illuminate the nature of genre conventions (Bukatman 2003, 2016; carrington 2016). Graphic novels have contributed original tales of science fiction to the tradition, and the genre continues to thrive in series like Garry Mac's *Gonzo Cosmic* (2012) and anthologies like Sfé Monster's *Beyond* (2015). Adaptations like John Jennings and Damian Duffy's version of *Kindred*, by Octavia Butler (2017), present new perspectives on landmark works in the genre.

Critical approaches to comics that take authors rather than genres as their point of departure also rely on speculation to make inferences at a structural level. Thierry Groensteen ([1999] 2007) pursues comics criticism by situating prototypical artists such as Switzerland's Rodolphe Töpffer in the context of historical developments in expressive cultural traditions, encouraging readers to develop systematic approaches to the work of *mangaka* like Osamu Tezuka and memoirists like Alison Bechdel. In the same fashion that literary criticism and art history speculate about links among biography, history, political economy, and creative expression, chroniclers like Trina Robbins (1996), Michael Tisserand (2016), and a burgeoning generation of graphic journalists including Joe Sacco, Charles Bowden, Alice Briggs (2010), and the Spanish team of Jorge Carrión and Sagar Fornies (2015) engage in serious storytelling that belies the connotations of the term *comic*.

Aimee Bahng argues, "The future is on the move, and though finance capitalism attempts to monopolize it through speculative instruments that render it a profitable space, the future remains profoundly unknowable and unpredictable" (2018, 16). Comics grow into new niches all the time in the contemporary economic and technological environment. Future investigations that extrapolate from discrete interventions to posit trends in comics might observe how comics devised in an educational context, such as Nick Sousanis's *Unflattening* (2015), may highlight the emergent teachable and therapeutic properties of sequential art. Tee Franklin's groundbreaking *Bingo Love* and *Jook Joint*, for instance, share the twin objectives of telling engrossing stories with the aim, in her words, "to educate people at the same time," in the markedly divergent genres of romance and horror (McMillan and Franklin 2018). Individual creative directions can signal affinities among artists or between artists and publics, while patterns in how comics and other texts are received suggest tentative links between the ways readers make meaning across media. Anglophone critics of Francophone comics, including Mark McKinney (2008, 20) and Laurence Grove (2010, 49), revisit the language of modernism in order to liken formal experimentation in bande dessinée to French new wave cinema and the new novel (*nouveau roman*) movement of the 1950s. The scholarship of Tejumola Olaniyan (2013) and Peter Limb (Limb and Olaniyan 2018) features comics as a field of contestation where African cartoonists, their subjects, and their readers struggle with power in public by querying and sometimes countermanding colonial, nationalist, and despotic discursive maneuvers. Grounded research on the fan cultures of comics, as well as a great deal of scholarship on manga, lends credence to the study of leisure and popular culture as a means to understand social formations organized by age, gender, education, and class. Across cultural frames of reference, speculation regarding the economic, psychological, and political relevance of comics yields important insights into cultural production writ large.

47

Superhero

Benjamin Saunders

The superhero comes in many varieties but can be loosely defined as a type of fictional character gifted with extraordinary powers and dedicated to a program of justice that often (but not always) takes the form of vigilantism. As such, the superhero constitutes one of the most successful popular fantasy figures of the past one hundred years.

Cultural commentators of all stripes—psychologists, sociologists, literary critics, scholars of religion, creative writers, and journalists—have offered different theories to explain this phenomenal popularity. Some liken costumed crime fighters to the gods and heroes of pagan myth (Arnaudo 2013; Reynolds 1992). Others tap into a residual river of Judeo-Christian religiosity flowing beneath the putatively secular surface of the superhero genre; superheroes, they say, slake an abiding thirst for the divine that persists in the face of modern skepticism (Oropeza 2008; Stevenson 2020). Then there are those who see the superhero as a nineteenth-century folk hero reimagined for a postindustrial, technologized, urban-capitalist environment: the gunslinging cowboy who rides a horse that never needs feeding transmuted into a gadget-wielding millionaire who drives a car that never gets stuck in traffic (Wright 2001). Still others put superheroes on the psychologist's couch and interrogate them as emblematic representatives of our individual neuroses, anxieties, and desires (Fingeroth 2004; Rosenberg 2008).

More hostile critics locate the appeal of superheroes in our basest instincts, diagnosing their popularity as symptomatic of numerous social and political ills. Some have claimed that superhero fantasies conflate moral right with physical might and are thus inherently fascistic (Wertham 1954). Others have explored the ways that superhero comics can express an aggressively nationalist political agenda (Dittmer 2013). The transmedia dominance of superhero franchises during the first decades of the twenty-first century has also been linked to the US's response to the traumatic events of September 11, 2001. According to one version of this argument, because superheroes have the capacity to reshape the world according to their own ethical standards—righting wrongs that, for whatever reason, the ordinary institutions of law and justice are incapable of redressing—superhero stories make excellent vehicles for the mobilization of inchoate feelings of victimization. These feelings are then pleasurably expiated in the orgiastic spectacle of righteous vengeance (Hassler-Forest 2012, 25–35). The contemporary success of the superhero fantasy may therefore be partly a function of its utility as a cover story for the destructive predations of American foreign policy.

But these disturbing suggestions must be weighed against the work of readers who emphasize the ways in which superhero stories explore the limits of our power fantasies and expose the historical contingency of our ethical values (Saunders 2011). Superhero stories can also serve as occasions for nuanced ruminations on the relationship between violence and the law (Curtis 2016). Of note, too, are those critics who interpret superpowers as a productive metaphor for the differences of gender, sexuality, race, class, and physical ability (Alaniz 2014; DiPaulo 2018; Fawaz 2016; Goodrum 2018; Robinson 2004; Saunders 2011). In the hands of these more sympathetic critics, superhero stories—and in particular, superhero *comics*, rather than the multimillion-dollar movie franchises that derive from them—emerge as one of the more progressive forms of popular imaginative literature available to us.

This multiplicity of interpretations tells us something about the elasticity of the superhero concept. But the range of critical responses also derives from the fact that superheroes have held a prominent place in US popular culture for several generations, and over the course of that lengthy history, perceptions of the target audience for the superheroic fantasy have altered dramatically. Primarily regarded (and widely dismissed) as entertainment for juveniles during the Great Depression in the 1930s, superhero stories were increasingly marketed to adults during the 1980s and today enjoy a genuinely intergenerational (and international) appeal. This shift in attitudes has been broadly consonant with accompanying changes in both thematic content and storytelling modes and a marked increase in levels of generic self-consciousness (Klock 2002). In other words, as conceptions of the audience for superheroes have changed, critical conceptions regarding the kinds of cultural work superheroes can do have recalibrated accordingly.

The variety of interpretive responses also owes something to the complex relationship between the content of superhero fantasies and the variety of media forms in which they appear. Although primarily associated with comic books (at least until quite recently), the superhero has always been a transmedia phenomenon. Following his comic book debut in 1938, Superman began appearing in newspapers in 1939 (thereby reaching millions of readers on a daily basis) and was captivating home audiences with a thrice-weekly radio series by 1940. During that same decade, he also appeared as the star of an expensive animated cartoon and a low-budget live-action movie serial, and when television displaced radio as the primary form of in-home entertainment, Superman jumped almost immediately (in one mighty bound) from one medium to the other, making his small-screen debut in the fall of 1952. To the extent that "the medium is the message," as Marshall McLuhan famously wrote, then the message of the superhero has been plural from the beginning.

Of course, to phrase it thus is to imply broad agreement that the superhero phenomenon begins with the runaway success of Superman, but inevitably things aren't quite so cut and dried. While Superman's arrival on the scene marks a pivotal moment in the history of both the superhero genre and the comic book medium, he was not even the first costumed crime fighter to appear in an American comic book; that honor goes to a more obscure character called the Clock, who debuted in 1936 (Sadowski 2009). Moreover, when we look beyond the boundaries of the comic book form, we can identify numerous possible superheroic antecedents, potentially going back to the dawn of human storytelling; there are commentators whose histories of the superhero begin with Gilgamesh (Gavaler 2015). But the atavistic aspects of the superhero fantasy should not obscure the fact that superheroes today are fundamentally products of modernity—with all that entails for our understanding of transformations in technology, communication, urbanization, immigration, nationalism, work, leisure, and so on (Gordon 1998). Thus while it may be possible to draw lines of connection back from Superman to ancient Greek legends or the *Poetic Edda*, the origins of modern superhero comic books can be more precisely traced to two immediately prior cultural forms: pulp magazines and newspaper comic strips.

A populist spin-off of the nineteenth-century illustrated magazine, the pulps were delivering sensationalist genre fiction to readers across the US by the 1920s. Early pulp heroes such as Doc Savage and the Shadow are clear precursors to Superman and Batman, respectively. Newspaper strips quickly registered the impact of the pulps; characters such as Tarzan and Buck Rogers were directly adapted from the pulps for the Sunday comics pages, and dramatic narrative increasingly came to encroach upon the once humor-dominated "funnies" throughout the 1930s (Walker 2004, 122–23). Considered in such a context, the first appearance of Superman represents a developmental culmination or end point as well as a site of origin.

But the superhero concept has hardly remained static since Superman first exploded on the scene; indeed, it is possible to identify at least four distinct eras or epochs in the development of the superhero since his 1938 debut. These eras are distinguished both by shifts in the economic structure of the comic book industry and also by larger patterns of historical and ideological change.

The first wave of superheroes rose and broke between 1938 and 1948. During this period, superheroes were instrumental in transforming the comic book industry from a vestigial organ of periodical publication into a lucrative form of mass entertainment. The bare statistics speak volumes: in 1936, two years before Superman's appearance, a handful of comic book publishers produced maybe eight monthly titles between them, almost all composed of reprinted newspaper strips; by 1940, two years after Superman's debut, there were twenty-three comic book publishers in the US, producing about 150 all-original monthly titles between them, the majority of which were spearheaded by a costumed crime fighter (Benton 1989, 18–32). By one estimate, more than seven hundred different costumed do-gooders saw their debut over the course of a decade (Benton 1992, 65).

In this fervid commercial atmosphere (perhaps comparable to that of the popular-music explosions of subsequent decades), publishers and creators frantically chased after hits but could not always accurately predict the readers' tastes. Consequently, most early superhero comics are marked by formulaic repetitiousness and even outright plagiarism with regard to devices thought

to boost sales (hence, for example, the proliferation of teenage "sidekicks"). But the fact that the conventions of the genre were still being codified also enabled a kind of wild creativity, to which the idiosyncratic vision of William Moulton Marston and H. G. Peter's *Wonder Woman*, the moral absolutism of Bob Fujitani's *Hangman*, or the near-deranged excesses of Fletcher Hanks all bear witness. At the same time, America's entry into the war in 1941 helped cement the figure of the superhero in the public consciousness during a relatively unusual period of ideological unity, with the various social tensions and political differences of the culture temporarily obscured by the magnitude of the Nazi threat (Murray 2011; Wright 2001).

A perfect storm of commercial, aesthetic, historical, and ideological factors thus combined to create the cultural conditions in which one comic book superhero in particular—Superman—could come to stand as synecdoche for the (sometimes contradictory) American principles of individualism, democracy, the work ethic, and consumerism: the "American way." Despite Superman's remarkable accrual of symbolic capital, however, comic book superheroes saw a sharp decline in popularity after the war; eventually, all but a handful were canceled, while romance, teen, funny animal, crime, and horror comics all blossomed.

The second wave of superheroes gathered force more gradually, starting in the mid- to late 1950s in the wake of an industry-wide recession fostered by a moral panic over the effects of comics on children and exacerbated by the rise of television. The publishers who survived this time of crisis turned again to what had seemed a failing genre just a few years before; at the very least, superheroes seemed less likely than crime and horror titles to provoke a sales-damaging controversy. Starting with DC's decision to revive the Flash in 1956 and gathering steam with the reinvention of the superhero at Marvel

Comics in the early 1960s, this second wave was marked by a new degree of self-consciousness about the genre (Schelly 2013, 145–53). For example, for the origin story of the "new" Flash, Barry Allen, Bob Kanigher wrote a scene showing the character reading an old *Flash* comic shortly before the accident that gives him his powers. At Marvel, Stan Lee, Jack Kirby, and Steve Ditko would combine this kind of self-referential wit with a new approach to continuity, in which all the characters shared a single universe—thereby creating the impression that their separate adventures combined into one master narrative and heightening fan engagement. The new Marvel characters also exhibited a wider range of emotional dynamism than was found in first-wave superheroes; they squabbled, suffered from everyday problems (such as money troubles), and were often misunderstood by the public they strove to protect. As much defined by their flaws as they were by their courage and fortitude, they projected vulnerability and weakness as well as power and strength. The more individualist ethos emblematized by Superman in the 1950s was also somewhat mitigated during this period by a new emphasis on the collectivist potential of the superteam in titles such as *Justice League of America*, *The Fantastic Four*, *The Avengers*, and *The X-Men*. And as the 1960s gave way to the 1970s, the (always) white and (almost always) male ranks of the superhero also slowly began to diversify, while the boundaries between superhero fantasy and the "real world" continued to erode in stories exploring themes of racial intolerance, political corruption, and social inequality. The reinvestment of comic book publishers in the superhero may have begun as an essentially conservative act of retrenchment—but the results were more politically complex. The second wave of superheroes thus represented a significant evolution of the genre in both aesthetic and ideological terms.

The superhero survived another period of transformation during the 1980s, once again in concert with a transformation in the economics of comic book distribution: the emergence of the so-called direct market, which catered not to newsstand vendors but rather to specialist comic book stores (Kidman 2019, 144–46). The growth of this alternative retail network permanently redrew the creative contours of the superhero genre for a third time, fostering change in two main ways. First, because "direct-sales-only" comic books were sold exclusively through specialist stores, they were not subject to the restrictions of the Comics Code Authority (an industry censor first established during the aforementioned moral panic of the 1950s). Material that would once have been declared too political, sexual, or violent for the youngest members of the newsstand audience was therefore no longer out-of-bounds. Second, while traditional methods of periodical distribution were too unreliable to support a comic book miniseries, such self-contained formats now became viable; this liberated comic book writers from the restrictive narrative logics of endless serialization.

The advent of the direct market thus dissolved at a stroke two structural barriers that had prevented superhero comics from operating within the relatively expansive thematic, formal, and aesthetic parameters enjoyed by most other popular genre fictions. The superhero had always been a hybrid of science fiction, crime, romance, and Western genre conventions. But only after the establishment of the direct market could superhero comics address political, philosophical, and sexual themes in the same manner as those foundational popular genres at their most sophisticated. It was in this context that works such as *Watchmen* and *Batman: The Dark Knight Returns* became possible—superhero comics that raised corrosive questions about the ideological limits of the genre that remain relevant today.

The economic conditions, aesthetic potential, and ideological possibilities of the superhero genre have continued to evolve, however, and it seems reasonable to suggest that we entered a fourth epoch of the genre in the first years of the twenty-first century, with the near-simultaneous events of 9/11 and Hollywood's (re)discovery of the market potential of the superhero fantasy. With movies such as *The Dark Knight*, *The Avengers*, *Black Panther*, and *Aquaman* generating enormous revenues, the perceived financial value of even supposedly "second-tier" superheroes has increased exponentially. This increased value encourages closer scrutiny from corporate owners and brand assurance division heads, whose primary motivation is to protect the property from damaging associations or controversies. This position is understandable but may also be incompatible with aesthetic bravery. Would today's Captain America be allowed to take the same bold stance as his comic book counterpart in the 1970s, when he renounced both flag and shield in the wake of Nixon's abuse of power, now that he is worth billions of dollars as a corporate IP?

As a corollary, it's also worth recalling that some of the most groundbreaking works in the superhero genre, such as Lee and Kirby's *The Fantastic Four* (1960), Moore and Gibbons's *Watchmen* (1986), and Bendis and Gaydos's *Alias* (2001), only saw the light of day because the economic risk they represented to their parent companies was relatively low. When the stakes for a contemporary superhero franchise are that much higher, it seems inevitable that further aesthetic and political evolution will be difficult to achieve, at least with regard to older, more established properties. Whatever the future holds, however, the ongoing transformation of the superhero will continue to constitute an object lesson in the dynamic interaction of two of our grandest theoretical abstractions: art and commerce.

48

Superman

Ian Gordon

Superman first appeared in *Action Comics* #1 with a publication date of June 1938, although the issue was almost certainly on newsstands in April 1938 because of prevailing magazine distribution processes. Created by Jerry Siegel and Joe Shuster, the success of Superman created a new genre of comic book feature, the superhero comic, which featured costumed heroes with powers obtained through accident, birth, science, or effort. Superman, then, refers to a specific character but is also used more generally to refer to someone with extraordinary qualities. This latter usage predates the origin of the superhero character with newspapers like the *New York Times* often labeling a person or character—for example, President Herbert Hoover or Fu Manchu—a superman (May 10, 1931, and November 27, 1932).

Two related issues figure in any consideration of Superman: first, the origin of the word and, second, the nature of superheroes who mostly operated outside of legal frameworks. The origins of the use of *superman* as a common word lay in the loose English translation of Friedrich Nietzsche's *übermensch*, a word more complex in meaning than simply a superman. Nietzsche's *übermensch* and the associated will to power (understood in part as making oneself a superman through self-discipline and thus achieving broader power and overcoming the individual self) cast a negative, fascist-like shadow on much of the use of *superman*. Used by George Bernard Shaw in his 1903 play *Man and Superman*, the word rapidly became bastardized to refer to people capable of outstanding feats. Nonetheless, the term *superman* retained its negative connotations, and indeed Jerry Siegel's first use of it occurred in a 1933 fanzine story illustrated by Joe Shuster in which a man empowered by a scientific development uses his new superskills only to enrich himself (Regalado 2007). Just why Siegel called his character the "Superman" is unknown. In the five years preceding that story's publication, however, over two hundred *New York Times* articles contained a mention of a "superman."

The word *superman* then carried a range of connotations, from the heroic to the villainous, and any consideration of superhero comics should pay some attention to the ways in which being super constructs their characters. Siegel and Shuster's use of it for their 1938 character gave the word a heroic inference, but their hero was given to taking action without necessarily thinking of the consequences, For instance, in *Action Comics* #8 (January 1939), Superman knocks down slum housing so the government will be forced to replace it with splendid high-rise apartments. The action places him outside of the law, even if the local police chief admires his action and shows little concern for the daily lives of the slum residents who, although evacuated before the destruction, have no say in the decision and live with the consequences. The tension between the valiant nature of characters and the conceit of the rightness of their cause simply because of their superness has been an issue of some debate over the years, and the reflex action of academics has been to link this to fascist ideology. In 1945, a Jesuit priest, Walter Ong, claimed that Superman and by extension superheroes were true to their source in Nietzschean philosophy, although he suggested that the mere name damned the character by association rather than making an argument. Later, in the early 1970s, Wolfgang Max Faust (1971), a German

academic, argued that mere publication of superhero stories created fascist-like dependency on heroic individuals because readers of such comics would infer the irrelevance of their own agency. If these opinions contained a kernel of truth, they lacked any analytical force based as they were on assertions and the thinnest awareness of the contents of Superman stories. Ong cites no comics, and Faust based his argument on just the title page of *Action Comics* #368 (October 1968); his argument ignores the thrust of the two-part story by Otto Binder in that issue and the next that questions the premise of Superman's greatness and reveals him to be flawed in his understanding of the need for heroics.

The Second World War threw the problem of Superman's superness into sharp relief for his publisher, DC Comics, not so much because of associations of his name with fascism, but because a creature so empowered could easily finish the war. The solution was that DC had Superman affirm his faith in the American people as the purveyors of democracy and capable of defeating fascism without his help. Thereafter, from the 1950s to the 1980s, Superman's powers were attenuated by a variety of factors: a weakness to Kryptonite, his human identity as Clark Kent, his pal Jimmy Olsen, his girlfriend Lois Lane, and a series of very human problems that played out in *Superman* comics alongside the heroic stories.

The tension contained in the word *superman* also finds expression in different interpretations of Superman's character. Superman, in his first comic book story, arrived fully formed as Superman. His powers were simply part of his being and not acquired. Yet to realize those powers, Superman had to behave in human ways. Many comic book stories had Superman try to be Superman without Clark Kent or Clark Kent without Superman. The question of whether or not Superman is a human or an alien entity also crops up from time to time. The resolution of these stories usually insists that he is both: Superman cannot be Superman without being Clark Kent and vice versa. Superman learning to be Superman by coming to terms with his humanity first—and by extension with the powers he possessed—found major expression in the 1978 film *Superman*, in which Christopher Reeve as Superman only appears almost a third of the way into the film. The narrative possibilities of that approach were strong enough to carry ten seasons of the television series *Smallville* (2001–11), in which Clark Kent only donned the Superman uniform and took that name in the final episode.

In his 2004 film *Kill Bill: Volume 2*, director and screenwriter Quentin Tarantino had the eponymous Bill offer a monologue on Superman in which he argued, "Clark Kent is how Superman views us. And what are the characteristics of Clark Kent? He's weak, he's unsure of himself, he's a coward. Clark Kent is Superman's critique on the whole human race." Tarantino's monologue drew heavily on Jules Feiffer's 1965 book *The Great Comic Book Heroes* in its understanding of Clark Kent being the disguise. But Feiffer made the point that Kent's purpose was to humanize the character, to suggest that the mild-mannered (readers of the comic book) might just aspire to more. As Tarantino has Bill frame the issue, Superman's alter ego is a decision he made, but of course Siegel and Shuster's Superman is not real and was created by the writer and artist. For all the iterations and bastardization of Siegel and Shuster's Superman, just maybe this is the essential meaning of their Superman: aspiring to be more, to be better than our found or known selves. That Superman in the hands of many creators has not met that challenge is in some ways yet more proof that this figure is a very human undertaking subject to failure—which is to say, Superman is not always particularly a superman.

But then again, the demands of the Superman serial narrative stretched over eighty years require the character to be super. Alan Moore and Dave Gibbon's 1986 comic *Watchmen* is often held up as the moment when writers began to examine the nature of superheroes, but Otto Binder took tentative steps in that direction in the aforementioned 1968 story, and in *Superman* #247 (January 1972), writer Elliot Maggin more directly did so when he had Superman question whether he had been making decisions—and enforcing them because he could—without regard to the role of self-responsibility in the development of human potential. This story was one of the first to open up the narrative possibilities of this tension in the nature of Superman and superheroes as vigilantes or benevolent potentates, which has become one of the mainstays of superhero stories in comics and films, including *Watchmen* and Marvel's *Civil War* comic books and the 2016 film *Captain America: Civil War*.

The Superman name has become iconic in American—and indeed global—culture in part because of the sheer amount of product bearing the name. Superman exists or has existed in a comic strip, radio serial, several live-action television series, animation of various sorts, and numerous films, just to name his media incarnations (Gordon 2017). Legal scholar Mitchell Adams has shown the international reach of Superman through an analysis of DC Comics' extensive filing of trademark registrations for its characters across numerous countries, including the European Union, Brazil, and Korea (2019). These filings underpin Superman's widespread appearances in, or on, a variety of goods and services. These appearances, in particular the use of the Superman symbol from his chest insignia or chevron, circulate the notion of Superman more broadly, often without using the word itself (Gordon 2016). Like the Nazi swastika before it and the Nike swoosh tick after it, the Superman symbol is an emblem that is recognized throughout the world, as are the characteristics attributed to the symbol. However, unlike Nike, which in addition to the swoosh needs a slogan, "Just Do It," Superman is his own slogan, recognizable the world over as a comic book superhero. Yet just what Superman designates even simply as a "superhero" is a situational negotiation between power and the need to hold it in check with notions of human limitations. For comics scholars, there is much to be limned here in the many ellipses necessary in Superman's narrative for this tension to be an effective storytelling prospect.

49

Trans-/*
Cáel M. Keegan

Signifying the complex of identifications and theorizations arising from transgender life, *trans-/** is a hybrid formation with an uncertain and largely unexplored relation to comics. The identifying prefix *trans* has been attached to the practices and identities of various sex and gender minority groups since the early 1960s: past usages include *transvestite*, *transsexual*, and *transgenderist* (Rawson and Williams 2014). Since the 1990s, it has been more commonly affixed to *gender* to form *transgender*—an umbrella term that now categorizes gender nonconforming identities largely outside the framework of sexuality (Feinberg 1998; Love 2014; Valentine 2007). Today, the term *trans* is often used as shorthand to collect together various forms of gender nonconforming behavior and identification, while the terms *trans-* and *trans** are used to describe modes of theorization and inquiry grounded in transgender knowledges and cultural praxes (Stryker, Currah, and Moore 2008; Hayward and Weinstein 2015).

Due to the relatively recent appearance of *transgender* as an identificatory term, trans comics have been largely indistinguishable from queer comics, which currently constitute one of the fastest-growing areas of comics production and study (Chute 2017, 349). However, this queer wave has not yet given much attention to the relevant specificities of trans comics authorship and consumption, which have long been operative within and alongside gay/lesbian and queer comics histories. For example, *No Straight Lines* (J. Hall 2012), the first major collection of queer comics since *Gay Comix* (1980–88), opens with an introduction from one of the world's most influential transgender artists—Hollywood film director Lana Wachowski. In what amounts to an understated coming-out letter, Wachowski returns to comics as the medium that unlocked her aesthetic awareness of the body's potential, describing how in 1974, *Zap Comix* introduced her to a radical new morphological imaginary in which women could have hairy legs and Wonder Woman might pee standing up. Wachowski's position as an introductory voice in *No Straight Lines* points to the central if largely obscured role that transgender readers and creators have played in the last four decades of comics history—a point that the subsequently released all-trans comics anthology *We're Still Here* (2018) makes emphatically with its title.

As an identificatory adjective, *trans* is important to the struggle for representation in comics—the desire for the medium to address transgender people's cultural marginalization and erasure through character and story. While transgender writers and illustrators have worked in both underground comics and commercial illustration for decades—Vaughn Bodē, Jeffrey Catherine Jones, Rachel Pollack, and Joey Allison Sayers are examples—there are few instances of transgender characters in comics before the year 2000. Early representational cases include Nazario's *Anarcoma* (1978), David Kottler's "I'm Me" (1983), the character Danny the Street in Grant Morrison's run on *Doom Patrol* (1990), and Diana Green's *Tranny Towers* (1993–96). However, the postmillennial era has ushered in an explosion of queer- and trans-authored print and webcomics featuring transgender characters and narratives, such as *Tranny Toons* (2001), *T-Gina* (2001), *How Loathsome* (2003–4), *Glamazonia: The Uncanny Super-Tranny* (2010), *Curveball* (2015), *Bitch Planet* (2014–present), *Kim and Kim* (2016–present), and *As the Crow Flies* (2017).

This "transgender tipping point" (Steinmetz 2014) has delivered comics readers an unprecedented rush of transgender images but has also generated critiques from trans cultural producers and scholars who view such representations as partial and insufficient marks of social and political inclusion (Gosset, Stanley, and Burton 2017). Such criticisms point to how transgender content does not necessarily shift the power dynamics of authorship or consumer access (which are sharply tiered by race and class), nor does it guarantee that representations are diverse, accurate, or nonstigmatizing. Moreover, a narrow focus on identifiably transgender content alone limits the history and aesthetic potential of trans comics, which may not always feature transgender characters and may instead express transgender subjectivity through style or technique. Because transgender subjectivity involves fine attention to the differences between sex and gender, surface and interior, and performance and essence, it is important that studies of trans comics "separate form from content" (McCloud 1993, 5), examining not only representation but also the medium's formal capacities to express transgender experience. Transgender characters are indeed crucial representational achievements, but transgender subjectivity may also be captured by how comics confront the established visual grammars of sensation and embodiment—for example, by the psychedelic feminine sensuality of Jeffrey Catherine Jones's *Idyl* (1972–75) or by Ben Grimm's morphological transformations in Marvel's *The Fantastic Four* (1961–present; Fawaz 2016, 80).

To consider the transgender capacities of comics form, we must move from the question of object to that of relation. This gesture traces the development of trans-/* studies, an interdisciplinary field that distinguishes itself from nominalist study of the transgender object by redefining *trans-* as a tool for examining *relations between forms*. The hyphenated *trans-* takes up Sandy Stone's call in "The *Empire* Strikes Back: A Post-transsexual Manifesto" for new modes of "juxtaposition" that would "fragment and reconstitute the elements of gender in new and unexpected geometries" (2006, 231). Formalizing the touching of two genders within one life, *juxtaposition* is a foundational element of transgender cultural production that in *trans-* becomes a broader theory for considering the "inextricability and mutual relatedness of trans- phenomena" (Stryker, Currah, and Moore 2008, 12). Gender is no longer the "proper object" (Butler 1994) of *trans-*, which can be brought into contact with any number of unexpected referents.

The use of juxtaposition as an aesthetic praxis might therefore inform trans-/* analyses of comics as a medium: Comics' anarchic seriality—their unpredictable sequential unfolding into a potentially indefinite space—illustrates the unexpected temporal, spatial, and morphological juxtapositions that characterize transgender experience, in which we might find ourselves undergoing puberty (again) in midlife, confronting inversely gendered images of ourselves, or anxiously entering a bathroom only ten feet away from the one we used to use. The shock of such spatiotemporal and anatomical juxtapositions is a formal element of Joe Brainard's "If Nancy Was" series (1972–75; 2008), crystallizing in his drawing "If Nancy Was a Boy," which features the iconic cartoon girl Nancy lifting her skirt with a gentle expression to reveal a small penis: this image fills in the imaginative gap created by Nancy's familiar dress yet simultaneously destabilizes her gender by juxtaposing different forms of gender embodiment, social ascription, and self-identification. Juxtaposition is also formally important to the ambivalence of *How Loathsome* (2003–4), in which the lead character Catherine's gender is not perceived consistently across panels, and to the bricolage of diverse trans male narratives in Dylan Edward's *Transposes* (2012). However, trans-juxtaposition is perhaps most elegantly articulated through the "interrelations and contestations" (Tensuan 2009, 176) of Cuban/US identity in Jamie Cortez's *Sexile* (2004) and by the dreamlike transitions between times, colors, and directions in Scout Tran's *Failing Sky* (2014–present)—a nonlinear webcomic designed to "subconsciously pattern" (Tran, n.d.) the flow of transgender life and memory.

Beyond comics form, however, there is the medium's aesthetic process. To analyze how comics work within and on the reader, we might turn to a more recent wave of theorization in which *trans-* becomes *trans**—moving from a theory of relation toward a theory of event. In this body of theory, the asterisk in trans* transforms the adjective into a wildcard "prepositional force" (Hayward and Weinstein 2015, 196) that expresses an infinite number of causal relations simultaneously across vectors of both time and space. Trans* is reconceptualized not as a meeting between previously defined forms but as a "paratactical" (Hayward and Weinstein 2015, 198) or sticky impetus by which forms themselves might cohere in any shape or direction. The force that drives the "transubstantiation of things" (Snorton 2017, 60), trans* is the energy by which one thing might become another. Trans* therefore names the processual energy by which vitality moves through and across its various iterations, allowing for change in forms to happen and therefore for meaning to occur. Trans* becomes the movement that produces form, enacting the "*event*ualization of life" itself (Hayward and Weinstein 2015, 196). It is this same force that allows gender to cohere as a material happening across discrete acts in time.

This definitional expansion brings trans* curiously into line with one of the most mystifying functions of comics—the agglutinating force called "closure" (McCloud 1993, 63) that concatenates and symbolically sutures comics across the gutters on a page. Closure requires the conscious and active participation of the reader, who assembles the comic into a chain of meaning by inventing an eventualization between panels or images, stitching static frames together into an occurrence. Like trans*, this basic operation of comics is also a paratactics, having no inherently subordinating or syntactical rules for the order of meaning that is created. Each encounter with a comics page is therefore a bit like gender transition, in which form must be continually relinquished for the meaning of the event to happen. Comics and transgender expression therefore both work through *happening*, bringing what is imagined into formal realization through the invention of meaning across discrete points in time. In comics, as in transgender ideation, whatever is believed can manifest as an event. This shared processual force operates at the deepest level of both comics and transgender self-revelation, as in Edie Fake's graphic novel *Gaylord Phoenix*, which illustrates hormonal transition ("Rad Queers: Edie Fake" 2014) as a phantasmagory that peels back layers of reality, memory, and sensation to recover a lost self—an eventualized body that "conforms to the shape of [one's] dreams" (Cremins 2013, 312). Similarly, Joey Allison Sayers's one-page comic "Springtime" (2008; in J. Hall 2012, 188) humorously reveals how all gender is processual by tracking the development of her breasts across panels. Sayers invites us to laugh with her understated "yay" as her breasts pop into full legibility, even as we realize that they are merely the visual manifestation of a far more complex, ongoing event.

While comics may be "formally queer" (Scott and Fawaz 2018, 202), it remains to be considered how trans-/* might already be operative both within and without queer analyses of the medium. Queer theorizations of desire as an orientation across space and through time (Ahmed 2006; Freeman 2010) have made queer comics studies centrally concerned with sequence and recursivity—with how the medium permits new directional mappings of desire while unmooring readers from the linear constraints of heteronormative and white temporalities (Fawaz 2017b; carrington 2018; McCullough 2018). Trans-/* studies, by contrast, has been more committed to theorizing the relation between the body's proprioception and the external perception of its forms (Prosser 1998; Salamon 2010). A trans-/* approach to comics studies might therefore emphasize how the comics reader uses closure to eventualize disparate panels into a contingent and morphological body of meaning. Trans-/* studies allows us to notice how queer attention to the reversal or disruption of sequence often presupposes form, in that sequence implies a reordering of known objects. What makes sequence happen versus how it is ordered or where it leads is a question that a trans-/* comics studies would be well positioned to investigate.

50

Universe

Anthony Michael D'Agostino

A superhero "universe" is both a spatial and textual conceit. Not limited by commitments to realism or the constraints of special-effects technology, the comic book superhero's setting is a theater of engagement intergalactic and cross-dimensional in scope. Indeed, the origin of the first superhero, Superman, begins not in the fictional American city of Metropolis but on the doomed planet Krypton, from which he is desperately rocketed to Earth, an interplanetary refugee. It is something of a cartographic necessity, then, to think of the superhero as existing within not the spatial limitations of a "world," as in a "planet," but the maximally inclusive category of a "universe." Some critics chart a specific historical relationship between the figure of the superhero and the high-tech city of American modernity, whether through the proxy of fictional urban spaces like DC's Gotham City or Marvel's sustained, focused, and realistic rendering of Manhattan (Bukatman 2003). However, closely related to the genres of science fiction and fantasy, superhero stories radically reimagine the terrestrial, adding to their Earths lost continents (DC and Marvel's Earths both contain versions of the mythological undersea kingdom of Atlantis) and geopolitically charged fictional nation-states (like Marvel's afro-futuristic Wakanda or DC's Middle Eastern Kahndaq) while maintaining intergalactic (and even extradimensional) breadth by exploring alien civilizations and interplanetary politics (like DC's passionate warrior civilization of the planet Tamaran or Marvel's competing imperial space-faring powers, the Shi'ar and Kree). Superhero comics' expansion of readers' sense of "world" to include whole universes of widely varying species of sentient beings that cooperate for the greater good, some argue, positions the superhero as a model for ethically encountering racial, cultural, and sexual difference and a figure for universal citizenship (Fawaz 2016).

In pop-cultural parlance, the term *universe*—as in the "Marvel Universe"—refers to a fictional world shared by and depicted in multiple texts, whether they be movie franchises, TV shows, or comic book magazines. Actions performed or events occurring in one movie, TV show, or comic book will have repercussions not merely in the sequels of the same movie franchise, the following issues of a comic book, or new episodes of an ongoing TV show but any other media (including but not limited to novels, video games, animated movies, or role-playing games) within a *shared universe*. Universal storytelling is premised upon the interconnection of relatively separate or autonomous narratives into grander metanarratives that include and transcend their source material, producing a metatextual and multiplatform mode of creative production, storytelling, and cultural consumption that has its roots in the textual and editorial complexities of superhero comic books.

The concept of "universe" acts as a principal of selection, organization, and interrelation responding to a problem not so much unique to but felt with singular intensity by the comic book medium—namely, How do the perpetually proliferating texts of serialized storytelling relate to one another? How do editors, creators, and readers of varying commitment cross-classify the ever-growing pool of stories, events, and characters produced by a given entertainment company? The word *universe*, in its ambivalent tendency to include "all existing matter, space, time [and] energy" and yet also delimit a set of relevant factors by the exclusion of all others, when applied to objects of popular culture, produces, curates, and defines relationships between stories and ideas, whether they be fictional, imaginary, canon, fanfic, personal canon, novelistic, cinematic, or graphic literary (*OED Online 2020*). In effect, *universe* is not merely a grandiose reconceptualization of setting but the possibility of structuring the infinite imaginative possibilities of storytelling.

In its simplest formulation, *universe* refers to a fictional world in which multiple entities coexist and potentially interact. In the beginning, so to speak, the comic book superhero of the 1930s, their supporting cast, and perhaps their setting constituted a single universe, a self-contained and consistently rendered fictional reality of one comic book serial or even a single story.

Umberto Eco famously argued that comic book stories existed in a state of timeless repetition called "an oneiric climate," where every story, no matter how action packed, ended with the same states of affairs as it began (1972). Comic book universes grow in complexity as characters from different comic book serials are made to interact, dragging their settings, archenemies, allies, and backstories into relation with one another, a common or shared universe. In *Marvel Mystery Comics* #8 (1940), Timely Comics' first superhero, the Human Torch, battled the antihero the Sub-Mariner, in what is now considered the first *crossover*, a story in which two preexisting characters (or sets of characters) usually isolated within their own textual space/times coexist in a text depicting a common present and, usually, a shared universe. According to Marv Wolfman, the writer of DC Comics' *Crisis on Infinite Earths*, crossovers initiated a sea-change in the temporality and psychological complexity of the comic book superhero (2005). After *Marvel Mystery Comics* #8, for instance, successive appearances

of the Human Torch and the Sub-Mariner were expected to reflect the events of the two heroes' past interactions. The crossover chipped away at the repetitive timelessness of the comic book superhero; no longer would "what has happened before and what has happened after" a given comic book "appear . . . extremely hazy," as in the forever present of Eco's "oneiric climate" (1972). Instead, the backstory preceding the opening page of any single issue of a superhero title would be a question of canonicity involving textual evidence, informed speculation, and authoritative selection undertaken by not only the editors and writers of the comics themselves but their readers in a critical discourse housed in comics' letter pages, in independently published fanzines and, now on the internet.

By featuring stories that substantially altered the fictional world in which they occurred, comic books began to develop *continuity*, a consistency (though not necessarily coherence) of event, character, and/or status (usually the relative power levels of different heroes) across multiple texts (Reynolds 1992). Universes cohere and populate themselves through continuity, and continuity assembles itself in the form of universe through the self-reinforcing representation of a fictional reality that conforms, to some extent, with its own continually rewritten past.

In superhero comic books, continuity, despite its linear connotations, accounts for not only a universe's past but the speculative histories and variant presents of *parallel* or *alternate universes* (also sometimes called an *alternate reality*) that explore the consequences of differing turns of events in canonical story lines ("What If . . . the Avengers Had Formed during the 1950s?") or place familiar characters and franchises in unexpected settings or wholly different genres (*Batman: Gotham by Gaslight*). Many comic books also depict future worlds as the destinies of a present universe (*Superboy and the*

Legion of Super-Heroes is set in the thirtieth century of the DC Universe), while others explore *possible futures*, whose relation to the primary fictional universe is contingent on the outcomes of the present adventures of a given superhero franchise ("Days of Future Past" in *The Uncanny X-Men* #141–42). When possible futures are foreclosed by present story lines, stock superhero plots reveal those alternate timelines to be preserved as alternate universes.

The multiplication of alternate universes connects to the vicissitudes of the publishing industry. In the 1950s, for instance, superhero comics went out of style, prompting the cancellation of all but a few monthlies until 1956, when Julius Schwarz resurrected the genre and initiated the Silver Age of comics by creating new versions of familiar characters. Julius Schwartz's Silver Age Flash stands as the first major *reboot*, a story that brackets (whether as in a *hard reboot*, completely eliminating, or as in a *soft reboot*, merely making nonessential the reading of) previous continuity to start a new story from the beginning, reintroducing or sometimes even re-creating a character or concept with a fresh slate and making the character more accessible to new readers.

When reboots leave behind the continuity of the universe that comes before it, they effectively create new universes. However, these new universes only reproduce the question of continuity—specifically, Whatever happened to the universe the reboot replaced, and how does it relate to the new universe? Gardner Fox addresses this question in 1961's "Flash of Two Worlds," in which the Flash of the Silver Age, Barry Allen, a denizen of the primary DC Universe referred to as "Earth-1," uses his superhuman speed to traverse the "vibrational barrier" that separates his universe from others to visit the Flash of DC Comics' Golden Age, Jay Garrick, who still exists, now aged and retired, in an alternate universe called "Earth-2." In 1983, DC Comics would acquire the rights

to Fawcett Comics' *Captain Marvel* characters and Charlton Comics' superheroes, each of which would reside in their own alternate universe, Earth-4 and Earth-S, respectively, alongside Earth-1 and Earth-2 in DC's shared *multiverse*, or the collection of related alternate universes.

For simplicity's sake, a comic book company's "universe" will often refer to a single, primary timeline or mainstream universal story, like DC's Earth-1 or Marvel's Earth-616. However, comic book universe encyclopedias like *The Official Handbook of the Marvel Universe* or *Who's Who in the DC Universe*, both of which include entries on characters and settings from various alternate realities, also use *Universe* with a capital *U* to refer to a multiverse. More recently, Marvel and DC have revealed that the universal stories of defunct comic book imprints like Marvel's *New Universe*, canceled TV adaptations like the early 1990s *X-Men* animated series, and video games like DC Comics' *Injustice: Gods among Us*, all once considered universes (or multiverses) firmly outside the multiverses of comic book continuity, survive as alternate realities within Marvel and DC's multiverses. In these instances, the terms *multiverse*, *universe*, and *alternate universe* become interchangeable. *Universe* acts as a modular umbrella term for any or all the others and a narrative device for the preservation and organization of ideas, concepts, and stories without a textual home.

The multiplication of universes and alternate universes provide a context for time-travel and dimension-hopping stories that build multiversal continuity. Marvel's *Excalibur* (1988) and *Exiles* (2001) feature superheroes exploring and producing interaction among alternate realities and possible futures. If universal storytelling produces continuity horizontally, along an x-axis of time, these *multiversal* stories generate continuity vertically, along a y-axis that cuts across and links multiple presents or parallel universes. Continuity also develops transversally when events link comic book presents to possible futures and variant pasts. Bishop and Rachel Summers of the X-Men franchise are both canonical characters originating from different possible futures who travel backward in time to become permanent fixtures of the X-Men's present-day story line, paradoxically interweaving multiple futures into the X-Men's shared past.

By the 1980s and 1990s, superhero comics had amassed decades of shared continuity spanning multiple pasts, presents, and futures of multiverses containing multiple iterations of the same characters, and many said this was making comic books impossible to read confidently, not to mention write and edit. The complexity of universal and multiversal storytelling, it is thought, constitutes a bar to easy reading and thus lowers sales (Riesman 2015).

This point of perceived ineffectual storytelling puts a universe or multiverse into "crisis," named for the first and most well-known narrative attempt to simplify and make comics more readable—DC's *Crisis on Infinite Earths*, a 1985 twelve-issue maxiseries intended to reboot the entirety of the DC Universe in one fell swoop: first, making all prior continuity null and void, including destroying most of the alternate universes of the multiverse, eliminating and/or "killing" significant numbers of beloved characters; second, allowing (almost) all franchises to start from new beginnings; and third, streamlining DC's multiverse by integrating key parallel or alternative universes into a single, cohesive DC Universe with a fresh, linear history. The *Crisis* story is now a staple of the superhero genre. DC and Marvel regularly stage crises to reboot and retcon, or retroactively change, their hermetic continuity and merge intellectual property acquisitions and their own canceled imprints into their mainstream universes.

However, the yearning for simplicity and coherence in the face of crisis that precipitates a reboot has been critiqued by literary critics, fans, and even comics creators who cite the complexity of comics continuity as, first, impossible to truly evade (because comic fandom never truly forgets ejected continuity) and, second, an essential part of the pleasure of the superhero genre (Wandtke 2007). Creators like Mark Gruenwald, Mark Waid, and Grant Morrison envisage not merely a multiverse but an intertextuality-inflected approach to continuity wherein all ideas, no matter what their ontological or canonical status, exist together in a maximally inclusive "omniverse" or "hypertime." In a story that could perhaps be considered an anticrisis, 1999's *The Kingdom*, Mark Waid's point-of-view character, Rip Hunter, reveals "hypertime . . . [, a] vast, interconnected web of parallel time-lines which comprise all reality. . . . The possibilities of hypertime are infinite . . . and humble the power of any man." Rip Hunter's metaphysics of hypertime is also a theory of speculative fiction that cuts against that of Marv Wolfman and his crisis-oriented ilk, whom Waid-as-Hunter positions as "Linear Men. . . . vested in enforcing an inflexible view of reality . . . [and who] think orderly, catalogued continuity is preferable to a kingdom of wonder." The ebb of "crisis" and flow of "kingdom of imagination" is the heartbeat-like rhythm of superhero universes' symphonic narratives.

The shifting, morphing, and overlapping concepts of universe, continuity, alternate universe, multiverse, crisis, and hypertime that make the superhero's "universe" so complex and dynamic generate a politically powerful self-awareness. Since multiversal storytelling's beginning in "The Flash of Two Worlds" in which the Golden Age Earth-2 is revealed to exist on the Silver Age's Earth-1 as a *comic book universe*, the ontological relationship between alternate realities has paralleled the relationship between fiction and reality. Multiversal stories, then, are metafictional, including their real-life audiences in their own fictional reality. Universes and alternate realities are often, as in DC's *Final Crisis* and *Dark Metal*, self-consciously referred to as stories, dreams, and ideas whose destruction and re-efflorescence signify not simply the narrativized "deaths" or resurrections of fictional characters and settings but very real acts of longtime readership or fandom, editorial decision-making, and politicized publishing. Marvel's Ultimate Universe and DC Comics' Earth-23 (numbered for Chicago Bulls' Michael Jordan's number) are alternate universes that have reconceived Spider-Man and Superman, respectively, as men of color, signifying the comic book industry's recognition of their increasingly racially diverse readership. DC's Earth-11 features a world of familiar superheroes of reversed genders, slyly suggesting that the genre's much-maligned centering of maleness isn't a necessary condition of its existence. In these cases, the alternate universe provides an ontological margin where the marginalized can be centered, making the multiverse a place where hegemonic "realities" can be rewritten. The comic book universe's inclusion of its readers in its multiverse is a part of the self-conscious narrative framing that empowers the superhero multiverse to participate in the reader's social world.

51

Watchmen
Andrew Hoberek

In summer 1986, DC Comics published the first issue of *Watchmen*, a twelve-issue maxiseries by a trio of English comic book creators: writer Alan Moore, artist Dave Gibbons, and colorist John Higgins. *Watchmen* begins with police discussing the dead body of a former vigilante-turned-government agent named the Comedian. Another vigilante named Rorschach investigates the Comedian's death, drawing in a range of former superheroes and eventually discovering a massive conspiracy set in motion by one of their colleagues—although a linear plot summary scarcely does justice to the complicated structure of flashbacks, flash-forwards, and textual intercutting that composes the story. Widely acknowledged as a landmark work in the history of comics, *Watchmen* also merits consideration as an example of a host of changes to the comics form that occurred, or were set in motion, during the 1980s.

Set in a universe distinct from the one that featured DC's core heroes such as Superman, Batman, and Wonder Woman, *Watchmen* was a superhero story that defied the conventions of the genre. The title, for instance, referred not to a superhero team, as one might expect, but instead alluded to the phrase (finally quoted in the series' eleventh issue) "Who watches the watchmen?" Drawing on other popular genres, including mystery, science fiction, and alternate history, *Watchmen* also featured elements of realism that, while not unprecedented in the superhero genre, had never before been taken to quite the extent that Moore and Gibbons did.

The year 1986 is frequently cited as an annus mirabilis for comics, since it saw the publication of *Watchmen*'s first issues, Frank Miller's revisionist Batman series *Batman: The Dark Knight Returns*, and what would become the first volume of Art Spiegelman's *Maus*. It is hard to overestimate the impact of this moment in comics history. In the late 1930s, Superman and Batman appeared and formalized the superhero genre. In the early 1960s, Stan Lee, Jack Kirby, and Steve Ditko wedded angst and soul-searching to superhero comics—essentially importing the tropes of the romance comics that Kirby had helped create—to reinvigorate the moribund genre. In the late 1960s, Justin Brown, Robert Crumb, Trina Robbins, and others bypassed mainstream publishers' adherence to the self-censoring Comics Code to give the world underground comix. The transformation of the form during the 1980s, characterized by the rise of alternative comics and mainstream publishers' increasing openness to more sophisticated stories, constituted its fourth great quantum leap.

While Spiegelman helped inaugurate the alternative comics movement dedicated to showing that comics could do more than tell superhero stories, *Watchmen* and *Dark Knight* sought to explore the underdeveloped complexity of the superhero genre. These two works, like the cinematic versions of the superhero genre today, emphasized the idea that people who put on costumes and fight criminals might have fraught and at times dark motivations. Relatedly, if we think that the superhero genre has been ruined by what is commonly called the "grim and gritty" mode of storytelling, we have these two works to blame. It is no coincidence that this shift took place in the 1980s. The superhero genre achieved mass popularity in the late 1930s and experienced a renaissance in the early 1960s, arguably the two high-water marks of US citizens' faith in the power of government, as a force transcending individuals, to do good in the world. From the first appearance of Superman in the New Deal era, the superhero stood as a figure for the liberal welfare state, a point Norman Mailer grasped when he identified John F. Kennedy as a real-life superhero. In the 1980s, the distrust of government activism that brought Ronald Reagan and Margaret Thatcher to power infiltrated comics in the form of a new cynicism about superheroes and their motivations. Beginning with *Watchmen* and *Dark Knight*, this cynicism ushered in a new wave of superhero stories centered on violent antiheroes like the Punisher (a previously minor Marvel character whose first solo series debuted, to immediate popularity, in 1987) or Deadpool (who began his career as a villain in 1991 but who by stages evolved into his current role as self-aware metaparody of the superhero genre).

Whereas Moore, unlike Miller, has remained a self-identified leftist, it is worth noting that the villain of *Watchmen* is a do-gooder liberal celebrity who thinks he can devise technological solutions to the world's problems—and is willing to sacrifice millions of people to put them into effect. In addition, while the series clearly takes a critical stance toward the violent, right-wing vigilante Rorschach, it also makes him—as readers correctly intuit—the center of the story. Despite Moore's protestations about the cinematic adaptation of *Watchmen*, then, there is something about the book that made the notoriously dark and humorless Zach Snyder a reasonable choice to direct the film.

Of course, Moore has frequently and explicitly criticized the grim and gritty turn in superhero stories, and much of his later work, like his run on the Superman pastiche *Supreme* (1996–2000), has been dedicated to celebrating the genre's more innocent and hopeful elements. Gibbons claimed in an interview published in Mark Salisbury's *Artists on Comic Art* (2000) that the focus on *Watchmen* as a "grim and gritty kind of thing" led people to miss "the joy and romance" of what was, for him, "a wonderful celebration of superheroes as much as anything else" (96). While it is true that *Watchmen* has elements of the violence and vigilantism that characterized *Dark Knight* and the revisionist superhero narratives that followed, it is also the case that its realism mostly inhered in a kind of quotidian sadness centered on failed relationships, loneliness, and disappointed expectations. In this respect, the series also bears comparison with the approach to superhero narratives found in Chris Ware's *Jimmy Corrigan: The Smartest Kid on Earth* (2000), Daniel Clowes's *The Death-Ray* (2011), or at a less critical remove, Jeff Lemire's post-2016 series *Black Hammer*.

Moreover, *Watchmen*'s innovations go well beyond its more realistic/cynical approach to superhero narratives. Moore, Gibbons, and Higgins investigate the formal possibilities of not only the superhero genre but the comic book medium in a way similar to that which the famous art historian Clement Greenberg imputed to expressionistic painting in the 1940s and 1950s. Moore, in thinking about the distinction between comics and film, has made the convincing argument that comics' formal distinctiveness lies in the way that the form lets the reader move backward and forward through the narrative at will, an idea *Watchmen* makes concrete via the character of Dr. Manhattan, who can simultaneously see but not change the past, present, and future. Gibbons contributes powerful visual rhymes whose meanings reverberate far beyond the level of plot. And Higgins's palette departs from the primary colors red, yellow, and blue favored by the pre-digital comics printing process to the secondary colors orange, purple, and green, a choice that mutes the

heroic tone of the images on the page in favor of a more washed-out, melancholic look. In this regard, we might see *Watchmen*—which engages in programmatic formal experimentation and self-consciously interrogates its medium's conventions in the interests of telling a more complex story—as something like the *Ulysses* of comics' modernist moment.

Watchmen was made possible by a number of technological and institutional changes to comics as a medium. One was the fax machine, which made it possible for Moore and Gibbons to collaborate on pages in England and then send them to DC's headquarters in New York City. Another perhaps even more important change was the rise of the direct market, pioneered by comics distributor Phil Seuling in the early 1970s and based on selling comics not through newsstands but through dedicated specialty shops. This shift meant that comics, no longer dependent on juvenile readers, could dispense with the Comics Code in targeting an older audience. It also meant that they no longer needed to feature ads—allowing each issue of *Watchmen* to appear as an autonomous aesthetic object and giving the creators room for back pages of putative found documents from the characters' world.

Watchmen also sought to transcend the constraints of the medium by aspiring to the status of a self-contained work of art, with each issue serving as a chapter rather than an installment in a theoretically unending story. Published in 1987 as a complete trade paperback, *Watchmen* arguably played just as great a role as Spiegelman's *Maus* in ushering in the era of the so-called graphic novel. Moore had first outlined the story as a vehicle for a group of characters that DC had acquired from the defunct comic book company Charlton, but when informed that he wouldn't be able to kill these characters for the sake of his story, he instead invented new ones. In the end, corporate publishing and intellectual property—which Moore pointedly critiques in his script—triumphed over his desire for creative closure. DC had not only licensed the series for a film adaptation but also returned to Moore's creations for the 2012 prequels collected under the title *Before Watchmen*. Beginning in late 2017 in the series *Doomsday Clock*, DC brought Moore and Gibbons's characters into the universe of Superman and Batman.

Watchmen remains a groundbreaking work whose impact resonates well beyond the comics medium. A 2017 special issue of *Cinema Journal* features a number of essays that discuss the series' influences not only from but also on film. *Watchmen* influenced a number of then-young comics readers, too, who would go on to become recognized literary figures. The most notable *Watchmen* reader who became a literary figure is Junot Díaz, whose 2008 Pulitzer Prize–winning novel, *The Brief Wondrous Life of Oscar Wao*, takes the series as an explicit intertext.

Watchmen perhaps appeals to filmmakers and the current generation of literary writers (who are more committed to popular genres than their predecessors) because it is immensely entertaining without sacrificing any of its formal or intellectual complexity. At least for now, the series continues to unfold new possibilities for critical analysis. We can see its critique of political liberalism differently than readers did in the 1980s. The title contains a story of sexual assault subsequently forgiven by the victim that likely resonates differently—and not necessarily to its creators' credit—in an era of sexual assault activism, now popularly referred to as the #MeToo movement. *Watchmen* was deeply of its time, but in giving alternative aesthetic shape to that time, it allows us to see it, and our own, in a usefully refracted mirror. That is at least one definition of what we expect from art.

52

Webcomics
Leah Misemer

As of this writing in 2019, webcomics are easy to stumble upon: you can follow cartoonists on the image-centric Instagram or Tumblr platforms, friends share them in social media feeds, and excerpts commonly appear in Reddit discussion threads. Internet users commonly convert individual comics panels into sharable memes that morph as they travel the web, blurring the lines between artist and user and between comics and other digital media. Despite this reach, webcomics are one of the most understudied forms of comics, which signifies a disconnect between scholarship and culture.

Sometimes called "digital native" comics, webcomics are originally shared through online posting. As with many types of online texts, they can be posted on social media or through the artist's own website, and series are generally most successful when they post new content on a regular schedule (Guigar 2014). Webcomics can range from one-time illustrations to multiyear-long serial narratives and cover a range of topics and genres, often refusing to fit standard genre expectations. Webcomics are distinguished from "digital comics," or "e-comics," which are often printed comics rendered in digital form, much like ebooks. As T. Campbell (2006) points out, webcomics are hugely influenced by the development of internet technology, with approaches to webcomic creation, posting, and even marketing shifting alongside technological change. The openness of webcomics—their lack of gatekeepers and the fact that anyone can post anything online—has made them a diverse form that can be difficult to pin down, especially as the evolution of digital technology has enabled a multitude of approaches to sharing media. Yet as comics easily shared and reposted via social media, webcomics arguably have a broader reach than print comics, and this ability to reach a larger, often more diverse audience makes them worthy of more thorough scholarly treatment.

Informed by the lack of gatekeeping that stems from their digital nature, webcomics have a flexibility that print comics rarely achieve (Fenty, Houp, and Taylor 2005). For webcomics creators, genre is a fluid concept. For example, *Questionable Content* falls into the slice-of-life genre, but author Jeph Jacques includes elements normally found in science fiction (e.g., robots, space stations) while describing the relationships of characters who work in coffee shops and libraries. While some webcomics, much like print comics, tell the story of a set of characters as they evolve over time, with each installment serving as a new piece of one continuous narrative, others reject narrative continuity over time in favor of posts that stand on their own. On the one hand, webcomics like Minna Sundberg's *Stand Still, Stay Silent*, set in postapocalyptic Iceland and running at 974 posts, or Ashley Cope's *Unsounded*, a fantasy epic following the exploits of the Daughter of the Lord of Thieves and her rotting-corpse companion, immerse the reader in a rich, cohesive story world. On the other hand, webcomics that reject narrative continuity do not have to remain in one genre throughout their run, since the author determines content with no oversight, yet the continuous posting still helps build an audience. *The Oatmeal*, one of the most popular webcomics, includes comics on all kinds of subjects, from why you shouldn't feed your tyrannosaurus crack cocaine, to the proper use of semicolons, to the difficulty of getting people to change set beliefs, to how to tell if your cat is plotting to kill you. Sometimes this variation in content stems from cartoonists using humorous posts to help build an audience that allows the author to broach more serious subjects. For example, in *Hyperbole and a Half*, Allie Brosh shared funny stories about her childhood and her dogs until she posted "Depression Part 1," which related her struggles with mental health issues. Sites like *The Nib* deploy this opportunity for variety in yet another way, with content centered on social justice topics that take advantage of the immediate nature of digital media to respond to current events. Unlike many of the other webcomics I mention, handled by a single creator or a stable creative team, *The Nib* is a site that hosts comics created by a variety of cartoonists, serving as a sort of webcomics anthology similar to those popular during the era of underground comix in the 1960s and 1970s.

Their diversity of form and subject matter has made theorizing webcomics a difficult prospect. Despite how much the internet has developed since *Reinventing Comics*' publication in 2000 and creators' negative response to his recommendations, Scott McCloud's *Reinventing Comics* remains the touchstone for scholarly conversations of webcomics. His notion of the "infinite canvas," meaning the ability for webcomics to stretch in all directions without the limits of the pages that bind printed comics, has held particular staying power, influencing the few scholarly treatments of the form to date. Both Bramlett (2018) and Kashtan (2018a) turn to examine alt text in webcomics, which refers to text that appears when a user hovers their mouse over the panels, and while this scholarship is valuable because of the way it focuses on aspects of webcomics connected to the mode of digital technology, there is a tendency to focus on the exceptional rather than returning to theorize webcomics more completely as a form. As both Kashtan and Bramlett acknowledge, not many webcomics use the alt-text feature. Aside from single book chapters and journal articles, webcomics have received little scholarly treatment with no chapters devoted to the subject in recent comics studies guides (Bramlett, Cook, and Meskin 2017; Aldama 2018a; Baetens, Frey, and Tabachnik 2018), and books on the subject are generally limited to practical advice for webcomics creators (Guigar 2014). As they have become a more important genre for marginalized creators, monographs have begun to devote a small amount of space to the genre, with Kunka (2017a) spending part of a chapter on Jennifer Cruté's *Jennifer's Journal* in his book on autobiographical comics and Whaley (2015) discussing web cartoonists Liesl Adams and Michelle Billingsley in a chapter on Black women in postmodern comics, but there are still ample opportunities for deeper exploration of the form.

The close association with the development of the mode (digital technology) and the medium (webcomics) suggests that webcomics ought to be studied alongside other digital media, yet this is seldom the case. The content of early webcomics was determined by the fact that only authors with enough tech savvy had the skills to post material. Subjects centered on video games (*Penny Arcade*) or web technologies (*User Friendly*) during this period because those topics spoke to the audience of "nerds" who read webcomics. However, with the development of free hosting, as well as the evolution of comics-creation software like MangaStudio and the increased functionality of programs like Adobe Photoshop, the skill barrier lowered and the content of webcomics became more diverse (T. Campbell 2006).

An approach to webcomics that considers them not just comics but a series of webpages has the potential to contribute to both comics studies and digital media studies. Such an approach would consider webcomics within the larger context of their pages and sites, thinking through what it means to experience a comic among ads, banners, links, comments, and the blog-like news posts that authors sometimes write to accompany the posted comic. We might, for instance, consider how webcomics operate within the "attention economy" of the internet (Lanham 2006), where views determine economic value. Or we might consider the fan interactions as acts of "produsage" that break down the barriers between producers and consumers as so many forms of digital media do today (Bruns 2008). Theorizing the comments sections, in particular, would provide an opportunity for comics studies to inform digital media studies, as the comments sections of webcomics tend toward being supportive rather than antagonistic spaces. Studying, for example, what creates that accepting and supportive tone might provide strategies for other forms of digital media attempting to combat trolling or bullying on the internet and other hostile behavior.

In considering webcomics as a form of digital media, which tends toward rapid change, we also must consider scholarly claims within particular historical contexts. Though it may seem odd to others in the humanities to discuss historical context within a twenty-year span, the swift development of digital technology necessitates this contextualization if research is to remain relevant over time. McCloud feels outdated because he fails to historicize, and the internet he knew is long gone, morphed by the advent of social media and crowdfunding sources like Kickstarter and Patreon. We can see this shift in examining the evolution of long-running serial stories as well as in paying attention to the expansion of style and content of webcomics as the internet developed. As Baudry (2018) notes, this change has not always followed a technologically determinant linear path, yet shifts are still visible over time. This history has been fraught with cartoonists attempting to find ways to monetize their work through techniques ranging from cross-promotional collectives and paywalls in the early 2000s to merchandising through companies like

Topatoco to the selling of collected print editions. These economic shifts are visible in the blog-like news posts that follow posted comics or on authors' social media accounts, as authors link to merchandise or write about their upcoming book releases. These pleas call attention to the fact that while capturing attention may help webcomic authors reach more people and build a bigger fan base, attention ultimately will not pay the bills and, for American artists, provide health insurance. This has resulted in the intertwining of webcomics and print, with many series posting comics online to gain the audience they need to purchase the print editions (Allen 2007; Kashtan 2018b). C. Spike Trotman's story, which began with her publishing the Glyph Comics Award–winning webcomic *Templar, Arizona*; continued with numerous well-known crowd-funded print anthologies, such as the sex-positive *Smut Peddler* anthology; and led to the establishment of indie-darling Iron Circus Comics, an internationally distributed publishing company, arguably represents the most famous transition from web to print. The web helped her gain a following that then crowd-funded Kickstarter projects, allowing her to establish an imprint that published books containing the kind of content for and about marginalized individuals that had previously been the purview of webcomics and underground zines.

Despite the economic barriers most webcomics artists face, as with many digital media, webcomics on all kinds of subjects have found their internet niche, an opportunity that has been particularly important for marginalized audiences and creators (Hellekson and Busse 2006). There are webcomics about history (*Hark! A Vagrant*) and LGBTQIA+ relationships (*Girls with Slingshots, Check, Please!*), steampunk webcomics (*Girl Genius*), fantasy webcomics (*Agents of the Realm, Tea Dragon Society*), and even webcomics about grammar (e.g., *Hyperbole and a Half*'s "The A Lot Is Better Than You

at Everything" and *The Oatmeal*'s "How to Use a Semicolon," "How to Use an Apostrophe," "When to Use i.e. in a Sentence") or coping with illness (*Mom's Cancer*). Beyond the variety of subjects, Hatfield (2016) points out that webcomics form essential communities for trans audiences and suggests we learn from their interactivity, while Cunningham (2018) discusses how trans creators, such as A. Stiffler and K. Copeland (*ChaosLife*), Kylie Wu (*Trans Girl Next Door*), and Sam Orchard (*Rooster Tails*), use autobiographical webcomics to complicate existing models of gender perception and recognition. Robbins (2013) highlights how many women have found a career as webcomics creators, and the success of cartoonists like Trotman, Aminder Dhaliwal (*Women World*), and Keith Knight (*The K Chronicles*) suggests that authors of color have also found the web a welcoming space. Hence studying webcomics would allow for more inclusion of marginalized individuals within comics studies.

Along with this potential to include more marginalized creators in comics studies, the very popularity of the form demands its theorization. In comics studies, we might consider webcomics, the most likely type of comics that almost all audiences will have been exposed to, as the comics vanguard. This high exposure rate stems from their spreadability as digital media and their ability to be excerpted, shared, and quickly read by anyone with access to digital technology (Jenkins, Ford, and Green 2013). Those outside the field of comics studies may never have picked up a paper newspaper or a comic book, but they more than likely have seen webcomics come across their social media feeds, particularly because webcomics tend to play into the visually dominant algorithms that govern such sites today (Long 2013). Though many creators continue to maintain archives on their websites, new archives at the Global Webcomics Web Archive out of Columbia University and the Webcomics Web Archive from the Library of

Congress promise to preserve this popular form for scholarly study. By paying attention to webcomics now, when the field is young, comics studies can avoid some of the criticisms leveled at other disciplines regarding relevance and representation.

53

Wonder Woman
Phil Jimenez

Wonder Woman was originally created as a feminist, antiwar icon in the 1930s by a queer polyamorous thrupple. But over eight decades of storytelling, her mostly male creators and audience have consistently pushed her into more traditional, heteronormative storytelling spaces, including ones that downplay queerness and glorify war. Today, as more women creators reclaim the character, her thematic roots are being challenged again, as they ponder portrayals of feminism, queer identity and war, and challenge their relationship to each other as portrayed in the comics themselves.

Best known globally from her portrayals on the 1970s TV show featuring Lynda Carter and the 2017 film starring Gal Godot and considered by many to be the most prominent female comic book superhero of all time, Wonder Woman made her debut in *All-Star Comics* #8 (All-American Publications, Winter 1941) just after the Japanese attacks on Pearl Harbor. The original *Wonder Woman* comics were imbued with creator William Moulton Marston's highly fetishized ideas about women, emotional intellect, and romantic, sexual, and political power; his interest in BDSM practices; and a surrealist approach to story within the comics themselves (and substantial input from his wife, Elizabeth Holloway Marston; their spouse, Olive Byrne; and artist H. G. Peter).

Depicted as a thick, raven-haired Amazon in star-spangled culottes and a red-and-gold, eagle-emblazoned bustier, the physically dominant and defiantly sexual Wonder Woman was conceived as "psychological propaganda for a new type of woman" Marston believed should "rule the world." Marston's intent was to promote in both boys and girls the belief that women were superior to men and that, as society's "love leaders," women could teach men to sublimate their violent urges by submitting to their "loving authority," mitigating their desire for bloodshed and war. Marston used comic books to deliver his message, knowing that, at the time, the medium was inexpensive and accessed by millions of young people. Between 1941 and 1948—encompassing World War II and its aftermath—Wonder Woman and her comics shamelessly promoted female superiority, queer identity, antiwar sentiment, and feminist-utopian ideals focused on women's intellectual acuity, athletic prowess, sexual liberation, and scientific curiosity and invention. This kind of social agenda-driven storytelling was not unusual in early superhero comics, although it has been challenged vociferously in today's marketplace, particular by older consumers who "see a hard push by social justice warriors" into their hobby, particularly through "forced diversity" (Del Arroz 2018).

Marston believed that "the world was primarily defined by gender conflict, as opposed to by class, religious, or cultural strife" (DiPaolo 2011, 73). Thus in Wonder Woman's comics, Mars, the ancient god of war, was the Amazons' greatest enemy, directly responsible for World War II; Hitler and the Axis Powers were minions of the war god and did his bidding. After Wonder Woman's official "reboot" in 1986 under storyteller George Perez, Mars's better-known Greek form, Ares, manipulated US and Russian zealots into nearly igniting a nuclear conflagration, a World War III; Ares assigned Wonder Woman the mission of preventing mankind from succumbing to his thrall (war depicted as having

no positive outcome but annihilation and extinction) and destroying themselves. In nearly all iterations of Wonder Woman's world through the mid-1980s, war and its consequent violence were conflated with hegemonic masculinity; indeed, Wonder Woman and the Amazons were created by their goddesses exclusively to thwart Mars and thereby male masculinity's destructive power on Earth (female masculinity was a decidedly lesser issue for Marston or any subsequent creator and was heavily embraced in-story from the 1990s onward).

Wonder Woman, then, has shouldered the exceptional yet unequal burden of being the ultimate feminist, queer, and female character for nearly a century in both mainstream superhero comics and arguably all of American popular culture. As a consequence, she has been the subject of constant discourse over her responsibility to adequately represent and embody the values, aspirations, and histories of those identity categories. Yet her other less considered but inherent and integral character attribute is her inextricable link to war as a driving (and distinctly male) ideology for culture.

When Marston (and perhaps Holloway and Byrne) revealed Wonder Woman's origins, he did so by upending and queering established takes on Greek mythology. Instead of a barbarous military sect born of Mars (fathered by war), feared for their battle prowess and murder of men, Marston's Amazons were reimagined as the fatherless, magically born offspring of Aphrodite and Athena (love and wisdom, respectively). Ruled by the benevolent Queen Hippolyta, the Amazons lived on Paradise Island, a magical utopia populated exclusively by superpowered women, clearly influenced by earlier fictional expressions of all-female utopian nations like Charlotte Perkins Gilman's *Herland* (1915).

Free from the strife and wars of men, the Amazons spent their days using "Amazon training"—a form of "mind over matter" self-help guru Marston championed—to channel their mental energies into creating unimaginable technology, to speak every known language, and in physical competitions tinged with reference both subtle and overt to bondage (mirroring sorority indoctrinations of the day) and other sexual fetishes, including extreme anthropomorphic play (*Wonder Woman #3*, February/March 1943). Thus established, Wonder Woman begat questions not just about female and feminist characters and their depiction in superhero comics (especially their bodies and costumes) but also about war and its wasteful use of resources. If war is the product of misdirected masculine energy, can it also be a feminist ideal? Does feminist ideology justify warfare in upholding war making as a "noble, heroic calling"? Should a queer, feminist superheroic character like Wonder Woman embody and glorify war, when we know that warfare "by its nature requires mass subordination to [patriarchal] norms of loyalty and obedience," mobilization around nativism, and a demand that "we dismantle our moral universe" to serve war's cause (Boggs and Pollard 2007, 18)?

For decades, it was nearly impossible to contemplate Wonder Woman and conceptions of feminine power, queer representation, and masculinity and war without considering the impact of Fredric Wertham's moral condemnation of comics, *Seduction of the Innocent* (1954), and the subsequent emergence of the self-censoring Comics Code Authority, which forced conservative guidelines upon the publishing industry to prevent government intervention. In the wake of Wertham's crusade against comics, Wonder Woman's open defiance of patriarchal norms plagued new editor/writer Robert Kanigher, particularly because of Wertham's claim that Wonder Woman was a bondage-loving lesbian promoting same-sex desire and eroticism (by Marston's admission, a fact not far from the truth); the character became a sales conundrum for decades, hampered further by

constant reinvention that stripped her of her most provocative traits. Yet because Wonder Woman's published adventures have mostly, though certainly not exclusively, been chronicled by male creators and targeted to male consumers, their conversations about women, feminist politics, and war—along with queer representation, the male gaze (straight and gay), and utopian society—have largely been defined creatively by cisgendered men, and Marston and Perez in particular.

In 1986, during the height of the Cold War, thirty-two-year-old superstar creator George Perez reinvented Wonder Woman (along with famed editor Karen Berger) and her world from the ground up in a company-wide relaunch meant to restore DC Comics' publishing prominence and make the publisher more competitive with Marvel Comics. Once committed, Perez declared his own agenda, stating he wanted to do a "humanist, rather than a strictly feminist," nonconfrontational character (quoted in Daniels 2001, 171). Many if not all modern takes on the character are rooted in George Perez's reboot of *Wonder Woman* from 1986, and nearly all modern creators have, in some way, used his vision for her as the basis for theirs. As a consequence, the book, though extremely popular among women and gay readers, became vastly less queer. The Amazons were restored to classic Bronze Age warriors—they were still created by the Olympian goddess, but now Artemis, not Aphrodite or Athena, was their patron. The Amazons were no longer technologically advanced love leaders; instead, they were warrior refugees on a hidden island that was the seal to Tartarus. Gone were overt themes of bondage, domination, and sex, and while some of the Amazons were made explicitly lesbian, Wonder Woman herself remained a chaste virgin. Instead of an all-knowing, transgressive, queer, feminist warrior, she was a naive stranger in a strange land. Nonetheless, if the scientific advancements and fetishized play of Marston's Amazons were absent from Perez's Wonder Woman (both the character and the series), the themes of love, equality, and the power of women and feminine energy permeated the material. Perez's Amazon was also a decidedly religious character, utterly devoted to her goddesses, whom she experienced as living, connected beings she could commune with and actually stand beside. While violence was often the last resort with this Wonder Woman, she would gladly—and with little reservation—execute her foe if she saw no other alternative.

This was the most notable of Perez's challenges to Marston's take and antiwar propaganda. Historically, rather than simply imprisoning or killing her foes, Wonder Woman worked most often to rehabilitate them; "Reform Isle" sat just off the shore of Paradise Island, a penal colony devoted to transformation through love, not punitive punishment. In Perez's *Wonder Woman*, lethal force was now sanctioned by a character whose original incarnation had been designed explicitly to denounce such violent force as conflict resolution and provide a loving alternative. This was a seismic shift in the world of Wonder Woman and an enormous readjustment of the character and her world. Though these sorts of reinventions were not uncommon to Wonder Woman, Perez's incarnation—buoyed by fantastic artwork, a respectful restoration of classic mythology, symbolic reference to other female warrior icons like Ellen Ripley and Sarah Connor, and a general prowar/prosoldier sentiment—was a popular one as well that has resonated for decades. For even though Perez's Amazons forsook their weapons and warfare the first moment they could (*Wonder Woman* vol. 2, #14, Perez and Wein, DC Comics), subsequent, less sensitive writers took hold of Wonder Woman's new edge and her "badass" Amazon sisters and ran with it throughout the 1990s.

After Perez and Berger's departure, *Wonder Woman* comics suffered mediocre sales and further creative disorganization and confusion so common to the character historically, so much so that "Who Is Wonder Woman?" became a regular editorial catchphrase as in-house debates about Wonder Woman's characterization and appearance—representing everything from fetishized sex object to neoliberal hellion—flourished. The answer changed numerous times, but one constant remained: in-story gravitas no longer came by spreading the gospel of love and sex or feminine power but by enforcing fear, by making war while downplaying overt feminist and queer messaging. The "warrior for peace," who used her sword as much as her magic lasso, was a vision of the character many consumers and creators preferred. So did corporate parent Warner Bros., who had to sell her to a global market with no consistent view on women and expressions of social, political, and physical power and was beholden to a niche marketplace and its single distribution channel (comic book specialty stores) that catered almost exclusively to male collectors. As I've stated in lectures I give at universities and comics conventions, "She was familiar in this incarnation, buttressing conventional wisdom about women and war instead of bucking it, while her Otherness and hints of defiant queerness were all but erased." As such, even left-leaning male writers and artists struggle to imbue Wonder Woman stories with a profemale feminist spirit while only passively commenting on, but rarely subordinating, the oft conservative political tone of the material, particularly the positioning of heterosexuality, masculinity, and men; the promotion of militarization common in entertainment; and the spectacle of romanticized war.

As DiPaolo points out, many of these depictions, including some of her most popular—including *Wonder Woman: Spirit of Truth*, *Kingdom Come*, *DC: The New*

Frontier, and *Infinite Crisis*—"collectively seem to rebuke Wonder Woman" as they try to "restore her to prominence" in the comic book world, making her "strong and admirable but also frightening and reckless" and sometimes "ruthless and sexless," often suffering "great public disgrace, penance, and physical beatings" before her peers Superman and Batman give their approval or forgiveness.

Perhaps the greatest rebuke so far was to change Wonder Woman's character from a once-subversive, fatherless, antiwar (and antimasculinity) advocate to a daughter of Zeus and God of War; this shift embraced the masculine nomenclature and purview of Wonder Woman's once-greatest enemy, the being (and metatextually, the ideologies) she was created to thwart (*Wonder Woman* vol. 4 #23, Azzarello and Chiang, DC Comics, 2013). While controversial, this take was a commercial and critical success, although later undone in an attempt to restore some of the Perezian take, and her queerness was restored, made explicitly homosexual but far less sociopolitically radical (*Wonder Woman: Rebirth*, Rucka, 2016, DC Comics). This phenomenon suggests that a singular creative vision; an ideological sympathy; strong, editorial guidance; a supportive corporate infrastructure; and a sensitivity to zeitgeist are all required to sustain Wonder Woman creatively and commercially, though the resulting character might not always seem the same—and consequently that not every incarnation (like some myths) will "speak" to every generation or gender.

The heavy leaning into violence in superhero adventure comic books, conflating battle dominance with prestige, is important to contemplate as more female creators take the reins of Wonder Woman's modern legacy. Clearly, some are interested in examining women-specific stories, masculine warfare, action heroes, and feminist icons. In retelling Diana's birth story, author Gail Simone etches into Wonder Woman lore a tale so personal, it is unlikely any man could have written the story (*Wonder Woman: The Circle*, Simone and Terry Dodson, DC Comics, 2008).

However, it seems just as clear that many simply want to feed their intense hunger to see female characters in epic adventures like their male counterparts. Modern female chroniclers of Wonder Woman's adventures may or may not consider "warrior cultures from training to combat . . . a repository of patriarchal values," nor might they care that the "predominantly male mythology of warfare evolved built upon the motif of fighting off demons and evil orders with maximum force, on imposing order by violent means to a chaotic world" (Boggs and Pollard 2007, 37–38). For both men and women, "warrior protagonists . . . rebuild psyches beset with anxiety, risk, defeat, and impotence, and war gives visceral expression to patriotic valor, technological virtue, and masculine conquest" (Boggs and Pollard 2007, 24). After all, it was Marston's often uncredited wife, Elizabeth Holloway, who understood this and insisted his new superhero creation should be a woman. In the fairly conservative milieu of modern superhero comics, which still equate "might makes right," this may be exactly the kind of storytelling Wonder Woman requires to speak to the culture and to make money for DC Comics.

In the 1970s, feminist activist Gloria Steinem used her influence to push her childhood idol Wonder Woman (and the female friendships the original series book exalted) back to prominence by placing her on the cover of the inaugural issue of *Ms. Magazine* in 1973. Soon after she reprinted a variety of classic Marston *Wonder Woman* story lines in a hardcover volume, which introduced modern audiences to the feminist values of the original series. Simultaneously, Lynda Carter's iconic embodiment of Wonder Woman first aired in 1975. The live-action adventure show's lighthearted but pointedly feminist commentary and Lynda Carter's physical beauty, costume, and famous transformational spin made her a defining vision of the character that has endured for generations, particularly as a gay icon. Powerful and globally recognized, these versions were rooted in Marston's "love-leader" ideology if not his BDSM and drag iconography.

But if those versions of Wonder Woman came to be seen as too frivolous, sexualized, and lacking the physical power and gravitas of war to make the character a serious contender for superheroine supreme, director Patty Jenkins and actress Gal Godot's *Wonder Woman* (2017) was seen as an epic achievement for female superheroes and for this one in particular and a rare critical and commercial success that catapulted Wonder Woman to the star of the DCU; the film more fully embraced Wonder Woman's Perezian, warrior-for-truth roots. Politically active female practitioners both pre- and post-Perez have differing responses to a war-making Wonder Woman. Like most other creators, their takes are as much a response to Marston, Carter, and Perez as a reclamation of the character for themselves. While some prefer her as a kind, war-eschewing feminist and humanist, others celebrate a more violent warrior Wonder Woman. In this incarnation, she is a visual representation of revolution and violent uprising as a protest against systematic oppression. However, it is more likely that Wonder Woman, a corporate product, will focus less on the transformation of a culture by violence and more on violence as a resource to uphold and buttress the culture she was created to critique. It is doubtful Wonder Woman will ever be written or drawn to overthrow anything other than metaphoric symbols of the systems that continue to marginalize and other.

Wonder Woman's current brand of subversion can perhaps be found instead in the character's reexamination of the expectations of feminist and queer representation and the depiction of war in modern comics and genre fiction. Contemporary scholars criticize the conflation of queer and feminist identity and politics, demanding a more supple exploration of the ways they overlap and diverge. And modern practitioners like Kelly Sue DeConnick, writer of *Wonder Woman: Historia*, the DC Comics / Black Label graphic novel, and the first woman to retell the origin of the Amazons, has stated that she rejects Marston, challenging the burden of perfection he has placed on women (as it so happens, I am the artist on this series). DeConnick aims to deconstruct the assumption that comics about women need to be for men (and their presumed psychological evolution) and the very idea that war is an enemy of modern feminists, or at least not compatible with their agenda. Only time will tell if DeConnick's Amazons, alongside Jenkins's and Jill Thompson's and G Willow Wilson's—who are as defiantly antipatriarchal, antitraditional, and antiassimilationist as Marston's—will affect Wonder Woman's messaging and if she will continue to teach women and girls to raise their swords while encouraging boys and men to lay theirs down and extend their hands in peace instead.

54

X-Men

Alexandro Segade

How many times have the X-Men died? The outcast team of mutant superheroes, whose stories have been ongoing in Marvel Comics for over fifty-five years, has through time travel created a multiverse of alternate futures in which their deaths are predetermined. In one future, they are hunted by the federal government, wanted posters pasted on dystopian brick walls, their faces marked "Slain" or "Apprehended." Those captured are neutralized with power-dampening collars and sent to concentration camps, where they unsuccessfully attempt a rebellion that leads to their destruction by the Sentinels, giant robots with weapons in their palms. In another future, the "Age of Apocalypse," the X-Men simply do not exist. The characters are instead warring factions whose power creates a conundrum: what to do with the humans not born superior, like them? The ensuing civil war leaves few mutants, or humans, standing. And if we forget the future and look at the ways the X-Men die in the continuous timeline we've been following all this time, they have been blown up in a high-rise while the world watches on TV; they have been blown up in a school bus; they have been crucified on their own front lawn; they have succumbed to a virus that only they can catch; and they have died of a poison only toxic to them. Across the years, nearly all of the main characters who have made up the X-Men have been killed at least once. Like the oppressed they represent, the X-Men's death is foretold.

But like oppression, the X-Men are still with us. Defined by their mantra, "To protect a world that hates and fears them," the team redefined the superhero comic in the early 1960s, expanding its repertoire of genres, from soap opera to space opera to body horror to speculative fiction, in a diverse pastiche of unstable forms used, in this case, to explore "otherness." It is fitting that a comic book story that takes prejudice as its subject would find its setting in a school: academia being an agonistic way out of class-, gender-, and race-based discrimination for many "gifted" people. Of course, Xavier's School for Gifted Youngsters, the "special" academy where young mutants are recruited and trained to master their extraordinary powers, could also be seen as a paramilitary revolutionary cell training a generation of child soldiers for a coming race war. In any case, otherness, it seems, is a subject particularly suited to comics. The medium can show us the others to identify with—"us" being the deeply "othered" nerds who read such things. If DC Comics' Justice League provides mythic bodies as surrogates for the nation (in the iconic figures of Superman, Batman, and Wonder Woman, among others), and Marvel Comics' the Avengers brand bodies with powers siphoned from capitalism (think of Iron Man's seemingly limitless access to machine technology), then the X-Men can be seen as bare lives whose marked bodies band together to survive the onslaught of those forces. How could you not identify?

The X-Men, created by Stan Lee and Jack Kirby, first appeared in 1963, the students of wheelchair-bound telepath Professor X. Instead of a convoluted mélange of conflicting origin stories, they all shared one: they were mutants, the "next step in human evolution," born with a mysterious X-gene that manifested outré abilities with uneven use values. Cyclops had to wear a visor or else his eyes would shoot red blasts at whatever he looked at; Beast had big feet and hands; Iceman could turn into a snowman; Marvel Girl could set the table with her mind. White kids with strained relationships with their parents, the X-Men were prep schoolers who, by virtue of the fact that they were born different (even from each other), shared an alienation from the hostile society into which they were attempting to integrate. Their mandate was to fight so-called evil mutants, such as the loutish Blob or the inconsistent Mimic, in order to convince the larger society to accept them. The primary antagonist to this plan was Magneto—an exceptionally powerful master of ill-defined "magnetism"—whose Brotherhood of Evil Mutants proposed a reversal, in which the disempowered use their superpowers to subjugate their oppressors, a bigoted humanity. It has been largely accepted that the early X-Men's mutancy served as a metaphor for the Jewishness of their creators, however latent this conceptualizing may have been for Lee (given name: Lieber) and Kirby (born Jacob Kurtzberg). Lee and Kirby were churning out a "house of ideas" and did not spend all that much on this one, which had flagging sales and didn't seem to stick.

After a spotty publication history, the X-Men returned in 1975, when writer Len Wein teamed up with the visionary artist Dave Cockrum to reimagine the "Uncanny" whiteness of the original team as an international, interracial explosion of "All-New, All-Different"–ness. The new cast was composed of weather-controlling Storm (a Black woman from Kenya, with white hair!), acrobatic Nightcrawler (covered in blue with a tail and from Bavaria!), and metallic Colossus (from the USSR during the Cold War!), not to mention the more stereotypical Apache Thunderbird, Japanese Sunfire, and Irish Banshee. "Small world" tokenism aside, these new X-Men nonetheless put pressure on the following concept: If mutants can be anyone, why was the previous generation all-white, all-American? This generation of X-Men, newly immigrated to the United States, was emblazoned in bold colors, not limited to their costumes. Cockrum drew the new group hurtling toward the viewer on the cover of *Giant-Size X-Men* #1, astonished expressions on the faces of the original team, here made into a surface the new group was ripping apart. In the 1970s, the X-Men could begin to reflect, and represent, the multiculturalism that their creators were experiencing in the streets of New York City, and just as American society at large began to reorient its self-image toward a kind of contested inclusivity, the X-Men became a space in superhero comics where those themes were readily available to explore. Of interest is the effect this diversifying of the group had on the aforementioned Jean Grey, a.k.a. Marvel Girl, who soon evolved from a meek telepath and budding telekinetic into a fully self-actualized if doomed (but oft revived) Phoenix, a feminist awakening echoing the shifts in women's political power of the time. Cyclops, whose eyes were a weaponized disability, now found himself confronted with his own (white cis male) privilege, unable to cope with his girlfriend's transformation into a cosmic god. And soon, the team was joined by intangible teenage genius Kitty Pryde, whose Jewishness was not metaphorical. Racial and cultural difference was no longer communicated exclusively in code.

With writer Chris Claremont at the helm, the series' popularity grew, spawning spin-offs such as *The New Mutants* (1983–91), about a younger and more specifically multicultural student body, and *X-Factor* (1986–98), which depicted the complicated lives of the aging original team. Joined by a host of talented cartoonists including John Byrne, Terry Austin, Paul Smith, Bill Sienkewicz, Art Adams, Walt Simonson, and John Romita Jr., as well as influential editors and writers Louise Simonson and Ann Nocenti, the creative team built an entire X-world, with few connections to the larger Marvel Universe. The one constant: the X-Men were hated and feared because they were different, and they had to deal with that, as well their fellow teammates and their differences, all the time. While mutancy is the primary factor in bringing these collectives together, the X-gene is not always present: in the building of the world, Claremont and company introduced defective clones, rebellious aliens, and ambivalent supernatural entities into the ranks. Feeling different was enough to make one identify and bond with other "others," a supposition that began to suggest, if not actualize, the inclusion of sexuality into this constellation of differences. Reading old issues of X-Men from the first Claremont era (1975–91), it is clear that there is a queer subtext to many of the relations of the characters, including but not limited to Cypher and Warlock's techno-organic merging into a single being in *The New Mutants* and the long-term relationship of villainesses Mystique and Destiny. Not-so-subtle hints lead to a prevalent fandom head canon surrounding the relationships of Kitty and Magik, Storm and Phoenix, Kitty and Storm, Storm and Rogue, and Storm in general, particularly when she trades in her flowing goddess gear for a Mohawk and leather jeans, thereby taking on some of the iconic cultural accoutrements of butch lesbian identity. But like race before it, homosexuality in the era of the Comics Code was unrepresentable, even if the culture wars of the 1980s colored all the X-Men's exploits with a queer tinge.

The success of the comic reached a high point in 1991, when a relaunched *X-Men* #1 by Claremont and artist Jim Lee sold enough copies to become the *Guinness Book of World Records* "Best Selling Comic Book of All Time." In 1992, the animated hit *X-Men* premiered on Fox Kids, a cartoon that hewed closely to the story lines in the comics. The X-Men became increasingly baroque in this period, introducing characters such as Cajun thief Gambit, gun-toting Black time cop Bishop, and one-eyed, cyber-armed Cable (Cyclops's son from the future!), whose overstuffed backstories, overblown powers, and overadorned costumes festooned the steroidal übermenschen drawn by artists such as Lee, Wilce Portacio, and Rob Liefeld. This expanded mutant body of the 1990s suggested a shift from mutant-as-outcast to mutant-as-outlier, from picked-on wimp to aggrieved alpha. New teams were introduced to explore these bodily themes. The flamboyant *X-Force* (1991–2001), by Rob Liefeld and Fabian Nicieza, fetishized prosthetic cyborg limbs and other weaponized technological appendages attached to an androgynous muscularity that engorged both the male and female characters. The counter to this was the disturbing, grunge-inflected *Generation X* (1994–2001), by Scott Lobdell and Chris Bachalo, a meditation on the body's lack of integrity. Characters such as Chamber, Husk, and Skin all pointed to body-as-container, a form that could explode, rip, and stretch, mostly uncontrollably. The protagonist of both the animated series and *Generation X* was Jubilee, a Chinese American teenage "mall rat" who commented on these excesses of the Clinton years with a sassy, sour jouissance that exploded from her word balloons just like the nuclear fireworks that exploded from her hands.

And that's also when the queer characters started to appear, beginning in 1992 with the Quebecois mutant Northstar's declaration, "I am gay!" in another spin-off book, *Alpha Flight* (1983–94), about Canadian superheroes. Northstar would later join the X-Men, and in 2004, he married his partner, the African American human Kyle (in *Astonishing X-Men* #51, written by Marjorie Liu). The ceremony was attended by mutants from both sides of the Canada–United States border, but because their marriage was not legal in the US at that time, Northstar then faced deportation, putting a strain on the couple. During this period, several new queer characters were introduced, such as the lizard boy Anole, the gem-skinned daughter of hip-hop producers Bling, and the bisexual, mixed-race miscreant Daken. But what is most striking is that queerness was always with the X-Men, and with the desublimation of queer desire, readers of the various books saw a series of comings out: Karma from *The New Mutants*, always asexual before, became a lesbian, and Rictor and Shatterstar, from *X-Force*, whose relationship was always confusingly close in that book, became boyfriends in a relaunched *X-Factor* (2005–13). Most surprisingly, Iceman, from the original team, was outed by telepathic Jean Grey, in *All-New X-Men* #40 (2015), by Brian Michael Bendis and Mahmud Asrar. With this, the character's five decades of failed heterosexual relationships were retconned, or rewritten from the perspective of the present, into a repressed homosexuality. Iceman has since starred in solo titles, the first gay Marvel Comics superhero to headline an ongoing series (2017–18). Iceman's latest self-titled miniseries (2018–19), also by Sina Grace, introduced nonbinary mutant Madin, along with the first drag queen mutant, Shade (who has since inspired real-life drag queens, such as *RuPaul's Drag Race*'s Nina Bonina Brown, to dress up as her). In the relaunched *Generation X* of 2017, by Christina Strain and Amilcar Pinna, Jubilee, now a single mom, becomes the teacher of a mostly queer-identified group of Generation Z students at the Xavier Institute, a cohort whose powers had little use in combat but served as great metaphors for sexuality, intimacy, coming out, and growing up.

We, however, may have outgrown the need for a "mutant metaphor," as survival for minoritarian subjects is now at odds with such coding, the struggle having morphed into a crisis of political representation. In the movie *Deadpool 2*, the eponymous lead (first appearance: *New Mutants* #98, 1991) spits out a line about the datedness of this "metaphor for civil rights." Deadpool was right, though not for the reasons he might think. It is not because "civil rights" is resolved but because of

the urgency we now have in confronting the racism of a system that elected a white supremacist demagogue president, backed by an evangelical cartoon villain vice president straight out of the classic graphic novel *X-Men: God Loves, Man Kills* (1982). While the powers the mutants possess still carry metaphorical potential, the metaphorical "identity" has become as repressive as identity in the real world. The X-Men's mutations have become a metonym for difference, part of the larger potential of "otherness." The metaphor served when we couldn't talk about ourselves.

So . . . what do we mean when we say "X-Men"? The *X* is a signifier without signified, an always incomplete sign that complicates, and potentially negates, whatever it's attached to. The X-Men could be read as "not men." Surely, one of their greatest contributions has been women characters: Storm, Rogue, Emma Frost, and Psylocke among the most popular in contemporary fandom. But the *X* also stands in for the shifting political positions of these "not men" within a system that continually attempts to subjugate, control, and kill them. This has resulted in a destabilization of the fundamental binary of comics: hero versus villain. Magneto, whose separatism marked him as evil when he first appeared, now finds his radicalism linked to his history as a Holocaust survivor and has since become an ambivalent protagonist. This deconstruction has gone both ways, with "heroes" such as Phoenix, Cyclops, and Professor X all committing a variety of atrocities, while long-term bad guys like Mystique and Sabertooth have saved the day more than once. Perhaps this collapse of moral absolutism is most clearly articulated in the claw-brandishing antihero Wolverine. With his endless capacity to heal, Wolverine nonetheless carries the emotional wounds of mutant-phobia under his skin, and his reproduction of trauma, enacted through homicide, is instrumental in the project of deconstructing the very idea of the superhero. Like Wolverine's body, which gets taken apart only to regrow, deconstruction continues to be one of the X-Men's most enduring legacies.

The 2019 "X-Men Disassembled" story line in *The Uncanny X-Men* deconstructs the mutant as a stand-in for the oppressed when a messiah called X-Man uses his powers to erase organized religion, resurrect extinct species, and create world peace. Produced collaboratively by writers Ed Brisson, Kelly Thompson, and Matthew Rosenberg and artists Mahmud Asrar, Adriano Di Benedetto, Yildiray Cinar, R. B. Silva, Rochelle Rosenberg, and Pere Perez, the collective talent behind this comic book making echoes its enormous cast, co-led by Jean Grey, Storm, and Armor, who represents a bloc of dissident X-kids. The would-be savior X-Man is Nate Grey, Jean's omnipotent adult son from an alternate timeline; the action is framed by a philosophical debate between mother and son about the ethics of psychically eradicating prejudice. In the end, X-Man concludes the X-Men are a crucial part of the cycle of oppression and blasts them into oblivion—or so it seems! Announcements accompanying this event tease the "Age of X-Man" (2019), a slew of new titles taking place in a utopian universe where mutants run a perfect world. Orwell's *1984* (1949), referenced in the "Days of Future Past" story line (*The Uncanny X-Men* #141–42, 1981), is set aside for Huxley's *Brave New World* (1929). The makers of X-Men are set to reimagine these posthuman others as empowered world leaders.

And as I am writing this, Wolverine is also going through his umpteenth resurrection in current continuity, after spending a few years dead. In tracing what *X-Men* could mean as a "keyword," I have looked at five decades of storytelling, character development, and world-building, and yet like the *X* in the name, I find it difficult to fix. The X-Men are an uncanny entanglement, contiguous with the exhausting debates around race and racism that characterize our time. Society demands oppression, and the X-Men, whether victims or perpetrators, will die again and again. For now, it appears the X-Men will keep coming back, but I wish they didn't have to.

55

Zine

Mimi Thi Nguyen

Let us start with a succinct definition of *zine* from Janice Radway, echoed across the academic literature: "Until zines emerged as digital forms, they were generally defined as handmade, noncommercial, irregularly issued, small-run, paper publications circulated by individuals participating in alternative, special-interest communities" (2011, 140). From here, the familiar story of the zine unfolds: the term *zine* is a recent derivation of *fanzine*, itself coined in the 1930s to refer to self-published magazines of science fiction, punks in the 1970s adopted the form to create an alternative infrastructure for a global phenomenon, and (some) girls and young women in the 1990s used zines to build a revolution of some kind—what kind exactly remains up for debate—upon a foundation of emotional intimacy and immediacy. Indeed, in academic studies and adjacent histories, the zine is most often heralded as a material form for the marginalized, as a medium of self-expression (without editors, advertisers, or censors) made through accessible means (using low-cost technologies of reproduction) in search of community (rather than audience) and infused with the tempo of immediacy, even urgency. These qualities of self-expression and community building are common themes for zine study, as found in Stephen Duncombe's *Notes from Underground* (1997), the first academic monograph about zines and "alternative culture": "The tension in the punk scene between the individual and the community, between freedom and

rules, is a microcosm of the tension that exists within all the networked communities of the zine scene. Zines are profoundly personal expressions, yet as a medium of participatory communication they depend upon and help create community" (65).

Zines are also often narrated either as continuation, extending or building upon preexisting print formats from earlier periods, or as eruption, expressively bursting forth with oppositional energies. In the former, zines are given a genealogy through continuity of form. From the pamphlet wars of seventeenth-century England between the Diggers and Levelers, both political movements committed to popular sovereignty; to the French Revolution and the wide circulation of anonymous or multiple-authored tracts arguing against the "unnatural" tyranny of the aristocracy; to the 1930s and the self-publication of science fiction fanzines in an era of censorship in the name of "decency"; to the early twentieth-century avant-garde movements of futurists, Dadaists, surrealists, and Situationists and their competing, clashing manifestoes; and to the late 1960s, when mimeographed feminist manifestos decried the gender politics of revolutionary discourses that privileged a "generic" masculine revolutionary. Across these varied historical and aesthetic movements, the zine is often described as a living artifact that continues to articulate the distinction between a radical egalitarianism and "the establishment." In nearly all these movements, small-scale self-publication challenged the supposed universalism of democratic cultural formations through this alternative form of public address. Thus it is at the same time that the zine is described through eruption—not in its form but by virtue of its content. Through the pamphlet, the broadside, the tract, the fanzine, the manifesto, anarchists, revolutionaries, "losers" (Duncombe 1997), or marginalized subcultures (nerds, punks, or teenage girls) express at times oppositional opinions, arguments, and feelings (none of these be-ing distinct bodies) that have no forum in "dominant" cultures or mainstream publications. It is as such, as Radway observes so well, that zines are described as "po-litical because it challenges established hierarchies of forms and voices, the selection of those who are at-tended to as legitimate, authorized denizens of the ma-jor institutions that comprise contemporary knowledge production" (2011, 145). This form is often narrated then as facilitating a nonalienated relation to labor (thus it is a do-it-yourself endeavor) that often spills into or implies otherwise a nonalienated, or at least *less* alienated, relation to self and to others (Gunder-loy 1990; Duncombe 1997). For instance, Mary Celeste Kearney and Elke Zobl connect the girl zine to life writ-ing, whether through words or comics, as at least semi-autobiographical work (Kearney 2006; Schilt 2003; Zobl 2004). Because of this sensibility of nonalienation (real or imagined or somewhere in between), zines are often assigned a temporality of immediacy; these missives capture a moment in time and are an aid for commu-nion with others, as soon as possible. *Revolution, Girl-Style Now*, as it were (Piepmeier 2009).

Zines are thus invoked as minor objects taken to diagnose certain normative conditions, whether the technologies and conditions for publicity, the mate-rial or felt experience of outsiderness, the failures of politics as usual, the exigencies of girlhood, whatever (Nguyen 2012). But what else can be said about zines, either besides or apart from the usual story? How and why do concepts of self-expression and community so often appear as transparent social goods through this particular medium? How do we think about the tempo-rality of zines decades later? Consider the aesthetics of intimacy and its forms, bringing together the histories of expressive interiority with the particularity of the zine as a rhetorical and aesthetic medium for publicity.

The form itself, often photocopied or printed half-sized sheets of paper or smaller, creates that sense of intimacy through scale and material. Whether comic or mani-festo (as examples of what might be found inside), genre conventions and boundaries might be stretched or dis-carded, and at the same time, an aesthetic of authentic-ity or accessibility might cohere yet another structure of affective expectation. As one zine writer, for instance, related to Alison Piepmeier in her study of girl zines, "I really hated when people would be like, 'Oh, it's all just girls in their bedrooms, sprawled out writing in their diaries, and then they'll send them to each other.' I'm like, that's an aesthetic choice. You're still construct-ing something when it looks like a diary entry. I wasn't photocopying my diary, or if I was, it was for a specific reason." At the same time, she asserted, "I'm creating this kind of media that's literally from my most sacred place to somebody else's most sacred place" (2009, 90). In such a fantasy of unmediated intimacy—with one-self, with others—we might observe after Lauren Berlant the "unfinished business" of sentimentality, the prem-ise of "a world of strangers who would be emotionally literate in each other's experience of power, intimacy, desire, and discontent, with all that entails" (2008, 5). Zines, as Duncombe argues, personalize politics—what this means, however, is not guaranteed (1997, 28).

Thus we would do well to also reconsider what Mi-randa Joseph calls *the romance of community*. What does it mean, exactly, to build community? Just as intimacy (with its associations to *real* experience) is often counterposed to theory, community (as *real* communion) is often counterposed to capital (Joseph 2002). The concept of community building often nar-rates the exclusion of populations from public and political cultures, especially when and where an idea of the universal emerges; at the same time, as Janet Lyon argues in her study of the manifesto, the form might also reproduce a dichotomy, claiming a "we" as an often-undifferentiated population (Duncombe's "freaks, geeks, nerds and losers," for instance, or "girl culture") even as the idea of a coherent "we" is being contested (1999). Thus is community central to the rhetorical forms—academic and otherwise—that invoke the zine as a foundation or a network, but this seeming self-evidence bears further critique (Nguyen 2012). It would be useful, for instance, to pay attention to how communities and publics are "overdetermined and also organized differently" through their forms of address (Berlant 2008, 8). Lauren Berlant's work on intimate publics and the fantasies of collectivity that adhere to them through sentimental modes, for instance, might be brought to bear upon claims of emotional accessibility and communion. How might we otherwise perceive the temporality of the zine, the relation between an aesthetics of intimacy and an aesthetics of urgency? What is the push of the "here" and the "now" that generates the address?

It is also important to consider that we do much more with zines than make them or read them. They are material objects too, and not only do we make them, but we scan them, sell them, distribute them, collect them, donate them, categorize them, make examples of them, copy them (in multiple senses of the word), teach them, lose them (to others who never return them), and destroy them. How else, then, might we consider the zine and its aesthetic of immediacy and those practices that extend their lives into the present or future?

In the years since its most proliferate era—after personal computers but before digital media—the zine as a material object has had its conditions of possibility changed dramatically. In the 1990s, the largest distributor of zines was Tower Records, mainstreaming the zine form for a moment, and during that time, some zines reached print runs in the thousands; in 2006, Tower Records declared bankruptcy and closed all its retail locations throughout the United States. Since the 1990s, other independent distributors—of records and comics as well as zines—have closed or struggled. Yet despite the passing of the copy machine into relative obscurity (including the closure of hundreds of independent copy stores, the transformation of thousands of twenty-four-hour Kinko's into daytime FedEx Offices, and increased security to remaining photocopiers, rendering commercial copy scams nearly impossible) or because of it (thus enhancing their auratic qualities), zines became a much-heralded medium for self-expression or communication—an analog form in a digital age. Its reputation for authenticity, even ground-up democracy, has been seized upon by "cutting-edge" brands (selling everything from clothes or a lifestyle concept to trend forecasting or vague promises of "innovation"), which publish glossy publications miming the aesthetic of self-expression and community for guerilla or viral (or otherwise buzzwordy) marketing. Zines are taught in workshops and classrooms as a craft activity or creative assignment—a substitute for the research paper, for instance. Since the 1990s, zine fests have been organized in Chicago, Los Angeles, and New York City, as well as in smaller locales throughout the country. Such fests reflect changes in independent publishing, including the financial nonviability of print; for instance, *Maximumrocknroll*—the longest regularly published punk print magazine since 1984—ended its run in 2019. In this era, writers and artists printing small runs for zine fests or limited distribution is more feasible than submission to alternative press or underground magazines that no longer exist or to digital platforms that do not offer compensation.

Furthermore, zines are now amassing in library collections and institutional archives, academic studies and popular press anthologies republish images and passages alongside close readings and remembrances, and papers are scanned, compressed, reformatted, re-edited, uploaded, remixed, downloaded, and shared on public digital platforms—the conditions for encountering zines, then, are radically changed (Freeman 2010; Eichhorn 2010; Kumbier 2014). As zines are increasingly subject to archival and other forms of preservation, J. B. Brager and Jami Sailor in *Archiving the Underground* issue a useful caution. First published in 2011, *Archiving the Underground*, a zine exploring the tensions that accompany "the academic project of archiving and 'academicizing' the subcultural practices in which we [zinesters] participate," included interviews with several scholars and archivists (some based in universities and some not) such as Lisa Darms, archivist from the Fales Library at New York University; Adela Licona, author of *Zines in Third Space: Radical Cooperation and Borderlands Rhetoric*; Alison Piepmeier, author of *Girl Zines: Making Media, Doing Feminism*; and Milo Miller from the nonaffiliated Queer Zine Archive Project. Brager and Sailor put to them questions about the codification of a canon, concerns about the misrepresentation and appropriation of zines and other underground cultures, and the relationship between academics, archivists, and artists and cultural producers. Together, Brager and Sailor write, "Like a whispered secret, the truths that zines contain may be ephemeral. They shift and change and from issue to issue, like the identities, situations and addresses of their creators. The danger in archiving individual issues in zines is that it cements a particular whisper. And the danger of publishing a book about zines is that you are projecting that whisper, far beyond its original and perhaps intended audience" (2011).

Zine study is often narrowly located in the moment of publication, stretched out through an insistently presentist premise decades later. Thus some zine makers are inscribing "DO NOT ARCHIVE" in their zines to combat both the institutionalization of their output as well as its temporal seizure. Such concerns also inform their digitization; Peipmeier, in her study of "girl zines," cites a former zinester who observes of her own efforts to take old zines offline: "Zines are tangible, are material. The writing is contained in an object that physically ages. Ink fades. Paper yellows. Holding a zine from even just ten years ago feels like holding a historical document. It's easier to place it, the writing inside, and the person who wrote it, in a particular moment in time, to contextualize it. Words appearing on a computer screen, even if they are date-stamped, seem the opposite: decontextualized, ahistorical, atemporal" (2009, 16). Also of concern is how zine collections are amassed (through donation or solicitation), how permissions—if any—are sought from the original creators, and how collections then come to institutionalize partial histories or then aim to identify and "correct" archival absences. As someone who is herself "collected" and who has an ambivalent-to-hostile relationship to being so, I have asked elsewhere, To what ends is the minor object—like the zine—recruited beyond what documentation, preservation, and circulation claim to do, especially as an object identified as the "correction" or resolution to a crisis of knowledge production (Nguyen 2015)? Janice Radway proposes that zines cannot be read only through their immediate moment and their "short-term futures," as if possessed of "half-lives"; instead, she pursues a longitudinal study of zines and their *afterlives*. Toward this end, she argues, "It will be critical to understand how zines functioned over time as aesthetic, rhetorical, and social technologies for making a range of things happen" (2011, 148).

There is still much to consider with regard to zine aesthetics (which vary widely, after all), their irregular serial and temporal rhythms (months, even years might go by between issues), and institutional or informal collection and classification apart from or alongside other print media—zines, newsletters, flyers, and so on—as "disposable" forms. Their study might also inform genealogies of the aesthetic and ideological properties of authenticity, improvisation, spontaneity, and community (such as the fest or the network; Relyea 2013). Finally, these creative works might be hailed as a revolt against former modes of capitalist production (rationalization, standardization, systematization, and bureaucracy) while eliding or accepting as a matter of course the dangers implicit or impending in reorganizing or regularizing modes of short-term, more varied, and autonomous labor, even the labor of love.

Appendix

CAPITALISM

Figure A.1. Art Young, "Capitalism," *Good Morning*, January 1, 1920. See *Cartoon*.

Figure A.2. Naji al-Ali, October 1980. See *Cartoon*.

Figure A.3. Marko introduces Alana. Brian K. Vaughan (w) and Fiona Staples (a), *Saga*, vol. 2 (2012). See *Reader*.

Figure A.4. Thomas Nast, "The Ignorant Vote—Honors Are Easy," *Harper's Weekly*, December 9, 1876. See *Cartoon* and *Race*.

Figure A.5. Page 57, *Black Orchid*, by Neil Gaiman and Dave McKean. Copyright DC Comics, 1991. See *Sequence*.

References

Abel, Jessica. 2008. *La Perdida*. New York: Pantheon.

Abrirached, Zeina. 2012. *A Game for Swallows: To Die, to Leave, to Return*. Minneapolis: Graphic Universe.

Acham, Christine. 2004. *Revolution Televised: Prime Time and the Struggle for Black Power*. Minneapolis: University of Minnesota Press.

Adams, Mitchell. 2019. "The Secret Commercial Identity of Superheroes: Protecting the Superhero Symbol." In *The Superhero Symbol: Media, Culture, and Politics*, edited by Liam Burke, Ian Gordon, and Angela Ndalianis, 89–104. New Brunswick, NJ: Rutgers University Press.

Adkins, Lisa, and Maryanne Dever. 2017. "Archives and New Modes of Feminist Research." *Australian Feminist Studies* 32, no. 91–92, 1–4.

Ahmed, Sara. 2004. *The Cultural Politics of Emotion*. Edinburgh: Edinburgh University Press.

———. 2006. *Queer Phenomenology: Orientations, Objects, Others*. Durham, NC: Duke University Press.

al-Ali, Naji. 2009. *A Child in Palestine: The Cartoons of Naji al-Ali*. New York: Verso Books.

Alaniz, José. 2014. *Death, Disability, and the Superhero: The Silver Age and Beyond*. Jackson: University Press of Mississippi.

———. 2016. "Standing Orders: Oracle, Disability and Retconning." In *Disability in Comic Books and Graphic Narratives*, edited by Chris Foss, Jonathan Gray, and Zach Walen, 59–79. London: Palgrave.

Alcaraz, Lalo. 2004. *La Cucaracha*. Kansas City, MI: Andrews McMeel.

Aldama, Frederick Luis. 2009. *Your Brain on Latino Comics: From Gus Arriola to Los Bros Hernandez*. Austin: University of Texas Press.

———, ed. 2010. *Multicultural Comics: From Zap to Blue Beetle*. Austin: University of Texas Press.

———. 2016. *Latinx Comic Book Storytelling: An Odyssey by Interview*. San Diego: Hyperbole.

———. 2017. *Latinx Superheroes in Mainstream Comics*. Tucson: University of Arizona Press.

———, ed. 2018a. *Comics Studies Here and Now*. New York: Routledge.

———, ed. 2018b. *Tales from la Vida: A Latinx Comics Anthology*. Columbus: Ohio State University Press.

Aldama, Frederick Luis, and Christopher González, eds. 2016. *Graphic Borders: Latino Comic Books Past, Present, and Future*. Austin: University of Texas Press.

Allen, Graham. 2000. *Intertextuality*. New York: Routledge.

Allen, Henry. 1972. "Horror Comics from the '50s Are Alive! (Choke!): Horror Comics Are Alive!" *Washington Post*, September 24, 1972, F1.

Allen, Todd. 2007. *The Economics of Web Comics: A Study in Converting Content to Revenue*. Self-published.

Alleyne, Sonia. 2003. "A Superhero's Story." *Black Enterprise* 34, no. 1, 107.

Andrae, Thomas. 1987. "From Menace to Messiah: The History and Historicity of Superman." In *American Media and Mass Culture: Left Perspectives*, edited by Donald Lazure, 124–38. Berkeley: University of California Press.

Andreyko, Marc, Sarah Gaydos, and Jamie S. Rich. 2017. *Love Is Love*. New York: DC Comics.

Arjana, Sophia Rose. 2018. *Veiled Superheroes: Islam, Feminism, and Popular Culture*. New York: Lexington.

Arnaudo, Marco. 2013. *The Myth of the Superhero*. Baltimore: Johns Hopkins University Press.

Ashby, LeRoy. 2012. *With Amusement for All: A History of American Popular Culture since 1830*. Lexington: University of Kentucky Press.

Ashcraft, Brian, and Luke Plunkett. 2014. *Cosplay World*. New York: Prestel.

Atanasoski, Neda. 2013. *Humanitarian Violence: The U.S. Deployment of Diversity*. Minneapolis: University of Minnesota Press.

Ault, Donald. 1997. "'Cutting Up' Again: Lacan on Barks on Lacan." *Indy Magazine* 17:30–33.

———. 2000. "'Cutting Up' Again Part II: Lacan on Barks on Lacan." In *Comics and Culture: Analytical and Theoretical Approaches to Comics*, edited by Anne Magnussen and

Hans-Christian Christiansen, 123–40. Copenhagen: Museum Tusculanum Press.

———. 2009. "Imagetextuality: 'Cutting Up' Again, Pt. III." *ImageTexT: Interdisciplinary Comics Studies* 1, no. 1 (Spring). http://imagetext.english.ufl.edu.

Avery, Tara, and Jeanne Thorton, eds. 2018. *We're Still Here: An All-Trans Comics Anthology*. Dana Point, CA: Stacked Deck.

Ayaka, Carolene, and Ian Hagues, eds. 2018. *Representing Multiculturalism in Comics and Graphic Novels*. New York: Routledge.

Bacon-Smith, Camille. 1991. *Enterprising Women: Television Fandom and the Creation of Popular Myth*. Philadelphia: University of Pennsylvania Press.

Baetens, Jan, and Hugo Frey. 2015. *The Graphic Novel: An Introduction*. Cambridge: Cambridge University Press.

Baetens, Jan, Hugo Frey, and Stephen Tabachnik, eds. 2018. *The Cambridge Companion to the History of the Graphic Novel*. Cambridge: Cambridge University Press.

Bahng, Aimee. 2018. *Migrant Futures: Decolonizing Speculation in Financial Times*. Durham, NC: Duke University Press.

Bainbridge, Jason, and Craig Norris. 2013. "Posthuman Drag: Understanding Cosplay as Social Networking in a Material Culture." *Intersections: Gender and Sexuality in Asia and the Pacific* 32. http://intersections.anu.edu.au.

Bakhtin, Mikhail. (1984) 1997. *Problems of Dostoevsky's Poetics*. Minneapolis: University of Minnesota Press.

Banta, Martha. 2003. *Barbaric Intercourse: Caricature and the Culture of Conduct, 1841–1936*. Chicago: University of Chicago Press.

Barker, Deborah E., and Kathryn McKee. 2011. "Introduction: The Southern Imaginary." In *American Cinema and the Southern Imaginary*, edited by Deborah E. Barker and Kathryn McKee, 1–23. Athens: University of Georgia Press.

Barry, Lynda. 2005. *One Hundred Demons*. Seattle: Sasquatch.

———. 2008. Introduction to *The Best American Comics*, edited by Lynda Barry, xi–xx. Boston: Houghton Mifflin.

Barthes, Roland. (1967) 2001. "The Death of the Author." In *The Norton Anthology of Theory and Criticism*, edited by Vincent B. Leitch, 1466–70. New York: Norton.

———. 1975. *The Pleasure of the Text*. Translated by Richard Miller. New York: Hill and Wang.

Barzilai, Maya. 2016. *Golem: Modern Wars and Their Monsters*. New York: New York University Press.

Baudry, Julien. 2018. "Paradoxes of Innovation in French Digital Comics." *Comics Grid: Journal of Comics Scholarship* 8, no. 1. https://comicsgrid.com.

Bazin, André. 1967. "The Evolution of the Language of Cinema." Translated by Hugh Gray. In *What Is Cinema?*, vol. 1, edited by Hugh Gray, 23–40. Berkeley: University of California Press.

Beaty, Bart. 2005. *Fredric Wertham and the Critique of Mass Culture*. Jackson: University Press of Mississippi.

———. 2012. *Comics versus Art*. Toronto: University of Toronto Press.

Beaty, Bart, and Benjamin Woo. 2016. *The Greatest Comic Book of All Time: Symbolic Capital and the Field of American Comic Books*. New York: Palgrave Macmillan.

Beaty, Bart, Benjamin Woo, and Nick Sousanis. n.d. What Were Comics? Accessed July 30, 2018. www.whatwerecomics.com.

Bechdel, Alison. 1998. *The Indelible Alison Bechdel: Confessions, Comix, and Miscellaneous Dykes to Watch Out For*. New York: Firebrand.

———. 2007. *Fun Home: A Family Tragicomic*. New York: Houghton Mifflin.

Beerbohm, Robert L. 1999. "Secret Origins of the Direct Market, Part One." *Comic Artist* 6 (Fall): 80–91.

———. 2000. "Secret Origins of the Direct Market, Part 2: Phil Seuling and the Undergrounds Emerge." *Comic Book Artist* 1, no. 7 (February): 116–25.

Benton, Mike. 1989. *The Comic Book in America: An Illustrated History*. Dallas: Taylor.

———. 1992. *Superhero Comics of the Golden Age: The Illustrated History*. Dallas: Taylor.

Berger, A. A. 1974. *The Comic-Stripped American: What Dick Tracy, Blondie, Daddy Warbucks, and Charlie Brown Tell Us about Ourselves*. Baltimore: Penguin.

Berlant, Lauren. 2008. *Female Complaint: The Unfinished Business of Sentimentality in American Culture*. Durham, NC: Duke University Press.

Berlatsky, Noah. 2015. *Wonder Woman: Bondage and Feminism in the Marston/Peter Comics, 1941–1948*. New Brunswick, NJ: Rutgers University Press.

Berman, Margaret Fink. 2010. "Imagining an Idiosyncratic Belonging: Representing Disability in Chris Ware's *Building Stories*." In *The Comics of Chris Ware: Drawing Is a Way of Thinking*, edited by David M. Ball and Martha B. Kuhlman, 191–205. Jackson: University Press of Mississippi.

Bessette, Jean. 2017. *Retroactivism in the Lesbian Archives: Composing Pasts and Futures*. Carbondale: Southern Illinois University Press.

Bibler, Michael. 2016. "Introduction: Smash the Mason-Dixon! or, Manifesting the Southern United States." *PMLA* 131, no. 1, 153–56.

Biskind, Peter. 1999. *Easy Riders, Raging Bulls: How the Sex-Drugs-and-Rock 'n' Roll Generation Saved Hollywood*. New York: Simon and Schuster.

Blackbeard, Bill, and Martin Williams, eds. 1977. *The Smithsonian Collection of Newspaper Comics*. Washington, DC: Smithsonian Institution Press.

Blackwell, Maylei. 2017. "Indigeneity." In *Keywords in Latina/o Studies*, 100–105. New York: New York University Press.

Blood Syndicate. 1994. "Lair of the White Roach" #15. Ivan Velez Jr. (w.), J. H. Williams III (p.). New York: DC Comics.

Blouin, Francis X., and William G. Rosenberg. 2011. *Processing the Past: Changing Authorities in History and the Archives*. New York: Oxford University Press.

Boggs, Carl, and Tom Pollard, eds. 2007. *The Hollywood War Machine: US Militarism and Popular Culture*. New York: Paradigm.

Bolling, Ben, and Matthew J. Smith, eds. 2014. *It Happens at Comic-Con: Ethnographic Essays on a Pop Culture Phenomenon*. Jefferson, NC: McFarland.

Bolter, Jay David, and Richard Grusin. 1999. *Remediation: Understanding New Media*. Cambridge: MIT Press.

Booth, Paul. 2015. *Playing Fans: Negotiating Fandom and Media in the Digital Age*. Iowa City: University of Iowa Press.

Bowden, Charles, and Alice Leora Briggs. 2010. *Dreamland: The Way Out of Juárez*. Austin: University of Texas Press.

Boyer, Jack. 1953. "Kids Quiz: What Our Younger Generation Thinks." *Honolulu Advertiser*, August 9, 1953, 13.

Brager, J. B., and Jami Sailor. 2011. *Archiving the Underground* #1. Self-published.

Brainard, Joe. 2008. *The Nancy Book*. Edited by Lisa Pearson and Ron Padgett. Los Angeles: Siglio.

Brakhage, Stan. 1976. "Metaphors on Vision." Special issue, *Film Culture* 30 (Fall).

Bramlett, Frank. 2016. "Comics and Linguistics." In *Routledge Companion to Comics*, edited by Frank Bramlett, Roy T. Cook, and Aaron Meskin, 380–89. New York: Routledge.

———. 2018. "Linguistic Discourse in Web Comics: Extending Conversation and Narrative into Alt-Text and Hidden Comics." In *The Language of Popular Culture*, edited by Valentin Werner, 72–91. New York: Routledge.

Bramlett, Frank, Roy T. Cook, and Aaron Meskin, eds. 2017. *The Routledge Companion to Comics*. New York: Routledge.

Bravo, Sophia. n.d. "Whitewashing vs. Racebending and the Politics of Race and Cosplay." Worship the Fandom. Accessed May 12, 2018. www.worshipthefandom.com.

Brienza, Casey. 2016. *Manga in America: Transnational Book Publishing and the Domestication of Japanese Comics*. New York: Bloomsbury Academic.

Brienza, Casey, and Paddy Johnston, eds. 2016. *Cultures of Comics Work*. New York: Palgrave Macmillan.

Broadnax, Jamie. 2015. "#28DaysOfBlackCosplay: More Than Just a Hashtag." Black Girl Nerds, February 5, 2015. https://blackgirlnerds.com.

Brock, Nettie A. 2017. "The Everyday Disney Side: Disneybounding and Casual Cosplay." *Journal of Fandom Studies* 5, no. 3 (September): 301–15. https://doi.org/10.1386/jfs.5.3.301_1.

Brown, Chester. 2003. *Louis Reil: A Comic-Strip Biography*. Montreal: Drawn & Quarterly.

Brown, Jeffrey A. 1999. "Comic Book Masculinity and the New Black Superhero." *African American Review* 33, no. 1, 25–42.

———. 2001. *Black Superheroes, Milestone Comics, and Their Fans*. Jackson: University Press of Mississippi.

———. 2011. "Supermoms? Maternity and the Monstrous-Feminine in Superhero Comics." *Journal of Graphic Novels and Comics* 2, no. 1, 77–87.

Brunetti, Ivan. 2011. *Cartooning: Philosophy and Practice*. New Haven, CT: Yale University Press.

Bruno, Michael. n.d. "Cosplay: The Illegitimate Child of SF Masquerades." Millennium Costumers Guild. Accessed March 26, 2015. http://millenniumcg.tripod.com.

Bruns, Axel. 2008. *Blogs, Wikipedia, Second Life, and Beyond: From Production to Produsage*. New York: Peter Lang.

Buell, Lawrence. 2014. *The Dream of the Great American Novel*. Cambridge: Harvard University Press.

Bui, Thi. 2017. *The Best We Could Do*. New York: Abrams ComicArts.

Bukatman, Scott. 2003. *Matters of Gravity: Special Effects and Supermen in the 20th Century*. Durham, NC: Duke University Press.

———. 2016. *Hellboy's World: Comics and Monsters on the Margins*. Berkeley: University of California Press.

Burke, Liam. 2015. *The Comic Book Film Adaptation*. Jackson: University Press of Mississippi.

Butler, Judith. (1991) 2006. *Gender Trouble: Feminism and the Subversion of Identity*. New York: Routledge Classics.

———. 1993. "Imitation and Gender Insubordination." In *Lesbian and Gay Studies Reader*, ed. Henry Abelove, Michele Aina, and David Halperin, 307–20. New York: Routledge.

———. 1994. "Against Proper Objects." *differences: A Journal of Feminist Cultural Studies* 6, no. 2–3: 1–26.

Campbell, Eddie. 2010. "Eddie Campbell's Graphic Novel Manifesto." *Don MacDonald* (blog). Accessed July 24, 2018. http://donmacdonald.com.

Campbell, James. 2017. *Experiencing William James: Belief in a Pluralistic World*. Charlottesville: University of Virginia Press.

Campbell, T. 2006. *A History of Webcomics: "The Golden Age": 1993–2005*. San Antonio: Antarctic.

Carrier, David. 2001. *The Aesthetics of Comics*. State College: Penn State University Press.

carrington, andré m. 2016. *Speculative Blackness: The Future of Race in Science Fiction*. Minneapolis: University of Minnesota Press.

———. 2018. "Desiring Blackness: A Queer Orientation to Marvel's Black Panther, 1998–2016." *American Literature* 90, no. 2, 221–50.

Carrión, Jorge, and Sagar Fornies. 2015. *Barcelona: Los vagabundos de la chatarra*. Barcelona: Norma.

Cendrowski, Mark, dir. 2013. *The Big Bang Theory*. Season 6, episode 13, "The Bakersfield Expedition." Aired January 10, 2013, on CBS. www.cbs.com.

Chaney, Michael. 2011a. "Animal Subjects of the Graphic Novels." *College Literature* 38, no. 3 (Summer): 129–49.

———. 2011b. *Graphic Subjects: Critical Essays on Autobiography and Graphic Novels*. Madison: University of Wisconsin Press.

———. 2017. "The Saga of the Animal as Visual Metaphor for Mixed-Race Identity in Comics." In *Animal Comics: Multispecies Storyworlds in Graphic Narratives*, edited by David Herman, 99–107. New York: Bloomsbury.

Chapman, Robyn. 2012. *Drawing Comics Lab: 52 Exercises on Characters, Panels, Storytelling, Publishing & Professional Practices*. London: Quarry Books.

Choo, Kukhee. 2008. "Girls Return Home: Portrayal of Femininity in Popular Japanese Girls' Manga and Anime Texts during the 1990s in *Hana Yori Dango* and *Fruits Basket*." *Women: A Cultural Review* 19, no. 3, 275–96.

Christiansen, Hans-Christian. 2000. "Comics and Film: A Narrative Perspective." In *Comics and Culture: Analytical and Theoretical Approaches to Comics*, edited by Anne Magnussen and Hans-Christian Christiansen, 107–21. Aarhus, Denmark: Museum Tusculanum Press.

Chute, Hillary L. 2008. "Comics as Literature? Reading Graphic Narrative." *PMLA* 123, no. 2 (March): 452–65.

———. 2010. *Graphic Women: Life Narrative and Contemporary Comics*. New York: Columbia University Press.

———. 2014. *Outside the Box: Interviews with Contemporary Cartoonists*. Chicago: University of Chicago Press.

———. 2015. "The Space of Graphic Narrative: Mapping Bodies, Feminism, and Form." In *Narrative Theory Unbound*, edited by Robyn Warhol and Susan S. Lanser, 194–209. Columbus: Ohio State University Press.

———. 2016. *Disaster Drawn: Visual Witness, Comics, and Documentary Form*. Cambridge: Belknap.

———. 2017. *Why Comics? From Underground to Everywhere*. New York: Harper.

Chute, Hillary L., and Marianne DeKoven. 2006. "Introduction: Graphic Narrative." *Modern Fiction Studies* 52, no. 4 (Winter): 767–82.

———. 2012. "Comic Books and Graphic Novels." In *The Cambridge Companion to Popular Fiction*, edited by David Glover and Scott McCracken, 175–95. Cambridge: Cambridge University Press.

Clarke, M. J. 2012. *Transmedia Television: New Trends in Network Serial Production*. London: Bloomsbury.

Clowes, Daniel. 2005. *Ice Haven*. New York: Pantheon.

Coates, Ta-Nehisi. 2015. *Between the World and Me*. New York: Spiegel & Grau.

———. 2016. *Black Panther: A Nation under Our Feet*. New York: Marvel.

Cocca, Carolyn. 2016. *Superwomen: Gender, Power, and Representation*. New York: Bloomsbury.

Cohen, Michael Mark. 2007. "'Cartooning Capitalism': Radical Cartooning and the Making of American Popular Radicalism in the Early Twentieth Century." *International Review of Social History* 52:35–58.

Cohn, Neil. 2010. "The Limits of Time and Transitions: Challenges to Theories of Sequential Image Comprehension." *Studies in Comics* 1, no. 1, 127–47.

Cohn, Neil, Ray Jackendoff, Phillip J. Holcomb, and Gina R. Kuperberg. 2014. "The Grammar of Visual Narrative: Neural Evidence for Constituent Structure in Sequential Image Comprehension." *Neuropsychologia* 6, no. 4, 63–70.

Comic Book Legal Defense Fund. n.d. "The Comics Code of 1954." Accessed November 19, 2020. http://cbldf.org.

Coogler, Ryan, dir. 2018. *Black Panther*. Los Angeles: Walt Disney Studios Motion Pictures.

Cooke, Jon B. 2019. *The Book of Weirdo*. San Francisco: Last Gasp.

Coover, Colleen. 2017. *Small Favors: The Definitive Girly Porno Collection*. Portland: Oni.

Coppa, Francesca. 2006. "A Brief History of Media Fandom." In *Fan Fiction and Fan Communities in the Age of the Internet: New Essays*, edited by Karen Hellekson and Kristina Busse, 41–59. Jefferson, NC: McFarland.

Cortez, Jamie. 2005. *Sexile: A Graphic Novel Biography of Adela Vazquez*. New York: Institute for Gay Men's Health.

Costello, Brannon. 2017. *Neon Visions: The Comics of Howard Chaykin*. Baton Rouge: Louisiana State University Press.

Costello, Brannon, and Qiana Whitted. 2012. Introduction to *Comics and the U.S. South*, edited by Brannon Costello and Qiana Whitted, vii–xvi. Jackson: University Press of Mississippi.

Couser, G. Thomas. 2018. "Is There a Body in This Text? Embodiment in Graphic Somatography." *a/b: Auto/Biography Studies* 33, no. 2, 347–73.

Cox, Christopher. 2018. "'Ms. Marvel,' Tumblr, and the Industrial Logics of Identity in Digital Spaces." *Transformative Works and Cultures* 27. https://journal.transformativeworks.org.

Crafton, Donald. 1993. *Before Mickey: The Animated Film, 1898–1928*. Chicago: University of Chicago Press.

Crane, Tristan, and Ted Naifa. 2004. *How Loathsome*. New York: Comics Lit.

Cremins, Brian. 2013. "Bodies, Transfigurations, and Bloodlust in Edie Fake's Graphic Novel *Gaylord Phoenix*." *Journal of Medical Humanities* 34, no. 2 (June): 301–13.

Crisis on Infinite Earths: Absolute Edition. 2005. Marv Wolfman (w.), George Perez (p.). New York: DC Comics.

Crist, Judith. 1948. "Horror in the Nursery." *Collier's*, March 29, 1948.

Culp, Jennifer. 2016. *Cosplay: Roleplaying for Fun and Profit*. New York: Rosen.

Cumberbatch, C. 2013. "I'm a Black Female Cosplayer and Some People Hate It." xoJane. Accessed February 14, 2017. www.xojane.com.

Cunningham, Sidney. 2018. "How the 'Non-duped' Pass: Gender Perception and Belonging in 'Postgender' Space." *TSQ: Transgender Studies Quarterly* 5, no. 1, 49–66.

Curtis, Neal. 2016. *Sovereignty and Superheroes*. Manchester: Manchester University Press.

Cutter, Martha J., and Cathy J. Schlund-Vials. 2018. Introduction to *Redrawing the Historical Past: History, Memory, and Multiethnic Graphic Novels*, edited by Martha J. Cutter and Cathy J. Schlund-Vials, 1–18. Athens: University of Georgia Press.

Cvetkovich, Ann. 2003. *An Archive of Feelings: Trauma, Sexuality, and Lesbian Public Cultures*. Durham, NC: Duke University Press.

———. 2008. "Drawing the Archive in Alison Bechdel's *Fun Home*." *WSQ: Women's Studies Quarterly* 36, nos. 1–2: 111–28.

———. 2012. *Depression: A Public Feeling*. Durham, NC: Duke University Press.

Czerwiec, M. K., Michael Green, Kimberly Myers, Susan Squier, Scott Smith, and Ian Williams. 2015. *Graphic Medicine Manifesto*. University Park: Penn State University Press.

Dainotto, Robert. 2017. "South by Chance: Southern Questions on the Global South." *Global South* 11, no. 2. https://doi.org/10.2979/globalsouth.11.2.03.

Daniels, Les. 2001. *Wonder Woman: The Complete History*. New York: Chronicle.

Danziger-Russell, Jacqueline. 2012. *Girls and Their Comics: Finding a Female Voice in Comic Book Narrative*. Lanham, MD: Scarecrow.

Darley, Lionel S. 1965. *Introduction to Bookbinding*. London: Faber and Faber.

Darms, Lisa, and Kate Eichhorn, eds. 2015. "Radical Archives." *Archive Journal* 5 (Fall). www.archivejournal.net.

Darnton, Robert. 1982. "What Is the History of Books?" *Dædalus* 111, no. 3, 65–83.

Darowski, Joseph J. 2014. *X-Men and the Mutant Metaphor: Race and Gender in the Comic Books*. Lanham, MD: Rowman & Littlefield.

Davis, Blair. 2017. "In Focus: *Watchmen*." *Cinema Journal* 56, no. 2 (Winter): 114–50.

Davis, Eleanor. 2017. *You & a Bike & a Road*. Toronto: Koyama.

Davis, LaRose. 2016. "Future Souths, Speculative Souths, and Southern Potentialities." *PMLA* 131, no. 1, 191–92.

Davis, Lennard J. 2013. "Constructing Normalcy." In *The Disability Studies Reader*, edited by Lennard J. Davis, 3–16. London: Taylor and Francis.

DeConnick, Kelly Sue, and Valentine De Landro. 2017. *Bitch Planet Book 2: President Bitch*. Portland: Image Comics.

De Falco, Tom. 2004. *Comics Creators on Spider-Man*. London: Titan.

DeGuzmán, María. 2017. "Latinx: ¡Estamos Aquí!, or Being 'Latinx' at UNC-Chapel Hill." *Cultural Dynamics* 29, no. 3, 214–30.

De Haven, Tom. 2010. *Our Hero: Superman on Earth*. New Haven, CT: Yale University Press.

Del Arroz, Jon. 2018. "What Is #Comicsgate?" *Jon Del Arroz* (blog), July 19, 2018. http://delarroz.com.

Denison, Rayna. 2007. "It's a Bird! It's a Plane! No, It's DVD! Superman, Smallville, and the Production (of) Melodrama." In *Film and Comic Books*, edited by Ian Gordon, Mark Jancovich, and Matthew P. McAllister, 160–79. Jackson: University Press of Mississippi.

Denning, Michael. 1987. *Mechanic Accents: Dime Novels and Working-Class Culture in America*. New York: Verso.

Derrida, Jacques. 1996. *Archive Fever: A Freudian Impression*. Translated by Eric Prenowitz. Chicago: University of Chicago Press.

Díaz, Junot. 2007. *The Brief Wondrous Life of Oscar Wao*. New York: Riverhead.

DiPaolo, Marc. 2011. *War, Politics, and Superheroes: Ethics and Propaganda in Comics and Film*. New York: McFarland.

———, ed. 2018. *Working-Class Comic Book Heroes: Class Conflict and Populist Politics in Comics*. Jackson: University Press of Mississippi.

Di Ricco, Massimo. 2015. "Drawing for a New Public: Middle Eastern 9th Art and the Emergence of a Transnational Graphic Movement." In *Postcolonial Comics: Texts, Events, Identities*, edited by Binita Mehta and Pia Mukherji, 187–203. London: Routledge.

Dittmar, Linda, and Joseph Entin, eds. 2016. "Archives and Radical Education." *Radical Teacher* 105:1–6.

Dittmer, Jason. 2007. "The Tyranny of the Serial: Popular Geopolitics, the Nation, and Comic Book Discourse." *Antipode* 39, no. 2, 247–68.

———. 2013. *Captain America and the Nationalist Superhero: Metaphors, Narratives, and Geopolitics*. Philadelphia: Temple University Press.

———. 2014. "Serialization and Displacement in Graphic Narrative." In *Serialization in Popular Culture*, edited by Rob Allen and Thijs van den Berg, 124–40. New York: Routledge.

Draaisma, Douwe. 2013. *The Nostalgia Factory: Memory, Time and Ageing*. New Haven: Yale University Press.

"*Drawn & Quarterly Manifesto* for Booksellers, The." (2003) 2015. In *Drawn & Quarterly: Twenty-Five Years of Contemporary Cartooning, Comics, and Graphic Novels*, edited by Tom Devlin, 26–29. Montreal: Drawn & Quarterly.

Duck, Leigh Ann. 2006. *The Nation's Region: Southern Modernism, Segregation, and U.S. Nationalism*. Athens: University of Georgia Press.

Duffy, Damian, and John Jennings. 2017. *Octavia E. Butler's Kindred: A Graphic Novel Adaptation*. New York: Abrams.

Duncan, Randy, and Matthew J. Smith. 2009. *The Power of Comics: History, Form and Culture*. New York: Continuum.

Duncombe, Stephen. 1997. *Notes from Underground: Zines and the Politics of Alternative Culture*. London: Verso.

Dunn, Lloyd. n.d. "*PhotoStatic Magazine* and the Rise of the Casual Publisher." *PhotoStatic Magazine Retrograde Archive*. Accessed November 18, 2020. http://psrf.detritus.net.

Earle, Harriet E. H. 2017. *Comics, Trauma, and the New Art of War*. Jackson: University Press of Mississippi.

Eco, Umberto. 1972. "The Myth of Superman." *Diacritics* 2, no. 1, 14–22.

———. 1994. *The Limits of Interpretation*. Bloomington: Indiana University Press.

Edwards, Dylan. 2001. *Tranny Toons*. Seattle: Northwest.

———. 2012. *Transposes*. Seattle: Northwest.

Eichhorn, Kate. 2008. "Archival Genres: Gathering Texts and Reading Spaces." *Invisible Culture* 12 (Spring). https://ivc.lib.rochester.edu.

———. 2010. "DIY Collectors, Archiving Scholars, and Activist Librarians: Legitimizing Feminist Knowledge and Cultural Production since 1990." *Women's Studies* 39, no. 6, 622–46.

———. 2013. *The Archival Turn in Feminism: Outrage in Order*. Philadelphia: Temple University Press.

Eisner, Will. 1985. *Comics and Sequential Art*. Tamarac, FL: Poorhouse.

———. (1986) 2008. *Graphic Storytelling and Visual Narrative: Principles and Practices from the Legendary Cartoonist*. New York: W. W. Norton.

El Refaie, Elisabeth. 2012a. *Autobiographical Comics: Life Writing in Pictures*. Jackson: University Press of Mississippi.

———. 2012b. "Of Men, Mice, and Monsters: Body Images in David Small's *Stitches: A Memoir*." *Journal of Graphic Novels and Comics* 3, no. 1, 55–67.

Enstad, Nan. 1999. *Ladies of Labor, Girls of Adventure: Working Women, Popular Culture, and Labor Politics at the Turn of the Twentieth Century*. New York: Columbia University Press.

Fake, Edie. 2010. *Gaylord Phoenix*. Los Angeles: Secret Acres.

Fanon, Franz. (1952) 1984. *Black Skin, White Masks*. London: Pluto.

Faughnder, Ryan. 2017. "Global Box Office Barely Grew in 2016. Blame It on China." *Los Angeles Times*, March 22, 2017. www.latimes.com.

Faust, Wolfgang. 1971. "Comics and How to Read Them." *Journal of Popular Culture* 5, no. 1 (Summer): 194–202.

Fawaz, Ramzi. 2016. *The New Mutants: Superheroes and the Radical Imagination of American Comics*. New York: New York University Press.

———. 2017a. "Notes on Wonder Woman." *Avidly* (blog), July 16, 2017. http://avidly.lareviewofbooks.org.

———. 2017b. "Stripped to the Bone: Sequencing Queerness in the Comic Strip Work of Joe Brainard and David Wojnarowicz." *ASAP/Journal* 2, no. 2 (May): 335–67.

———. 2018. "Legions of Superheroes: Diversity, Multiplicity, and Collective Action against Genocide in the Superhero Comic Book." *Social Text* 36, no. 4, 21–55.

———. 2019. "A Queer Sequence: Comics as a Disruptive Medium." *PMLA* 134, no. 3, 588–94.

Fawkes, Ray. 2014. *The People Inside*. Portland: Onix.

Feiffer, Jules. 1965. *The Great Comic Book Heroes*. New York: Bonanza.

Feinberg, Leslie. 1998. *Trans Liberation: Beyond Pink or Blue*. Boston: Beacon.

Fenty, Sean, Trena Houp, and Laurie Taylor. 2005. "Webcomics: The Influence and Continuation of the Comix Revolution." *ImageTexT: Interdisciplinary Comics Studies* 1, no. 2 (Winter). http://imagetext.english.ufl.edu.

Fernandez L'Hoeste, Hector, and Juan Poblete, eds. 2009. *Redrawing the Nation: National Identity in Latin/o American Comics*. London: Palgrave.

Fernández Rodríguez, Carolina. 2015. "Latina Super-Heroines: Hot Tamales in Tights vs. Women Warriors, Wrestlers and Guerrilla Fighters of La Raza." *Complutense Journal of English Studies* 23:115–36.

Fielder, Tim. 2017. *Matty's Rocket: Book One*. New York: Dieselfunk.

Figa, A. 2015a. "Trans, Genderqueer, and Genderfluid Cosplayers on Finding Their Safe Space in Conventions." Mary Sue, March 12, 2015. www.themarysue.com.

———. 2015b. "Queersplay Cosplay Creates Safe Spaces at Cons." Women Write about Comics. Accessed May 10, 2017. http://womenwriteaboutcomics.com.

Fingeroth, Danny. 2004. *Superheroes on the Couch*. London: Bloomsbury.

Finkelstein, Victor. 1980. *Attitudes and Disabled People*. New York: World Rehabilitation Fund.

Fiore, R. 2009. "The Experience of Comics." *Comics Journal* 1, no. 300, 252–58.

Fiske, John. (1989) 2011. *Reading the Popular*. New York: Routledge.

———. 1989. *Understanding Popular Culture*. New York: Routledge.

Foss, Chris, Jonathan W. Gray, and Zach Whalen, eds. 2016. *Disability in Comic Books and Graphic Narratives*. New York: Palgrave Macmillan.

Freccero, Carla. 1999. *Popular Culture: An Introduction*. New York: New York University Press.

Freeman, Elizabeth. 2010. *Time Binds: Queer Temporalities, Queer Histories*. Durham, NC: Duke University Press.

Gabilliet, Jean-Paul. 2009. *Of Comics and Men: A Cultural History of American Comic Books*. Jackson: University Press of Mississippi.

Gaiman, Neil, and Dave McKean. 1991. *Black Orchid*. New York: Vertigo / DC Comics.

Gaines, Maxwell Charles. 1942. "Narrative Illustration: The Story of the Comics—Author Bio." *Print, a Quarterly Journal of the Graphic Arts* 3, no. 2, 1–24.

———. 1943. "Good Triumphs over Evil—More about the Comics." *Print, a Quarterly Journal of the Graphic Arts* 3, no. 3, 19.

Galvan, Margaret. 2015. "Archiving Grassroots Comics: The Radicality of Networks and Lesbian Community." *Archive Journal* 5 (Fall). www.archivejournal.net.

———. 2017. "Archiving *Wimmen*: Collectives, Networks, and Comix." *Australian Feminist Studies* 32, nos. 91–92, 22–40.

———. 2018. "'The Lesbian Norman Rockwell': Alison Bechdel and Queer Grassroots Networks." *American Literature* 90, no. 2, 407–38.

Gans, Herbert J. 1999. *Popular Culture and High Culture*. New York: Basic Books.

Gaonkar, Dilip Parameshwar, and Elizabeth A. Povinelli. 2003. "Technologies of Public Forms: Circulation, Transfiguration, Recognition." *Public Culture* 15:386–97.

García, Enrique. 2017. *The Hernandez Brothers: Love, Rockets, and Alternative Comics*. Pittsburgh: University of Pittsburgh Press.

García, Santiago. 2015. *On the Graphic Novel*. Jackson: University Press of Mississippi.

Gardner, Jared. 2006. "Archives, Collectors, and the New Media Work of Comics." *Modern Fiction Studies* 52, no. 4, 787–806.

———. 2012. *Projections: Comics and the History of Twenty-First-Century Storytelling*. Palo Alto: Stanford University Press.

Garland-Thomson, Rosemarie. 1997. *Extraordinary Bodies: Figuring Physical Disability in American Culture and Literature*. New York: Columbia University Press.

Gartley, Elizabeth. 2017. "Speaking Language? The Politics of Language and Power in *Saga*." *Studies in Comics* 8:51–68.

Garza, Margarito C. 1977. *¡Relámpago!* Self-published.

Gateward, Frances, and John Jennings, eds. 2015. *The Blacker the Ink: Constructions of Black Identity in Comics and Sequential Art*. New Brunswick, NJ: Rutgers University Press.

Gavaler, Chris. 2015. *On the Origin of Superheroes*. Iowa City: University of Iowa Press.

Gay Comix. September 1980–July 1988. Northampton, MA: Kitchen Sink.

Gearino, Dan. 2017. *Comic Shop: The Retail Mavericks Who Gave Us a New Geek Culture*. Athens, OH: Swallow.

Geissman, Grant. 2005. *Foul Play! The Art and Artists of the Notorious 1950s E.C. Comics!* New York: HarperCollins.

Gilligan, Sarah. 2011. "Heaving Cleavages and Fantastic Frock Coats: Gender Fluidity, Celebrity and Tactile Transmediality in Contemporary Costume Cinema." *Film, Fashion, and Consumption* 1, no. 1, 7–38. https://doi.org/10.1386/ffc.1.1.7_1.

Gillman, Melanie. 2017. *As the Crow Flies*. Chicago: Iron Circus Comics.

Glaser, Jennifer. 2013. "Picturing the Transnational in Palomar: Gilbert Hernandez and the Comics of the Borderlands." *ImageTexT: Interdisciplinary Comics Studies* 7, no. 1 (Summer). http://imagetext.english.ufl.edu.

Gobineau, Arthur. (1853) 1967. *An Essay on the Inequality of the Human Races*. Translated by Adrian H. Collins. New York: H. Fertig.

Goldstein, Nancy. 2008. *Jackie Ormes: The First African American Woman Cartoonist*. Ann Arbor: University of Michigan Press.

Gooden, Tai. 2016. "Unmasking the Cosplay Community's Sexism and Racism Problem." Establishment, May 12, 2016. https://theestablishment.co.

Goodley, Dan. 2011. *Disability Studies: An Interdisciplinary Introduction*. Los Angeles: SAGE.

Goodman, Kenneth S. 2014. "A Process of Reading in Nonalphabetic Languages: An Introduction." In *Making Sense of Learners Making Sense of Written Language: The Selected Works of Kenneth S. Goodman and Yetta M. Goodman*, 75–85. New York: Routledge.

Goodrum, Michael, Tara Prescott, and Philip Smith, eds. 2018. *Gender and the Superhero Narrative*. Jackson: University Press of Mississippi.

Gopalakrishnan, Kaveri. 2015. "Basic Space?" In *Drawing the Line: Indian Women Fight Back*, edited by Priya Kuriyan, Larissa Bertonasco, Ludmilla Bartsct, and Nicole Marie Burton, 141–49. New Delhi: Zubaan.

Gordon, Ian. 1998. *Comic Strips and Consumer Culture: 1890–1945*. Washington, DC: Smithsonian Institution Press.

———. 2012. "Writing to Superman: Towards an Understanding of the Social Networks of Comic-Book Fans." *Participations: Journal of Audience and Reception Studies* 9:120–32.

———. 2016. "Refiguring Media: Tee Shirts as a Site of Audience Engagement with Superheroes." *Information Society* 32, no. 5, 301–5.

———. 2017. *Superman: The Persistence of an American Icon*. New Brunswick, NJ: Rutgers University Press.

Gosset, Reina, Eric A. Stanley, and Johanna Burton, eds. 2017. *Trap Door: Trans Cultural Production and the Politics of Visibility*. Cambridge: MIT Press.

Gravett, Paul. 2013. *Comics Art*. New Haven, CT: Yale University Press.

Gray, Brenna Clarke, and David N. Wright. 2017. "Decentering the Sexual Aggressor: Sexual Violence, Trigger Warnings and Bitch Planet." *Journal of Graphic Novels and Comics* 8, no. 3, 264–76.

Gray, Jonathan, Cornell Sandvoss, and C. Lee Harrington, eds. 2007. *Fandom: Identities and Communities in a Mediated World*. New York: New York University Press.

Green, Justin. 2009. *Binky Brown Meets the Holy Virgin Mary*. San Francisco: McSweeney's.

Green, Karen. n.d. "Research Guides: The American Graphic Novel: Archival Collections." Columbia University Libraries. Accessed August 7, 2018. http://guides.library.columbia.edu.

Greeson, Jennifer Rae. 2010. *Our South: Geographical Fantasy and the Rise of National Literature*. Cambridge: Harvard University Press.

Gregory, Chase. 2012. "'In the Gutter': Comix Theory." *Studies in Comics* 3, no. 1, 107–28.

Griepp, Milton, and John Jackson Miller. 2017. "Comics and Graphic Novel Sales Up 5% in 2016." Comichron: A Resource for Comics Research. Accessed January 4, 2019. www.comichron.com.

Grierson, John [The Moviegoer, pseud.]. 1926. "Flaherty's Poetic *Moana*." *New York Sun*, February 8, 1926. In *The Documentary Film Reader: History, Theory, Criticism*, edited by Jonathan Kahana, 86–87. Oxford: Oxford University Press.

———. 1933. "The Documentary Producer." *Cinema Quarterly* 2, no. 1 (Autumn): 7–9. In *The Documentary Film Reader: History, Theory, Criticism*, edited by Jonathan Kahana, 215–16. Oxford: Oxford University Press.

Grimes, William. 2013a. "Al Jaffee's Work Is Going to Columbia." *New York Times*, October 6, 2013. www.nytimes.com.

———. 2013b. "Columbia Rare Book Library Gets the Kitchen Sink." *ArtsBeat* (blog), December 31, 2013. http://artsbeat.blogs.nytimes.com.

Groensteen, Thierry. 2007. *The System of Comics*. Translated by Bart Beaty and Nick Nguyen. Jackson, MS: University Press of Mississippi.

———. 2009. "Why Are Comics Still in Search of Cultural Legitimization?" Translated by Shirley Smolderen. In *A Comics Studies Reader*, edited by Jeet Heer and Kent Worcester, 3–11. Jackson: University Press of Mississippi.

———. 2013. *Comics and Narration*. Translated by Ann Miller. Jackson: University Press of Mississippi.

Groth, Gary. 1991. "Zap: An Interview with Robert Crumb." *Comics Journal* 143. Accessed March 2, 2017. www.tcj.com.

———. 2004. "One of the Main Reasons to Go On Living Is I Still Think I Haven't Done My Best Work." In *R. Crumb: Interviews, Comix, and Color Gallery*, 13–66. Vol. 3 of *Comics Journal Library*. Seattle: Fantagraphics.

———. 2013. "Gary Groth and the Brothers." In *The* Love and Rockets *Companion*, edited by Marc Sobel and Kristy Valenti, 10–79. Seattle: Fantagraphics.

Grove, Laurence. 2010. *Comics in French: The European Bande Dessinée in Context*. New York: Bergahn.

Gruber, Christian. 2019. *The Praiseworthy One: The Prophet Muhammad in Islamic Texts and Images*. Bloomington: Indiana University Press.

Guigar, Brad. 2014. *The Webcomics Handbook*. Philadelphia: Greystone Inn Comics.

Guigar, Brad, Dave Kellett, Scott Kurtz, and Kris Straud. 2008. *How to Make Webcomics*. Berkeley, CA: Image Comics.

Gunderloy, Mike. 1990. "Zines: Where the Action Is; the Very Small Press in America." *Whole Earth Review* 68 (Fall): 58–60.

Gunnels, Jen. 2009. "'A Jedi like My Father before Me': Social identity and the New York Comic Con." *Transformative Works and Cultures* 3. https://doi.org/10.3983/twc.2009.0161.

Gustines, George Gene. 2011. "The X-Men Go to College." *ArtsBeat* (blog), November 11, 2011. http://artsbeat.blogs.nytimes.com.

Habell-Pallán, Michelle. 2005. *Loca Motion: The Travels of Chicana and Latina Popular Culture*. New York: New York University Press.

Hajdu, David. 2009. *The Ten-Cent Plague: The Great Comic-Book Scare and How It Changed America*. New York: Picador.

Halberstam, Jack. 2011. *The Queer Art of Failure*. Durham, NC: Duke University Press.

———. 2017. "Suffering Sappho! Wonder Woman and Feminism." *Bullybloggers* (blog), July 5, 2017. https://bullybloggers.wordpress.com.

Hale-Stern, Kaila. 2018. "Our New Favorite Wonder Woman Cosplayer Went as Patty Jenkins." Mary Sue, April 11, 2018. www.themarysue.com.

Hall, Justin. 2012. *No Straight Lines: Four Decades of Queer Comics*. Seattle: Fantagraphics.

Hall, Stuart. 2002. *Stuart Hall: Representation and the Media*. Video lecture produced, directed, and edited by Sut Jhally. Northampton, MA: Media Education Foundation.

Halloran, Fiona Deans. 2012. *Thomas Nast: The Father of Modern Political Cartoons*. Chapel Hill: University of North Carolina Press.

Hamlin, Janet. 2013. *Sketching Guantanamo: Court Sketches of the Military Tribunals 2006–2012*. Seattle: Fantagraphics.

Haraway, Donna. 1988. "Situated Knowledges: The Science Question in Feminism and the Privilege of Partial Perspective." *Feminist Studies* 14, no. 3, 575–99.

Harrison, Claire. 2003. "Visual Social Semiotics: Understanding How Still Images Make Meaning." *Technical Communication* 50:46–60.

Hartman, Saidiya. 2008. "Venus in Two Acts." *Small Axe* 12, no. 2, 1–14.

Harvey, Robert C. 2001. "The Graphic Novel, Will Eisner, and Other Pioneers, Part 2." *Comics Journal*, no. 234 (June): 92–97. www.tcj.com.

———. 2016. "Outcault, Goddard, the Comics, and the Yellow Kid." *Comics Journal*, June 9, 2016. www.tcj.com.

Harvey, Robert C., and Gus Arriola. 2000. *Accidental Ambassador Gordo: The Comic Strip Art of Gus Arriola*. Jackson: University Press of Mississippi.

Hassler-Forest, Dan. 2012. *Capitalist Superheroes: Caped Crusaders in a Neoliberal Age*. Winchester: Zero.

Hatfield, Charles. 2005. *Alternative Comics: An Emerging Literature*. Jackson: University Press of Mississippi.

———. 2011. "Redrawing the Comic-Strip Child: Charles M. Schulz's *Peanuts* as Cross-Writing." In *The Oxford Handbook of Children's Literature*, edited by J. L. Mickenberg and L. Vallone, 167–87. New York: Oxford University Press.

———. 2014. "Do Independent Comics Still Exist in the US and Canada?" In *La bande dessinée en dissidence* [Comics in dissent], edited by Christophe Dony, Tanguy Habrand, and Gert Meesters, 59–78. Belgium: Presses Universitaires de Liège.

Hatfield, Nami Kitsune. 2016. "Transforming Spaces: Transgender Webcomics as a Model for Transgender Empowerment and Representation within Library and Archive Spaces." *Queer Cats Journal of LGBTQ Studies* 1, no. 1, 58–73.

Hayles, N. Katherine. 2002. *Writing Machines*. Cambridge: MIT Press.

Hayot, Eric. 2012. *On Literary Worlds*. Oxford: Oxford University Press.

Hayward, Eva, and Jami Weinstein. 2015. "Introduction: Tranimalities in the Age of Trans* Life." *TSQ: Transgender Studies Quarterly* 2, no. 2 (May): 195–208.

Healey, Karen. 2009. "When Fangirls Perform: The Gendered Fan Identity in Superhero Comics Fandom." In *The Contemporary Comic Book Superhero*, edited by Angela Ndalianis, 144–63. New York: Routledge.

Heer, Jeet. 2013. *In Love with Art: Françoise Mouly's Adventures in Comics with Art Spiegelman*. Toronto: Coach House Books.

Heer, Jeet, and Kent Worcester. 2009. Introduction to *A Comics Studies Reader*, edited by Jeet Heer and Kent Worcester, xi–xv. Jackson: University Press of Mississippi.

Hellekson, Karen, and Kristina Busse, eds. 2006. *Fan Fiction and Fan Communities in the Age of the Internet*. Jefferson, NC: McFarland.

Herman, David, ed. 2017. *Animal Comics: Multispecies Storyworlds in Graphic Narratives*. New York: Bloomsbury.

Hernandez, Gilbert. 2007a. *Beyond Palomar*. Seattle: Fantagraphics.

———. 2007b. *Chance in Hell*. Seattle: Fantagraphics.

———. 2007c. *Heartbreak Soup*. Seattle: Fantagraphics.

———. 2007d. *Human Diastrophism*. Seattle: Fantagraphics.

———. 2007e. "Poison River." In *Beyond Palomar*, 7–192. Seattle: Fantagraphics.

———. 2008. "BEM." In *Amor y Cohetes*, by Gilbert Hernandez, Jaime Hernandez, and Mario Hernandez, 9–48. Seattle: Fantagraphics.

———. 2009. *The Troublemakers*. Seattle: Fantagraphics.

———. 2013. *The Children of Palomar*. Seattle: Fantagraphics.

———. 2014a. *Fatima: The Blood Spinners*. Milwaukee: Dark Horse.

———. 2014b. *Loverboys*. Milwaukee: Dark Horse.

———. 2014c. *Luba and Her Family*. Seattle: Fantagraphics.

———. 2015. *Ofelia*. Seattle: Fantagraphics.

Hernandez, Jaime. 2007a. *The Girl from H.O.P.P.E.R.S.* Seattle: Fantagraphics.

———. 2007b. *Maggie the Mechanic*. Seattle: Fantagraphics.

———. 2007c. "Mechan-X." In *Maggie the Mechanic*, 7–14. Seattle: Fantagraphics.

———. 2010. *Penny Century*. Seattle: Fantagraphics.

———. 2011. *Esperanza*. Seattle: Fantagraphics.

———. 2012. *God and Science: Return of the Ti-Girls*. Seattle: Fantagraphics.

———. 2014. *The Love Bunglers*. Seattle: Fantagraphics.

Hilmes, Michelle. 2009. "Nailing Mercury: The Problem of Media Industry Historiography." In *Media Industries: History, Theory and Method*, edited by Alisa Perren and Jennifer Holt. London: Blackwell.

Hlozek, R. 2004. "Cosplay: The New Main Attraction." *Jive Magazine*, May 2004. www.jivemagazine.com.

Holland, Sharon P. 2016. "Hum/animal: All Together." *PMLA* 131, no. 1, 167–69.

Holt, Jennifer, and Alisa Perren, eds. 2009. *Media Industries: History, Theory and Method*. London: Blackwell.

Honey, Maureen. 1984. *Creating Rosie the Riveter: Class, Gender, and Propaganda during World War II*. Amherst: University of Massachusetts Press.

Hong, Christine. 2015. "Illustrating the Postwar Peace: Miné Okubo, the 'Citizen-Subject' of Japan, and Fortune Magazine." *American Quarterly* 67, no. 1, 105–40.

Horton, Andrew, and Stuart Y. McDougal. 1998. Introduction to *Play It Again, Sam: Retakes on Remakes*, edited by Andrew Horton and Stuart Y. McDougal, 1–11. Berkeley: University of California Press.

Howard, Sheena. 2018. "Situating *Cyberzone*: Black Lesbian Identity in Comics." *Journal of Lesbian Studies* 22, no. 4, 402–14.

Howard, Sheena C., and Ronald L. Jackson II, eds. 2013. *Black Comics: Politics of Race and Representation*. New York: Bloomsbury.

Hutcheon, Linda. 1985. *A Theory of Parody*. Cambridge: Methuen.

———. 1989a. "Historiographic Metafiction: Parody and the Intertextuality of History." In *Intertextuality and Contemporary American Fiction*, edited by Patrick O'Donnell and Robert Con Davis, 3–32. Baltimore: Johns Hopkins University Press.

———. 1989b. *The Politics of Postmodernism*. New York: Routledge.

———. 2006. *A Theory of Adaptation*. New York: Routledge.

Ignacio, Abe Enrique de la Cruz, Jorge Emmanuel, and Helen Toribio, eds. 2004. *The Forbidden Book: The Philippine-American War in Political Cartoons*. San Francisco: T'Boli.

Inge, M. Thomas. 2012. "Li'l Abner, Snuffy, and Friends: The Appalachian South in the American Comic Strip." In *Comics and the U.S. South*, edited by Brannon Costello and Qiana Whitted, 3–28. Jackson: University Press of Mississippi.

"Interviews with Women Comic Artists: Trina Robbins." 1979. *Cultural Correspondence*, no. 9 (Spring): 10–12.

Jackson, Sarah J., Moya Bailey, and Brooke Foucault Welles. 2017. "#GirlsLikeUs: Trans Advocacy and Community Building Online." *new media & society* 20, no. 5, 1–21.

Jacobi, Charles Thomas. 1888. *The Printers' Vocabulary*. London: Chiswick.

Jacobs, Dale. 2020. "Text, Object, Transaction: Reconciling Approaches to the Teaching of Comics." In *With Great Power Comes Great Pedagogy: Teaching, Learning, and Comic Books*, edited by Susan Kirtley, Peter Carlson, and Antero Garcia, 23–37. New York: Routledge.

Jacobs, Frank. 1973. *The Mad World of William M. Gaines*. New York: Bantam.

James, William. 1890. *The Principles of Psychology*. New York: Holt.

Janson, Klaus. 2003. *The DC Guide to Inking Comics*. New York: Watson-Guptill.

Jee, Yein. 2008. "Origin of the Word Cosplay." *Yein Jee's Asian Blog*, July 3, 2008. https://yeinjee.com.

Jenkins, Henry. 1992. *Textual Poachers: Television Fans and Participatory Culture*. New York: Routledge.

———. 2008a. *Convergence Culture: Where Old and New Media Collide*. New York: New York University Press.

———. 2008b. "'Just Men in Tights': Rewriting Silver Age Comics in an Era of Multiplicity." In *The Contemporary Comic Book Superhero*, edited by Angela Ndalianis. New York: Routledge.

Jenkins, Henry, and N. Carpentier. 2013. "Theorizing Participatory Intensities: A Conversation about Participation and Politics." *Convergence* 19, no. 3, 265–86. https://doi.org/10.1177/1354856513482090.

Jenkins, Henry, Sam Ford, and Joshua Green, eds. 2013. *Spreadable Media: Creating Value and Meaning in a Networked Culture*. New York: New York University Press.

Johnson, Derek. 2013. *Media Franchising: Creative License and Collaboration in the Culture Industries*. New York: New York University Press.

Jones, Gerard. 2004. *Men of Tomorrow: Geeks, Gangsters and the Birth of the Comic Book*. New York: Basic Books.

Jones, Jeffrey Catherine. (1975) 1979. *Idyl*. Dragon's Dream.

Joseph, Miranda. 2002. *Against the Romance of Community*. Minneapolis: University of Minnesota Press.

Juno, Andrea, and Diane Noomin. 1997. "Diane Noomin" (interview). In *Dangerous Drawings: Interviews with Comix and Graphix Artists*, 176–87. New York: Juno.

Juno, Andrea, and Art Spiegelman. 1997. "Art Spiegelman" (interview). In *Dangerous Drawings: Interviews with Comix and Graphix Artists*, 6–27. New York: Juno.

Kamentsky, Gina. 2002. *A Transgendered Gal's Search for Validation and a Decent Cup of Coffee. T-Gina*. T-Gina Comics. Self-published.

Kaplan, Caren. 1992. "Resisting Autobiography: Out-Law Genres and Transnational Feminist Subjects." In *De/Colonizing the Subject: The Politics of Gender in Women's Autobiography*, edited by Sidonie Smith and Julia Watson, 115–38. Minneapolis: University of Minnesota Press.

Karasik, Paul, and Mark Newgarden. 2017. *How to Read Nancy: The Elements of Comics in Three Easy Panels*. Seattle: Fantagraphics.

Kashtan, Aaron. 2017. "'Those Aren't Really Comics': Raina Telgemeier and the Limitations of Direct-Market Centrism." Paper presented at the International Comic Arts Forum, Seattle, November 3, 2017.

———. 2018a. *Between Pen and Pixel: Comics, Materiality, and the Book of the Future*. Columbus: Ohio State University Press.

———. 2018b. "Change the Cover: Superhero Fan Identity in an Age of Diversification." *Journal of Fandom Studies* 6, no. 3 (September): 243–61.

Kasilag, Giselle. 2003. "Today's Mindless Purchase May Be Tomorrow's Nest Egg: Comic Books as Investments." *BusinessWorld*, November 10, 2003, 1.

Kaye, Julia. n.d. *Up and Out*. Accessed February 4, 2019. http://upandoutcomic.tumblr.com.

Kearney, Mary Celeste. 2006. *Girls Make Media*. New York: Routledge.

Kidman, Shawna. 2019. *Comic Books Incorporated: How the Business of Comics Became the Business of Hollywood*. Oakland: University of California Press.

Kirkpatrick, Ellen. 2013. "Playing Gods: Identity in the Superhero Genre and Cosplay." MPhil thesis, Bristol University.

———. 2015. "Toward New Horizons: Cosplay (Re)imagined through the Superhero Genre, Authenticity, and Transformation." *Transformative Works and Cultures* 18. http://journal.transformativeworks.org.

———. 2017. "Recovering the Radical Promise of the Superhero Genre: Transformation, Representation, Worldmaking." PhD diss., Kingston University.

———. 2019. "On [Dis]play: Outlier Resistance and on the Matter of Racebending Superhero Cosplay." *Transformative Works and Cultures* 29. https://doi.org/10.3983/twc.2019.1483.

Kirkpatrick, Ellen, and Suzanne Scott. 2015. "Representation and Diversity in Comics Studies." *Cinema Journal* 55, no. 1 (Fall): 120–24.

Kitabayashi, Ken. 2004. "The Otaku Group from a Business Perspective: Revaluation of Enthusiastic Consumers." *NRI Papers* 84 (December 1): 2–8. www.nri.com.

Kline, Stephen. 1993. *Out of the Garden: Toys and Children's Culture in the Age of TV Marketing*. New York: Verso.

Klock, Geoff. 2002. *How to Read Superhero Comics and Why*. New York: Continuum.

Kohlert, Frederik Byrn. 2012. "Female Grotesques: Carnivalesque Subversion in the Comics of Julie Doucet." *Journal of Graphic Novels and Comics* 3, no. 1, 19–38.

Kristeva, Julia. 1980a. "The Bounded Text." In *Desire in Language: A Semiotic Approach to Literature and Art*, edited by Leon S. Roudiez, 36–63. Translated by Thomas Gora, Alice Jardine, and Leon S. Roudiez. New York: Columbia University Press.

———. 1980b. "Word, Dialogue, and Novel." In *Desire in Language: A Semiotic Approach to Literature and Art*, edited by Leon S. Roudiez, 64–91. Translated by Thomas Gora, Alice

Jardine, and Leon S. Roudiez. New York: Columbia University Press.

Kumbier, Alana. 2014. *Ephemeral Material: Queering the Archive*. Sacramento: Litwin.

Kunka, Andrew J. 2017a. *Autobiographical Comics*. London: Bloomsbury.

———. 2017b. "*A Contract with God, The First Kingdom*, and the 'Graphic Novel': The Will Eisner / Jack Katz Letters." *INKS* 1, no. 1 (Spring): 27–39.

Kunka, Andrew, and Derek Royal. 2018. "Catching Up with the Hernandez Brothers." In *Full Bleed: The Comics & Culture Quarterly*, edited by Dirk Wood and Ted Adams, 13–29. San Diego: IDW/Woodworks.

Kunzle, David. 2007. *Father of the Comic Strip: Rodolphe Töpffer*. Jackson: University Press of Mississippi.

Labio, Catherine. 2011. "What's in a Name? The Academic Study of Comics and the 'Graphic Novel.'" *Cinema Journal* 50, no. 3 (Spring): 123–26.

Lamb, Chris. 2004. *Drawn to Extremes: The Use and Abuse of Editorial Cartoons*. New York: Columbia University Press.

Lamerichs, Nicolle. 2010. "Stranger Than Fiction: Fan Identity in Cosplay." *Transformative Works and Cultures* 7. https://doi.org/10.3983/twc.2011.0246.

———. 2018. "Nicolle Lamerichs." *Fan Fashion, or How Creative Designers Appropriate Pop-Culture*. January 24, 2018. https://nicollelamerichs.com.

Landis, Winona. 2016. "Diasporic (Dis)identification: The Participatory Fandom of *Ms. Marvel*." *South Asian Popular Culture* 14, no. 1–2: 33–47. https://doi.org/10.1080/14746689.2016.1241344.

Lanham, Richard. 2006. *Economics of Attention: Style and Substance in the Age of Information*. Chicago: University of Chicago Press.

Lassiter, Matthew D., and Joseph Crespino. 2010. "Introduction: The End of Southern History." In *The Myth of Southern Exceptionalism*, edited by Matthew D. Lassiter and Joseph Crespino, 3–22. Oxford: Oxford University Press.

Lee, Benjamin, and Edward LiPuma. 2002. "Cultures of Circulation: The Imaginations of Modernity." *Public Culture* 14:191–213.

Lee, Stan, and Jack Kirby. (1961) 2013, 2018. *The Fantastic Four Omnibus*, vols. 1 and 2. New York: Marvel Comics.

LeFevre, P. 2017. "Newspaper Strips." In *The Routledge Companion to Comics*, edited by Frank Bramlett, Roy T. Cook, and Aaron Meskin, 16–24. New York: Routledge.

Leng, Rachel. 2013. "Gender, Sexuality, and Cosplay: A Case Study of Male-to-Female Crossplay." *Phoenix Papers: First Edition*, April 2013. https://dash.harvard.edu.

Lepore, Jill. 2015. *The Secret History of Wonder Woman*. New York: Vintage.

Lethem, Jonathan. 2004. "The Return of the King, or, Identifying with Your Parents." In *Give Our Regards to the Atomsmashers! Writers on Comics*, edited by Sean How, 2–23. New York: Pantheon.

Levine, Lawrence. 1988. *Highbrow/Lowbrow*. Cambridge: Harvard University Press.

Lewis, A. David, and Martin Lund, eds. 2017. *Muslim Superheroes: Comics, Islam, and Representation*. Cambridge: Harvard University Press.

Lhamon, W. T., Jr. 1998. *Raising Cain: Blackface Performance from Jim Crow to Hip Hop*. Cambridge: Harvard University Press.

Library of Congress Collections Policy Statements. 1994. Washington, DC: Library of Congress.

Licona, Adela. 2005. "(B)orderlands' Rhetorics and Representations: The Transformative Potential of Feminist Third-Space Scholarship and Zines." *NWSA Journal* 17:104–29.

Limb, Peter, and Tejumola Olaniyan, eds. 2018. *Taking African Cartoons Seriously: Politics, Satire, and Culture*. East Lansing: Michigan State University Press.

Linde, Jess. 2014. "Cosplay Is Not Consent: Exploring the Dark Side of Adult Dress-Up." *Vice*, July 15, 2014. www.vice.com.

Linnaeus, Carl. (1759) 1964. *Systema Naturae*. 10th ed. New York: Stechert-Hafner Service Agency.

Lizardi, Ryan. 2014. *Mediated Nostalgia: Individual Memory and Contemporary Mass Media*. Lanham, MD: Lexington.

Long, Geoffrey. 2013. "(Sp)Reading Digital Comics." Spreadable Media. Accessed June 5, 2015. http://spreadablemedia.org.

Lopes, Paul. 2009. *Demanding Respect: The Evolution of the American Comic Book*. Philadelphia: Temple University Press.

Lopez, Lori Kido. 2011. "Fan Activists and the Politics of Race in *The Last Airbender*." *International Journal of Cultural Studies* 15, no. 5, 431–45.

Lopez, Marco, Desiree Rodriguez, Hazel Newlevant, Derek Ruiz, and Neil Schwartz. 2018. *Puerto Rico Strong*. St. Louis: Lion Forge.

Love, Heather. 2014. "Queer." *Transgender Studies Quarterly* 1, no. 1–2, 172–76.

Love, Jeremy. 2009, 2010. *Bayou*, vols. 1 and 2. New York: DC Comics.

Lowe, Lisa. 2015. *The Intimacies of Four Continents*. Durham, NC: Duke University Press.

Luque, Nazario. 2017. *Anarcoma: Obra Grafica Completa*. Barcelona: La Cupula.

Lyon, Janet. 2009. *Manifestoes: Provocations of the Modern*. Ithaca, NY: Cornell University Press.

Mac, Garry. 2012. *Gonzo Cosmic* #1. Glasgow: Unthank Comics.

Maher, Bill. 2018. "Adulting." *Real Time with Bill Maher Blog*, November 16, 2018. www.real-time-with-bill-maher-blog.com.

Marrone, Daniel. 2016. *Forging the Past: Seth and the Art of Memory*. Jackson: University Press of Mississippi.

Marshall, Daniel, Kevin P. Murphy, and Zeb Tortorici, eds. 2014. "Special Issue: Queering Archives: Historical Unravelings" *Radical History Review* 14, no. 3 (Fall).

Martinbrough, Shawn. 2007. *How to Draw Noir Comics: The Art and Technique of Visual Storytelling*. New York: Watson-Guptill.

Mazur, Dan, and Alexander Danner. 2014. *Comics: A Global History, 1968 to the Present*. London: Thames and Hudson.

Mazzucchelli, David. 2009. *Asterios Polyp*. New York: Pantheon.

Mbembe, Achille. 2017. *Critique of Black Reason*. Translated by Laurent Dubois. Durham, NC: Duke University Press.

McAllister, Matthew P., Ian Gordon, and Mark Jancovich. 2006. "Blockbuster Meets Superhero Comic, or Art House Meets Graphic Novel? The Contradictory Relationship between Film and Comic Art." *Journal of Popular Film and Television* 34, no. 3, 108–14.

McCabe, Caitlin. 2016. "Columbia University Acquires Personal Archives of Seminal Comics Creator Howard Cruse." *Comic Book Legal Defense Fund* (blog), September 8, 2016. http://cbldf.org.

McCay, Winsor, dir. 1918. *The Sinking of the Lusitania*. New York: Jewel Productions.

McClancy, Kathleen. 2018. "Comics and History." *Feminist Media Histories* 4, no. 3, 1–11. https://doi.org/10.1525/fmh.2018.4.3.1.

McCloud, Scott. 1993. *Understanding Comics: The Invisible Art*. New York: HarperCollins.

———. 2000. *Reinventing Comics: The Evolution of an Art Form*. New York: HarperCollins.

———. 2006. *Making Comics*. New York: HarperCollins.

———. 2018. "A Bill of Rights for Comics Creators." Scott McCloud. www.scottmccloud.com.

———. n.d. "The 'Infinite' Canvass." Scott McCloud. Accessed July 11, 2018. www.scottmccloud.com.

McCullough, Kate. 2018. "The Complexity of Loss Itself: The Comics Form and *Fun Home*'s Queer Reparative Temporality." *American Literature* 90, no. 2 (June): 377–405.

McGuire, Richard. 2014. *Here*. New York: Pantheon.

McInnis, Jarvis. 2015. "That 'the Land Would One Day Be Free': Reconciling Race and Region in African American and Southern Studies." *Mississippi Quarterly* 68, no. 1–2, 15–20.

McIsaac, Molly. 2012. "What Is Cosplay and Why Do People Do It?" iFanboy, June 12, 2012. https://ifanboy.com.

McKenzie, Donald F. 1999. *Bibliography and the Sociology of Texts*. New York: Cambridge University Press.

McKinney, Mark. 2008. "Representations of History and Politics in French-Language Comics and Graphic Novels: An Introduction." In *History and Politics in French-Language Comics and Graphic Novels*, edited by Mark McKinney, 3–24. Jackson: University Press of Mississippi.

McLelland, Mark, and Romit Dasgupta, eds. 2005. *Genders, Transgenders and Sexualities in Japan*. London: Routledge.

McMillan, Graeme. 2016. "'Rebirth': Geoff Johns Talks about Bringing Hope Back to the DC Universe." *Hollywood Reporter*, May 25, 2016. www.hollywoodreporter.com.

McMillan, Graeme, and Tee Franklin. 2018. "Inside Image's Socially Conscious Horror Comic 'Jook Joint.'" Heat Vision. *Hollywood Reporter*, June 19, 2018. www.hollywoodreporter.com.

McPherson, Tara. 2003. *Reconstructing Dixie: Race, Gender and Nostalgia in the Imagined South*. Durham, NC: Duke University Press.

McRuer, Robert. 2006. *Crip Theory: Cultural Signs of Queerness and Disability*. New York: New York University Press.

Meehan, Eileen. 2005. *Why TV Is Not Our Fault: Television Programming, Viewers, and Who's Really in Control*. Lanham, MD: Rowman & Littlefield.

Melamed, Jodi. 2011. *Represent and Destroy: Rationalizing Violence in the New Racial Capitalism*. Minneapolis: University of Minnesota Press.

Merino, Ana. 2009. "The Bros Hernandez: A Latin Presence in Alternative U.S. Comics." In *Redrawing the Nation: National Identity in Latin/o American Comics*, edited by Hector Fernández L'Hoeste and Juan Poblete, 251–69. New York: Palgrave Macmillan.

Metz, Christian. 1982. *The Imaginary Signifier*. Bloomington: Indiana University Press.

Micheline, J. A. 2015. "Cosplaying While Trans: Exploring the Intersection between Cosplay and Gender Identity." *Vice*. www.vice.com.

Mickwitz, Nina. 2016. *Documentary Comics: Graphic Truth-Telling in a Skeptical Age*. New York: Palgrave Macmillan.

Millán, Isabel. 2016. "Anya Sofía (Araña) Corazón: The Inner Webbings and Mexi-Ricanization of Spider-girl." In *Graphic Borders: Latino Comic Books Past, Present, and Future*, edited by Frederick Luis Aldama and Christopher González, 203–23. Austin: University of Texas Press.

Miller, Ann. 2017. "Formalist Theory: Academics." In *The Secret Origins of Comics Studies*, edited by Matthew J. Smith and Randy Duncan, 150–63. New York: Routledge.

Miller, John Jackson. 2017. "FAQ: Postal Sales Data for Comic Books." Comichron: A Resource for Comics Research. www.comichron.com.

Miranda-Rodriguez, Edgardo. 2018. *Ricanstruction: Reminiscing and Rebuilding Puerto Rico*. New York: Somos Arte.

Misemer, Leah. 2018. "Hands across the Ocean: A 1970s Network of French and American Women Cartoonists." In *Comics Studies Here and Now*, edited by Frederick Luis Aldama, 191–210. New York: Routledge.

Mitchell, David T., and Sharon L. Snyder. 2000. *Narrative Prosthesis: Disability and the Dependencies of Discourse*. Ann Arbor: University of Michigan Press.

Mitchell, W. J. T. 1984. "The Politics of Genre: Space and Time in Lessing's *Laacoon*." *Representations* 6, no. 1, 98–115.

———. 1986. *Iconology*. Chicago: University of Chicago Press.

———. 1995. *Picture Theory: Essays on Verbal and Visual Representation*. Chicago: University of Chicago Press.

———. 2004. *What Do Pictures Want? The Lives and Loves of Images*. Chicago: University of Chicago Press.

Mitchell, W. J. T., and Art Spiegelman. 2014. "Public Conversation: What the %$&# Happened to Comics?" In "Comics and Media," edited by Hillary Chute and Patrick Jagoda, special issue, *Critical Inquiry*, Spring 2014, 20–35.

Molotiu, Andrei, ed. 2009. *Abstract Comics*. Seattle: Fantagraphics.

———. 2012. "Abstract Form: Sequential Dynamism and Iconostasis in Abstract Comics and Steve Ditko's *Amazing Spider-Man*." In *Critical Approaches to Comics: Theories and Methods*, edited by Matthew J. Smith and Randy Duncan, 84–100. New York: Routledge.

Monster, Sfé, ed. 2015. *Beyond: The Queer Sci-Fi and Fantasy Comic Anthology*. Portland, OR: Beyond Press.

Moore, Alan, and Melinda Gebbie. (2006) 2018. *Lost Girls*. London: Knockabout Comics.

Moore, Alan, Dave McKean, and John Higgins. 1987. *Watchmen*. New York: DC Comics.

Moore, Alan, Rick Veitch, and Al Williamson. 1985. "The Jungle Line." *DC Comics Presents* 85 (September). New York: DC Comics.

Moore, Mignon R. 2006. "Lipstick or Timberlands? Meanings of Gender Presentation in Black Lesbian Communities." *Signs* 32, no. 1, 113–39.

Morrison, Grant. 2012. *Supergods*. New York: Spiegel & Grau.

Morris-Suzuki, Tessa. 2005. *The Past within Us: Media, Memory, History*. London: Verso.

Morton, Samuel George. 1839. *Crania Americana*. London: Simpkins, Marshall.

Muñoz, José Esteban. 2009. *Cruising Utopia: The Then and There of Queer Futurity*. New York: New York University Press.

Murray, Christopher. 2011. *Champions of the Oppressed: Superhero Comics, Popular Culture, and Propaganda in America during World War II*. Creskill, NJ: Hampton.

Nama, Adilifu. 2009. "Brave Black Worlds: Black Superheroes as Science Fiction Ciphers." *African Identities* 7, no. 2, 133–44.

Nama, Adilifu, and Maya Haddad. 2016. "Mapping the Blatino Badlands and Borderlands of American Pop Culture." In *Graphic Borders: Latino Comic Books Past, Present, and Future*, edited by Frederick Luis Aldama and Christopher González, 253–68. Austin: University of Texas Press.

Nast, Thomas. 1876. "The Ignorant Vote—Honors Are Easy." *Harper's Weekly*, December 9, 1876, cover.

Navasky, Victor S. 2013. *The Art of Controversy: Political Cartoons and Their Enduring Power*. New York: Alfred Knopf.

Ndalianis, Angela. 2009. "Enter the Aleph: Superhero Worlds and Hypertime Realities." In *The Contemporary Comic Book Superhero*, edited by Angela Ndalianis, 270–90. New York: Routledge.

New York Times. 1943. "Publisher Shares Profit: 10 Groups Benefit from Bible Stories in Comic Strip Form." December 30, 1943, 15.

Nguyen, Mimi Thi. 2012. "Riot Grrrl, Race, and Revival." In "Punk Anteriors: Genealogy, Performance, Theory," edited by Beth Stinson and Fiona I. B. Ngô, special issue, *Women & Performance* 22, no. 2–3 (July–November): 173–96.

———. 2015. "Minor Threats." In "Queering Archives," edited by Kevin Murphy, Daniel Marshall, and Zeb Tortorici, special issue, *Radical History Review* 122 (May): 11–24.

Nicholson, Hope. 2017. *The Spectacular Sisterhood of Superwomen: Awesome Female Characters from Comic Book History*. Philadelphia: Quirk.

Norcliffe, Glen, and Olivero Rendace. 2003. "New Geographies of Comic Book Production in North America: The New Artisan, Distancing, and the Periodic Social Economy." *Economic Geography* 79, no. 3, 241–63.

Norris, Craig, and Jason Bainbridge. 2009. "Intersections: Selling Otaku? Mapping the Relationship between Industry and Fandom in the Australian Cosplay Scene." *Intersections: Gender and Sexuality in Asia and the Pacific* 20 (April). http://intersections.anu.edu.au.

North, Sterling. 1941. "The Antidote for Comics." *National Parent-Teacher*, March 1941.

Norton, Bonny, and Karen Vanderheyden. 2004. "Comic Book Culture and Second Language Learners." In *Critical Pedagogies and Language Learning*, edited by Bonny Norton and Kelleen Toohey, 201–21. New York: Cambridge University Press.

Nyberg, Amy Kiste. 1998. *Seal of Approval: The History of the Comics Code*. Jackson: University Press of Mississippi.

———. 2016. "The Comics Code." In *The Routledge Companion to Comics*, edited by Frank Bramlett, Roy T. Cook, and Aaron Meskin, 25–33. New York: Routledge.

OED Online. 2020. "Universe, n2." Oxford: Oxford University Press. Accessed November 19, 2020. www.oed.com.

Oh, Stella. 2017. "Laughter against Laughter: Interrupting Racial and Gendered Stereotypes in Gene Luen Yang's *American Born Chinese*." *Journal of Graphic Novels and Comics* 8, no. 1, 20–32.

O'Keefe, Carly. 2006. "Sparta Residents Offer Hope to Herrin after Plant Closing." KFVS12, May 12, 2006. www.kfvs12.com.

Oksman, Tahneer. 2016. *"How Come Boys Get to Keep Their Noses?": Women and Jewish American Identity in Contemporary Graphic Memoirs*. New York: Columbia University Press.

Okubo, Miné. (1946) 2014. *Citizen 13660*. Seattle: University of Washington Press.

Olaniyan, Tejumola. 2013. AfricaCartoons. Accessed September 25, 2018. africacartoons.com.

Oliver, Michael. 1990. *The Politics of Disablement: A Sociological Approach*. London: St. Martin's.

Ong, Walter J. 1945. "The Comics and the Super State." *Arizona Quarterly* 1, no. 3 (Autumn): 34–48.

———. 1986. "Writing Is a Technology That Restructures Thought." In *The Written Word: Literacy in Transition*, edited by Gerd Baumann, 23–50. New York: Oxford University Press.

Ornasaka, Junko. 2006. *Feminist Revolution in Literacy: Feminist Bookstores in the United States*. New York: Routledge.

Oropeza, B. J., ed. 2008. *The Gospel According to Superheroes: Religion and Popular Culture*. New York: Peter Lang.

O'Sullivan, Judith. 1990. *The Great American Comic Strip: One Hundred Years of Cartoon Art*. Boston: Little, Brown and Company.

Pande, Rukmini. 2018. "Who Do You Mean by 'Fan'? Decolonizing Media Fandom Identity." In *A Companion to Media Fandom and Fan Studies*, edited by Paul Booth, 319–32. Hoboken, NJ: John Wiley & Sons.

Panter, Gary. 2005. *Satiro-plastic: The Sketchbook of Gary Panter*. Montreal: Drawn & Quarterly.

Park, Chan-wook, dir. 2003. *Oldboy*. Seoul: Show East.

Penrose, Walter Duvall, Jr. 2017. "More Than an Amazon: Wonder Woman." *Oxford University Press Blog*, July 27, 2017. https://blog.oup.com.

Pérez, Laura E. 2007. *Chicana Art: The Politics of Spiritual and Aesthetic Altarities*. Durham, NC: Duke University Press.

Perren, Alisa, and Laura E. Felschow. 2018. "The Bigger Picture: Drawing Intersections between Comics, Fan, and Industry Studies." In *The Routledge Companion to Media Fandom*, edited by Melissa A. Click and Suzanne Scott, 309–18. New York: Routledge.

Perren, Alisa, and Gregory Steirer. 2021. *The American Comic Book Industry and Hollywood*. London: Bloomsbury.

Pett, Emma. 2016. "Cosplay Rey: Intergenerational Fandom and the Importance of Play at the 2016 Star Wars Celebration, London." *Deletion*, November 24, 2016. www.deletionscifi.org.

Pickens, Therí A., ed. 2017. "Blue Blackness, Black Blueness: Making Sense of Blackness and Disability." Special issue, *African American Review* 50, no. 2, 93–103.

Piepmeier, Alison. 2009. *Girl Zines: Making Media, Doing Feminism*. New York: New York University Press.

Pilcher, Tim, and Gene Kannenberg Jr. 2008. *Erotic Comics: A Graphic History from Tijuana Bibles to Underground Comix*. New York: Abrams.

Pitkethly, Clare. 2009. "Derrida, Deleuze and a Duck: The Movement of the Circulating Differential in Comic Book Analysis." *Animation: An Interdisciplinary Journal* 4, no. 3, 283–302.

Pizzino, Christopher. 2016. *Arresting Development: Comics at the Boundaries of Literature*. Austin: University of Texas Press.

Plunkett, Luke. 2014. "Where the Word 'Cosplay' Actually Comes From." *Kotaku*, October 10, 2014. https://kotaku.com.

Postema, Barbara. 2013. *Narrative Structure in Comics: Making Sense of Fragments*. Rochester, NY: RIT Press.

Powell, Nate. 2011. *Any Empire*. Marietta, GA: Top Shelf.

Priego, Ernesto. 2010. "The Comic Book in the Age of Digital Reproduction." PhD diss., University College London. http://dx.doi.org/10.6084/m9.figshare.754575.

Prorokova, Tatiana, and Nimrod Tal, eds. 2018. *Cultures of War in Graphic Novels: Violence, Trauma, and Memory*. New Brunswick, NJ: Rutgers University Press.

Prosser, Jay. 1998. *Second Skins: The Body Narratives of Transsexuality*. New York: Columbia University Press.

Prough, Jennifer S. 2011. *Straight from the Heart: Gender, Intimacy, and the Cultural Production of Shōjo Manga*. Honolulu: University of Hawai'i Press.

Pustz, Matthew. 1999. *Comic Book Culture: Fanboys and True Believers*. Jackson: University Press of Mississippi.

———. 2016. "Comics and Fandom." In *The Routledge Companion to Comics*, edited by Frank Bramlett, Roy T. Cook, and Aaron Meskin, 267–74. New York: Routledge.

Quesenberry, Krista. 2017. "Intersectional and Non-human Self-Representation in Women's Autobiographical Comics." *Journal of Graphic Novels and Comics* 8, no. 5, 417–32.

Quinby, Lee. 1992. "The Subject of Memoirs: The Woman Warrior's Technology of Ideographic Selfhood." In *De/Colonizing the Subject: The Politics of Gender in Women's Autobiography*, edited by Sidonie Smith and Julia Watson, 297–320. Minneapolis: University of Minnesota Press.

Rabinowitz, Paula. 2014. *American Pulp: How Paperbacks Brought Modernism to Main Street*. Princeton, NJ: Princeton University Press.

Rad Queers. 2014. "Rad Queers: Edie Fake." Accessed July 30, 2018. https://vimeo.com.

Radway, Janice. 1984. *Reading the Romance: Women, Patriarchy, and Popular Literature*. Chapel Hill: University of North Carolina Press.

———. 1997. *A Feeling for Books: The Book-of-the-Month Club, Literary Taste, and Middle-Class Desire*. Chapel Hill: University of North Carolina Press.

———. 2011. "Zines, Half-Lives, and Afterlives: On the Temporalities of Social and Political Change." *PMLA* 126, no. 1, 140–50.

Rahman, D., L. Wing-Sun, and B. Cheung. 2012. "'Cosplay'—Imaginative Self and Performing Identity." *Fashion Theory: The Journal of Dress, Body and Culture* 16, no. 13, 317–42.

Raven, James. 2014. "'Print Culture' and the Perils of Practice." In *The Perils of Print Culture: New Directions in Book History*, edited by Jason McElligott and Eve Patten, 218–37. New York: Palgrave Macmillan.

Rawson, K. J., and Aaron Devor, eds. 2015. "Archives and Archiving." *TSQ: Transgender Studies Quarterly* 2, no. 4.

Rawson, K. J., and Cristan Williams. 2014. "Transgender*: The Rhetorical History of a Term." *Present Tense* 3, no. 2, 1–9.

Redfield, James W. 1852. *Comparative Physiognomy: Or, Resemblances between Men and Animals*. New York: Redfield.

Regalado, Aldo. 2007. "*Unbreakable* and the Limits of Transgression." In *Film and Comic Books*, edited by Ian Gordon, Mark Jancovich, and Matthew P. McAllister, 116–36. Jackson: University Press of Mississippi.

Reid, Calvin. 2011. "X-Men Writer Chris Claremont Donates Archive to Columbia University." *PublishersWeekly.com* (blog), November 14, 2011. www.publishersweekly.com.

———. 2013a. "Columbia Acquires Kitchen Sink Press Comics Archive." *PublishersWeekly.com* (blog), December 18, 2013. www.publishersweekly.com.

———. 2013b. "Columbia University Acquires Complete 'Elfquest' Comics Archive." *PublishersWeekly.com* (blog), February 26, 2013. www.publishersweekly.com.

Reid, Robin Anne. 2017. "Bending Culture: Racebendin.com's Protests against Media Whitewashing." In *Dis-orienting Planets: Racial Representations of Asia in Science Fiction*, edited by Isiah Lavender, 189–203. Jackson: University Press of Mississippi.

Relyea, Lane. 2013. *Your Everyday Art World*. Boston: MIT Press.

Reynolds, Richard. 1992. *Superheroes: A Modern Mythology*. Jackson: University Press of Mississippi.

Rieder, John. 2017. *Science Fiction and the Mass Cultural Genre System*. Middletown, CT: Wesleyan University Press.

Riesman, Abraham. 2015. "The Secret History of Ultimate Marvel, the Experiment That Changed Superheroes Forever." *Vulture*, May 25, 2015. www.vulture.com.

Rifas, Leonard. 2010. "Race and Comix." In *Multicultural Comics: From Zap to Blue Beetle*, edited by Frederick Luis Aldama, 27–38. Austin: University of Texas Press.

Rivera, Gabby. 2016. *Juliet Takes a Breath*. New York: Riverdale Avenue Books.

Robb, Jenny E. 2009. "Bill Blackbeard: The Collector Who Rescued the Comics." *Journal of American Culture* 32, no. 3, 244–56.

Robbins, Trina. 1993. *A Century of Women Cartoonists*. Northampton, MA: Kitchen Sink.

———. 1996. *The Great Women Superheroes*. Northampton, MA: Kitchen Sink.

———. 1999. *From Girls to Grrrlz: A History of ♀'s Comics from Teens to Zines*. San Francisco: Chronicle.

———. 2001. *The Great Women Cartoonists*. New York: Watson-Guptill.

———. 2013. *Pretty in Ink: North American Women Cartoonists 1896–2013*. Seattle: Fantagraphics.

Robbins, Trina, and Catherine Yronwode. 1985. *Women and the Comics*. Columbia, MO: Eclipse.

Robinson, David. 1917. "Caricature in Ancient Art." *Bulletin of the College Art Association of America* 1, no. 3 (November): 65–68.

Robinson, Lillian S. 2004. *Wonder Women: Feminisms and Superheroes*. New York: Routledge.

Rodríguez, Juana María. 2014. *Sexual Futures, Queer Gestures, and Other Latina Longings*. New York: New York University Press.

Rodríguez, Richard T. 2016. "Revealing Secret Identities." In *Graphic Borders: Latino Comic Books Past, Present, and Future*, edited by Frederick Luis Aldama and Christopher González, 224–37. Austin: University of Texas Press.

———. 2017. "X Marks the Spot." *Cultural Dynamics* 29, no. 3, 202–13.

Rogers, Sean, and Jeet Heer. 2015. "A History of *Drawn & Quarterly*." In *Drawn & Quarterly: Twenty-Five Years of Contemporary Cartooning, Comics, and Graphic Novels*, edited by Tom Devlin et al., 13–57. Montreal: Drawn & Quarterly.

Rohy, Valerie. 2010. "In the Queer Archive: *Fun Home*." *GLQ: A Journal of Lesbian and Gay Studies* 16, no. 3, 341–61.

Rosenbaum, Jonathan. 1980. *Moving Places: A Life at the Movies*. New York: Harper and Row.

Rosenberg, Robin, ed. 2008. *The Psychology of Superheroes*. New York: Pop Smart.

Round, Julia. 2014. *Gothic in Comics and Graphic Novels: A Critical Approach*. Jefferson, NC: McFarland.

Royal, Derek Parker. 2007. "Introduction: Coloring America: Multi-ethnic Engagements with Graphic Narrative." *MELUS* 32, no. 3 (September): 7–22.

Rubin, Joan Shelley. 1992. *The Making of Middlebrow Culture*. Chapel Hill: University of North Carolina Press.

Rutledge, J. Howard, and Peter B. Bart. 1955. "Comic Books: Slight Sales Recovery Leaves Volume below Pre-'Clean Up' Days Smaller Publishers." *Wall Street Journal*, October 5, 1955.

Sabeti, Shari. 2011. "The Irony of 'Cool Club': The Place of Comic Book Reading in Schools." *Journal of Graphic Novels and Comics* 2, no. 2, 137–49.

Sabin, Roger. 1996. *Comics, Comix and Graphic Novels: A History of Comic Art*. London: Phaidon.

Sadowski, Greg, ed. 2009. *Supermen! The First Wave of Comic Book Heroes 1936–1941*. Seattle: Fantagraphics.

Salamon, Gayle. 2010. *Assuming a Body: Transgender and Rhetorics of Materiality*. New York: Columbia University Press.

Salisbury, Mark. 2000. *Artists on Comic Art*. London: Titan.

Salkowitz, Rob. 2012. *Comic-Con and the Business of Pop Culture: What the World's Wildest Trade Show Can Tell Us about the Future of Entertainment*. New York: McGraw-Hill Education.

Salzberg, Charles. 1983. "Cashing in on Comic Books." *Fact* 2, no. 6, 68–71.

Sammond, Nicholas. 2018. "Meeting in the Archive: Comix and Collecting as Community." *Feminist Media Histories* 4, no. 3, 96–118.

Sanders, J. S., ed. 2016. *The Comics of Hergé: When the Lines Are Not So Clear*. Jackson: University Press of Mississippi.

Satrapi, Marjane. (2000) 2004. *Persepolis*. New York: Pantheon.

Sattouf, Riad. 2015. *The Arab of the Future: A Childhood in the Middle East, 1978–1984*. New York: Metropolitan.

Saunders, Ben. 2011. *Do the Gods Wear Capes? Spirituality, Fantasy, and Superheroes*. London: Bloomsbury.

Savage, William. 1841. *Dictionary of the Art of Printing*. London: Longman, Brown, Green, and Longmans.

Saxey, Esther. 2006. "Desire without Closure in Jaime Hernandez' *Love and Rockets*." *ImageTexT: Interdisciplinary Comics Studies* 3, no. 1 (Summer). www.english.ufl.edu.

Scalenghe, Sara. 2014. *Disability in the Ottoman Arab World, 1500–1800*. Cambridge: Cambridge University Press.

Schelly, Bill. 1995. *The Golden Age of Comic Fandom*. Ellettsville, IN: Hamster.

———. 2013. *American Comic Book Chronicles: The 1950s*. Raleigh: TwoMorrows.

———. 2015. *Harvey Kurtzman: The Man Who Created MAD and Revolutionized American Humor*. Seattle: Fantagraphics.

Schickel, Richard. 1999. *Matinee Idylls: Reflections on the Movies*. Chicago: Ivan R. Dee.

Schilt, Kristen. 2003. "I'll Resist with Every Inch and Every Breath: Girls and Zine Making as a Form of Resistance." *Youth and Society* 35:71–97.

Scott, Darieck. 2014. "Big Black Beauty: Drawing and Naming the Black Male Figure in Superhero and Gay Porn Comics." In *Porn Archives*, edited by Tim Dean, 183–212. Durham, NC: Duke University Press.

Scott, Darieck, and Ramzi Fawaz. 2018. "Introduction: Queer about Comics." *American Literature* 90, no. 2, 197–219.

Scott, Suzanne. 2015. "'Cosplay Is Serious Business': Gendering Material Fan Labor on Heroes of Cosplay." *Cinema Journal* 54, no. 3, 146–54.

Sedgwick, Eve. 1990. *Epistemology of the Closet*. Berkeley: University of California Press.

Senate Committee on the Judiciary, Subcommittee to Investigate Juvenile Delinquency. 1954. "Investigation of Juvenile Delinquency in the United States." 83rd Congress, 2nd session, April 21, 1954.

Serrato, Phillip. 2011. "Latino/a." In *Keywords for Children's Literature*, edited by Philip Nel and Lissa Paul, 133–37. New York: New York University Press.

Seymour, Jessica. 2018. "Racebending and Prosumer Fanart Practices in Harry Potter Fandom." In *A Companion to Media Fandom and Fan Studies*, edited by Paul Booth, 333–48. Hoboken, NJ: John Wiley and Sons.

Shakespeare, Tom. 2014. *Disability Rights and Wrongs Revisited*. London: Routledge.

Shep, Sydney J. 2010. "Imagining Postnational Book History." *Papers of the Bibliographical Society of America* 104, no. 20, 253–68.

Sheppard, Alice. 1994. *Cartooning for Suffrage*. Albuquerque: University of New Mexico Press.

Shetterly, Will, and Vince Stone. 1991. "Hero Worship: Last Fair Deal Gone Down." *Captain Confederacy* 2, no. 2 (December). New York: Epic Comics.

Shindler, Dorman T. 2006. "Alan Moore Leaves Behind His *Extraordinary Gentlemen* to Dally with *Lost Girls*." *Science Fiction Weekly*, August 7, 2006.

Simone, Gail. 1999. Women in Refrigerators. March 1999. Accessed January 10, 2019. https://lby3.com/wir.

Singer, Marc. 2013. "The Myth of Echo: Cultural Populism and Comics Studies." *Studies in Comics* 4, no. 2, 355–66.

———. 2019. *Breaking the Frames: Populism and Prestige in Comics Studies*. Austin: University of Texas Press.

Siwek, Stephen E. 2017. *Video Games in the 21st Century*. Washington, DC: Entertainment Software Association. www.theesa.com.

Smith, Greg M., Thomas Andrae, Scott Bukatman, and Thomas LaMarre. 2011. "Surveying the World of Contemporary Comics Scholarship: A Conversation." *Cinema Journal* 50, no. 3, 135–47.

Smith, Jon, and Deborah Cohn. 2004. "Introduction: Uncanny Hybridities." In *Look Away! The U.S. South in New World Studies*, edited by Jon Smith and Deborah Cohn, 1–19. Durham, NC: Duke University Press.

Smith, Matthew J., and Randy Duncan, eds. 2017. *The Secret Origins of Comics Studies*. New York: Routledge.

Smith, Scott, and José Alaniz, eds. 2019. *Uncanny Bodies: Disability and Superhero Comics*. University Park: Penn State University Press.

Smith, Sidonie, and Julia Watson. 2017. *Life Writing in the Long Run: A Smith and Watson Autobiography Studies Reader*. Ann Arbor: Michigan Publishing, University of Michigan Library.

Snorton, C. Riley. 2017. *Black on Both Sides: A Racial History of Trans Identity*. Minneapolis: University of Minnesota Press.

Sobel, Marc, and Kristy Valenti, eds. 2013. *The* Love and Rockets *Companion*. Seattle: Fantagraphics.

Sontag, Susan. 1969. "The Pornographic Imagination." In *Styles of Radical Will*, 35–73. New York: Farrar, Straus, and Giroux.

Sorese, Jeremy. 2015. *Curveball*. London: Nobrow.

Sousanis, Nick. 2015. *Unflattening*. Cambridge: Harvard University Press.

———. 2017. "A Life in Comics." *Columbia Magazine*, Summer 2017. http://magazine.columbia.edu.

Southern Illinoisan. 1951. "Sparta Plant Turns Out Six Million Comic Books a Month." January 8, 1951, 10.

Sperzel, Edith. 1948. "The Effect of Comic Books on Vocabulary Growth and Reading Comprehension." *Elementary English* 25:109–13.

Spiegelman, Art. 1986. *Maus I: A Survivor's Tale: My Father Bleeds History*. New York: Pantheon.

———. 1992. *Maus II: And Here My Troubles Began*. New York: Pantheon.

———. 2006. "Drawing Blood: Outrageous Cartoons and the Art of Outrage." *Harper's Magazine*, June 2006.

———. 2007. *Art Spiegelman: Conversations*. Edited by Joseph Witek. Jackson: University Press of Mississippi.

———. 2013. *Co-mix: A Retrospective of Comics, Graphics, and Scraps*. Montreal: Drawn & Quarterly.

Spiegelman, Art, and Chris Ware. 2014. Interview by Hillary L. Chute, 2008. In *Outside the Box: Interviews with Contemporary Cartoonists*, edited by Hillary L. Chute, 217–52. Chicago: University of Chicago Press.

Spillar, Kathy. 2017. "Wonder Woman Is Back on the Cover of *Ms*." Ms. *Magazine Blog*, July 6, 2017. http://msmagazine.com.

Spurgeon, Tom. 2016. *We Told You So: Comics as Art*. Seattle: Fantagraphics.

Squier, Susan. 2008. "Literature and Medicine, Future Tense: Make It Graphic." *Literature and Medicine* 27, no. 2, 124–52.

Steedman, Carolyn. 2001. *Dust: The Archive and Cultural History*. Manchester: Manchester University Press.

Steinberg, Marc. 2012. *Anime's Media Mix: Franchising Toys and Characters in Japan*. Minneapolis: University of Minnesota Press.

Steinmetz, Katy. 2014. "The Transgender Tipping Point." *Time*, May 29, 2014. www.time.com.

Steirer, Gregory. 2014. "No More Bags and Boards: Collecting Culture and the Digital Comics Marketplace." *Journal of Graphic Novels and Comics* 5, no. 4, 455–69.

Stevenson, Gregory, ed. 2020. *Theology and the Marvel Universe*. New York: Lexington.

Stone, Amy L., and Jaime Cantrell, eds. 2015. *Out of the Closet, into the Archives: Researching Sexual Histories*. Albany: State University of New York Press.

Stone, Sandy. 2006. "The *Empire* Strikes Back: A Posttranssexual Manifesto." In *The Transgender Studies Reader*, edited by Susan Stryker and Stephen Whittle, 221–35. London: Routledge.

Straw, Will. 2010. "The Circulatory Turn." In *The Wireless Spectrum: The Politics, Practices, and Poetics of Mobile Media*, edited by Barbara Crow, Michael Longford, and Kim Sawchuk, 17–28. Toronto: University of Toronto Press.

———. 2017. "Some Things a Scene Might Be." In *Scene Thinking: Cultural Studies from the Scenes Perspective*, edited by Benjamin Woo, Stuart R. Poyntz, and Jamie Rennie, 192–201. London: Routledge.

Streeby, Shelley. 2002. *American Sensations: Class, Empire, and the Production of Popular Culture*. Berkeley: University of California Press.

———. 2017. "Reading Jaime Hernandez's Comics as Speculative Fiction." In *Altermundos: Latin@ Speculative Literature, Film, and Popular Culture*, edited by B. V. Olguin and Cathryn Josefina Merla-Watson, 147–66. Seattle: University of Washington Press.

———. 2018. "Heroism and Comics Form: Feminist and Queer Speculations." *American Literature* 90, no. 2, 449–59.

Strinati, Dominic. 1995. *An Introduction to Theories of Popular Culture*. New York: Routledge.

Strub, Whitney. 2011. *Perversion for Profit: The Politics of Pornography and the Rise of the New Right*. New York: Columbia University Press.

Stryker, Susan, Paisley Currah, and Lisa Jean Moore. 2008. "Trans, Trans-, or Transgender?" *Women's Studies Quarterly* 36, no. 3–4, 11–22.

Swafford, Brian. 2012. "Critical Ethnography: The Comics Shop as Cultural Clubhouse." In *Critical Approaches to Comics: Theories and Methods*, edited by Matthew J. Smith and Randy Duncan, 291–302. New York: Routledge.

Swirski, Peter. 2005. *From Lowbrow to Nobrow*. Montreal: McGill-Queen's University Press.

Szczepaniak, Angela. 2014. "A Series of Thoughts on Seriality in Daniel Clowes' *Eightball*." In *Serialization in Popular Culture*, edited by Rob Allen and Thijs van den Berg. New York: Routledge.

Tagame, Gengoroh. 2013. *The Passion of Gengoroh Tagame: Master of Gay Erotic Manga*. Translated by Anne Ishii. New York: PictureBox.

Tarantino, Quentin, dir. 2004. *Kill Bill: Volume 2*. Los Angeles: Miramax.

Tensuan, Teresa M. 2009. "Crossing the Lines: Graphic (Life) Narratives and Co-laborative Political Transformations." *Biography* 32, no. 1 (Winter): 175–89.

Thompson, Jason, and Atsuhisa Okura. 2007. "How Manga Conquered America." *Wired*, November 2007.

Thorkelson, Nick. 1979. "Cartooning." *Radical America* 13, no. 2 (March/April): 27–51.

Tilley, Carol L. 2012. "Seducing the Innocent: Fredric Wertham and the Falsifications That Helped Condemn Comics." *Information and Culture* 47, no. 4, 383–413.

———. 2014. "Comics: A Once-Missed Opportunity." *Journal of Research on Libraries and Young Adults* 4 (May 5). www.yalsa.ala.org.

———. 2015. "Children and the Comics: Young Readers Take on the Critics." In *Protest on the Page: Essays on Print and the Culture of Dissent Since 1865*, edited by James Baughman, Jennifer Ratner-Rosenhaugen, and James Danky, 161–79. Madison: University of Wisconsin Press.

———. 2016. "Guest Post: Found in the Collection: 'The Uncanny Adventures of (I Hate) Dr. Wertham.'" Billy Ireland Cartoon Library and Museum (Ohio State University) blog, February 23, 2016. https://library.osu.edu.

———. 2017a. "Banned, Burned, and Now Rebuilding: Comics Collections in Libraries." *OUPblog* (blog), September 25, 2017. https://blog.oup.com.

———. 2017b. "Educating with Comics." In *The Secret Origins of Comics Studies*, edited by Matthew J. Smith and Randy Duncan, 3–11. New York: Routledge.

———. 2018. "Superheroes and Identity: The Role of Nostalgia in Comic Book Culture." In *Reinventing Childhood Nostalgia: Books, Toys and Contemporary Media Culture*, edited by Elisabeth Wessling, 51–65. New York: Routledge.

———. 2019. "Starting Small . . ." *Hogan's Alley* 22:90.

Tisserand, Michael. 2016. *Krazy: George Herriman, a Life in Black and White*. New York: Harper.

Tongson, Karen. 2011. *Relocations: Queer Suburban Imaginaries*. New York: New York University Press.

Tran, Scout. n.d. "About." Failing Sky. Accessed July 30, 2018. http://failingsky.com.

Tye, Larry. 2012. *Superman: The High-Flying History of America's Most Enduring Hero*. New York: Random House.

Ullén, Magnus. 2009. "Pornography and Its Critical Reception: Toward a Theory of Masturbation." *Jump Cut: A Review of Contemporary Media* 51 (Spring): 1–24.

Valentine, David. 2007. *Imagining Transgender: An Ethnography of a Category*. Durham, NC: Duke University Press.

Vargas, Deborah R., Nancy Raquel Mirabal, and Lawrence La Fountain-Stokes, eds. 2017. *Keywords for Latina/o Studies*. New York: New York University Press.

Vaughan, Brian, and Fiona Staples. 2014. *Saga: Volume 2*. Portland: Image Comics.

Velez, Ivan, Jr. 1994. "A Writer Dreams of Comic Epics and a Closet-less Culture." *New York Times*, July 24, 1994.

Visaggio, Madeline, and Eva Cabrera. 2016. *Kim and Kim*. Los Angeles: Black Mask Studios.

Vo, Lam Thuy. 2012. "Comics Get Scholarly Treatment at Columbia." *WSJ Blogs—Metropolis*, September 17, 2012. http://blogs.wsj.com.

Walker, Brian. 2004. *The Comics before 1945*. New York: Harry Abrams.

Wandtke, Terrence R., ed. 2007. *The Amazing Transforming Superhero*. Jefferson, NC: McFarland.

Wanzo, Rebecca. 2009. "Wearing Hero-Face: Black Citizens and Melancholic Patriotism in *Truth: Red, White, and Black*." *Journal of Popular Culture* 42, no. 2, 339–62.

———. 2018. "The Normative Broken: Melinda Gebbie, Feminist Comix, and Child Sexuality Temporalities." *American Literature* 90, no. 2 (June): 347–75.

———. 2020. *The Content of Their Caricature*. New York: New York University Press.

Ware, Chris. 2015. "Chris Ware on Cartooning and Memories." YouTube video, 1:37. https://youtu.be/OGV7zcInb20.

———. 2000. *Jimmy Corrigan: The Smartest Kid on Earth*. New York: Pantheon.

Warhol, Robyn. 2011. "The Space Between: A Narrative Approach to Alison Bechdel's 'Fun Home.'" *College Literature* 38, no. 3, 1–20.

Warner, Kristen J. 2015. "ABC's *Scandal* and Black Women's Fandom." In *Cupcakes, Pinterest, and Ladyporn*, edited by Elana Levine, 32–50. Champaign: University of Illinois Press.

Warner, Michael. 2002. "Public and Counterpublics." *Public Culture* 14, no. 1.

Warshow, Robert. 2001. "Paul, the Horror Comics, and Dr. Wertham." In *The Immediate Experience: Movies, Comics, Theatre and Other Aspects of Popular Culture*, 53–74. Cambridge: Harvard University Press.

Waskul, Dennis D., and Phillip Vannini. 2006. "Introduction: The Body in Symbolic Interaction." In *Body/Embodiment: Symbolic Interaction and the Sociology of the Body*, edited by Dennis D. Waskul and Phillip Vannini, 1–18. New York: Ashgate.

Watson, Julia. 2008. "Autographic Disclosures and Genealogies of Desire in Alison Bechdel's *Fun Home*." *Biography* 31, no. 1, 27–58.

Waugh, Thomas. 2002. *Out/Lines: Underground Gay Graphics before Stonewall*. Vancouver: Arsenal Pulp.

Wertham, Fredric. 1948. "The Comics—Very Funny!" *Saturday Review of Literature*, May 29, 1948.

———. 1954. *Seduction of the Innocent*. New York: Rinehart.

Whaley, Deborah Elizabeth. 2015. *Black Women in Sequence: Re-inking Comics, Graphic Novels, and Anime*. Seattle: University of Washington Press.

White, David M., and Robert H. Abel, eds. 1963. *The Funnies: An American Idiom*. Glencoe, IL: Free Press.

Whitlock, Gillian. 2006. "Autographics: The Seeing 'I' of the Comics." *Modern Fiction Studies* 52, no. 4 (Winter): 965–79.

Whitted, Qiana J. 2012. "Of Slaves and Other Swamp Things: Black Southern History as Comic Book Horror." In *Comics and the U.S. South*, edited by Brannon Costello and Qiana J. Whitted, 187–213. Jackson: University Press of Mississippi.

———. 2019. *EC Comics: Race, Shock, and Social Protest*. New Brunswick, NJ: Rutgers University Press.

Williams, Randall. 2010. *The Divided World: Human Rights and Its Violence*. Minneapolis: University of Minnesota Press.

Williams, Raymond. 1978. *Marxism and Literature*. Oxford: Oxford University Press.

———. 1986. "The Uses of Cultural Theory." *New Left Review* 158:19–31.

Winchester, Mark D. 2017. "Litigation and Early Comic Strips: The Lawsuits of Outcault, Dirks, and Fisher." In *Drawing the Line: Comics Studies and INKS 1994–1997*, edited by Lucy Shelton Caswell and Jared Gardner, 52–68. Columbus: Ohio State University Press.

Winge, T. 2006. "Costuming the Imagination: Origins of Anime and Manga Cosplay." *Mechademia* 1:65–76.

Witek, Joseph. 1989. *Comic Books as History: The Narrative Art of Jack Jackson, Art Spiegelman, and Harvey Pekar*. Jackson: University Press of Mississippi.

———, ed. 2007. *Art Spiegelman: Conversations*. Jackson: University Press of Mississippi.

Woo, Benjamin. 2011. "The Android's Dungeon: Comic-Bookstores, Cultural Spaces, and the Social Practices of Audiences." *Journal of Graphic Novels and Comics* 2, no. 2, 125–36.

———. 2012. "Understanding Understandings of Comics: Reading and Collecting as Media-Oriented Practices." *Participations: Journal of Audience and Reception Studies* 9, no. 2, 180–99.

———. 2018a. *Getting a Life: The Social Worlds of Geek Culture*. Montreal: McGill-Queen's University Press.

———. 2018b. "Is There a Comic Book Industry?" *Media Industries* 5, no. 1, 27–46.

Wright, Bradford W. 2001. *Comic Book Nation: The Transformation of Youth Culture in America*. Baltimore: Johns Hopkins University Press.

Wyburn, John, and Paul Roach. 2012. "An Hedonic Analysis of American Collectable Comic-Book Prices." *Journal of Cultural Economics* 36, no. 4, 309–26.

Yagoda, Ben. 2009. *Memoir: A History*. New York: Penguin.

Yang, Gene Luen. 2006. *American Born Chinese*. New York: Square Fish.

Young, Art. 1928. *On My Way: Being the Book of Art Young in Text and Picture*. New York: H. Liveright.

Zobl, Elke. 2004. "Persephone Is Pissed? Grrrl Zine Reading, Making and Distributing across the Globe." *Hecate* 30, no. 2, 156–75.

About the Contributors

José Alaniz is Professor of Slavic Languages and Literatures and Comparative Literature (adjunct) at the University of Washington, Seattle. He is the author of *Komiks: Comic Art in Russia* and *Death, Disability, and the Superhero: The Silver Age and Beyond*.

Frederick Luis Aldama is Arts and Humanities Distinguished Professor of English at the Ohio State University. He is the award-winning author, co-author, and editor of forty books, including *Your Brain on Latino Comics*; *Graphic Borders: Latino Comic Books Past, Present, and Future*; and *Graphic Indigeneity: Comics in the Americas and Australasia*.

Bart Beaty is Professor of English at the University of Calgary. He is the author of *Twelve-Cent Archie*, *Comics versus Art*, and *Unpopular Culture: Transforming the European Comic Book in the 1990s*, among other works.

Ian Blechschmidt received his PhD in communication studies from Northwestern University. He is currently a lecturer at the School of the Arts Institute of Chicago, where he teaches courses in international comics and visual rhetoric. He has written extensively on gender in American underground comix and the Vietnam War comics series *The 'Nam*.

Frank Bramlett is a linguist at the University of Nebraska at Omaha. He is the editor or co-editor of several volumes of comics scholarship, including the *Routledge Companion to Comics* and *Linguistics and the Study of Comics*, among others.

Scott Bukatman is Professor of Film and Media Studies in the Department of Art and Art History at Stanford University. He has published widely on playful embodiment in media phenomena ranging from cyberspace and Jerry Lewis to animation, musicals, comics, and superheroes. His most recent book is *Hellboy's World: Comics and Monsters on the Margins*.

andré carrington is Associate Professor of English at the University of California, Riverside. In his first book, *Speculative Blackness: The Future of Race in Science Fiction*, he interrogates the cultural politics of race in the fantastic genres through studies of fanzines, comics, film, television, and other speculative-fiction texts. He is currently at work on a second book, *Audiofuturism*, on the cultural politics of race in science fiction radio drama.

Michael Chaney is Professor of English at Dartmouth College and is the author of *Reading Lessons in Seeing*.

Sara Biggs Chaney is a lecturer and Associate Coordinator of the Mellon Mays Undergraduate Fellowship Program at Dartmouth College.

Michael Mark Cohen is Associate Teaching Professor of African American Studies and African Diaspora Studies at the University of California, Berkeley. He is the author of *The Conspiracy of Capital: Law, Violence, and American Popular Radicalism in the Age of Monopoly*.

Brannon Costello is James F. Cassidy Professor of English at Louisiana State University. He is the author of *Neon Visions: The Comics of Howard Chaykin*, winner of the Comics Studies Society's inaugural Charles Hatfield Prize, and *Plantation Airs: Racial Paternalism and the Transformations of Class in Southern Fiction*.

Anthony Michael D'Agostino is a postdoctoral fellow in English at Fordham University. His work concentrates on the nineteenth-century novel, superhero comics, queer theory, and feminism. His articles, "Flesh-to-Flesh Contact: Marvel Comics' Rogue and the Queer Feminist Imagination" and "Telepathy and Sadomasochism in *Jane Eyre*," appear in *American Literature* and *Victorians: A Journal of Culture and Literature*, respectively.

Blair Davis is Associate Professor of Media and Cinema Studies in the College of Communication at DePaul University in Chicago. His books include *The Battle for the Bs: 1950s Hollywood and the Rebirth of Low-Budget Cinema, Movie Comics: Page to Screen/Screen to Page*, and *Comic Book Movies*. His comics-related essays are featured in such anthologies as *The Blacker the Ink* and *Working-Class Comic Book Heroes* and in such journals as *Cinema Journal* and *Inks*.

Ramzi Fawaz is Associate Professor of English at the University of Wisconsin–Madison. He is the author of *The New Mutants: Superheroes and the Radical Imagination of American Comics*. With Darieck Scott, he co-edited the special issue of *American Literature*, "Queer about Comics," which won the 2018 best special issue award

from the Council of Editors of Learned Journals. His new book, *Queer Forms*, explores the influence of feminist and queer politics on American popular culture in the 1970s. *Queer Forms* will be published by New York University Press.

Margaret Galvan is Assistant Professor of Visual Rhetoric in the Department of English at the University of Florida. She is at work on a book, *In Visible Archives of the 1980s: Feminist Politics & Queer Platforms*, under contract with the University of Minnesota Press, which examines how publishing practices and archives have shaped understandings of the visual within feminist and queer activism. Her published work can be found in journals like *American Literature, Archive Journal, Inks, Journal of Lesbian Studies*, and *WSQ: Women's Studies Quarterly*.

Enrique García is Associate Professor of Hispanic Visual Culture at Middlebury College. He teaches classes about Hispanic sports, film, comic books, and music and has published articles that focus on a variety of subjects, from analyzing Robert Rodríguez's *Planet Terror* to addressing the representation of Taíno culture in Puerto Rican comic books. He has published two academic books, one about Cuban cinema (*Cuban Cinema after the Cold War*) and another about Mexican American comic book artists Jaime and Gilbert Hernandez (*The Hernandez Brothers: Love, Rockets, and Alternative Comics*).

Jared Gardner is Professor of English and Director of Popular Culture Studies at the Ohio State University. He has authored and edited several volumes in comics studies, including *Projections: Comics and the History of Twenty-First-Century Storytelling*.

Ian Gordon is the author of a number of monographs, including *Superman: The Persistence of an American Icon*, the Eisner-nominated *The Comics of Charles Schulz, Ben Katchor Conversations*, and *The Superhero Symbol: Media, Culture, and Politics*. His other works include *Kid Comic Strips: A Genre across Four Countries* and *Comic Strips and Consumer Culture*. He teaches cultural history and media studies in Singapore.

Jonathan W. Gray is Associate Professor of English at the CUNY Graduate Center and John Jay College. His first book, *Civil Rights in the White Literary Imagination*, traces the white literary responses to the period between the Brown case and the death of Martin Luther King Jr. His forthcoming project, *Illustrating the Race*, investigates how the twin understandings of illustration—the creative act of depiction and the political act of bringing forth for public consideration—function in the representation of African Americans in comics and graphic narratives published since 1966.

Sean Guynes is a cultural historian, critic, and writer who lives in Ann Arbor, Michigan. He is the author of the forthcoming books *Whiteness* (MIT Press) and *Starship Troopers* (Auteur Publishing) and a co-editor of the *Encapsulations: Critical Comics Studies* book series for University of Nebraska Press, two journal special issues, and several books—including *Unstable Masks: Whiteness and American Superhero Comics*.

Justin Hall is Associate Professor of Comics at the California College of the Arts and the creator of the comics series *Hard to Swallow* (with Dave Davenport), *True Travel Tales*, and *Glamazonia*. He has stories published in the *Houghton Mifflin Best American Comics*, *QU33R*, *Best Erotic Comics*, and the *SF Weekly*,

among others, and has exhibited his art in galleries and museums internationally. He edited the Lambda Literary Award–winning, Eisner-nominated *No Straight Lines: Four Decades of Queer Comics*, which he is now producing as a feature-length documentary film.

Charles Hatfield is Professor of English at California State University, Northridge. He is the author of *Alternative Comics* and *Hand of Fire: The Comics Art of Jack Kirby*, a co-editor (with Jeet Heer and Kent Worcester) of *The Superhero Reader*, and the curator of the 2015 CSUN Art Galleries exhibition *Comic Book Apocalypse: The Graphic World of Jack Kirby*.

Andrew Hoberek is Catherine Paine Middlebush Professor of English at the University of Missouri. He is the author of *Considering Watchmen: Poetry, Property, Politics, and the Comics/Graphic Novels* and an editor at the *Los Angeles Review of Books*.

Yetta Howard is Associate Professor of English and Comparative Literature and a codirector of the LGBTQ Research Consortium at San Diego State University. Howard is the author of *Ugly Differences: Queer Female Sexuality in the Underground* and the editor of *Rated RX: Sheree Rose with and after Bob Flanagan*.

Phil Jimenez is an Inkpot, Diamond, and Wizard Award–winning writer and artist who has worked for DC Comics, Marvel Comics, and a host of other comic book companies for over twenty-five years. Jimenez is best known for his work on *Tempest, JLA/Titans, Planetary/Authority, The Invisibles, New X-Men, Wonder Woman, Infinite Crisis, The Amazing Spider-Man, The Transformers, DC: Rebirth*, and *Superwoman* and for his creator-owned project, *Otherworld*. He is currently drawing *Historia*, the Black Label graphic novel written by Kelly Sue DeConnick for DC Comics.

Aaron Kashtan is a lecturer in the University Writing Program at the University of North Carolina, Charlotte. He received his PhD in English from the University of Florida and has also taught at Georgia Tech and Miami University, Ohio. His first book, *Between Pen and Pixel: Comics, Materiality, and the Book of the Future*, was published by Ohio State University Press in spring 2018.

Cáel M. Keegan is Assistant Professor of Women, Gender, and Sexuality Studies and Integrative, Religious, and Intercultural Studies at Grand Valley State University. He is the author of *Lana and Lilly Wachowski: Sensing Transgender* and a co-editor of *Somatechnics 8.1*, "Cinematic Bodies." His writing has also appeared in *Genders*, *Queer Studies in Media and Popular Culture*, *Transgender Studies Quarterly*, *Mediekultur*, *Spectator*, and *Journal of Homosexuality*.

Adam L. Kern earned a PhD in Japanese literature from Harvard University, where he was on the faculty for nearly a decade before joining the University of Wisconsin–Madison as Professor of Japanese Literature and Visual Culture. Kern's books include *Manga from the Floating World: Comicbook Culture and the* Kibyōshi *of Edo Japan*, a second edition of which has just been published.

Joo Ok Kim is Assistant Professor of International and Interdisciplinary Studies in the Department of American Studies at the University of Kansas. Her work has appeared in *Journal of Asian American Studies*, *Verge*, and *South*, among others.

Ellen Kirkpatrick is an independent scholar. She received her PhD in comics, culture, and identity at Kingston University, London. Her research examines how fantasy inspires and intersects with real-world politics, media fandom, (counter)storytelling, and activism. Her monograph, *Superhero Culture: A Multimodal (Counter) Story* is forthcoming. Her work has appeared in *Transformative Works and Cultures*, *Cinema Journal*, In Media Res, *Feminist Review*, and the collection *Seeing Fans* (edited by Lucy Bennett and Paul Booth).

Susan Kirtley is Professor of English, Director of Rhetoric and Composition, and Director of Comics Studies at Portland State University. Her research interests include visual rhetoric and graphic narratives, and she has published pieces on comics for the popular press and academic journals. Her book, *Lynda Barry: Girlhood through the Looking Glass*, was the 2013 Eisner Award winner for Best Educational/Academic Work.

Joshua Abraham Kopin received his PhD in American studies at the University of Texas at Austin. He recently completed a dissertation that frames comics as a nineteenth-century technology of time and space. His work has appeared in *American Literature* and *Inks*.

Isabel Millán is Assistant Professor in the Department of Women's, Gender, and Sexuality Studies at the University of Oregon. Recent publications include "Contested Children's Literature: Que(e)ries into Chicana and Central American Autofantasías" in *Signs: Journal of Women in Culture and Society* and "Engineering Afro-Latina and Mexican Immigrant Heroines: Biopolitics in Borderlands Speculative Literature and Film" in *Aztlán: A Journal of Chicano Studies*. Millán has also published chapters in *Graphic Borders: Latino Comic Books Past, Present, and Future* and *The Routledge Companion to Latina/o Popular Culture*.

Leah Misemer is a Marion L. Brittain Postdoctoral Fellow at the Georgia Institute of Technology. Her upcoming book projects include *Comics Correspondents: The Counterpublics of Seriality* and *Invisible Made Visible: Comics and Mental Illness*, co-authored with Jessica Gross.

Mimi Thi Nguyen is Associate Professor of Gender and Women's Studies and Asian American Studies at the University of Illinois at Urbana-Champaign. Her first book is *The Gift of Freedom: War, Debt, and Other Refugee Passages*. Her following project is called *The Promise of Beauty*. She has also published in *Signs*, *Camera Obscura*, *Women & Performance*, *positions: asia critique*, *Radical History Review*, and *ArtForum*.

Dr. Amy Kiste Nyberg joined the faculty in the journalism program at Seton Hall University in 1993. She is the author of *Seal of Approval: The History of the Comics Code* as well as numerous articles and book chapters on various aspects of comic book censorship. She also conducts research into comics journalism and its creators.

Tahneer Oksman is Associate Professor of Academic Writing at Marymount Manhattan College. She is the author of *"How Come Boys Get to Keep Their Noses?": Women and Jewish American Identity in Contemporary Graphic Memoirs* and a co-editor of the anthology *The Comics of Julie Doucet and Gabrielle Bell: A Place inside Yourself*. She is the graphic novel editor for *Women's Review of Books*.

Dr. Osvaldo Oyola is a public scholar, editor, and member of the International Comic Arts Forum executive board. His work has appeared in the *Los Angeles Review of Books*, *Shelfdust*, and *Apex Magazine*,

and he has a chapter in the forthcoming *Unstable Masks: Whiteness and American Superhero Comics*. He is the first winner of the Gilbert Seldes Prize for Public Scholarship, awarded by the Comics Studies Society.

Christopher Pizzino is Associate Professor of English at the University of Georgia. He is the author of *Arresting Development: Comics at the Boundaries of Literature*, and his essays are featured in *Comics Studies Here and Now*, *Cambridge History of the Graphic Novel*, and *Comics Memory: Archive and Styles*, among others.

Barbara Postema is Senior Lecturer of English at Massey University in New Zealand. Her monograph, *Narrative Structure in Comics*, was published with RIT Press in 2013. She has contributed work on comics to *Image and Narrative*, *Journal of Graphic Novels and Comics*, and *International Journal of Comic Art*, as well as collections such as *The Routledge Companion to Comics and Graphic Novels*. She is a co-editor (together with Candida Rifkind and Nhora Lucía Serrano) of a new book series from Wilfred Laurier University Press, *Crossing the Lines: Transcultural/Transnational Comics Studies*.

Stacey Robinson is Assistant Professor of Graphic Design at the University of Illinois. As part of the collaborative team Black Kirby with artist John Jennings, he creates graphic novels, gallery exhibitions, and lectures that deconstruct the work of artist Jack Kirby to reimagine Black resistance spaces inspired by hip-hop, religion, the arts, and sciences. His latest graphic novel, *I Am Alfonso Jones*, with writer Tony Medina is available from Lee & Low Books.

Nicholas Sammond is Director of the Centre of the Study of the United States and Professor of Cinema and Media Studies at the University of Toronto. He is the author of

Birth of an Industry: Blackface Minstrelsy and the Rise of American Animation and *Babes in Tomorrowland: Walt Disney and the Making of the American Child, 1930–1960.* Both books received the Katherine Singer Kovacs Award from the Society for Cinema and Media Studies.

Dr. Benjamin Saunders is Professor of English at the University of Oregon, where he founded the undergraduate minor in comics studies. He is the author of *Desiring Donne: Poetry, Sexuality, Interpretation*, short-listed by *Choice* magazine as an Outstanding Academic Title of the Year, and *Do the Gods Wear Capes? Spirituality, Fantasy, and Superheroes*, which has been described by novelist and comic book writer Greg Rucka as "the best critical work on the meaning and impact of superheroes that has ever been written." Saunders is a co-editor (with Charles Hatfield) of *Comic Book Apocalypse: The Graphic World of Jack Kirby.*

Cathy Schlund-Vials is Board of Trustees Distinguished Professor of English and Asian / Asian American Studies at the University of Connecticut. She is also Associate Dean for Humanities in UConn's College of Liberal Arts and Sciences. She has co-edited a number of volumes on race, human rights, and historical trauma, including *Redrawing the Historical Past: History, Memory, and Multiethnic Graphic Novels* and *Keywords for Asian American Studies.*

Darieck Scott is Associate Professor of African American Studies at the University of California, Berkeley. Scott is the author of *Extravagant Abjection: Blackness, Power, and Sexuality in the African American Literary Imagination*, winner of the 2011 Alan Bray Memorial Prize for Queer Studies from the Modern Language Association. Scott is also the author of the novels *Hex* and *Traitor to the Race* and the editor of *Best Black Gay Erotica*. With Ramzi Fawaz, he is a co-editor of the *American Literature* special issue, "Queer about Comics," which was awarded the 2018 Best Special Issue by the Council of Editors of Learned Journals.

Alexandro Segade is an interdisciplinary artist whose solo performance work has appeared at the Broad, the Roy and Edna Disney/CalArts Theater, and LAXART in Los Angeles; Yerba Buena Center for the Arts in San Francisco; and MoMA PS1, among others. Since 2000, Segade has worked with Malik Gaines and Jade Gordon in My Barbarian, an art collective included in the Whitney Biennial, and is the subject of a solo exhibition at the New Museum in 2016 and a survey at the Whitney in 2020. Segade also cofounded ARM, a collective exploring queer histories in art projects at the Whitney and High Line, New York; Rogaland Kunstcenter, Norway; and Espacio Odéon, Bogota, Colombia.

Matt Silady was raised in the Chicagoland area, where he taught public school before studying creative writing at the University of California, Davis. He published the Eisner-nominated graphic novel *The Homeless Channel.* Since then, Matt accepted a teaching position at California College of the Arts (CCA), where he helped expand the college's undergraduate comics curriculum and founded CCA's MFA in Comics Program. His recent projects include FOLIO Award–nominated "The Great Wine Heist" for *Sonoma Magazine.*

Christopher Spaide is a lecturer in the Department of English at Harvard University, where he focuses on twentieth- and twenty-first-century American literature. His essays and reviews have appeared or are forthcoming in *Cambridge Quarterly, College Literature, Contemporary Literature, Poetry*, and the *Yale Review*.

Jessica Quick Stark is a poet and scholar that lives in Durham, North Carolina. She is currently working on her first scholarly book project on experimental poets' use of comics, cartoons, and pictorial media in twentieth-century US American poetry. Her first full-length poetry collection, *Savage Pageant*, is forthcoming with Birds LLC in 2020. She writes poetry reviews for *Carolina Quarterly* and serves as a poetry reader for *Split Lip Magazine*. She writes an ongoing poetry comics zine called *INNANET*.

Gregory Steirer is Assistant Professor of English at Dickinson College. His work focuses on media industries, intellectual property law, and digital culture and has appeared in a variety of journals and edited collections. His book on the American comic book industry and Hollywood, co-authored with Alisa Perren, will be published by BFI/Bloomsbury in 2020.

Shelley Streeby is Professor of Ethnic Studies and Literature at the University of California, San Diego. She is the author of *American Sensations: Class, Empire, and the Production of Popular Culture*, which received the American Studies Association's 2003 Lora Romero First Book Prize; *Radical Sensations: World Movements, Violence, and Visual Culture*; and *Imagining the Future of Climate Change: World-Making through Science Fiction and Activism*.

Carol L. Tilley is Associate Professor in the School of Information Sciences at the University of Illinois. Her scholarship focuses on the intersection of comics, libraries, and young people, particularly in the United States in the mid-twentieth century. She is a former

president of the Comics Studies Society and a 2016 Eisner Award judge.

Rebecca Wanzo is Associate Professor of Women, Gender, and Sexuality Studies at Washington University in St. Louis. She is the author of *The Suffering Will Not Be Televised: African American Sentimental Storytelling* and *The Content of Our Caricature: African American Comic Art and Political Belonging*. Her work can also be found in journals such as *American Literature, Camera Obscura: Feminism, Culture, and Media Studies, differences: A Journal of Feminist Cultural Studies*, and *Women & Performance*.

Deborah Elizabeth Whaley is Professor of American and African American Studies at the University of Iowa. Her books include *Black Women in Sequence: Re-inking Comics, Graphic Novels, and Anime* and *Disciplining Women: Alpha Kappa Alpha, Black Counterpublics, and the Cultural Politics of Black Sororities*. With Ramzi Fawaz and Shelley Streeby, she is a co-editor of *Keywords in Comics Studies*.

Benjamin Woo is Associate Professor of Communication and Media Studies at Carleton University (Ottawa, Canada). He is the director of the Comic Cons Research Project, the author of *Getting a Life: The Social Worlds of Geek Culture*, co-author (with Bart Beaty) of *The Greatest Comic Book of All Time: Symbolic Capital and the Field of American Comic Books*, and a co-editor (with Stuart R. Poyntz and Jamie Rennie) of *Scene Thinking: Cultural Studies from the Scenes Perspective*.

Nicholas Yanes earned a doctorate in American studies from the University of Iowa and is a co-editor of two books, one on the representations of Obama in popular culture and the other on fan responses to the Hannibal Lecter franchise, both published by McFarland Press. He is currently an entertainment journalist and freelance writer.

Matt Yockey is Associate Professor of Theater and Film at the University of Toledo. He is the author of *Batman* and the editor of *Make Ours Marvel: Media Convergence and a Comics Universe*.